AD LITTERAM

NOTRE DAME CONFERENCES IN MEDIEVAL STUDIES
Number III

Institute of Medieval Studies
University of Notre Dame
John Van Engen, Director

Ad litteram

Authoritative Texts and Their Medieval Readers

EDITED BY

Mark D. Jordan and Kent Emery, Jr.

UNIVERSITY OF NOTRE DAME PRESS
NOTRE DAME   LONDON

Library of Congress Cataloging-in-Publication Data

Ad litteram : authoritative texts and their medieval readers / edited
  by Mark D. Jordan, Kent Emery, Jr.
       p.   cm. — (Notre Dame conferences in medieval
  studies ; no. 3)
     Includes bibliographical references and index.
     ISBN 0-268-00632-6
     1. Canon (Literature)   2. Literature, Medieval — History
  and criticism.   3. Bible — Criticism, interpretation, etc. —
  History — Middle Ages, 600–1500.   4. Learning and scholarship — History — Medieval, 500–1500.   5. Reading.
  6. Transmission of texts.   I. Jordan, Mark D.   II. Emery,
  Kent, 1944-   .   III. Series: Notre Dame conferences in medieval studies ; 3.
  PN81.A348   1992
  001.2'09'02 — dc20   91-50563
                                                                   CIP

Contents

Contributors

L.-J. Bataillon, O.P., is a member of the Commissio Leonina, Grotta-ferrata.

Marcia L. Colish is Frederick B. Artz Professor of History in Oberlin College.

Kent Emery, Jr., teaches in the Program of Liberal Studies and the Medieval Institute, University of Notre Dame.

Gillian R. Evans is a Fellow of Fitzwilliam College and Lecturer in History in Cambridge University.

Margaret T. Gibson is Reader in History in the University of Liverpool.

Mark D. Jordan teaches in the Medieval Institute, University of Notre Dame.

Raymond Macken, O.F.M., is the General Editor of *Henrici de Gandavo Opera omnia.*

A. J. Minnis is Professor of Medieval Literature and Co-Director of the Centre for Medieval Studies in the University of York.

Mary A. Rouse is the Managing Editor of *Viator.*

Richard H. Rouse is Professor of History in the University of California, Los Angeles.

Daniel J. Sheerin in Professor of Classical Languages at the University of Notre Dame.

Siegfried Wenzel is Professor of English in the University of Pennsylvania.

Albert Zimmermann is Director of the Thomas-Institut in the Universität zu Köln.

Introduction

ACCORDING TO JOHN OF SALISBURY, it was Bernard of Chartres who confected the familiar image in which medieval scholars were dwarfs sitting on the shoulders of ancient giants (*Metalogicon* 3.4). The image has been studied most for what it suggests of the tension between tradition and innovation, but we ought to remember as well that Bernard's giants are authors and that his image captures the dependence of medieval learning on the exegesis of inherited authoritative texts. Peter of Blois makes this clear: "We are like dwarfs on the shoulders of giants; by their aid, we can gaze farther than they did. Clinging to the ancients' treatises, we rediscover their finer judgments — banished from memory by ages past, forgotten by men — and raise them as from death to new life" (*Epist.* 92).

No one doubts that the reading of authoritative texts lies at the center of medieval theology, philosophy, and letters, and yet reiterated efforts to explain that reading have not been persuasive. Some efforts fail to persuade because they impose, unreflectively or contentiously, anachronistic "theories" of interpretation. Many others fail because they cannot hold together the different disciplines united in the medieval practice of reading. Thus, a modern reader may have a good sense for the medieval exegesis of one kind of text, but fail entirely to see that the exegesis is justified for medieval readers only because of its analogies to readings of other, quite different texts.

The essays that follow are intended to counteract both causes of failure. On the one hand, the modern reader must replace his or her presumptions about historically pure reading or critically creative reading with the different assumptions evident in the learned culture of the Middle Ages. Medieval readers, too, recognized a conflict between letters and logic, between reconstruction and extension. They knew the "battle of the arts" in popular and sophisticated versions. But their hierarchy of the arts of the trivium is not our own, and so their resolutions of the battle cannot be ours. The modern reader must rediscover what

is plausible in medieval combinations of exegetical sensitivity with dia-
lectical boldness or reverent construction. When Alan of Lille remarks
that an authority has a nose of wax which can be bent to different
meanings, he is not undoing historical accuracy so much as asserting
that texts enter arguments as active interlocutors.

On the other hand, the analogies of reading that bind medieval
letters, philosophy, and theology must be made to stand forth. The
reading of Scripture cannot be understood without looking to the
reading of Seneca and of Aristotle, though the three readings are by
no means the same. Thus while Thomas Aquinas denies that any text
but Scripture has the plurality of spiritual senses built upon the literal,
he nonetheless tacitly uses Scripture as a remote paradigm for varieties
of meaning possible to philosophy. Indeed, and quite generally, almost
nothing can be understood of medieval reading without a sympathetic
understanding of its scriptural exegesis.

The authors of these essays share no program or agenda beyond
the intention to recover medieval readings, whenever possible, in the
manner that the texts themselves suggest. Oddly enough, that intention distinguishes the essays' methods from many other methods now
prevailing. Much theological historiography, for example, either inserts the interpretation of the texts within narrative histories of religious life and "mentalities," or criticizes the texts for their ignorance —
or naiveté —about historical sources. The latter point has been pressed
particularly against medieval exegesis of Scripture. Texts of medieval
philosophy, in turn, are too often stripped of single passages thought
to contain interesting logical puzzles or to illustrate some present
problem in ontology or epistemology. In literature, the tyranny of premature theory has led to interesting self-examination by critics, but
has also encouraged forgetfulness of the particular precedures of the
medieval texts.

Against every attempt to concentrate on medieval texts in relation to modern readers, to our own theories or disunities, the following essays reply that we must first understand how medieval readers
established their own relations to authoritative texts. In becoming
authors themselves, medieval readers knew that they had both inherited
and rejuvenated powerful accounts of what is now called "textuality."
They demanded of themselves and of their future readers some adept-
ness in complementary arts of rhetoric and reading as they understood
them. To acknowledge this point of interpretation is scarcely new,
though it seems now especially needful.

Earlier versions of all of these essays were invited for a conference at the Medieval Institute, University of Notre Dame, in April 1989. The conference was made possible through the generosity of the National Endowment for the Humanities, the Conway Foundation, and Notre Dame's College of Arts and Letters. The editorial work in collecting these essays into this volume was the joint effort of Kent Emery, Jr., and Mark D. Jordan. Both editors wish to express their gratitude to the institutions for their support and to their colleagues who shared their time and their labor.

Abbreviations

BGPTMA	Beiträge zur Geschichte der Philosophie und Theologie des Mittelalters
CCCM	Corpus Christianorum, Continuatio Mediaevalis
CCSL	Corpus Christianorum, Series Latina
CSEL	Corpus Scriptorum Ecclesiasticorum Latinorum
EETS	Early English Text Society
GCS	Die griechischen christlichen Schriftsteller der ersten drei Jahrhunderte
HBS	Henry Bradshaw Society Publications
PG	Patrologiae Graecae cursus completus, ed. J.-P. Migne
PL	Patrologiae Latinae cursus completus, ed. J.-P. Migne
PMLA	Publications of the Modern Language Society of America
RTAM	Recherches de Théologie ancienne et médiévale
SC	Sources Chrétiennes
TU	Texte und Untersuchungen zur Geschichte der altchristlichen Literatur

The Place of the *Glossa ordinaria* in Medieval Exegesis

M. T. GIBSON

1. WHO WROTE THE *GLOSSA ORDINARIA*?

EVERY SCHOOLBOY KNOWS that the *Glossa ordinaria* is in two parts: the marginal gloss was written by Walafrid Strabo in the early ninth century, while the interlinear annotation is the work of Anselm of Laon in the later eleventh. Every schoolboy also knows that this is *wrong*. Since the late 1920s the *Glossa ordinaria* has been identified as one of the achievements of the twelfth-century Renaissance, first planned on the hilltop at Laon and subsequently completed by a miracle of teamwork among the masters of Auxerre, Laon, and Paris.[1] The date is set broadly at *c.* 1080–1130, but (as I have argued elsewhere[2]) the manuscripts belong to the next generation, *c.* 1140–1170, and beyond. What is more, manuscripts of the *Glossa ordinaria* after 1220 are almost as rare as manuscripts before 1140. This is a text with a brief, intense flowering, and a long reputation thereafter. In a less romantic metaphor, the twelfth-century glossed Bible may be regarded as the hinge, the *Wendepunkt,* between the old exegesis and the new. The traditional exegesis of the Fathers and their Carolingian editors reaches its summation in the mid-twelfth–century *Gloss.* But even as these splendid manuscripts are being reproduced, the concept of exegesis is changing radically. The Paris masters of the same generation are writing commentaries that are new in form, in content, and in purpose.

"Walafrid Strabo wrote the marginal gloss." The truth within this heresy is that any Carolingian manuscript of the Psalter or other book of the Bible in which the annotation is integral to the layout of the page will have a marginal gloss only. The *glossa interlinearis,* as the old editors called it, is not a feature of such manuscripts before *c.* 1050. Conversely, the attribution of the interlinear gloss to Anselm of Laon is true in respect of the date at which interlinear glossing becomes common in manuscripts of the Bible — not casual notes by a variety of readers (be it understood), but a recognized element in the design of the page. From the later eleventh century a Bible with a marginal gloss will have an interlinear gloss as well, a double gloss such as to tax the vigilance of any scribe. The definitive version of this complex *mise-en-page* is the *Glossa ordinaria.* Visually it owes much to the moderns, but for its content we look to the Fathers, and for its basic structure we must return to the early Carolingians.

2. COLLECTORS' MANUSCRIPTS, 800–1050

The Frankfurt manuscript Stadt- und Universitätsbibliothek Barth. 32 (see Plate 1) is a complete text of the Psalter, followed by nine Canticles, which has survived by the accident of its donation to Frankfurt Cathedral in the mid-fourteenth century.[3] The practiced insular initials and the variety of insular scripts indicate a date *c.* 800. The text is in insular half-uncial, organized by major black and two-color initials at the beginning of each psalm. The gloss is in an insular minuscule with considerable stretches of early Carolingian minuscule intervening later in the manuscript. Little initials within the gloss mark both lemmata and new sections of the discussion. Each psalm is preceded by the brief *explanatio* that can in all likelihood be attributed to Bede.[4] These are written in a slightly arcane cursive, without internal initials, that is smaller than the script of the gloss and more uncompromisingly insular. The ordinary Carolingian reader would find it hard going. The routine *tituli* — "In finem psalmus Dauid canticum" (Plate 1) — are written in red in a script verging towards Carolingian minuscule. The concluding prayers — "Ellunde domine etc." (Plate 1) — also in red, are in a plain Carolingian script. The Psalter text is the *Romanum,* marked up for reading aloud.[5] Taking the page as a whole, it has been designed from the beginning as text and gloss: a tri-columnar page in which the two gloss columns together (65 and 75 mm.) well outweigh the central text column (95 mm.). The gloss and the Bedan *explanationes* are together contained within a panel separating them from the text. The text is ruled at 28 lines per page and the gloss is half-spaced against it to yield 55 lines: the Bedan *explanationes* are independent.

This Frankfurt manuscript belongs to the milieu of Fulda and Fritzlar, perhaps indeed to Fulda itself.[6] Manifestly the volume comes from a well-established insular scriptorium. The preparation of the page, the hierarchy of initials, the several scripts distinguishing the four elements in the text (Psalter-text, gloss, Bedan *explanationes* and prayers): all these speak of a very practiced operation indeed. There is nothing either makeshift or experimental about this manuscript. Yet as a glossed insular Psalter it is a unique survival. In the creationist argument of the early nineteenth century, God has put the fossils there to test our faith. Barth. 32 has a similar status in the history of the glossed Bible. If it is rationally explicable — and we are all committed to the assumption that it is — it implies the existence of other manuscripts of the same type in the generation prior to *c.* 800. What it cannot be is a one-off item; it is the chance survivor of a vanished genre. Such an insular genre offers a perspective on the more plentiful Carolingian manuscripts of the same type.

In the first place, Barth. 32 is designed primarily to be studied rather than used in choir, but it bears no signs of use in the schoolroom. Although it cannot be compared with the most splendid of the insular Gospel-books,[7] in its own fashion it is a display manuscript. The ample scale, the diversity of script and initials, and the comprehensive ancillary material in which the Psalter itself is set: all these are elements of a luxury volume. Only full-page illumination is absent. This is a volume from a major library: ecclesiastical, royal, or indeed aristocratic. The catalogue of books owned by Everard of Friuli is a salutary reminder of what the aristocratic collector could achieve in the mid-ninth century.

> I, Evrard the count, with Gisla my wife, have decreed that on our death our property is to be divided among our children as follows . . .
> The books in our chapel to be divided thus —
> UNROCH to have our double Psalter, our Bible, St. Augustine *De uerbis domini,* and the lawbook of the Franks, the Ripuarians, the Lombards, the Alamans, and the Bavarians; also the book *De re militari* . . .
> BERENGAR to have another Psalter written in gold, St. Augustine *De ciuitate Dei* and *De uerbis domini,* and the *Gesta pontificum* . . .
> ADALARD to have the third Psalter, which I have used myself, the commentary on the Pauline Epistles, and Augustine *De uerbis domini* . . .

RUDOLPH to have the glossed Psalter which Gisla has had for her
own use . . . and the daily missal which we have always had in
our chapel . . .

Due provision was then made for the four daughters.[8] The *Psalterium
duplex,*[9] the *Psalterium aureum,* the *Psalterium cum sua expositione:* Everard
and Gisla had them all.

Secondly, a major element in Barth. 32 is the marginal gloss.
It is essentially patristic, the dominant contributor being Cassiodorus.[10]
But whether the selection has been made directly for the present gloss
or whether it has a more complex history is not yet clear. The abridged
version of the *Expositio psalmorum* that is known principally in a Durham manuscript of *c.* 725–750 may yet prove to have had a wider circulation as marginalia in insular and Carolingian Psalters.[11]

In sum, however, Barth. 32 constitutes a base from which to consider glossed Psalters of the ninth century and beyond. These also
prove to be luxury volumes with a Cassiodoran gloss, at least initially.
Two such manuscripts and fragments of a third survive from St. Gall
c. 840–870.[12] In the wonderfully opulent Göttweig manuscript, Stiftsbibliothek 30 (see Plate 2), the very gloss begins in a Carolingian version of rustic capitals; in the rest of the volume, it descends to minuscule half-spaced with the text hand. Bernhard Bischoff has identified
the Göttweig manuscript as the textual model for a series of binding-
fragments in the Bischöfliche Zentralbibliothek at Regensburg and
the Staatsbibliothek in Munich.[13] The Göttweig manuscript and the
Regensburg-Munich fragments are notable for the elaborate "canon-
table" decoration of the litanies that precede the text of the Psalter.
The other complete manuscript, St. Gall, Stiftsbibliothek 27, is similar in size, disposition, and content.[14] As to the original owners of
these books, the role played by Abbot Grimalt of St. Gall at the court
of Louis the German in Regensburg permits the speculation that both
Göttweig 30 and the fragmentary volume were acquired by patrons
at Louis's court. Thereafter one volume remained in Regensburg and
the other travelled on down the Danube to Göttweig. South of the Alps
the principal witness is a fine volume that seems never to have left
its original home in the chapter library of Vercelli.[15] The region of
Milan has been proposed for the fragments of a slightly later volume
that was once easily its equal: these are now in the Schöyen Collection
in Oslo and the Kreis- und Studienbibliothek, Dillingen a. d. Donau.[16]
Damaged though they are, the Oslo-Dillingen fragments supply unique

evidence of a volume that had both a systematic gloss and major figural illustrations within the Psalter text (see Plate 3). This gloss owes a good deal to Augustine.[17]

West of the Rhine, the picture is obscure — unexpectedly so, given Leroquais's descriptive census of Psalter-manuscripts in all the public libraries of France. Laon 14 and Orléans 48 are solid examples of ninth-century Psalters with a planned, Cassiodoran gloss,[18] but they do not approach the splendor of the manuscripts from St. Gall and northern Italy. Conversely, the two finest illuminated Psalters of the period have long departed from France: the Utrecht Psalter from Rheims and the Stuttgart Psalter from St. Germain-des-Prés, both *c.* 820–830.[19] (The latter does have a gloss to Psalms 1–16:10,[20] but it is an addition not provided for in the original *mise-en-page.*) What we do find are luxury Psalters with extensive preliminary illustration and a systematic gloss being produced in France in the late tenth century and the first half of the eleventh. These have all the appearance of being in the same tradition, and we shall return briefly to them below. In the present state of our knowledge, however, the most accessible and complete examples of the Carolingian glossed Psalter are the books from St. Gall. Further inquiry may alter that balance in favor of France or Italy, but the principle stands: the luxury glossed Psalter, which was established by *c.* 800, continued and developed throughout the ninth century.

That other books of the Bible might be treated in a similar way is elegantly demonstrated by a group of manuscripts now in the Herzog August Bibliothek, Wolfenbüttel. They were all written in Alsace-Weissenburg *c.* 860: by, or under the direction of, the monk Otfrid. There are three volumes of the prophets (MSS Weissenburg 33, 32, and 36) and a fourth volume (MS Weissenburg 59) consisting of Acts, the catholic Epistles, and the Apocalypse.[21] All have systematic annotation, set at approximately half-spacing within panels to the right and left of the text (see Plate 4). What is more, they are much of a size; the layout of their pages is essentially the same, as is the reference system linking text and gloss. A fifth volume, containing the four Gospels (MS Weissenburg 26), has the same type of systematic gloss, but the dimensions are rather different and the gloss is by another scribe.[22] The details are expressed in Table 1.

The "boundary-columns" are those narrow columns between gloss and text which hold the reference signs; the signs themselves are in red in the first four manuscripts, and in black in the fifth. Why the Gospels diverge in this way is not at all clear. The temptation is to

Table 1.

MS	Contents	Page*	Text*	Lines	Outer gloss	Inner gloss	Boundary columns
33	Isaiah	304 × 258	222 × 114	27	50	57	9–11
32	Jeremiah	306 × 235	225 × 110	28	43	52	8–9
36	Minor Pr.	290 × 228	235 × 100	25	56	40	5–7
59	Acts, etc.	274 × 212	195 × 93	23	*c.* 50	35–40	8–9
26	Gospels	306 × 256	221 × 89	24	46	46	7–8

*Measured in mm.

postulate an entire Bible laid out according to the parameters of the other four manuscripts, or — casting caution to the winds — to see the Gospels as the sole surviving volume from yet another such series. Let us be content with what we have: date and provenance are certain, and the association specifically with Otfrid is widely accepted, even if it is a little difficult to define.[23]

In the four "matching" volumes, the annotation is based very closely on identifiable authors. The gloss to Isaiah depends on the abridgement of Jerome's commentary that was made in the late eighth century by Alcuin's pupil, Josephus Scottus.[24] The gloss to Jeremiah is effectively Rabanus, himself using Jerome but supplying the missing conclusion and the commentary to Lamentations.[25] For the Minor Prophets the glossator uses Jerome directly.[26] In the New Testament volume he is a faithful follower of Bede.[27] Essentially, then, the glossator is using the most recent reliable editions — as we would today. Where he has the choice of Jerome "straight" or the Carolingian adaptations by Josephus Scottus and Rabanus, he uses the latter. Some further difficulties have been clarified, and the *recherché* linguistic disquisitions have been abridged or cut entirely. In their lucid and convenient presentation of Carolingian exegesis, the Weissenburg volumes now stand alone. Unlike the glossed Psalters — which were to grow ever more splendid — these are plain text manuscripts, without major illumination, destined for a well-equipped, working monastic library. The likelihood is that other, comparable scriptoria produced comparable books.

The habit of glossing a Bible text and the expectation that a volume of Scripture would be systematically annotated, are dramatically illustrated by two manuscripts that were written in Reichenau over a century later. These are now Bamberg, Staatsbibliothek MSS bibl. 22 and 76. They are familiar to all students of Otto III as volumes from his personal library.[28] That they were designed specifically for the young king may be inferred from the prefatory illuminations. The Song of Songs begins with a unique image of the two major sacraments—a procession of bishops and kings from baptism to the Eucharist. The page facing shows Christ in majesty seated upon the initial 'O' of *O*sculetur (Plate 5).[29] The text continues at the foot of the page, SCVLETVR ME OSCVLO O, and on the verso RIS SUI (Plate 6). The page has been ruled for text and half-spaced gloss; both are executed by the same scribe. The gloss itself is based on Alcuin and the explanatory headings on Bede.[30] The second part of the same volume is a glossed Daniel, with two fine opening miniatures;[31] the companion volume is a glossed Isaiah, in the same format.[32] It is safe to say that these little books were never replicated. They are witness here simply to the principle of glossing the Bible and to the substance of that gloss. Whether or not in a Carolingian "revised edition," the annotation is substantially either patristic or (where the Fathers were lacking) the work of Bede. Of contemporary scholarship, whether in the form of a prologue or an alternative opinion, there is not a trace.

Meanwhile the luxury glossed Psalter continued in production. One of the finest was made in 999 for Odbert, abbot of St. Bertin. Three remarkable full-page miniatures precede the Psalter, and within the text itself approximately one psalm in four has a good historiated initial.[33] Another impressive volume, from St. Symphorian at Metz, survives now only in a single photograph and Leroquais's description.[34] St. Denis had a more modest version, but with a hymnal, in the early eleventh century; St. Germain-des-Prés had a related text, with two archaic miniatures, written between 1030 and *c.* 1060.[35] Finally, a Psalter from Angers Cathedral, written and used in the mid-eleventh century, when Berengar of Tours was an archdeacon there, again has ambitious full-page painted miniatures.[36] In these late witnesses to the Carolingian tradition, the pictorial canon is enlarged and the gloss, so far as it has been examined, has often diverged markedly from its Cassiodoran origins — often, but not always. The lost Metz manuscript seems to have been conservative and Cassiodoran. St. Bertin, St. Denis, and St. Germain-des-Prés, on the other hand, have related versions of the Augustine-based gloss that is already visible in Laon 14.[37] The Angers Psalter is the most innovative, possibly in response to archdeacon Rainald, master in the schools of Angers *c.* 1040–1060.[38]

A new and elegant *mise-en-page* was devised over the same de-

cades at Tegernsee in southern Bavaria. In four splendid and virtually identical Psalters, the Cassiodoran gloss constitutes the outer
column in a bicolumnar manuscript (Plate 7).[39] I say "virtually identical," because the ancillary material varies slightly in sequence and
in content, but essentially the four volumes are quadruplets from the
same scriptorium. The running title "BRVNO EPISCOPVS" that appears
throughout Rawl. G. 163 (Plate 7), and nowhere else, has long been
held to name the author of the gloss. If that is so, "Bishop Bruno"
should be sought in the ninth century, for the gloss is a slightly expanded version of that found in ninth-century St. Gall.[40] The man
who has been identified as the author since the late fifteenth century,
Bruno, bishop of Würzburg (*ob.* 1045), is immediately out of court.[41]
He may, of course, be the patron by whom that particular manuscript
was commissioned.[42] For our purposes, the Tegernsee manuscripts
continue the tradition of the luxury Psalter in a highly professional
form. They have fine gold display initials at the major divisions of
the text, a supporting hierarchy of lesser initials, and the ruling for
the text and gloss on a single, full- and half-space grid.[43] In structure
and content, and above all in style, they are the heirs of Frankfurt,
Barth. 32, the Fulda Psalter of *c.* 800.

3. THE BIBLE IN SCHOOL, 1050–1120

In Carolingian Europe, the Bible was the object of public reading and private reflection, but it was not the basis of elementary education. Mastery of Latin and the tricks of eloquence were still learned
from the well-tried antique manuals and from a limited canon of the
classical Latin poets and the learned authors of the fifth and sixth centuries. Carolingian manuscripts of these staple teaching texts have,
in addition to an often extensive marginal gloss, words and phrases
written between the lines. These interlinear notes are juxtaposed to
the words they explain, leading the student through his author's syntax phrase by phrase and marking unexpected perils on the way. Plate
10 shows a later-tenth-century manuscript of the *De consolatione philosophiae,* probably from the Rhineland:[44]

> Etenim licet Indica longe
> Tellus tua iura tremescat
> Et seruiat ultima Thyle . . .
>   (3 met.5, lines 5–7)

"Though you rule the world—from India to the Orkneys—if you cannot control your own instincts and moods, you have no power at all." The reference-letter D refers twice to the marginal gloss, which contains an exposition about a century older than the present manuscript. It locates India and "Ultima Thule," "only a day's journey from the frozen sea that we read of in Solinus."[45] But the real hazard is "tua": let the land, "tellus," tremble at your government, "tua iura." The master provides synonyms for "tremescat" (line 6) and "atras" (line 8) and, in the prose following (3 pr.6), a longer observation on "fallax" and a translation of the fragment of Euripides that begins on the bottom line. 'Reading' a text in this way, master and student came to understand it. They had not only learned the words, they had sought out the underlying questions and found solutions. Could they claim a comparable understanding of the Bible?

On the face of it, the answer was to use the Bible itself as the basic educational text, thus replacing the lies of the poets and the temptations of philosophy with Christian truth. The student would study within the framework of his own culture and beliefs. Bible-based education had been a live issue in the late fourth and early fifth centuries,[46] perhaps again in the time of Bede,[47] and certainly in the reforming circles of the 1040s and 1050s. Manegold of Lautenbach abandoned a successful career expounding Priscian, Cicero, and Ovid in the schools of northern France to "enter religion" and apply the same talents and the same method to the Psalter, the Pauline Epistles, and (it is said) several other parts of Scripture.[48] He was also increasingly involved in Gregorian politics. We may indeed speculate that insofar as education was on the program of the reformers attached to the papal court, these men would have wished to replace the old curriculum of the *artes* and *auctores* with studies based more narrowly on the Bible and on canon law. Whether such studies would be appropriate to a secular clerk, in an age when secular clerks were required to have increasingly sophisticated skills in administration, is quite another question.

Whether or not it was sound, whether or not it would prove workable, Bible-based education was a recognized phenomenon in the mid- and later-eleventh century. "I have heard of a man in Francia," wrote a former *scholasticus* of Bamberg cathedral, himself now a monk, *c.* 1060, "who used to be an outstanding teacher of dialectic. Now he has turned his attention to the learning of the Church and has sharpened the wits of many students by his intelligent exposition of the

Pauline Epistles and the Psalter."[49] These words may well refer to Lanfranc of Bec,[50] whom we know on other evidence to have applied to the Bible techniques learned and used in the study of the *artes.*[51] Lanfranc's exposition of the Pauline Epistles, together with other anonymous commentaries of the same type, survive in manuscripts which are predictably—it might be said, necessarily—in the format of the double gloss: they consist of marginal annotation and brief words or phrases between the lines. It is the long-familiar format of the glossed Virgil or Boethius (Plate 10), here applied to Scripture. The earliest example of the new-style gloss to the Pauline Epistles survives in what may be the original manuscript from St. Vincent, Metz, and in a much more elegant copy of the Metz manuscript that was made at Tegernsee *c.* 1050–1060.[52] The Metz manuscript is the more useful in that it names its authorities.

Metz-Tegernsee Gloss on Romans 2.2–5

2.2 *Scimus enim quoniam iudicium dei est secundum ueritatem in eos qui talia agunt.*
AMB. *Scimus:* Quia si nobis displicet. quanto magis deo qui uere iustus est et opus suum zelatur.[53]
L. *iudicium:* [interlinear] condemnationem dicit.
AMB. *secundum ueritatem:* [interlinear] terrorem eis incutit.
PEL. *agunt:* [interlinear] id est. sui similes iudicant.[54]
LANT. *Scimus:* Iam quod diceret. Si tu iniustus iniuste iudicas iniustum. quanto magis deus iustus te iuste iudicabit iniustum.
LANT. Ne forte aliquis sibi de impunitate blandiretur dicens. Misericors deus non patietur creaturam perire. hoc adiecit.
PEL. Numquid propterea tibi de impunitate blandiris quia deus in presenti non reddit?

2.4 *An diuitias bonitatis eius et patientiae et longanimitatis contemnis? Ignoras quoniam benignitas dei ad paenitentiam te adducit?*
SED. *An diuitias:* Diuitias bonitatis dei dicit quibus bona pro malis dat. Patientia uero est qua peccatores patienter tolerat. Longanimitas est qua longum spacium poenitentiae dat.[55]
LANT. *ignorans:* [interlinear] Deus tibi tempus poenitentiae concedit. sed tu eo male uteris.

2.5 *Secundum autem duritiam tuam et impenitens cor thesaurizas tibi iram in die irae et reuelationis iusti iudicii dei.*
ORIENIS *duritiam:* Cor durum in scripturis dici uidetur cum mens

humana uelut cera a frigore iniquitatis obstricta signaculum imaginis diuinae non recipit.[56]

AMB. *impenitens:* Impunitatem peccatorum sperans. non solum duras inconuertibilis. sed adhuc acerbius peccas.

LANT. *impenitens:* [interlinear] Cor autem impoenitens uocatur quod emolliri ad poenitentiam non potest.

AMB. *in die irae:* Dies irae est peccatoribus qua in eo sentiunt poenam.

So far as I have verified them, both the attributions and the verbal details of the quotations are soberly accurate. The order of the words has often been changed, and much has been omitted; but otherwise these glosses are pretty well verbatim 'Ambrosiaster', the Latin Origen, Pelagius, and Sedulius, as advertised. The identity of "Lant.," the only modern master and perhaps himself the excerptor of the patristic material, is still quite uncertain. He could well be Williram's master teaching in "Francia." That he is Lanfranc of Bec requires the hypothesis that Lanfranc wrote two quite distinct expositions of St. Paul: one giving rise to the "Lant." material in the Metz-Tegernsee Gloss, the other being the text known at Canterbury.[57] Here is the same passage of Romans in what we may call the "Canterbury text":

2.2 LANF. Auctoritate sua confirmat peccatores supradictorum scelerum generaliter esse damnandos.

secundum ueritatem: Id est secundum iustitiam. sine acceptione personarum (cf. 2.11).

2.3 LANF. Putare posset aliquis imperitus. quod tanto liberius peccare liceret. quanto diligentius alios a peccato compesceret.

2.4 AMB. Haec dicit. ut non iam se putet euasisse. si patitur illum diu peccantem.

contemnis: [interlinear] nolendo respicere.

2.5 AMB. *et reuelationis iusti iudicii dei:* Reuelabitur quod modo futurum negatur. Cum enim ostenditur quod non esse creditur reuelatur. His enim ostenditur qui negant quia credentibus manifestum est.

thesaurizas: [interlinear] auges.[58]

In this case we are reasonably confident that Lanfranc of Bec is both the glossator "Lanf." and the excerptor of the patristic material. His sources are 'Ambrosiaster', once more, and Augustine — a much narrower range than was laid under contribution for the Metz-Tegernsee commentary. We note the presence of "beginners" (*imperiti*) and the cross-referencing from verse to verse. From time to time Lanfranc introduces simple logical and rhetorical formulae:

> 1 Cor. 1.4 *In omnibus diuites facti estis in illo.*
> LANFRANC: **Totum pro parte** ponit. Non enim **omnes** in omnibus uirtutibus diuites erant. **Quosdam** enim in posterioribus redarguit.

Rightly used, logic is a fine exegetical tool. In the wrong hands, it might be dangerous, as Lanfranc illustrates sharply a few verses further on.

> 1 Cor. 1.17 *Non enim misit me Christus baptizare sed euangelizare, non in sapientia uerbi, ut non euacuetur crux Christi.*
> LANFRANC: **Sapientia,** ubi dialecticam dicit, per quam **crux,** id est mors Christi, eam simpliciter intelligentibus euacuari uidetur: quia —
>> Deus immortalis.
>> Christus autem deus.
>> Christus igitur immortalis.
>> Si autem immortalis, mori non potuit.

Sic de partu Virginis et quibusdam aliis sacramentis. Perspicaciter etiam intuentibus dialectica sacramenta dei non impugnat, sed cum res exigit — si rectissime teneatur — astruit et confirmat.[59]

The *artes* give an edge to Lanfranc's commentary, without in any sense dominating it. The verbal pyrotechnics of the Metz-Tegernsee Gloss — "Si tu iniustus iniuste iudicas iniustum. quanto magis deus iustus te iuste iudicabit iniustum" — were certainly not unfamiliar to Lanfranc nor beyond his competence,[60] but he thought them inappropriate to biblical commentary.

Scholars differed over the extent to which the *artes* might be applied to the study of the Bible and the elucidation of Christian doctrine, and conversely, over the use of the Bible as a school text. But to some extent and in some places, they were prepared to use Scripture as a basis for teaching elementary syntax and the techniques of argument — as a text like other texts, to be analyzed as well as learned. Their outlook is reflected in the new format of the biblical text for use in school: now the long-established marginal gloss is augmented with interlinear notes. The new function generated the new format. "Walafrid Strabo wrote the marginal gloss, Anselm of Laon wrote the interlinear": the dates at least are sound.

"He was prevented by the cares of administration from glossing the entire Bible," so Peter the Chanter, writing *c.* 1160.[61] As dean and eventually archdeacon, Anselm had a major role to play in a time of crisis between the cathedral of Laon and the city. In 1112 the cathedral was burned down and the bishop lynched.[62] The man who had to steer an even course through such disasters might well be distracted from glossing the Bible. The issue is not the existence of a complete commentary on the Bible (in some form that had existed since the time of Rabanus); it is the extent to which such commentary was cast in the form of a marginal and interlinear gloss. Undoubtedly the Psalter and the Pauline Epistles were available in that format.[63] For Anselm himself, and for the "school of Laon" in his time (*c.* 1080–1117), two questions were outstanding. Of the several alternative versions of the Psalter and Pauline Epistles with marginal and interlinear gloss, which were the best suited to schoolroom use at Laon? Could they be improved? Secondly, could or should the rest of the Bible be treated in the same way? Anselm's effective answer to the former may have brought him more credit than is strictly his due by way of answering the latter.

There is a widespread scholarly consensus that Anselm constructed the definitive gloss on the Psalter and the Pauline Epistles, the so-called *parva glosatura.*[64] Here is his exposition of Romans 2.1–5.

2.1 *Propter quod inexcusabilis:* Hic communiter de gentilibus et Iudaeis. Iudaeus iudicabit gentilem propter priorem statum. gentilis Iudaeum. uterque homo non spiritus. Si Iudaeus iudicat gentilem de idolatria. et ipsi idolatriae. Si gentilis Iudaeum de legis praeuaricatione. et ipse praeuaricator naturalis legis.

propter quod: [interlinear] Quia omnis faciens et consentiens dignus est morte.

inexcusabilis: Quia tu ipse testis est damnationis tuae, dum alium iudicas. Quare hoc? Quia eadem agis.

o homo: [interlinear] tam Iudaeus quam gentilis.

qui iudicas: In quo ostendit se esse quod non est. id est iustum.

qui iudicas: Hoc propter Iudaeos. etsi nondum eos nominatim exprimit. qui in lege gloriantur, et agunt quae damnant. et quia nondum nominatim eos exprimit ideo dicit, "Ira in omnem animam operantis malum, Iudaei et Graeci. Et gloria omni operanti bonum, Iudaeo et Graeco."

eadem enim agis: Inanem excusationem gentium et Iudaeorum sua auctoritate destruit Apostolus. posset enim excusationem peccati sui dicere Iudaeus. Etsi eadem. me Iudaeum defendit genus et lex. me gentilem ignorantia. Contra Apostolus.

agis: [interlinear] Quod uos ita opiniamini. nos autem scimus. Vel uere inexcusabilis es.

2.2 *enim:* [interlinear] uel autem.

secundum ueritatem: [interlinear] equitatem rei non personas.

in eos: [interlinear] contra.

qui talia agunt: [interlinear] siue Iudaeos siue gentiles.

2.3 *Existimas autem:* Communiter legitur hoc capitulum contra Iudaeos et gentiles.

existimas: [interlinear] Increpatio cum ironia. Nos ita scimus sed tu existimas. Opinaris.

o homo: [interlinear] carnalis.

qui iudicas: [interlinear] Quia haec potestas data est tibi. et non est in mundo qui te iudicet.

talia: [interlinear] quae.

quia tu effugies: Peccas dum tibi impunitatem promittis. grauius quia contemnis bonum dei et ignoras te contemnere. Et an hoc facis? Increpatio, quasi mirum.

quia tu: [interlinear] hoc subaudis, Quocunque modo.

2.4 *An diuitias:* Copiosa est bonitas quae multa uel multis peccantibus uel multa bona ministrat. blandiens ut ad paenitentiam attrahat. Copiosa patientia quae tot et tanta peccantes sustinet. nec cito punit et hoc est longanimitatis. quia non ad horam est. sed longa per multa expectans tempora. Haec contemnit qui non sic utitur ad paenitentiam ut deus intendit sed ad impunitatem uertit.

An: [interlinear] Cur ergo modo non punit? Quia bonus expectat quod ignoras, an diuitias.

diuitias: [interlinear] copiosam bonitatem.

patientiae: [interlinear] patientiam et longanimitatem.

longanimitatis: [interlinear] quia modo tempus est misericordiae.

ignoras: [interlinear] Seuere loquitur quia mala mens non reuocatur nisi timore. Ecce deum nescis misericordem.

adducit: [interlinear] quantum in se est.

patientiam: [interlinear] uel penitentiam.

2.5 *Secundum duritiam:* Sunt enim quidam quibus mala quae agunt displicent.

secundum duritiam: [interlinear] Sed quia tu durus. et in malo tuo pertinax. de quo nec corde penites.

thesaurizas: Accumulas tibi uindictam. deterius peccando. haec impoenitentia est blasfemia in spiritum sanctum.

iram: [interlinear] exercendam.

in die: [interlinear] quando omnia aperta. et quando reuelabitur quod a uobis modo nescitur.[65]

These few verses may well give us pause. Although the format of Anselm's exposition is appropriate to the schoolroom, its function is as much the convenient record of patristic opinion as the analysis of syntax and the teaching of rhetoric. The problem-solving element is much reduced. Or rather, it has been removed to the newly vigorous genre of "sentence-literature," which would develop rapidly over the next two generations by way of Abelard's *Sic et non* to the *IV Libri sententiarum* of Peter Lombard.[66] Thus the *parva glosatura* is paradoxically a more conservative work than the two earlier commentaries quoted above: it is solid patristic matter, with few modern additions.[67] As such, it set the tone for the *Glossa ordinaria.*[68]

4. THE *GLOSSA ORDINARIA* (*c.* 1130–*c.* 1160)

The *Glossa ordinaria* as it stood in the mid-twelfth century, and as we know it today, is the sum of the books of the Vulgate Bible laid out as a text with marginal and interlinear gloss. The classic *mise-en-page* is a central column of text with half-spaced glossing to left and right, and brief interlinear notes throughout. In format it derives both from the display Psalters of *c.* 800–*c.* 1050 and from the secular teaching texts of the same period. An entire glossed Bible consists of seven or eight such quarto volumes, with the proviso that some books — being in greater demand — were copied more frequently than others.[69] So far as it has been examined, the text remains remarkably stable, probably because the great bulk of the manuscripts was produced between the mid-twelfth and the early thirteenth century. Throughout the thirteenth and fourteenth centuries, the *Glossa ordinaria,* though widely available, was not constantly being transcribed; it was not, for instance, a set text in the universities. Thus the text suffered little contamination or evolution. This is well seen in the *editio princeps* of 1480, four stately volumes that have the twelfth-century *mise-en-page* and (with few exceptions) the twelfth-century text.[70]

The books of the glossed Bible are, with one exception, anonymous. The Lamentations of Jeremiah carries the colophon, "Sufficiant haec ad expositionem Lamentationum Ieremiae, quae de patrum fontibus hausi ego Gillebertus autisiodorensis ecclesiae diaconus."[71]

Gilbert of Auxerre, also known as "Vniversalis," was a theologian and lawyer who late in life became bishop of London. He may have studied or even taught at Laon.[72] It is not unlikely that he put his hand to other books than Lamentations, but the surviving data are scarce, late, and uncertain, as they are for Anselm and the school of Laon as a whole.[73] We cannot make bricks without straw. Rather than speculate on the authorship of individual books we should look at the institution or institutions that generated the *Glossa ordinaria*. The great days of the cathedral school at Laon were the last two decades of the eleventh century. Abelard visited *c*. 1110, when Master Anselm's reputation was already made and his powers (if we are to believe Abelard) were already on the wane.[74] What is more, if we believe one tenth of what Guibert of Nogent has to say about the state of the cathedral and city of Laon *c*. 1100–1115, it was not an atmosphere in which the arts of peace could flourish.[75] The manuscripts of the *Gloss* that survive today in the municipal library at Laon are for the most part not from the cathedral itself, but from the Cistercian house of Vauclerc (founded 1134).[76] There is, in sum, very little support for Peter the Chanter's suggestion that the gloss to the rest of the Bible was attempted in the cathedral school at Laon. Where, then? How can we explain the serried ranks of glossed Gospels, glossed Prophets, glossed Apocalypses of the mid-twelfth century?[77]

In an earlier essay, I flew the kite that the *Glossa ordinaria* was organized for the school of St. Victor.[78] That kite may be a rather more substantial craft. The educational philosophy of St. Victor falls in very easily with the *Glossa ordinaria,* even to the point of requiring some such correlation of patristic exegesis and biblical text.[79] The dates are credible. The *floruit* of St. Victor as an influential school is *c*. 1125–1160. Most crucial of all, the *Glossa ordinaria* is an example of the successful distribution of a definitive text over a very wide area: the same annotation down to the most curious details is found from Klosterneuburg to Durham. Relatively few institutions in the mid-twelfth century had the reputation and resources to effect such a distribution. I do not insist on St. Victor, merely on an institution of that kind at that date.

5. TWELFTH-CENTURY EXEGESIS

Several of the greatest scholars and teachers in the twelfth century gave their time to the study of the Bible. For them, the *Glossa ordinaria* was simply the best edition to use: the one that made patristic exegesis instantly and reliably available for any verse of Scripture. Their own biblical exegesis was never cast as text and gloss, but in the format of continuous commentary with lemmata, so the commentator can stick close to his text, resolving the minor cruxes of syntax and meaning. That accomplished, he can identify and address the major issue. Abelard's treatment of the passage in Romans quoted above is a fine example of the technique.[80] Having examined each verse in detail, only then does he fully consider the Last Judgment. The continuous commentary is flexible as to scale, easily revised, and readily transcribed in the cheap scholastic octavo written in "écriture microscopique." It has space for argument and reflection. It is the structure adopted without exception by the great exegetes of the twelfth century: Abelard himself, Rupert of Deutz, Gilbert de la Porrée, Hugh and Andrew of St. Victor—and reasonably so. These are the men at the forefront of biblical scholarship. Their work was in constant flux: criticized, adjusted, and radically recast. The *Glossa ordinaria* by contrast was static: the same indispensable work of reference in every good library. To return to my original metaphor, the *Glossa ordinaria* is the junction between traditional patristic exegesis and modern scholastic method. It is the side of the hinge that is fixed to the doorpost, while scholastic exegesis swings with the door. In that capacity, the *Glossa ordinaria* remained available and consulted, but essentially unchanged, until well into the fifteenth century. Only the ambitions of the early printers and the new demands of Reformation controversy radically altered first the format and then the content of the *Glossa ordinaria.*[81]

NOTES

1. B. Smalley, "Glossa Ordinaria," in *Theologische Realenzyklopädie* (1984) 13:452–457, with literature. See also C. F. R. de Hamel, *Glossed Books of the Bible and the Beginnings of the Paris Booktrade* (Woodbridge, 1984), 1–5.

2. M. T. Gibson, "The Twelfth-Century Glossed Bible," in E. A. Livingstone, ed., *Studia Patristica* 23 (1990): 232–244.

3. G. Powitz and H. Buck, *Die Handschriften des Bartholomaeusstift und des Karmeliterklosters in Frankfurt-am-Main*, Kataloge der Stadt- und Universitätsbibliothek Frankfurt-am-Main 3:ii (Frankfurt, 1974), 66–70.

4. PL 93:483C–1098C, *explanationes* only. See preeminently B. Fischer, "Bedae de titulis psalmorum liber," in *Festschrift Bernhard Bischoff zu seinem 65 Geburtstag*, ed. J. Autenrieth and F. Brunhölzl (Stuttgart, 1971), 90–110 and plate 2.

5. The *Romanum* is another sign of early date. On the Continent, it rapidly gave way to the *Gallicanum* in the first decades of the ninth century.

6. The text hand appears also in one Fulda Gospel-book (Oxford, Bodleian Library MS Laud lat. 102), and may be compared with the hand of another (Erlangen, Universitätsbibliothek MS. 9). For the latter see B. Bischoff and J. Hofmann, *Libri Sancti Kiliani,* Quellen und Forschungen zur Geschichte des Bistums und Hochstifts Würzburg 6 (Würzburg, 1952), 55–56, and the plates in R. Schilling, *Die illuminierten Handschriften und Einzelminiaturen des Mittelalters und der Renaissance in Frankfurter Besitz* (Frankfurt, 1929), plate 2 (initials fols. 61v, 120v). MS Barth. 32 was certainly in Fulda from the mid-eleventh century until the mid-fourteenth; see Powitz and Buck, *Bartholomaeusstift,* 68.

7. For examples, see most conveniently J. J. G. Alexander, *Insular Manuscripts 6th to the 9th Century,* A Survey of Manuscripts Illuminated in the British Isles 1 (London, 1978), nos. 9, 11, 22, 24, 26, 30, with the references.

8. P. E. Schramm and F. Mütherich, *Denkmale der deutschen Könige und Kaiser I,* 2d ed. (Munich, 1981), 93–94, at 94. The list of books is preceded by a splendid array of metalwork, gems, and ivory *de paramento nostro* (from our regalia).

9. It survives as Vatican, Bibliotheca Apostolica Reg. lat. 11, still having Everard's note of ownership. See E. A. Lowe, *Codices Latini Antiquiores* 1 (Oxford, 1934), no. 101, and its *Supplement* (Oxford, 1971), no. 101.

10. *Cassiodorus in Psalmos,* ed. M. Adriaen, CCSL 97–98 (Turnhout, 1958).

11. For Durham, Cathedral Library B.II.30, see Alexander, *Insular Manuscripts,* no. 17, with the references. A tenth-century fragment of the abridged Cassiodorus is now Halle, Universitäts- u. Landesbibliothek, Qu. Cod. 76, fol. 1–33: J. Fliege, *Die Handschriften der ehemaligen Stifts- und Gymnasialbibliothek Quedlinburg in Halle* (Halle [Salle], 1982), 49–50.

12. My debt here is equally to Dr. Bonifatius Fischer, whose study of the Bedan *tituli* (note 4 above: see his plates 3–6) first alerted me to these manuscripts, and to the generous encouragement and advice of Professor Bernhard Bischoff.

13. B. Bischoff, "Bücher am Hofe Ludwigs des Deutschen und die Privatbibliothek des Kanzlers Grimalt," in his *Mittelalterliche Studien* 3 (Stuttgart, 1981), 187–212, at 190, with references. For the Munich bifolium, Staatsbibliothek Clm 29315/3, see Schramm and Mütherich, *Denkmale,* 474 and plate 2. Thanks are due to the Hill Monastic Microfilm Library, Collegeville, for a microfilm of Göttweig 30, and to the Zentralbibliothek in Regensburg for excellent photographs of the fragments in their care.

14. A. Bruckner, *Scriptoria Medii Aevi Helvetica* 3 (Geneva, 1938), 59.

15. Vercelli, Chapter Library CXLIX, for which see G. Mazzatinti, *Inventari dei manoscritti delle biblioteche d'Italia* (Florence, 1925) 31:113–114; and B. Bischoff, *Die südostdeutschen Schreibschulen und Bibliotheken in der Karolingerzeit* (Wiesbaden, 1980) 2:189.

16. See Bernard Quaritch Ltd., *Bookhands of the Middle Ages III,* Catalogue 1088 (London, 1988), no. 56, now Oslo, Schöyen 74. The Dillingen fragment is number 25. I am very grateful to Messrs. Quaritch for allowing me to study the Schöyen fragment, and to Mr. Martin Schöyen for his ready assistance.

17. *Enarrationes in psalmos,* ed. E. Dekkers and J. Fraipont, CCSL 38–40 (Turnhout, 1956).

18. V. Leroquais, *Les Psautiers manuscrits latins des bibliothèques publiques de France* (Macon, 1940–1941), nos. 182 and 240.

19. For facsimiles with a critical introduction, see *Utrecht-Psalter,* ed. R. van der Horst and J. H. A. Engelbregt, Codices Selecti 75 (Graz, 1984); *Der Stuttgarter Bilderpsalter: bibl. fol. 23 Württembergische Landesbibliothek Stuttgart* (Stuttgart, 1968), with remarks on provenance at 2:25.

20. See H. Boese, *Die alte 'Glosa Psalmorum ex traditione seniorum': Untersuchungen, Materialen, Texte,* Vetus Latina 9 (Freiburg, 1982); compare B. Fischer, "Die Texte," in *Der Stuttgarter Bilderpsalter* 2:223–288, at 226–256.

21. H. Butzmann, *Die Weissenburger Handschriften,* Kataloge der Herzog-August-Bibliothek Wolfenbüttel NS 10 (Frankfurt 1964), 142–144, 147–148, 196–198.

22. Ibid., 134–136.

23. The principal studies of the Weissenburg scriptorium are Butzmann, *Weissenburger Handschriften,* 42–66, and W. Kleiber, *Otfrid von Weissenburg* (Munich, 1971). Kleiber regards Otfrid as being in charge of the scriptorium from the middle to the later ninth century and as being himself the scribe of MSS Weissenburg 26, 32, 33, 36, and 59. That is probably too sweeping a judgment: at least MS. 26 (the four Gospels) is in a markedly different hand.

24. Josephus's abridgement was available in MS Weissenburg 49; see Butzmann, *Weissenburger Handscriften,* 186–187, with references.

25. See PL 111:793–1272. Jerome himself breaks off at Jeremiah 32:44, Scilicet in Rabanus book 12, 111:1062.

26. *Commentarii in Prophetas,* ed. M. Adriaen, CCSL 76–76A (Turnhout, 1969–70).

27. Bede, *Expositio Actuum Apostolorum* and *In Epistolas VII Catholicas,* ed. M. L. W. Laistner, CCSL 121 (Turnhout, 1983). For Bede, *Explanatio Apocalypsis,* see still PL 93:129–206.

28. F. Mütherich, "The Library of Otto III," in *The Role of the Book in Medieval Culture,* ed. P. F. Ganz, Bibliologia 3 (Turnhout, 1986) 2:11–25, at 13.

29. Bamberg, Staatsbibliothek bibl. 22, fols. 4v (procession) and 5 (Christ: our Plate 5). See further Schramm and Mütherich, *Denkmale,* no. 109.

30. Alcuin, *Compendium in Canticum Canticorum,* PL 100:639–664; Bede, *In Cantica Canticorum,* ed. D. Hurst, CCSL 119B (Turnhout, 1983).

31. Bibl. 22, fols. 31 and 32. There is a good color plate of fol. 32 in J. J. G. Alexander, *The Decorated Letter* (London, 1978), plate 13; see also pp. 33 and 35.

32. Bibl. 76. See Schramm and Mütherich, *Denkmale* 1, no. 109 and plate of fol. 11.

33. Boulogne-sur-Mer, Bibliothèque Municipale 20. See Leroquais, *Les Psautiers manuscrits latins,* no. 76, with plates xv–xxi; and H. Steger, *David Rex et Propheta* (Nuremberg, 1961), nos. 21–22.

34. Metz, Bibliothéque Municipale 14, destroyed in 1944. See the detailed description by Leroquais, *Les Psautiers manuscrits latins,* 2:251–254, with plate xxii; and Steger, *David,* no. 24.

35. Paris, B.N. lat. 103 (St. Denis: Leroquais no. 274) and lat. 11550 (St. Germain-des-Prés: Leroquais no. 334, with plates xxx–xxxi). See also Steger, *David,* no. 30. For B.N. lat. 11550, see further C. Samaran and R. Marichal, *Catalogue des manuscrits en écriture latine portant des indications de date, de lieu, ou de copiste* 3 (Paris, 1974), 241.

36. Amiens, Bibliothèque de la Ville Fonds de l'Escalopier 2 (Leroquais no. 11, Steger no. 25).

37. See note 19, above.

38. See O. Guillot, *Le comte d'Anjou et son entourage au XI siècle* (Paris, 1972) 2:115, with the references there.

39. C. E. Eder, "Die Schule des Klosters Tegernsee im frühen Mittelalter im Spiegel der Tegernseer Handschriften," *Studien und Mitteilungen zur Geschichte des Benediktinerordens* 83 (1972): 103–106, nos. 70–73. See further note 44 below.

40. See Fischer, "Bedae de titulis psalmorum liber," 103–105, who first observed the relation of the Tegernsee commentary to St. Gall.

41. The *editio princeps* is anonymous (Reyser: *c.* 1485). Koberger's editions of 1494 and 1497 imply that Bruno is the author without actually saying so. See F. R. Goff, *Incunabula in American Libraries,* 3rd ed. (rptd. New York, 1973), P–1046 (Reyser: HC 4011*) and P–1050, P–1057 (Koberger: HC 4012*, HC 4013*). Cochlaeus (1533), who altered and expanded the text, accepts Bruno's authorship without question. Migne follows Cochlaeus's text and the ascription to Bruno (PL 142:39–530).

42. In the mid-ninth century, several manuscripts written for Hincmar of Rheims have the owner's name, "HINCMARVS," written along the lower margins of the text. See F. M. Cary, "The Scriptorium of Reims during the Archbishopric of Hincmar (845–882 A.D.)," in *Classical and Mediaeval Studies in Honor of Edward Kenneth Rand,* ed. L. W. Jones (New York, 1938), 41–60, at 49 and following.

43. Munich, Staatsbibliothek Clm 18121: page, 327 × 249 mm.; psalter-column, 89 mm.; gloss-column, 84 mm.; 23 lines of text, 45 lines of gloss. Oxford, Bodleian Rawl. G. 163 (Plate 7): page, 306 × 240 mm.; psalter-column, 93 mm.; gloss-column, 94 mm.; 23 lines of text and 45 lines of gloss. Oxford, Bodleian Laud lat. 96: page, 328 × 249 mm.; psalter-column, 93 mm.; gloss-column, 84 mm.; 23 lines of text, 45 lines of gloss. Vatican, Bibliotheca Apostolica Ross. lat. 184: page, 319 × 244 mm.; psalter-column, 88 mm.; gloss-column, 88 mm.; 23 lines of text, 45 lines of gloss.

44. London, BL Harley 3095, fol. 40v. See F. Troncarelli, *Boethiana Aetas* (Alessandria, 1987), no. 80, pp. 220–222.

45. E. T. Silk, *Saeculi noni auctoris in Boetii Consolationem philosophiae commentarius,* Papers and Monographs of the American Academy in Rome 9 (Rome, 1935), 136–137. Compare Solinus, *Collectanea rerum memorabilium* 22.9, ed. T. Mommsen, 2d ed. (Berlin, 1895), 102: "ultra Thylen accipimus pigrum et concretum mare."

46. Augustine, *De doctrina Christiana* 4 and throughout.

47. Bede, *De arte metrica* and *De schematibus et tropis,* ed. C. B. Kendall, CCSL 128A (Turnhout, 1975), 60–171. See also the older, "Christian" Donatus: L. Holtz, *Donat et la tradition de l'enseignement grammatical* (Paris, 1981), 256–258.

48. W. Hartmann, "Manegold von Lautenbach," in *Die Deutsche Literatur der Mittelalters: Verfasserlexikon,* ed. C. Stöllinger-Löser, 5 (Berlin and New York, 1985), columns 1214–1218.

49. Williram of Ebersberg, *Expositio in Cantica canticorum,* ed. E. H. Bartelmez (Philadelphia, 1967), 1.

50. Bartelmez records two readings, "LANTFRANCVM" (or "LANFRANCVM") and "LANTFRIDVM," without clarifying which is preferable. In some manuscripts, the prefatory letter is lacking totally.

51. M. T. Gibson, *Lanfranc of Bec* (Oxford, 1978), chap. 3.

52. The manuscripts are Berlin, Deutsche Staatsbibliothek Phill. 1650

(St. Vincent, Metz) and Munich, Staatsbibliothek Clm 18503A (Tegernsee). See further, and respectively, V. Rose, *Verzeichniss der lateinischen Handschriften* 1, Die Handschriften-Verzeichnisse der königlichen Bibliothek zu Berlin 12 (Berlin, 1893), no. 48, with Beryl Smalley, "La *Glossa ordinaria:* Quelques prédécesseurs d'Anselm de Laon," *Recherches de théologie ancienne et médiévale* 9 (1937): 365–400; and Eder, "Die Schule des Klosters Tegernsee," no. 93.

53. *Ambrosiastri qui dicitur commentarius in epistolas Paulinas,* ed. H. J. Vogels, CSEL 81 (Vienna, 1966), 62–66.

54. Pelagius. *Expositio in Romanos,* ed. A. Souter, Texts and Studies 9 (Cambridge, 1926), 19.

55. Sedulius Scottus, *Collectaneum in Epistolam ad Romanos,* PL 103:24B.

56. Origen, *Commentary on Romans,* trans. Rufinus, PG 14:875A.

57. Smalley, "La *Glossa ordinaria,*" 387–388.

58. As in PL 150:105D–406A, at 110B–111B. The text has been verified against Canterbury Cathedral Add. 162 (formerly Abbey 3186), fols. 11v–12r. See further M. T. Gibson, "Lanfranc's Commentary on the Pauline Epistles," *Journal of Theological Studies* NS 22 (1971): 86–112.

59. PL 150:157A–C.

60. Such linguistic juggling already interested Abbo of Fleury (*ob.* 1004). It is a passion with Anselm of Bec and equally with his brilliant younger contemporary, Guy the Carthusian. See notably Guy's *Meditations,* ed. A. Wilmart, Etudes de Philosophie Médiévale 22 (Paris, 1936), nos. 53–54, *et passim.*

61. Commentary on the Psalter, Paris, B.N. lat. 12011, f. 173v, quoted by B. Smalley, "Gilbert the Universal," *Recherches de théologie ancienne et médiévale* 9 (1937): 400.

62. Guibert of Nogent, *De uita sua* 3.4–10. See the excellent annotated translation by J. F. Benton, *Self and Society in Medieval France* (New York and Evanston, 1970), 151–184, with the references there.

63. Smalley, "La *Glossa ordinaria,*" throughout.

64. F. Stegmüller, *Repertorium biblicum medii aevi* 9 (Madrid, 1977), nos. 11801 (Psalter) and 11832 (Epistles). Anselm may also have written the psalter-commentary attributed to "Ansellus archidiaconus": V. I. J. Flint, "Some Notes on the Early Twelfth-Century Commentaries on the Psalms," *Recherches de théologie ancienne et médiévale* 38 (1971): 80–88. This is a continuous commentary with lemmata; see Stegmüller 2 (1950), no. 1357, but not Stegmüller 8 (1976), no. 1357.

65. Oxford, Bodleian MS Auct.D.1.13, fols. 3r–4r, collated with London, BL Royal IV.A.III, fol. 3r–v and the *editio princeps* of 1480 by Adolf Rusch of Strassburg (see note 70 below).

66. See O. Lottin, *Psychologie et morale aux 12 et 13 siècles* 5: *L'école d'Anselme de Laon et de Guillaume de Champeaux* (Gembloux, 1959).

67. The *parva glosatura* to the Psalter normally contains no "attributed"

comments by modern masters. For the Pauline Epistles, the tally is Berengar four times (Gal. 2:17, 3:1; Eph. 4:26; 2 Thess. 2:6) and Lanfranc once (Heb. 8:4).

68. Anselm's *parva glosatura* to the Psalter and the Pauline Epistles constitutes the *Glossa ordinaria* to these books. The argument that they were displaced by the *magna glosatura* of Peter Lombard (as made, e.g., by Smalley and de Hamel) seems to me ill-founded and ultimately unnecessary. Note that the glosses to the Pauline Epistles in Oxford, Bodleian Laud lat.9 (see note 69 below) and to the Psalter and the Epistles in Rusch's *editio princeps* are still the *parva glosatura.*

69. The two-volume folio is rare. See, e.g., Oxford, Bodleian Laud lat.9 (Proverbs-Apocalypse), mid-thirteenth-century French, and the summary description by O. Pächt and J. J. G. Alexander, *Illuminated Manuscripts in the Bodleian Library, Oxford* (Oxford, 1966), 1, no. 527 and plate 40. The single-volume glossed pandect is unknown.

70. Adolf Rusch of Strassburg: Hain 3173. For descriptions and references, see *Gesamtkatalog der Wiegendrucke* 4 (Leipzig, 1930), no. 4282; F. R. Goff, *Incunabula in American Libraries,* corrected reprinting (New York, 1973), no. B-607.

71. Oxford, Bodleian MS Auct.D.2.11, fol. 137v; Stegmüller 9 (1977), no. 11809; Rusch's *editio princeps, ad loc.*

72. B. Smalley, "Gilbertus Universalis, Bishop of London (1128-1134), and the Problem of the 'Glossa Ordinaria'," *Recherches de théologie ancienne et médiévale* 7 (1935): 235-262, and 8 (1936): 24-60.

73. B. Smalley, *The Study of the Bible in the Middle Ages,* 3rd ed. (Oxford, 1983), 49-51, and note 57 above.

74. *Historia calamitatum,* ed. J. Monfrin, 2d ed. (Paris, 1962), lines 164–240, pp. 68-70.

75. See note 62 above. Whatever his faults, Guibert was an eyewitness, who had direct personal knowledge of the clergy and laity of the city.

76. *Catalogue générale des manuscrits des bibliothèques publiques des Départments,* 4⁰ series, 1 (Paris, 1849), 41-255 (by F. Ravaisson).

77. C. F. R. de Hamel, *Glossed Books of the Bible and the Beginnings of the Paris Booktrade* (Woodbridge, 1974), plates 15, 17, 20.

78. Gibson, "The Twelfth-Century Glossed Bible."

79. Hugh of St. Victor, *Didascalicon* 4.1-2, ed. H. Buttimer (Washington, 1939), 70-72.

80. Abelard, *Commentaria in epistolam Pauli ad Romanos* 1, ed. E. M. Buytaert, CCCM 11 (Turnhout, 1969), 76-79.

81. See K. Froehlich in *Biblia Latina cum Glossa Ordinaria: Anastatical Reproduction of the First Printed Edition, Strassburg, c. 1480,* ed. K. Froehlich and M. T. Gibson (Louvain, 1991), xii-xv.

Sonus and *Verba:* Varieties of Meaning in the Liturgical Proclamation of the Gospel in the Middle Ages[1]

Daniel J. Sheerin

THIS ESSAY IS the result of reflections on some perennial criticisms of what was the most common mode of encounter with the text of the Gospels in the Middle Ages, i.e., in the form of pericopes chanted or read in Latin in the course of the eucharistic liturgy. Though vestiges of earlier patterns of serial if discontinuous readings from certain Gospels in certain seasons remained from earlier periods, by the Middle Ages the Gospels had been divided according to a variety of rationales into excerpts which were distributed into a rigid and very limited annual cycle.[2] This provided only a sporadic and partial reading,[3] as opposed to providing a greater number of readings systematically selected and distributed over an extended cycle.[4] The literary and theological unity of the individual Gospels and the relationships of the four Gospels were ignored, and in place of one or four Gospels, the people were left with a set of apparently isolated episodes which were no Gospel at all. In addition, the Western Church insisted on the use of Latin for the liturgical proclamation of the Gospel before congregations who had long ceased to understand that language or for whom it had never been the vernacular language, and thus that little of the Gospels which was read was incomprehensible to all save a clerical elite.

Reflection on these criticisms has led to the following perspectives: The proclamation of the Gospel in the course of the eucharistic liturgy necessarily involved a shift of contextuality of the Gospel text(s). Given this, the chanting or reading of the Gospels in isolated pericopes with attendant homiletic interpretation was an ideal medium for the communication of the Gospel from the points of view of (1) tradition, (2) the contextuality of the Gospels, and (3) analysis of the liturgical proclamation of the Gospel as a speech-literacy event.

1. TRADITION

It is appropriate to look for a precedent and paradigm for the liturgical proclamation of the Gospel in a Gospel pericope, and Luke 4:14–22 at once suggests itself.[5] It is the account of Christ's reading and preaching in the synagogue at Nazareth, the event cited in most of the so-called *Ordinals of Christ*[6] as the occasion when Christ fulfilled the ordained office of lector. The Lucan narrative reads as follows:

> And Jesus returned in the power of the spirit into Galilee, and the fame of him went out through the whole country. And he taught in their synagogues and was magnified by all. And he came to Nazareth where he was brought up: and he went into the synagogue according to his custom on the sabbath day; and he rose up to read. And the book of Isaias the prophet was delivered unto him. And as he unfolded the book, he found the place where it was written: "The Spirit of the Lord is upon me, wherefore he hath anointed me to preach the gospel to the poor, he hath sent me to heal the contrite of heart; to preach deliverance to the captives, and sight to the blind, to set at liberty them that are bruised, to preach the acceptable year of the Lord, and the day of reward." And when he had folded the book, he restored it to the minister, and sat down. And the eyes of all in the synagogue were fixed on him. And he began to say to them: This day is fulfilled this scripture in your ears. And all gave testimony to him; and they wondered at the words of grace that proceeded from his mouth, and they said: Is not this the son of Joseph? (Douay-Rheims)

We notice that Jesus' reading and teaching in the synagogue at Nazareth was not an isolated event, but occurred within the context of the ritual pattern of his society, a weekly assembly to listen to the reading of the word of God and to hear, as one historian of preaching has put it, "the interpretation and contemporization of the scriptural message."[7] Nor yet, Luke tells us, was the structure of the event at Nazareth an isolated event in Jesus' activities, rather, it was part of the regular pattern of his ministry. Both the preaching of Jesus' ministry and the ritual pattern of the synagogue were appropriated by the early Christians, and Origen maintained in his homily on this pericope[8] that Jesus' ministry could be indefinitely replicated in the Liturgy of the Word in these Christian assemblies:

> When you read "he taught in their synagogues and was magnified by all," do not think that they alone were blessed, and that you are deprived of his teaching. If the things which have been written are true, the Lord spoke not only then, in the assembly of the Jews, but he also speaks today, in this assembly. And Jesus teaches not only in this assembly, but also in other gatherings and in the entire world, seeking instruments through whom he can teach. Pray that he may find me also an instrument well-tuned and fit to play! For just as Almighty God sought out prophets at the time when mortals stood in need of prophecy, e.g. Isaiah, Jeremiah, Ezechiel, and Daniel, so Jesus seeks instruments through whom He can teach His word and instruct the peoples in the synagogues and "be magnified by all." Jesus is even more "magnified by all" now than when He was known only in a single province. (182:3–16)

The selection of the reading from Isaiah was not, Origen insists, a matter of chance, rather "it was the work of God's providence . . . that He found the book of Isaiah in particular; and not another reading, but this one which declared the mystery of the Anointed . . . one must not think that this occurred by whim or chance, but by the providence and economy of God" (182:20–183:2).

Origen proceeds to interpret the passage from Isaiah for his audience, just as Jesus had done for the congregation in Nazareth, providing, in effect, a contemporary equivalent to "This day is fulfilled this scripture in your ears." Then he returns to Luke's narrative to observe that the focused expectation of those assembled in the synagogue at Nazareth can and should be replicated:

> But when Jesus finished reading this, he rolled up "the scroll and gave it to the minister, and sat down, and the eyes of all in the synagogue were fixed on him." Even now, if you wish, in this synagogue, in this assembly, your eyes can be fixed on the Savior. For when you direct the highest gaze of your heart to Wisdom and Truth, to the contemplation of the Onlybegotten of God, your eyes gaze upon Jesus. Blessed the assembly of which Scrip-

ture attests "the eyes of all were fixed on him"! How I wish that
this gathering could have a like testimonial, that the eyes of all,
of the catechumens and of the faithful, of the women, of the men,
and of the children, not the eyes of body, but the eyes of the soul,
were gazing on Jesus! (184:11–20)

This pericope from Luke provided, as commentators ancient and
modern have observed, a paradigm for the assembled Christian people's encounter with the word of God. This encounter is a structured
event. It takes place in the ritual context of an assembly which gathers
at appointed times to listen to the reading and interpretation of a portion of a text of the canonical Scripture excerpted according to an approved pattern. The static visible code of the canonical written word
comes alive in sound, a literally vibrant presence. The assembly awaits
the ritual interpretation and application which the text requires, waits
to be told how "this day is fullfilled this Scripture in your ears."

This procedure for the communication of the word of God and
its interpretation/application by the reading aloud of a pericope from
Scripture followed by a homily arose from practical and ecclesial considerations (the practical efficiency and liturgical propriety of proclaiming the word in this way, the amount of time to be allowed for the
reading, the audience's attention span, the reader's physical energy,
the optimal reception of the word in community, the need for guid-
ance in interpretation and application of the word within a tradition,
etc.). This procedure for the communication of the word became itself a part of tradition, and this tradition and the practical and ecdle-
sial considerations that gave rise to it remained valid throughout the
Middle Ages and long after.

2. THE CONTEXTUALITY OF THE GOSPELS AND
THE GOSPEL PERICOPES

It is, perhaps, in this context of the liturgical encounter with Scripture that one can see best actualized Walter Ong's model of the Church
as "an oral-chirographic interpretive community, founded in oral-
traditional materials early interpreted in textual form and thereafter
interpreted in a historically continuous communal setting by continuous interaction of the oral and the textual."[9]

It was in the course of an essay which is an extended and enthusiastic response to Werner Kelber's monograph *The Oral and Written Gospel*[10] that Ong proposed this model as a supplement to those sketched by Avery Dulles in his celebrated book *Models of the Church*. To summarize and simplify Kelber's nuanced study and Ong's equally nuanced interpretation of it, a process is described whereby Christ's original oral kerygma and its oral transmission were subjected to a redactional, interpretive reprocessing which produced a written Gospel text wherein was edited and preserved, but forever altered, the original oral kerygma. Here is one of Kelber's descriptions of the momentous character of this undertaking:

> Mark's writing project is an act of daring rife with consequences. To the extent that the gospel draws on oral voices, it has rendered them voiceless. The voiceprints of once-spoken words have been muted. This is an extraordinary undertaking. If it is agreed that Jesus entrusted his message to the oral medium, the existence of a written gospel is nothing short of remarkable. For the moment, language has fallen silent; the ground of Jesus' speech and that of his earliest followers is abandoned. Sayings and stories are rescued, but at the price of their transportation into and, we shall see, transformation by a foreign medium. The text, while asserting itself out of dominant oral traditions and activities, has brought about the freezing of oral life into textual still life. In short, the oral legacy has been deracinated and transplanted into a linguistic construct that has lost touch with the living, oral matrix.[11]

One might view the composition of the written Gospel as a decontextualization[12] of the oral kerygma, meaning by decontextualization the severing of oral speech-events from what have been concisely termed "extra-linguistic expressive devices" and "extralingual circumstances" which provide the generative and interpretive context of speech.[13] Kelber describes the context of oral language in this way: "Oral language is bound up with a physiological, social, and environmental contextuality. Gestures and facial expressions, pitch and tone of voice, economic and political experience, and the very locale of discourse are crucial determinants in shaping meaning."[14]

Decontextualization of speech through textualization is sometimes viewed as a movement towards autonomy in language, though the pursuit of absolute autonomy is a snare and a delusion, or, as Ong puts it: "The quest for utterance that reveals all and never needs interpretation is a quest for a will-o-the-wisp."[15] Writing frees language from the limitations of time and space, but, as Ong observes,

> removing an utterance from its author is not removing it from discourse. No utterance can exist outside discourse, outside a transactional setting. Putting an utterance into script can only interrupt discourse. . . . When someone reads the text—only then does the text become an utterance and only then does the suspended discourse continue, and with it verbalized meaning. Texts have meaning only insofar as they are converted into the extratextual.[16]

Kelber, however, speaks of the writing of Mark's Gospel not in terms of decontextualization, but of "a shift of contextuality,"[17] and this formula will help to enlarge our consideration of the liturgical proclamation of the Gospel. If we can view Christ's oral kerygma as a contextualized speech event, and the writing up of the Gospels as a shift of contextuality, then we can, perhaps, view the oral proclamation of a pericope from the written Gospel as yet another shift of contextuality.[18]

Walter Ong sees an alternating continuum in the Church's encounter with the Gospel. An oral kerygma was given written form by the writing of the Gospel. This written text was then proclaimed and interpreted orally for illiterates (and, in the liturgy, for literates as well) for over a millennium. The expansion of literacy[19] and the availability of abundant copies of the Gospel through printing brought us, whether as an ideal or in fact, to the routine, potentially unmediated contact of the literate Christian with the written Gospel. The original oral kerygma and the Christ whose proclamation it was and is continue, however, to be absolutely central, and thus Ong describes the Church as an "oral-textual-oral-textual-oral interpretive community."[20]

3. PROCLAMATION OF THE GOSPEL AS A SPEECH-LITERACY EVENT

As a supplement to Ong's diachronic description of what might be regarded as successive shifts of contextuality of the Gospel over time, one could suggest a synchronic description of a contemporaneous shifting of contextuality of the Gospel in the interplay of written and oral gospel in the Christian community. What follows is a sketch

of such a synchronic description. This sketch is focused on the liturgical proclamation of the Gospel in the Middle Ages considered first
as a speech event and then as a literacy event of which the speech event
forms the major component,[21] another look, with a more specific focus
on what Graham describes as Scripture's "capacity to function simultaneously both as spoken and as written word."[22]

One must view the liturgical proclamation of the Gospel as what
Michael Silverstein has called an "embedded speech event," one of "those
which are part of such large-scale cultural enterprises as complex rituals including speech, song, dance, dress, etc., where the meaning of
the speech behavior in the speech events is usually integrally linked
to the presence of these other signalling media."[23] The liturgical proclamation of the Gospel was (and is) a speech event in which the speech
itself and the extralingual components attending it are ritualized, at
once a real and symbolic re-presentation and realization of the oral
kerygma of the Gospel.[24] The character of the Gospel proclamation
as speech event may be considered according to the following categories: the extralingual circumstances or occasion, speaker, and audience, the speech itself, extralingual elements, and interactive aspects.

The occasion, the Liturgy of the Word in the eucharistic liturgy,
provides the context for the speech event. The eucharistic assembly
constitutes what would be, in Silverstein's terms, the "prior speech
events"[25] which have shaped the speech event at hand and have conditioned the community for it. As ritual it is regularly repeated, in a
ritual space, and the procedures of the speech event follow conventions well known to audience and speaker alike. The occasion, to
some degree, generates the speech, and it is the speech which has in
part generated the occasion. The people assemble on a regular basis
in order, among other things, to listen to the proclamation of the
Gospel, and no other speech would be appropriate. Even so, it is the
existence of Gospel texts that can be repeated, that can be heard and
heard again, that has generated the community, Ong's oral-
chirographic-interpretive community, which assembles regularly to listen to its proclamation.[26] At the same time, however, while the same
ritual is almost invariably repeated, it is repeated on a variety of occasions, i.e., the feasts of the temporale and sanctorale of the liturgical
year, and it is assumed that the content of the speech, i.e., the Gospel
pericope, will vary appositely to the occasion according to a schema
the existence and operation of which is somehow assumed. In addition, the proclamation of the Gospel is only a part of the Liturgy of

the Word and would have been preceded by chants, another reading, and earlier interactions of reader and congregation; these also constitute "prior speech events" which would, along with the earlier experienced ritual pattern, predispose the audience to an assured, reverent attention to this particular speech-event.

The speaker, a deacon or presbyter, is a hierarchical figure chosen from the larger community and ordained for, among other things, the role of speaker, i.e., for the proclamation of the Gospel. Both his costume and his assigned location in the assembled community help to identify him as such. The audience, depending on the specific occasion, may represent various parts of the communal hierarchy, from catechumen to bishop, but each has his or her assigned place in the assembly and assigned role within the community and knows his or her appropriate attitude, mental and physical, towards the speech.

The speech itself, the reading of the Gospel pericope, occurs at the appointed and expected place in the ritual. It has been prepared for both by the congregation's prior experience of the liturgy and by reading(s) and chants from Scripture which precede the Gospel and to which its reading (and attendant homily) is the climax in the Liturgy of the Word. The Gospel text-speech is clearly marked as such by verbal, musical, and non-verbal indices discussed here. The speech is to a degree shaped by the occasion, for the occasion, because of both the practical considerations and the traditions which arose from these practical considerations requires the reading not of the whole of a Gospel, but of a selection, a pericope from it. In addition, the occasion, while generally unvarying in its format, varies by date according to an elaborated structure of feasts and seasons. The Gospel pericopes are appointed for the specific feasts and seasons because of their actual or assumed appositeness to them. This is, of course, an ideal; but whatever objective defect in appositeness there may be can be overcome by an assumption of appositeness which derives from the audience's expectation and can find ready support in the community's immediate and remote interpretive apparatus.[27] One might cite, in this connection, the pseudo-Hieronymian epistle *Quanquam licenter* prefixed to the *Liber comitis*[28] and the medieval aetiological myth of Jerome's having selected and arranged the pericopes of the ecclesiastical year.[29]

Among the extralinguistic elements of this speech event, gesture and intonation suggest themselves for consideration. The principal gesture on the part of the speaker is movement, at most an elaborate procession with the Gospel book to some place of eminence, at the least a movement to the north end of the altar, and thus his delivery of the speech occurs in a place reserved for it. Other ritual gestures — attitudes of prayer and obeisance by way of apologia or renewal of commission to proclaim the Gospel, signing of self and the Gospel book, veneration, incensation, illumination of the Gospel book—further contextualize the speech for the speaker and for the audience as well. I have been rather summary on this point, for, of course, the number and kind of the ceremonies and ministers' gestures preparatory to and following the speech act vary with the solemnity of the circumstances and according to period and liturgical use.[30]

I will be even more summary in the matter of intonation. Suffice it to say that the developed chanting of the Gospel text according to tones specifically assigned to it further contextualized and identified its proclamation as such. The chanting of the Gospel is a hieratic element, to be sure, but it can also be viewed as proceeding from a concern that as many as possible hear the speech and that it be delivered as clearly as possible, with due attention to pronunciation and punctuation of the text.[31] But even in situations in which the Gospel was merely read aloud, aloud is the operative word. The inscribed symbols of the text become vibrant sound, are reintroduced into the oral-aural sphere. Suspended discourse is renewed, the orality of the kerygma is reestablished, and the *scriptura* is, from this point of view at least, fulfilled in the congregation's *ears*.[32]

The audience has its own gestures which are variously listed and explained in most medieval commentaries on the liturgy. Standing up to hear the Gospel, removal by men of head coverings, removal of cloaks, setting aside of staves and of weapons, standing with head bowed, bowing or genuflecting at the name of Jesus, signing oneself at the beginning of the Gospel reading, and, in some traditions, at the end, all are crucial extralinguistic contextualizing elements.[33] The audience's utterance is limited to the few words we are about to consider under the rubric of interactive elements, but by way of a bridge to that topic, attention should be drawn to the audience's silence during the reading of the Gospel. This silence, universally insisted upon in medieval liturgical treatises and in pastoral and devotional manuals and even explicitly demanded in some earlier rituals for the proclamation of the Gospel,[34] is, as all pastors know, an ideal. Silence at liturgical functions is, in fact, an important cultural variable and deserves study as such. Suffice it to say that one could argue that the congregation's silence is also a crucial contextualizing element in this speech event and is as important, in a way, as the speaker's sound. This interplay of sound and silence, this acoustical continuum is crucial.

The last aspect to be considered in this account of the proclamation of the Gospel as a speech event is what Scinto calls "interactive potential." He observes, "Oral manifestations of language permit a greater degree of immediate language interaction due to the direct and immediate visual and auditory participation in the act of communication."[35] Obviously, the interactive potential in the speech event we are considering is going to be far greater than that in written discourse, but at the same time it will be considerably less, since the speech is the hieratic chanting or reading of a fixed written text, than in an informal conversation, in a dialogue, or even in an oration. Responsiveness of the speaker to the audience's non-verbal reactions is not a factor, nor can the audience react verbally with questions, nor probably with applause, to the reading of the Gospel. Interaction does take place, however, in ritual form in the dialogue of the speaker's greeting of the people and their response, his announcement of the Gospel and their acclamation, and, in some usages, in their pronouncement of "Amen" or another acclamation at the end of the reading.

If, however, we view the homily as a part of the speech event that is the proclamation of the Gospel, then the limited interactive potential of the Gospel reading is compensated for by the considerably greater interactive potential of the homily.[36] The homily is, in most instances, a monologic speech event,[37] though the patristic and medieval periods offer evidence of interaction on the part of the audience in the way of applause, acclamations, and remarks.[38] A skillful homilist has, however, depending on prevailing homiletic styles, a large repertory of devices to evoke, assume, and respond to his audience's reaction to and involvement in the readings and the homily. These devices are too many even to catalogue here, but we might cite, as of particular importance, direct address to the audience, requests for the congregation's prayers for the homilist, appeal to speaker and audience's shared experience of the feast at hand and their common listening to the pericope, and all the audience-involving devices traditionally associated with the diatribe which make a monologic speech an affective and effective dialogue.

For all this, the proclamation of the Gospel text itself, the focus of all else that might be interactive and/or spontaneous in this speech event, is a speech not at all spontaneous, nor one composed *ex tempore* according to preexisting patterns and structures like the eucharistic prayers of the early Church,[39] nor even a paraphrase, nor a harmony of the Gospels,[40] but a verbatim delivery, a reading aloud of the "verba composita," in Amalarius's phrase,[41] of a chirographically fixed text. Thus the proclamation of the Gospel as embedded speech event is best viewed, perhaps, as a speech event which forms a part or an aspect of a literacy event. The concept "literacy event" has been defined by Shirley Brice Heath:

> A literacy event is any occasion in which a piece of writing is integral to the nature of the participants' interactions and their interpretive processes. . . . In addition to having an appropriate structure, a literacy event has certain interactional rules and demands particular interpretive competences on the part of participants. Some aspects of reading and/or writing are required by at least one party, and certain types of speech events are appropriate within certain literacy events. Speech events may describe, repeat, reinforce, expand, frame, or contradict written materials, and participants must learn whether the oral or written mode takes precedence in literacy events.[42]

Heath's description is dense and multiplex, and we must proceed selectively, adopting some of the headings she suggests to analyze the Gospel proclamation as a literacy event and supplementing these with a few additional categories which seem required.

The liturgical reading of the Gospel may be considered a communal participation in literacy, one focused upon, but also radiating from, a particular written text.[43] Augustine told his congregation: "When you assemble at church, put away your idle talk. Pay attention to the Scripture. We are your books."[44]

Church was the locus of literacy in general for the masses of people in the Middle Ages. At church the liturgy was conducted and the sacraments were administered according to books, either immediately or at a very close remove. The Latin language in which the services were conducted was the language of literacy, symbolically and in some circumstances literally.[45] Most of what the people heard in church came from books or was about or based on texts contained in books.[46] Even the devotional and narrative paintings and sculptures which they saw there were depictions of people and events known primarily and ideally from books.[47]

Moreover, in contrast to modern congregational situations in which the congregation is invited to read along silently in their own Bibles the text read aloud or commented upon by the minister, or in which the audience automatically read silently in their leaflet missals the Gospel text being proclaimed to them orally, earlier congregations simply listened while an ordained member of the community, in some instances perhaps the only one present competent to do so, read out the Gospel text for them. This procedure coincides approximately with the three constraints which Jack Goody has identified as operative "upon direct access to written materials in early literate cultures."[48]

The first constraint is technological and economic: the scarcity of manuscript copies of the written text. The second is pedagogical: reading aloud slows the communication of the written text and shifts it into the oral-aural mode, with enhanced opportunity for question, answer, and comment. This opportunity arises in the homily when, even if question and answer do not occur, the homilist can pose hypothetical questions which might be raised by a part or the whole of the audience, or can set problems and questions apropos of the text which he proceeds to solve and answer. Goody describes the third constraint as follows: "Thirdly, and most importantly, by retaining control over the process of transmission, we render our jobs more secure," hence some of the socio-linguistic analysis of clerical resistance to a widely circulating vernacular Scripture in the Middle Ages.[49]

But however restricted we may suppose the congregation's immediate access to the written Gospel to have been, they did indeed have a ceremonial access through a member or members of the community whose putative expertise or charism was to read and explain the Gospel, as described in the prologue to the Middle English Northern Homily Collection:

> And wel bird ever ilk man,
> Lof God after than he kan,
> Lered men wit rihtwis lare,
> And laued folk wit rihtwis fare,
> Prestes wit matines and wit messe,
> And laued men wiht rihtwisnes,
> Clerk wit lar of Godes worde,
> For he haues in him Godes horde
> Of wisdom and of gastlic lare . . .[50]

Thus the proclamation of the Gospel can, I think, be regarded as a celebration of a communal, if not necessarily a collaborative, literacy:[51] access through a member or members of the community to the written word of God and to the written interpretive apparatus which attended the Scripture in varying degrees of proximity.[52]

Heath's definition of a literacy event requires certain "interpretive competences on the part of participants." In the case of the congregation, they can both see and hear (because of the otherness of the language, whether because of its style or foreign character) that they are listening to the reading/chanting of a written text from a book, a text, written in the Latin language, not a vernacular, oral retelling of an orally transmitted text, nor a spontaneous, vernacular paraphrase of a text transmitted chirographically in Latin. In addition, it is announced to them, and they manifest by their acclamation and behavior that they know that the text from the book is a portion of a Gospel, a text which is, in a sense, a synechdoche, the part standing for the whole.[53] The congregation assumes a competence on the reader's part to read the text to them and, *mutatis mutandis* according to time and place and personalities, a competence on the part of the reader or homilist to interpret the text for them. The reader may bring no more in the way of interpretive competence to the literacy event that an awareness of the nature of the text he is reading and an ability to read it aloud. More is expected and required ideally of a homilist who must rely on native ability and pastoral experience, and, at best, access to the intertextual system of which the Gospel pericope is a part.

This intertextual system may be analyzed under three headings: (1) the pericope as a segment of a Gospel, (2) the pericope as one of a number of written liturgical texts, readings, chants, and prayers, appointed for a particular feast,[54] and (3) the pericope as the focus of a corpus of interpretive texts which were generated by the Gospels and, in some instances, by the pericope (or which may have influenced the selection of the pericope), and which its interpretation to a degree assumes.

The pericope is a segment of a written Gospel, a kind of text which, in varying degrees, because of the character of its composition, is readily divided into those nuclear forms — discourses, dialogues, short narratives, etc. — in which the oral kerygma developed and in which it is assumed to have circulated during the oral phase of its transmission. From the opposite point of view, one of the capacities of a written Gospel, following Kelber's analysis, is for "inner reflexiveness."[55] Thus, though the pericopes are read in isolation, as having occurred "in illo tempore," these same isolated pericopes can be situated in the linear series of the written Gospel's narrative. Each pericope is a *sequentia sancti evangelii,* even if not a part of a *lectio continua* or *Bahnlesung* by reference to the Gospel text from which it was excerpted.

As the pericope was part of a written Gospel, so too was it a part of an array of written liturgical texts appointed to be chanted and read on a given feast.[56] Whether or not there was an objectively verifiable rationale of the relationship of the Gospel pericope to these other texts, the Gospel was in fact viewed as informing the other texts and elucidated by them. Rupert of Deutz, in a notable declaration which was later appropriated by Sicard of Cremona, Innocent III, and Durandus, tells us that "The holy Gospel is the foremost of all the things that are said at the Mass. For, just as the head is preeminent over the body and the rest of the members serve in subjection to it, so the Gospel is preeminent over the whole liturgy, and all that is read or chanted there are in harmony with it according to a comprehensible scheme."[57] Rupert applies this principle almost ubiquitously in his account of the texts for the feasts of the liturgical year, as does Durandus in his *Rationale.* One might cite also in this connection the *concordiae* or harmonies which Smaragdus inserted in his florilegium on the liturgical readings (*Collectiones epistolarum et evangeliorum de tempore et de sanctis*). These paragraphs are intended to help the careful reader, as Smaragdus described it, to discover quickly "how the readings respond harmoniously to one another and are suited to their seasons, feasts and [liturgical] acts."[58] The fourth book of the *Gemma animae* of "Honorius Augustodunensis" is entitled *De concordia officiorum.*[59]

This search for correspondences, for light of meaning reflected from one liturgical reading or chant onto another, has a sound basis in certain indications we have about the process of selection of liturgical texts, and, in some cases, in the liturgical texts themselves.[60] At the same time, such thoroughgoing analyses and harmonizations as those undertaken by "Honorius," Rupert of Deutz, and Durandus seem strained in some cases where texts have been displaced from their original location or seem to have been selected in isolation from the other chants and readings for the feast, for no apparent reason apart from some superficial appositeness or association. But medieval commentators on the liturgy, though not universally uncritical of the choice of texts, enjoyed a greater ease, for a number of reasons, in finding these intertextual relationships and harmonies. They lived unselfconsciously in the wide intertextual ambience of the multiple contexts in which scriptural texts could occur, whether in extended quotation and paraphrase, or in short excerpt or allusion, or even in ironic and satiric parody,[61] and their experience in multiplex scriptural hermeneutic made finding meaning in the juxtaposition of texts in the liturgy relatively easy.[62]

Yet another intertextual relationship of the Gospel pericope to other liturgical texts can be seen in the fact that the pericopes were frequently attended in the liturgy of the day by texts appointed specifically for their elucidation and interpretation, that is, patristic and later homilies and commentaries on the pericopes which served as readings at matins. The sermons of Ranulphe de la Houblonnière, to cite only one readily studied example, contain citations of the "expositio" or the "omelia hodierna," i.e., to the matins readings, as well as of office chants of the day, in sermons preached before various audiences.[63]

In addition, the proclamation of the Gospel pericope and its attendant homily moved congregations beyond the written Gospels of which the pericopes were a part and beyond the associated liturgical texts into the wider intertextual world of preachers' aids, exegesis, and theology, depending, of course, on the preacher's education, resourcefulness, and the materials at his immediate or remote disposal.[64] Preaching the word was, according to Peter the Chanter's much-quoted formulation, the roof of the edifice of biblical studies; raised on the foundation of *lectio* and the walls of *disputatio*, it "protects the faithful from the scorching heat and blasts of the vices."[65] Ideally, the homily, the goal of clerical education and religious study, expanded considerably the parameters of the literate world to which the congregation has access through its delegated literacy, as the resources of the literate world, selected and adapted to the needs of the congregation, were made available to them in a responsive, engaging, and suitable form through a regularly and easily accessible literacy event.[66]

4. *SONUS* AND *VERBA:* VARIETIES OF MEANING

This analysis of the liturgical proclamation of Gospel pericopes as an aspect of tradition and as a speech-literacy event suggests, I think, ways in which this procedure might be regarded as well suited both to the character of the Gospel text and to the residually oral-aural community in which its proclamation took place. But the account of the liturgical proclamation of the Gospel presented here is, in some respects, an idealized one, "decontextualized" in its own way from historical circumstances, and now some awkward realities must be considered.

"In omnem terram exivit sonus eorum, et in fines orbis terrae verba eorum." "Their sound has gone forth to the whole world, and their words to the ends of earth." Paul quotes this verse from the eighteenth Psalm at Romans 10:18 where he is discussing the role of preaching. Origen comments that what is being said is

> that the sound of the apostles of Christ has gone forth to the whole world, to be sure, but it is not their *sound,* but their *words* that have reached unto the ends of the earth. This can be understood thus because 'world' means all those who are ignorant and less capable of understanding. It is not the *words* which have reached these, the words wherein are contained the understanding of the faith and the elucidation of wisdom, but rather the *sound* of the faith, by means of ordinary, plain preaching.[67]

A little later Origen again describes the *sonus* as apostolic preaching "in which there is a straightforward proclamation of the faith, one adequate for the simpler sort." I want to borrow and adapt Origen's categories of *sonus* and *verba* in considering the relationship of the ideal so far described to a generalized medieval reality. One must ask: Did the people actually attend church and with what frequency? What in fact did the masses of the people understand of a Gospel not, perhaps, proclaimed, but, rather, mumbled to them in a foreign tongue which neither they nor, perhaps, the reader understood?[68] Was there preaching?[69] Was it competent? Did the preaching focus on the Gospel pericopes or was it overburdened by a vast weight of catechesis and exhortation extraneous to or abstracted from the Gospel text?[70] Did the people receive in the proclamation of the Gospel even that *sonus* which, Origen suggests, might be adequate for the simpler sort, or did they receive, in Vergil's words, only *sine mente sonum?*

Rather than look to contemporary social historians for skeptical or negative views on these questions, let us turn for a "worst-case scenario" to a famous invective of the English reformer Thomas Becon, his *The Displaying of the Popish Mass,* probably of the 1550s,[71] and focus on some relevant passages from this work. The first passage has to do with the necessity of preaching and its lack:

The chiefest jewel of all, I mean the preaching of God's word, is utterly exiled from your mass, as all goodness is besides. There is none of you all that stand up in the pulpit, that lift up your voice to declare unto the people either their wickedness, or preach unto them the most joyful, pleasant, and comfortable gospel of our Saviour Christ. If there be any preaching at all, the bells make it when the popish clerk ringeth unto mass. The bells, being hanged up, tell the people somewhat which they understand, namely, that there is a popish mass ready at hand, come hear it who list, and be never the better when ye have done. But ye speak nothing at all that the people understand, and so are ye worse than the bells. (p. 256)

The following excerpts are from Becon's account of the gospel ritual:

when ye have stand awhile pattering like a sort of asses ye know not what at the lower end of the altar, saying the *introite,* or office of the mass, as they call it, the *Kyries,* the *Gloria in excelsis,* the collects, the epistle, the gradual, the allcluia, the tract, or the sequence, — and all in Latin, because such as are there present should keep counsel and not betray your subtile secrets, — ye remove, as men soon weary of a place, from the one end of the altar to the other, and like pretty fellows ye take up the mass-book in your hands, making the people believe that now ye will speak somewhat whereby they shall greatly be edified and well-grounded in the knowledge of Christ.

But Becon shortly continues:

as God is neither in your heart nor in your mouth, so do ye not preach the holy gospel of God to the people; but only ye rehearse a few Latin sentences out of the gospel, which neither ye yourselves for the most part, nor yet the simple people understand. And notwithstanding, the silly, sheepish, simple souls solemnly stand up and give good ear, as though they should hear some notable thing, and go home the better instructed; but all in vain; for they learn nothing. Only when ye rehearse the name of Jesus, they learn to make solemn courtesy; and so, a piece of the gospel being once read, they stroke themselves on the head and kiss the nail of their right thumb, and sit down again as wise as they were afore. . . . (p. 257)

Becon reviews much of the same material in a later section:

> After that ye have mumbled over all these things, ye take up your
> mass-book, and away ye go to the other end of the altar to read
> the gospel . . . and all in Latin, because it shall do no man
> good. . . . Pope Anastasius . . . ordained that the people should
> stand up when the gospel is read, that they might hear and under-
> stand the doctrine of the gospel, and frame their lives according
> to the same. This use is observed at this day in the popish masses;
> I mean, the people stand up and make courtesy when they hear
> the name of Jesus, but they understand not one word. It were
> as good to be read on such sort to swine and dogs as to the chris-
> tian people, seeing they understand it not. (p. 264)

Now of the extent, quality, and kind of preaching on the Gospel
pericopes and on the Mass provided through the Middle Ages little
can be said here save that these are, of course, absolutely critical issues. A number of the defenses of the Latin liturgy in the writings
of Catholic apologists of the reformation period make the point that
the uneducated have an understanding sufficient for them of what takes
place at the eucharist because they have been instructed in these matters through preaching. Johann Eck provided the following spirited
defense of the use of Latin in the Mass:

> Even though the laity do not understand the words, nonetheless
> they understand all the mysteries which they have taken in from
> their cradle whether from the instruction of their parents or the
> preaching of pastors. On that account they conform themselves
> to the celebration of the Mass now by kneeling, now by stand-
> ing, now by bowing, now by knocking the breast, and making
> the sign of the cross. Thus this outward activity shows that they
> have a greater understanding of the mysteries of the Mass than
> if Cicero, Livy, and Varro, men most learned in Latin, were to
> hear the words without being instructed in the mysteries them-
> selves.[72]

Josse Clichtove employed a similar defense of the use of Latin specifically in the Liturgy of the Word:

> Nor yet, because of the fact that in the Western Church the epis-
> tles and gospels in the most sacred rite of the Mass are read in
> the Latin language is a plain understanding of them denied to

the people. Surely the meaning of the epistles and gospels is expounded more than adequately by a suitable explanation in the vernacular language to the whole people in the sermons which are customarily delivered on feast days. Those of the masses who burn with a desire to know the ideas contained in these readings of the divine Scripture should assemble at these public preachings of the divine word, nor should they demand that those ideas resound in their ears in the vernacular, bare, with no interpretation provided, everyday when they attend the sacred mysteries of the Mass.[73]

These passages from Eck and Clichtove point up the crucial roles of family[74] and preaching in religious formation and force us back to one of Becon's points, the fact that the masses of the people understood neither the words of the Mass (those they could hear) nor of the Gospel proclaimed within it. One must raise the questions: What sort of understanding of the Gospels in the Mass did the people in fact have? What was considered to have been sufficient for their needs? Further, was it, as Becon says, "as good to be read on such sort to swine and dogs as to the christian people," or could something of value be affirmed in spite of the failure to adjust the language of the Scripture in the liturgy to changes in the vernacular?

Students of medieval vernacular culture might tell us something of what the people understood, while those concerned with ecclesiastical legislation, church reform, and the preaching movements might tell us what degree of understanding was considered needful and/or lacking in the people.[75] An immediate, partial answer to these questions is available if we compare Thomas Becon's account of the Gospel at Mass with a set of vernacular English instructions on attendance at Mass of the fourteenth and fifteenth centuries.[76] This comparison suggests that congregations had learned, in some respects anyway, something of that minimum which was considered sufficient for them of the meaning of the liturgical proclamation of the Gospel. This, combined with the earlier analysis of the proclamation of the Gospel as a speech-literacy event provides some support for the contention that their encounter with the Gospel pericope in Latin was not as empty of meaning as might be supposed by modern and postmodern sensibilities.

Becon's account of the proclamation of the Gospel is, strictly speaking, post-medieval, but Becon had grown up and been ordained a priest

before the Reformation. Thus the correspondences between the details he mentions and those mentioned in the fourteenth- and fifteenth-
century instructions on attendance at Mass are not surprising, and
we can, I think, retroject the congregational behavior Becon describes
onto earlier congregations. The points of comparison are as follows:

(1) Becon mentions the movement of the missal to the other end
of the altar as a signal for attention. The B text of the so-called *Lay
Folks' Mass Book* identifies the time of the Gospel by the moving of the
book and the priest's signing the book and himself:

> for then tho prest flyttes his boke
> north to that other auter noke,
> and makes a cros vpon tho letter
> with his thoume, he spedes tho bette[r],
> and sithen an other open his face.[77]

So, too, the *Meditations for goostly exercyse in the tyme of the mass* provides
reflections suitable for the time "When the prest or Deacan redyth the
Gospell with hys faice agaynst the Northe,"[78] i.e., at the left hand side
of the altar or facing towards the north at an ambo.

(2) Becon reports that "the silly, sheepish simple souls stand up,
and give good ear." So also the *Lay Folks' Mass Book* advises:

> And when thou has this al done,
> knele doun on thi knese sone;
> If thai singe messe, or if thai saie,
> thi pater-noster reherce al-waie,
> til deken or prest tho gospel rede.
> stonde vp then & take gode hede.[79]

The treatise commonly called *How to Hear Mass* or *The Manner and
Mede of the Mass* advises:

> At the gospel, were ful good
> Studefastliche that ye stod,
>   ffor no thing that ye stured hit.[80]

John Mirk instructs parish priests to teach their congregations to stand
up and bless themselves at the beginning of the Gospel:

> And whenne the gospelle I-red be schalle,
> Teche hem thenne to stonde vp alle.
> And blesse [hem] feyre as they conne
> Whenne gloria tibi ys by-gonne.[81]

The *Lay Folks' Mass Book* also advises making a large cross on oneself at the beginning of the Gospel, with a prayer:

> At tho bigynnyng tent thou take,
> a large cros on the thou make,
> stonde & saye on this manere,
> als thou may se wryten here.
> In tho name of fadre, & son, & tho holi gost,
> a sothfast god of mightes most;
> Be gods worde welcome to me;
> Ioy & louying, lord, be to the.[82]

(3) They "give good ear," Becon says, "as though they should hear some notable thing." All the manuals advise silence and devout attention, as in the *Merita Missae:* "And when the gospelle shall be rede, / Lestene as thoue were adred."[83] The *Lay Folks' Mass Book* calls for meditative silence and recitation of a private prayer during the Gospel:

> Whils hit is red, speke thou noght,
> bot thenk on him that dere the boght,
> sayande thus in thi mynde,
> als thou shalt after wryten fynde.
> "Jhesu, myne, graunt me thi grace, *etc.*[84]

How to Hear Mass advises silence, close attention, and meditation:

> Al yor lykyng ther-on leith
> To wite what the prest seith,
>   Holliche that ye here hit.
> Thaugh ye vnderstonde hit nought,
> Ye may wel wite that god hit wrought,
>   And therfore wisdam were hit
> Ffor to worschupe al godes werkes,
> To lewed men that ben none clerkes.[85]

The *Meditations for goostly exercyse* recommends the following attitude:

> And lett ther be no lesse devocyon in your hart. to the said Gospell Rede on the Preist or on the Deakyn. then yf the holly Apostles Sainct Peter and Paule wer present. which prechyd yt. Allso lift up your hartes with all Devotyon and swettnes. And dylygence. and with all trew humble faithe. Loue and reuerence. to thos holly wordes, as the sone of God wer there and rede thayme. which was the furst precher of thame.[86]

(4) The simple people do not understand, Becon says, the "few Latin sentences out of the Gospel"; they learn nothing. *How to Hear Mass* provides an "Exemplum" to explain how the Gospel pericope, though in Latin and thus to a degree unintelligible to the uneducated, remains efficacious and should still be an object of reverence to all. The exemplum is an analogy derived in part from the deaf asp (here called an adder) of Ps 57:5–6 which hears not the charmer's voice:

> And whi ye schulde this lessun lere,
> Herkneth alle and ye may here,
>   Ther a Neddre hauntes,
> Ye may wel fynde an ye wol seche,
> He vnderstond nothing thi speche
>   Whon thou hire enchauntes,
> Neuertheles heo wot ful wel
> What is thi menynge eueri-del
>   Whon that thou hire endauntes.
> So fareth ther vnderstondyying fayles,
> The verrey vertu yow alle a-vayles
>   Thorw grace that god yow grauntes.[87]

(5) Becon says of the people that "When ye rehearse the name of Jesus," during the Gospel, "they learn to make a solemn courtesy." This recalls Canon 25 of the Second Council of Lyons (1274) which encouraged bowing the head, a genuflection of the heart, upon hearing the name of Jesus, especially during Mass,[88] and indicates an attention to the words of the Gospel sufficient to permit recognition of a familiar and sacred name.

(6) After the Gospel, Becon reports: "they stroke themselves on the head and kiss the nail of their right thumb." I am inclined to agree in seeing in this a reflection of the advice given in the *Lay Folks' Mass Book* at this point:

> Som-where bisyde, when hit is done,
> thou make a cros, and kys hit sone.[89]

The foregoing can serve to provide a partial indication of the simple instructions provided to the laity for their participation in the extralinguistic elements (and some linguistic elements: Name of Jesus, "Gloria tibi") of the proclamation of the Gospel, and these are only a few of the congregational gestures mentioned in the liturgical commentaries cited earlier. Becon's testimony, though not ideal, does indicate that these instructions found a hearing in at least some congregations of the later Middle Ages.

Nor yet, in many communities, was the congregation's ignorance of the content as great as might at first be assumed due to their general ignorance of Latin. Several factors contributed to this. The expectation of the appositeness of the Gospel pericopes to the days on which they were read was not frustrated in the case of many of the greater feasts commemorating events in the life of Christ and his Mother. Thus the assumption that the Gospels of the Nativity, of the Circumcision, of Epiphany, of the feast of the Purification, and so on through the liturgical year, narrated the events being commemorated was often a sound one. This assumption was reinforced and supplemented by the annual repetition of the same Gospel pericopes with the attendant possibility that if the congregation did not hear a homily on a given pericope in a particular year, it was likely that they had heard one in the not too distant past unless preaching was altogether absent or malapropos. So even if the congregation could not understand the Latin words of the Gospel, they may have had a general idea of what the Gospel was about and what it meant for them.

Now if with this selective review of the historical situation in mind we return to the analysis of the proclamation of the Gospel as a speech and literacy event, we are brought to an obvious, but intriguing conclusion: Even when the Gospel was proclaimed in a foreign, learned, hieratic language, the speech-literacy event remained intact in all respects save part of its referential function, and that only in the case of those who did not understand Latin, who did not comprehend (to use the term in a naive sense) the Latin Gospel text. We are confronted by a defect in what Michael Silverstein calls the "referential function" of speech, which he describes as "the function of *pure reference*, or, in terms more culturally bound than philosophical, the function of description or 'telling about,'" or "communication by propositions — predications descriptive of states of affairs — subject to verification in some cases of objects and events, taken as representations of the truth in other."[90]

This is, of course, to modern Western sensibilities a rather damaging defect,[91] but, as Silverstein observes, "Reference is only one kind of linguistic performance among many."[92] If we add to the linguistic elements of the speech event which do remain intact, even with the Gospel in a language which is, in terms of referentiality, incomprehensible to most who heard it, those extralinguistic details of circumstance, of speaker, audience, costume, gesture, and the interactive elements we have described earlier and have seen mentioned in medieval documents, we can see that if much was lost, much of meaning and significance still remained in the Gospel proclamation taken as whole.

If we turn to reconsider the proclamation of the Gospel as a literacy event, we find the same notable referential failure in the written text, or, rather, in its linguistic medium, but we also find that much of the literacy event remains intact. The reading or chanting of the Gospel pericopes continues to be a communal participation in literacy, a celebration of the community's access, at whatever remove, to the written word of God. If the reading of the Gospel was attended by a homily, the wider access to the Gospel's intertextual world was also available, as was yet another mode of encounter with the Gospel through translation or paraphrase in the homily. (Note that one of Erasmus's many defenses of his Latin *Paraphrases* of the New Testament was the contention that he was only doing for the well-educated readers of *bonae litterae* what vernacular preachers did by paraphrasing the Scriptures for their congregations, in effect making the Scriptures available in the suitable idiom.[93])

Again, if we view the proclamation of the Gospel as a performative speech event,[94] i.e., one which accomplishes something, we realize that, save for the one momentous defect in the referential function, the Gospel was, in fact, duly proclaimed to the people and they knew that it had been proclaimed to them. Success in the referential function, while important, to be sure, and perhaps all-important to moderns, has, one would think, been successfully dispensed with in the past and in other contemporary cultures. In the Western Middle Ages, and in other cultures, people have entered society, changed their status within it, and departed from it through performative speech events which were defective, so far as the uneducated were concerned, in their referential function, and yet these people have been successfully baptized, married, and buried for all that.

In addition, the use of Latin for the reading aloud or chanting of the Gospel pericopes was not without certain advantages. The use of Latin can be viewed as what Silverstein calls a "privacy function" of speech, i.e., the use of speech to "set social boundaries on an interaction."[95] This, as I suggested earlier, has been the focus of much of the socio-linguistic study of Latin in the Middle Ages. But there is another aspect of privacy function operative here, i.e., the protection of things holy from anticipated misuse or profanation. What the silent recitations of the Canon of the Mass, insisted upon through most of the Middle Ages, did, it was thought, to veil and protect the anaphora, this the Latin language accomplished for the portions of the Mass that were read aloud or chanted.[96] This reserve is hardly to modern taste, and, in my experience, it was most urgently advocated only once the translation of part or the whole of the eucharistic liturgy became a demand or a reality. Even so, this particular sense of the sacred must, I think, be taken into account in any understanding of the ritual behavior of a culture so very different from our own.

Moreover, the chanting or reading aloud of the Latin pericope conferred additional benefits by the fact of its being Latin aloud, of its being the audible, physical sound of Latin in church.[97]

First, the Latin of the Gospel and of the other audible parts of the liturgy was an onomatopoeia of the solemn and sacred. One might posit among the congregation's interpretive capacities at our literacy event an awareness that the Gospel was being read to them in Latin, and an awareness of how Latin sounded. Thus, if the vicar were one Sunday to read or chant the Gospel in Church Slavonic, a difference would have been noted. So there is a sense in which the Latin of the Gospel and of the other audible parts of the Mass provided the people with the sounds which were part of a sacred continuum of sound and silence, the sounds of which were probably, in the case of the naive, all the more sacred because of their limited intelligibility. Even the uneducated must also have had some capacity for recognition of repeated and/or significant words, like the formulae used to announce the Gospel, or the names of Jesus, Mary, and so on. (Even for the well-educated, the sound of the bizarre Latin of the Scripture and of the hieratic language of the liturgical texts will have been sufficiently different from that of other kinds of Latin texts that the Latin of the Mass was for these, too, an onomatopoeia of the sacred.[98])

Secondly, the sound of Latin in church was the sound of a literacy event. Even when a literary form of the vernacular was well developed, Latin was the language of literacy as was no other. Moreover, save for those educated or partially literate in Latin who would have been familiar with its secular or less intensely sacred uses, the sound of Mass was the sound of the world of sacred texts and of the intertextual world available to the masses of the community only through their ordained, literate delegates.

Third, the sound of the Latin Gospel was a sound of influence and power.[99] John Beleth asserts in his *Summa de officiis ecclesiasticis* that at Mass "While the gospel is being read, the devil is smitten as if with a sword."[100] One is not surprised to find, then, readings of a variety of Gospel pericopes in rituals for exorcism. In some cases a series of apposite pericopes, accounts of exorcisms by Christ, are read.[101] In one ritual it is simply the opening pericopes of the four Gospels, with the following conjuration: "May the Gospel of Our Lord Jesus Christ be to you, cursed spirit(s) N., an eternal fire, but to this servant of God, N., an unparalleled protection against your savage charms for the restoration of body and soul unto life eternal."[102] By analogy, in, e.g., the York and Sarum rituals for baptism in the late Middle Ages, two Gospel pericopes, Mark 9:17–29, an exorcism account (good protection, the Sarum Ritual explains, against epilepsy) and John 1:1–14, were read over the newly baptized child.[103]

In addition to their effect on individuals, Gospel pericopes were employed in attempts to control the environment, hence their use in blessings employed against inclement weather. Some blessings require the reading of Matthew 8:23–27 (Jesus' calming of the storm) or other apposite pericopes,[104] or the reading of the Johannine prologue.[105] Later rituals employ the beginning pericopes of all four Gospels, some even directing that a Gospel be read towards each of the four points of the compass.[106] In one ritual each Gospel is to be followed by this prayer: "Through these words of the holy Gospel and through the power of the word of God may Almighty God free us from sudden and unprovided for death, and from lightning and storm, and from all ills and dangers."[107]

You will recall Thomas Becon's invective where he tells the papist priests that the bells are better than they, for the bells "tell the people somewhat which they understand." But one should recall the medieval ritual for the blessing of bells, that bells were blessed to be rung for the expulsion from their vicinity of menaces and dangers, physical and spiritual, as well as for the increase of the faith. Consider the following words from the ritual for the blessing of bells from the Pontifical of William Durandus:

> that wheresoever its ringing may hereafter sound, the power of those who lie in ambush, the shadows of phantasms, the onset of winds, the fall of lightning, the damage of thunder, the catastrophe of storms, and every spirit of storms may withdraw far away, and that, when the children of Christians hear its ringing, an increase of devotion may grow in them, that hastening to the

> bosom of devoted Mother Church, they may sing a new song
> in the assembly of the saints. . . .[108]

Belief in the effectiveness of the inarticulate, inanimate, but sacred
and meaningful *sonus* of bells is no more bizarre than a belief in the
effectiveness of the articulate *sonus* of the reading of words of power
and comfort whose power and comfort were considered to be effective, to an extent, independently of their relational function.

Only a special pleader would, of course, attempt further to explain or defend the proclamation of the Gospel in Latin once vernacular versions were available. The insistence on this practice on the part
of the Western Church, an insistence which became even more stub-
born as the Middle Ages passed away, is, if not unique, then certainly
an extraordinary aberration in the history of Christianity. Whether
the proclamation of the Gospel in the vernacular and the wider availability of the vernacular Scripture has made that great a difference
to the success of Christianity is quite another question. One must observe that there are vast problems inherent in determining what we
might mean by the term "understanding" in the case of the Gospels,[109]
and I must remark, in closing, that Margaret Aston's description of
the literate Lollards and others similarly disposed as "direct auditors
of God" is, in its way, every bit as problematic as John Eck's insistence
that the language in which the Scripture is read at Mass does not matter because "the Holy Spirit speaks through it and instills it into hearts
in whatsoever languages."[110]

Real understanding of the Gospel in any language, at any time,
has proven a difficult and controversial business, for the Gospels are
the authoritative text, read *ad litteram* or otherwise. And yet, for all the
controversy, coercion, and extravagant learning which have complicated attempts to understand the Gospels, faithful people have not
ceased trying to do so. Perhaps they have taken comfort in the kind
of consolation apropos of Scripture which John Alcock, bishop of
Ely, offered to the Carthusians of Coventry at the end of the fifteenth
century:

> though thou haue not the holy perfyte intellect thereof, yet rede
> & here it. For ryghte as [a] man beying in a place full of swete
> oynements & herbes odofyferous, feleth the swetnes of them
> though nother he se them nor vnderstonde theyr nature, Ryght
> so the vertue of the words of God & his scrypture gyveth an In-

fluence of grace to hym that hereth and redeth it though he
vnderstondeth it not & be in synne or wretchednesse.[111]

NOTES

1. I wish to thank my colleagues Joseph Amar, Carl Dehne, and Patrick Gaffney for their advice and encouragement in the preparation of this essay.

2. For an account of the development of liturgical readings see Cyrille Vogel, *Medieval Liturgy: An Introduction to the Sources,* trans. and rev. William Storey and Niels Rasmussen (Washington, D.C., 1986), 291–355. There (300, 374–376) the common assumption of a primitive *lectio continua* of Scripture, whereby "the reader would have simply continued the sacred text where he had left off at the previous celebration," is rejected. Though use of *lectio continua* seems quite improbable, there is good evidence for the use of readings of discrete passages from the same book of Scripture, separated by omissions of varying length, in biblical order or with the biblical order scrambled, through the church year or at fixed seasons. A three-year cycle of readings of the Old Testament, the Gospel, and the Epistles at the time of Origen is postulated in Pierre Nautin, *Origène: Sa vie et son oeuvre* (Paris, 1977), 72–89. For other sorts of serial readings see, e.g. G. G. Willis, *St. Augustine's Lectionary,* Alcuin Club Collections 44 (London, 1962) and Reiner Kaczynski, *Das Wort Gottes in Liturgie und Alltag der Gemeinden des Johannes Chrysostomus* (Freiburg, 1974), 72–89.

3. For contemporary criticisms of the medieval system, see, e.g., William A. Graham, *Beyond the Written Word: Oral Aspects of Scripture in the History of Religion* (Cambridge, 1987), 120:

> in the Christianity of the Middle Ages, especially in Western Europe, the centrality of the bare scriptural word in liturgy, catechism, and sermon receded before the elaboration of the church liturgical tradition. This had presumably greatest effect upon the ordinary layperson, who, with few exceptions, no longer spoke or understood Latin, the language of liturgy and Bible in Western Christendom. Constant exposure to the biblical text, not to mention active scripture study and use, came to be largely the preserve of the monk, the scholar, and, to a lesser degree, the cleric. Thus the Word was available to the rank and file mainly through the evolved forms of the liturgy, biblical storytelling, or biblically inspired art, and much less, if at all, through substantial reading, recitation, and study of the holy words themselves.

See also Harold Coward, *Sacred Word and Sacred Text: Scriptures in World Religions* (Maryknoll, N.Y., 1988), 72:

Eventually only brief sections were read, with little attention to their larger contexts. As a result the scripture was heard only in bits and pieces, which sometimes were experienced as disconnected divine words descending directly from heaven.

See also the observations of L.-J. Bataillon in this volume.

4. Contemporary attempts to multiply the number of pericopes by expanding the timespan of the cycle of liturgical readings seem to have arisen more from biblical scholarship than from liturgical prudence; see, e.g., John Reumann, "*Redaktionsgeschichte* and Roman *Ordo:* Some Principles and Problems in Pericope Reform," in *Vita laudanda: Essays in Memory of Ulrich S. Leupold,* ed. E. R. W. Schultz (Waterloo, Ont., 1976), 25–58:

> The conclusion is apparent: the three-year cycle of readings in the *Ordo* often presents the reader and preacher with an opportunity, if not the necessity, to employ redaktionsgeschichte as never before. This lectionary development comes at a time when study of editorial tendencies and composition and the theology of each evangelist is on the rise. Whether all are aware of the implications or not, current scholarship and recent lectionary reform thus converge. (47)

Enlarged systems of pericopes have not met with universal approval; see, e.g., the remark of James H. Ware, *Not with Words of Wisdom: Performative Language and Liturgy* (Washington, D.C., 1981), 191–192: "One of the problems with lectionaries is that some scriptures are not repeated often enough because the cycle is too long. Some elements of scripture are more important than others and should be repeated more often. Repetition is essential to reinforcement and incorporation."

5. This text was employed as a Gospel pericope for the period after Theophany in the early Middle Ages, see Theodor Klauser, *Das römische Capitulare Evangeliorum: Texte und Untersuchungen zu seiner ältesten Geschichte,* Liturgiegeschichtliche Quellen und Forschungen, 28 (Münster, 1935), 14, 16, 103, 142, 173.

See the discussion of the significance of Luke 4:14–22 for early Christian preaching in Thomas K. Carroll, "Introduction: From Synagogue to Sanctuary," *Preaching the Word,* Message of the Fathers of the Church 11 (Wilmington, 1984), 9–20; *cf.* the citation of Luke 4:22, along with John 7:46, by Berthold of Regensburg in his treatment of the Gospel proclamation in a popular sermon on the Mass (printed in Adolph Franz, *Die Messe im deutschen Mittelalter: Beiträge zur Geschichte der Liturgie und des religiösen Volkslebens* [Freiburg, 1902], 743).

6. Roger E. Reynolds, *The Ordinals of Christ from their Origins to the Twelfth Century,* Beiträge zur Geschichte und Quellenkunde des Mittelalters 7 (Berlin and New York, 1978), *passim,* especially the comparative table on 165f.

7. Carroll, *Preaching the Word,* 13.

8. *In Lucam hom. XXXII* (GCS *Origines* 9:181–184). Origen's homilies on Luke have survived for the most part only in Jerome's translation, and in that form were widely read during the Western Middle Ages.

9. Walter J. Ong, "Text as Interpretation: Mark and After," in *Oral Tradition in Literature: Interpretation in Context,* ed. John Miles Foley (Columbia, Mo., 1986), 147–169; this quotation from pp. 167–168.

10. Werner H. Kelber, *The Oral and the Written Gospel: The Hermeneutics of Speaking and Writing in the Synoptic Tradition, Mark, Paul, and Q* (Philadelphia, 1983).

11. Ibid., 91.

12. See, e.g., the qualified view of Walter Ong ("Text as Interpretation," 153):

> Giving some linearity to the mosaic configuration of such an oral kerygma meant decontextualizing the oral sayings by means of writing — of course only to a degree, since the Gospel text often states the setting of a given saying, but to a highly significant degree because a verbally stated setting itself is necessarily of a different order of existence from a real setting. A real setting is dense, never fully verbalized or verbalizable, involving all sorts of elusive but real imponderables. The real setting contours the saying designed for it, or elicited by it.

13. Leonard F. M. Scinto, *Written Language and Psychological Development* (Orlando, Fla., 1986), 57.

14. Kelber, *The Oral and the Written Gospel,* 109.

15. Ong, "Text as Interpretation," 147.

16. Ibid., 148–149.

17. Kelber, *The Oral and the Written Gospel,* 109.

18. *Cf.* the remark of Robert Cabié in *The Eucharist,* trans. Matthew J. O'Connell, The Church at Prayer 2, 2nd ed. (Collegeville, Minn., 1982), 67: "The very fact of proposing a specific passage of Scripture for a given day and even the division into verses represent a kind of rereading of the Bible by the Church and a way of actualizing its message."

19. For an overview of the ebb and flow of the varieties of literacy in the Middle Ages, see Harvey J. Graff, *The Legacies of Literacy: Continuities and Contradictions in Western Culture and Society* (Bloomington, 1987), 34–106.

20. Ong, "Text as Interpretation," 167. For the situation of the early church, see the historical sketch provided by Graham in chapter 10 ("The Spoken Word of Christian Holy Writ") of his *Beyond the Written Word,* 119–125; see especially his chapter 12 ("Hearing and Seeing: The Rhetoric of Martin Luther," 141–154), wherein it becomes apparent that even with translation into the vernacular and wider access to the printed text of Scripture, the Reformation's emphasis on preaching gave prominence, if not priority, to the oral-aural encounter with Scripture.

Augustine sees the end of the alternating oral-textual continuum of Ong's formulation in eternity. Augustine insists, on the basis of 2 Cor. 13:8-10, on the transitoriness and partiality of present knowledge and the oral-textual means of obtaining it compared to the stability and immediacy of the experience of it in the Heavenly Jerusalem: "Nisi forte putat Caritas uestra . . . quod codex ibi nobis legendus est, aut tractandus sermo, quemadmodum uobis modo tractatur. Ideo modo tractatur, ut ibi teneatur; ideo modo per syllabas diuiditur, ut ibi totus atque integer contempletur. Non ibi deerit uerbum Dei; sed tamen non per litteras, non per sonos, non per codices, non per lectorem, non per tractatorem. Quomodo ergo? Sicut *in principio erat Verbum, et Verbum erat apud Deum, et Deus erat Verbum." (Enarr. in Ps. 103.3.3* [CCSL 40:1500-1501]).

21. Obviously these socio-linguistic categories are only one of many approaches which language study offers for the examination of the use of language and liturgy. See the menu offered by Josef Schermann, *Die Sprache im Gottesdienst,* Innsbrucker theologische Studien 18 (Innsbruck and Vienna, 1987).

22. Graham, *Beyond the Written Word,* 80.

23. Michael Silverstein, "Shifters, Linguistic Categories, and Cultural Description," in *Meaning in Anthropology,* ed. Keith H. Basso and Henry A. Selby (Albuquerque, 1976), 11-55 at pp. 13-14; earlier Silverstein defines a speech event as "some sequence of speech behaviors in which some speaker or speakers signal to some hearer or hearers by means of a system of phonetic sign vehicles called speech messages or utterances" (p. 13).

24. *Cf.* Graham's study of the chanting of the *Qur'an* in *Beyond the Written Word,* 96–109, esp. his observation that "Chanting the *Qur'an* is a reenactment of the revelatory act itself . . ." (p. 100).

25. Silverstein, "Shifters," 13.

26. Note the following lines from the prologue of the fourteenth-century Middle English Northern Collection of homilies on the Gospel pericopes: "The faur godspellers us schawes, / Cristes dedes and his sawes, / . . . And of thair spel in kirk at messe, / Er lezouns red bathe mar and lesse, / For at euer ilke messe we rede / Of Cristes wordes and his dede, / Forthi tha godspells that always / Er red in kirk on sundays, / Opon Inglis wil Ic undo, / Yef God wil gif me grace tharto, / For namlic on the sunnenday, / Comes lawed men thair bede to say / To the kirc, an for to lere / Gastlic lare that thar thai here, / For als gret mister haf thay, / to wit quat the godspel wil say / Als lered men, for bathe er bouht / Wit Cristes blod . . ." As in John Small, ed., *English Metrical Homilies from Manuscripts of the Fourteenth Century* (Edinburgh, 1852), 4-5.

27. See below note 57.

28. See edition provided by W. H. Frere in *The Roman Epistle-Lectionary* (*Studies in Early Roman Liturgy III*), Alcuin Club Collections 32 (Oxford, 1935),

75–76, and expanded versions prefixed to homiliaries, printed in Reginald Grégoire, *Homéliaires liturgiques médiévaux: Analyse de manuscrits*, Biblioteca degli *Studi medievali* 12 (Spoleto, 1980); see Klaus Gamber, "Der 'Liber Comitis' des Hieronymus. Ein wenig beachteter Zeuge der Vulgata," *Studia Evangelica* 6 (TU 112): 147–153.

29. See, e.g., "Honorius Augustodunensis," *Gemma animae* 1.88: "Hieronymus autem presbyter Lectionarium, et Evangeliarium ut hodie habet Ecclesia collegit." (PL 172:572–573); *cf. Gemma animae* 4.1 (PL 172:689C–D).

30. See the materials collected by Mario Righetti, *Manuale di storia liturgica*, vol. 3, *La Messa*, 3rd ed. (Milan, 1966),.260–268, and Josef A. Jungmann, *The Mass of the Roman Rite: Its Origin and Development*, trans. F. A. Brunner (New York, 1951–1955), 1:403–419.

For the significance of the gestures as set forth in medieval liturgical exegesis, see Rudolf Suntrup, *Die Bedeutung der liturgischen Gebärden und Bewegungen in lateinischen und deutschen Auslegungen des 9. bis 13 Jahrhunderts*, Münstersche Mittelalter-Schriften 37 (Munich, 1978).

In the dedicatory letter of his *Paraphrasis in Euangelium Ioannis* (Ep 1333:229–261), Erasmus provides a lengthy contrast of the reverence shown to the Gospel-book in the Gospel ceremonial to the non-observance of the Gospel message in the lives of Christians, concluding "Non improbo ceremonias, non exagito vulgi simplicis religionem. Sed tum demum ista fuerint nobis vsui, si quod signis visibilibus admonemur, re praestiterimus. Si vere Christiani sumus, hoc est si legitimi Euangelicae doctrinae professores, totum hoc quod illic foris geritur, intus in animis nostris peragatur." As in P. S. Allen, ed., *Opus epistolarum Des. Erasmi Roterodami* (Oxford, 1906–1948), 5:168–169.

31. The contrast of the classic techniques for chanting the Gospel with the concerns and techniques discussed by Charlotte I. Lee in a modern oral-interpretive manual, *Oral Reading of the Scriptures* (Boston, 1974) is illuminating.

32. Jack Goody observes that "Writing creates the possibility of the autodidact and makes the acquisition of information potentially less personal, less 'intensive'." See Goody, *The Interface between the Written and the Oral* (Cambridge, 1987), 114. The implications of this diminution of interpersonal exchange in the propagation and ongoing experience of the Gospel are momentous.

33. Lists of the congregation's gestures and responses can be found, e.g., in Amalarius of Metz, *Liber officialis* 3.187–211, ed. J. M. Hanssens, *Amalarii episcopi opera liturgica* 2, Studi e testi 139:309–310; John Beleth, *Summa de officiis ecclesiasticis* 39d–I (CCSL, CM 41A:71–73); Sicard of Cremona, *Mitrale* 3.4 (PL 213:108–112); Albert the Great, *De sacrificio missae* 2.7.7, in *B. Alberti Magni . . . Opera omnia* 38 (Paris, 1899), 56; Dionysius the Carthusian, *Expositio missae*, art. 13, in *Dionysii Cartusiani Opera omnia* 35 (Tournai, 1908), 346. Note also the succinct listing in the opening verses of the "De

evangelio" section of the *Versus de mysterio missae* attributed to Hildebert of Lavardin: "Inde sinistrorsum Domini sacra verba leguntur: / Plebs baculos ponit, stat, retetigitque caput. / Neve superveniens zizania seminet hostis, / Frontibus imprimitur mystica forma crucis" (PL 171.1178B–1179A).

34. See Righetti, *Manuale di storia liturgica* 3:266.

35. Scinto, *Written Language and Psychological Development,* 57.

36. While deprecating modern preoccupation with spontaneity in worship, Harold Coward finds some room for spontaneity in the homily: "Spontaneity does have a place in one aspect of worship, that of preaching. But even here spontaneity for its power depends on a store of deeply familiar word-use (prayer, scripture, and hymn) shared in common by preacher and listeners" (*Sacred Word and Sacred Text,* 185–186).

37. Limited exceptions are the chanted homilies, which have a refrain assigned to the congregation, the Syriac *madrasha* (and the homiletic-dramatic-dialogue, the *sogitha*), the Greek *kontakion,* and, to a degree, Augustine's *Psalmus contra partem Donati* and the imitations of it.

38. For the earlier period, see, e.g., Chrysostomus Baur, *John Chrysostom and His Time,* trans. Sr. M. Gonzaga (London, 1959) 1:222–223, 231 f, and F. van der Meer, *Augustine the Bishop: The Life and Work of a Father of the Church,* trans. Brian Battershaw, G. R. Lamb (London, 1961), 427–430; for the Middle Ages, see G. R. Owst, *Preaching in Medieval England* (Cambridge, 1926), 179–194. Erasmus, however, contrasts the energy and critical boldness of ancient congregations with the passivity and silence of those of his own time; see Ep. 1858.325–334 in *Opus epistolarum Des. Erasmi Roterodami* 7:136.

39. See Allan Bouley, *From Freedom to Formula: The Evolution of the Eucharistic Prayer from Oral Improvisation to Written Texts,* Catholic University of America Studies in Christian Antiquity 21 (Washington, D.C., 1981).

40. For the slight evidence of liturgical use of Gospel harmonizations in the West, see Vogel-Storey-Rasmussen, *Medieval Liturgy,* 378 n. 48; for the use of Gospel centos see p. 301.

41. Amalarius of Metz, *Liber officialis* 3.18.10, Studi e testi 139: 309.9.

42. Shirley Brice Heath, "Protean Shapes in Literacy Events: Ever-Shifting Oral and Literate Traditions," in *Spoken and Written Language: Exploring Orality and Literacy,* ed. Deborah Tannen (Norwood, N.J., 1982), 91–117, at p. 93.

43. Elsewhere (*"In Media Latinitate," Helios* 14 [1987]: 54–55) I have suggested that the whole of medieval Christian Europe might be regarded as, in a sense, a "textual community" along the lines described by Brian Stock. See his *The Implications of Literacy: Written Language and Models of Interpretation in the Eleventh and Twelfth Centuries* (Princeton, 1983), 90.

44. Augustine, *Sermo* 227 (SC 116:238): "Quando conuenitis ad ecclesiam, tollite fabulas uanas, intenti estote ad scripturas. Codices uestri sumus."

45. The term *literatus* commonly meant literate in Latin and educated

in much else besides; see the remarks of Harvey Graff, *The Legacies of Literacy*, 34–35, and of Brian Stock, *The Implications of Literacy*, 26–27, both building on the study of Herbert Grundmann, *"Literatus-Illiteratus:* Der Wandel einer Bildungsnorme vom Altertum zum Mittelalter," *Archiv für Kulturgeschichte* 40 (1958): 1–65. In his discussion of "written-oral diglossia," Jack Goody cites medieval England as an example of the situation in which a community's written and oral registers employ different languages, in this case, Latin for writing and English and French for speaking; see his *Interface between the Written and the Oral*, 280–282.

46. *Cf.* the following remark by Goody (*The Interface between the Written and the Oral*, 114): "Writing may affect the procedures (that is, the cognitive operations) and content of the knowledge of individuals in a society, even though they are unable to read, let alone to write. . . . Even non-literate peoples or cultures may acquire, be influenced by, even be dominated by, forms of knowledge developed through literacy."

47. See the concise treatment of the topos of pictures as the books of the masses and its use by orthodox apologists to counter the demand for wider access to the text of Scripture in Margaret Aston, "Devotional Literacy," in *Lollards and Reformers: Images and Literacy in Late Medieval Religion* (London, 1984), 101–133, at pp. 115–119.

48. Goody, *The Interface between the Written and the Oral*, 118–119.

49. See, e.g., Michael Richter, "A Socio-Linguistic Approach to the Latin Middle Ages," in *The Materials, Sources and Methods of Ecclesiastical History*, ed. Derek Baker, Studies in Church History 11 (Oxford, 1975), 69–82.

50. Small, *English Metrical Homilies*, 2.

51. For the concept of "collaborative literacy," see remarks and materials cited by Brian V. Street, "Literacy Practices and Literacy Myths," in *The Written World: Studies in Literate Thought and Action*, ed. Roger Säljö (Berlin, 1988), 59–72, at p. 70. One should note, however, that "contemporization" of the Gospel requires the collaboration of reader/preacher and congregation along the lines of the procedure followed in some literacy events in the contemporary community described by Heath ("Protean Shapes," 112).

52. That this communal literacy functioned only through restricted, hierarchical channels need not constitute a criticism of it unless one is predisposed to be critical on this point; see the remark of Brian V. Street ("Literacy Practices," 60): "Any ethnographic account of literacy will, in fact, bring out its significance for power, authority, and social differentiation in terms of the author's own interpretation of these concepts."

53. This contributes, perhaps, to the preacher's commonplace of the virtual all-sufficiency of the feast's pericope(s); e.g., in a model sermon of "Honorius Augustodunensis" for the first Sunday after Pentecost in *Speculum Ecclesiae:* "Si nulla Scriptura esset nisi hodiernum Evangelium, sufficeret fidelibus ad vitae exemplum" (PL 172:1038D).

54. Graham's contrasts between the liturgical and devotional use of the *Qur'an* and the Christian Bible (*Beyond the Written Word,* 88, 102) are not altogether accurate. One must add to the liturgical use of the Psalter (and canticles) the use of other biblical texts (including Gospel texts, sometimes in direct quotation, sometimes centonized) for the chants of the Divine Office and Mass, as well as allusions to biblical texts in prayers and hymns.

55. Kelber, *The Oral and the Written Gospel,* 108.

56. A canon which found its way into Gratian's *Decretum* (1.38.5) directs that a priest, really to be a priest, must know the following: "sacramentorum liber, lectionarius, antiphonarius, baptisterium, computus, canones penitentiales, psalterium, omeliae per circulum anni dominicis diebus et singulis festiuitatibus anni." See Aemilius Friedberg, ed. *Corpus Iuris Canonici* 1: *Decretum Magistri Gratiani* [Leipzig, 1879], 141. How often this ideal was even approached is another matter.

57. Rupert of Deutz, *Liber de divinis officiis* 1.37 (CCSL, CM 7:31.907–911): "Sanctum euangelium principale est omnium, quae dicuntur ad missae officium. Sicut enim caput praeeminet corpori et illi cetera membra subseruiunt, sic euangelium toti officio praeeminet et omnia, quae ibi leguntur uel canuntur, intellectuali ratione consentiunt"; Sicard of Cremona, *Mitrale* 5.1 (PL 213:202AB); Innocent III, *De sacro altaris mysterio* 2.47 (PL 217:826); William Durandus, *Rationale divinorum officiorum* 4.4 ("De Evangelio"); cf. the extensive addition to John Beleth's *Summa de ecclesiasticis officiis* 39 1a (CCSL, CM 41:31.51–64).

58. Smaragdus, *Collectiones* (PL 102:14CD): "quomodo sibi invicem concordi voce lectiones respondeant, temporibus, diebus, actionibus conveniant. . ."

59. See PL 172.689 ff.

60. See Righetti, *Manuale di storia liturgica,* 3:254–260, on thematically associated epistle/prophecy and Gospel pericopes.

61. For more elaborate examples, see the parodies of the Mass and of Gospel texts collected by Paul Lehmann, *Die Parodie im Mittelalter,* 2nd ed. (Stuttgart, 1963), 183–257.

62. Cf. Ralph Hexter's description of the liturgy as "an interactive system of texts and users," in his *"Latinitas* in the Middle Ages: Horizons and Perspectives," *Helios* 14 (1987): 69–92.

63. Nicole Beriou, ed., *La prédication de Ranulphe de la Houblonniere: Sermons aux clercs et aux simples gens à Paris au XIIIᵉ siècle* (Paris, 1987); see Index V.B.1, "Liturgie," 1:194.

64. Cf. the observations of the *Lay Folks' Mass Book* on the need of both reader and hearer for teaching: "bothe tho reders & tho herers / has mykil nede, me thenk, of lerers, / how thai shulde rede, & thai shulde here / tho wordes of god, so leue & dere"; "Clerkes heren on a manere, / bot lewed men bos another lere." (Text B: 163–166, 173–174; EETS, o.s. 71.16).

65. Peter the Chanter, *Verbum abbreviatum* 1 (PL 205:25AB): "Praedicatio vero, cui subserviunt priora, quasi tectum est tegens fideles ab aestu, et a turbine vitiorum."

66. Note the observation of the anonymous author of *The Cloud of Unknowing*, Chapter 35: "Alle is one in maner, redyng & heryng; clerkes redyn on bookes, & lewid men redyn on clerkes, whan thei here hem preche the worde of God," from *The Cloud of Unknowing and Related Treatises on Contemplative Prayer*, ed. Phyllis Hodgson, Analecta Cartusiana 3 (Salzburg, 1982) 39.32–34.

67. Origen, PG 14.1172A.

68. Even the reading of the Gospel could be, of course, botched, handled negligently, or otherwise vitiated. In an early, modest step in the reform of the Mass, Johann Oecolampadius substituted the vernacular for Latin in the epistle and Gospel readings of the Mass while he served as chaplain to Franz von Sickingen in spring of 1522. He wrote and published an epistle in defense of this innovation, *Quod expediat Epistolae et Euanglia in Missa vernaculo sermone plebi promulgari*, reprinted in *Briefe und Akten zum Leben Oekolampads, 1:1499–1526*, ed. Ernst Staehelin, Quellen und Forschungen zur Reformationsgeschichte 10 (Leipzig, 1927), 181–190. There he defends his actions by sarcastically contrasting the outcry over his handling of the Liturgy of the Word to the general ignorance, laziness, and misbehavior of others: "I have only changed the language [of the readings], and that, I think, not without good results. And this is such a great outrage?!? Those who read in Latin so incorrectly and miserably that neither the readers themselves nor their hearers can get any meaning from it, they obtain pardon! Those who mumble the readings to themselves so silently that no one would believe that they are reading, they are considered harmless! People who disrupt the reading with guffaws, lewd behavior, and disorderly conduct are hardly reproached for it!"(p. 182).

69. The necessity for parish priests to preach was insisted upon in ecclesiastical enactments throughout the Middle Ages. Canon 15 of the Council of Oxford (1222), for example, warns parish clergy that they must preach "ne canes muti merito iudicentur, cum salubri latratu a caulis dominicis luporum morsus non repellunt." See *Councils and Synods, with Other Documents Relating to the English Church II: A.D. 1205–1313*, ed. F. M. Powicke and C. R. Cheney (Oxford, 1964) 1:110.

70. A much copied statute (dated 1239?) of Robert Grosseteste, Bishop of Lincoln, required that parish priests know and preach regularly to the people on the Decalogue, the seven capital sins, and the seven sacraments (*Councils and Synods* 1:268). Canon 9 of the Council of Lambeth in 1281 required that at least four times per year the priests, "per se vel per alium," expound to their people in the vernacular, "absque cuiuslibet subtilitatis textura fantastica," the fourteen articles of the faith, the ten commandments,

the two precepts of the Gospel, the seven works of mercy, the seven capital sins with their offspring, the seven principal virtues, and the seven sacraments (*Councils and Synods* 2:900–901).

71. Becon's life and literary activities are described by Derrick Sherwin Bailey, *Thomas Becon and the Reformation of the Church in England* (Edinburgh, 1952). The date of the composition and publication of *The Displaying of the Popishe Masse* are uncertain (see Bibliographies, item 42, p. 145), but it has been situated approximately by Bailey in the 1550s. Quotations here are taken from the edition by John Ayre, *Prayers and Other Pieces of Thomas Becon, S.T.P.,* Parker Society Publications 4 (Cambridge, 1844), 253–286.

72. Johannes Eck, *Enchiridion locorum communium adversus Lutherum et alios hostes ecclesiae,* Version B of Ch 37: "Missas latine, non germanice, dicendas," ed. Pierre Fraenkel, Corpus Catholicorum 34 (Münster, 1987), 385. Compare the arguments of Hieronymus Dungersheim in *Hieronymus Dungersheim, Schriften gegen Luther,* ed. Theobald Freudenberger, Corpus Catholicorum 39 (Münster, 1987), 154.

73. John Clichtove, *Propugnaculum ecclesie adversus Lutheranos* (Cologne, 1526), 33.

74. See Aston, "Devotional Literacy," 128, for some famous instances of parental involvement in religious formation. First instructions on how to behave at Mass and on the significance of the feasts of the church year would, in many cases, have been provided by parents.

75. An introduction to the general topic of medieval preaching has been provided by Jean Longère, *La prédication médiévale* (Paris, 1983). A broader view is provided by J. B. Schneyer, *Geschichte der katholischen Predigt* (Freiburg, 1969). See also the overview provided by Longère in "Le pouvoir de prêcher et le contenu da la prédication dans l'occident chrétien," in *Preaching and Propaganda in the Middle Ages: Islam, Byzantium, Latin West* (Paris, 1983), 165–172. More focused studies, like that provided by L.-J. Bataillon in this volume, are much needed.

76. For this procedure and much else in this section, I am indebted to the stimulating study of John Bossy, "The Mass as a Social Institution 1200–1700," *Past and Present* 100 (1983): 29–61.

77. *Mass Book,* Text B 155–159 (EETS o.s. 71:16).

78. J. Wickham Legg, ed., *Tracts on the Mass,* Henry Bradshaw Society 27 (London, 1904), 22.

79. *Mass Book,* Text B 149–154 (EETS o.s. 71:16).

80. *How to Hear Mass,* lines 421–423 (EETS o.s. 117:504).

81. *Instructions for Parish Priests* 278–281 (EETS o.s. 31:9).

82. *Mass Book,* Text B 175–182 (EETS o.s. 71:18).

83. *Merita Missae,* 55–56 (EETS o.s. 71:149).

84. *Mass Book,* Text B 183–187 (EETS o.s. 71:18).

85. *How to Hear Mass,* 424–431 (EETS o.s. 117:504).

86. *Meditations,* HBS 27.22.

87. *How to Hear Mass,* 433–444 (EETS o.s. 117:504–505). Note the analogous reply to the objection that the layfolk do not understand the words of the Mass from Sermon 74 of the collection *Biga salutis* (Hagenau, 1497): "Nam et serpens non intelligit verba incantantis, sed si audierit, non potest incantanti nocere. Multo maiorem virtutem habet verbum divinum, unde ridiculum est, os habere in ecclesia et cor in foro" (quoted in Franz, *Die Messe,* 26 n. 1. On its author see Schneyer, *Geschichte der katholischen Predigt,* 225. Compare the words of Johann Eck quoted below in note 110.

88. The 25th canon of the Council of Lyons (1274) encouraged bowing the head upon hearing the name of Jesus, especially in the course of the Mass: ". . . et quod generaliter scribitur, ut in nomine Jesu omne genu flectatur (Phil 2:10), singuli singulariter in se ipsis implentes, praecipue dum aguntur Missarum sacra mysteria, gloriosum illud nomen quandocumque recolitur, flectant genua cordis sui, quod vel capitis inclinatione testentur" (Mansi 24:98). See Andre Cabassut, "La devotion au nom de Jesus dans l'église d'occident," *La vie spirituelle* 86 (1952): 46–69, at p. 57, for Gregory X's efforts to encourage this devotion through the preaching of the Dominicans.

Cf. the recommendation of genuflection at hearing the names of Jesus and Mary during the Mass in the following short didactic poem: "Tu Jesus in missa quociens audisve Maria / Et flectis genua, Johannes dat tibi papa / Et veniam scelerum triginta nempe dierum" (*A Glastonbury Miscellany of the Fifteenth Century,* ed. A. G. Rigg [Oxford, 1968], 95). Cf. Adolph Franz, *Die Messe im deutschen Mittelalter: Beiträge zur Geschichte der Liturgie und des religiösen Volkslebens* (Freiburg, 1902), 25 n. 1. See R. W. Pfaff, *New Liturgical Feasts in Later Medieval England* (Oxford, 1970), 62–83, on the liturgical cult and devotion to the Holy Name of Jesus in England.

89. *Mass Book,* Text B 195–196 (EETS o.s. 71:18). Text E reads "Sone besyde when hyt is done / thou make a + and kus hyt sone." The editor, T. F. Simmons (note *ad loc.* p. 220), is probably correct in seeing a connection between this directive and Becon's reference to the people kissing their right thumb-nail, the cross being both the sign of the cross made on their persons and that formed by the crossing of the thumb and index finger which they are directed here to kiss by way of veneration.

90. Silverstein, "Shifters," 14; Silverstein also uses the term "semanticity" to describe the property of speech that is "abstract reference or description" (15).

91. See Silverstein, "Shifters," 14: "It is this referential function of speech, and its characteristic sign mode, the semantico-referential sign, that has formed the basis for linguistic theory and linguistic analysis in the Western tradition."

92. Silverstein, "Shifters," 18. Compare his earlier remark: "When we speak of linguistic categories, we mean categories of this referential kind;

hence one of the principal reasons social functions of speech have not been built into our analyses of language: the sign modes of most of what goes on in the majority of speech events are not referential" (15).

93. Erasmus compares his efforts to those of preachers in *Ad exhortationem . . . Alberti Pii . . . Responsio*, LB 9:1115B; *Apologia brevis ad viginti quatuor libros Alberti Pii*, LB 9:1131F. Contrary to the impression created in LB, the words "sed cum eadem vulgari Lingua reddunt multo verborum ambitu, plane Paraphrastae sunt" are Erasmus's. In the *Responsio* (LB 9:1114E) Erasmus makes the point "since the New Testament was translated into the sort of Latin which was, at this time, the common language of the masses in general, whereas now the Latin language does not exist except among the educated, was it a sacrilege if, given these changes in circumstances, I translated the New Testament into more correct Latin (*Latinius vertissem novum Testamentum*)?"

94. For this sort of analysis of liturgical language, see James H. Ware, *Not with Words of Wisdom: Performative Language and Liturgy* (Washington, D.C., 1981). Ware sees the principal role of Scripture in liturgy as a form of "directive speech," i.e., one that contributes to "the process of directing a person's or a community's behavior within the lifestyle created by their ultimate concern" (40). Cf. Alexander of Hales's description of the Liturgy of the Word as "Illuminatio populi," the Gospel in particular being "Illuminatio populi, quae insinuatur, ut [homo] intelligat quod Christi mandatis est obediendum" (Franz, *Die Messe*, 460). Ware, however, also notes the multiplex use of Scripture in "enabling speech, covenant making, prayer and praise" as well (185). See note 54 above.

95. Silverstein, "Shifters," 17.

96. See, e.g., Clichtove, *Propugnaculum ecclesie*, 32:

Periret enim reuerentia illa et veneratio diuinorum verborum: in epistolis apostolicis et euangeliis contentorum. quinimmo sordescerent tandem et vilescerent populo, eadem verba sacratissima: si sublato latini sermonis operimento (quo condita: seruantur in sua dignitate) exponerentur omnium oculis et auribus . . . Omitto quod plerunque daretur rudi populo grauiter errandi occasio: si epistole sacre et euangelia in sermone vernaculo, quando sacra facit sacerdos, eius auribus passim ingerentur, *etc.*

Graham draws a parallel between the common Muslim prohibition of the use of the *Qu'ran* in translation and Roman-Catholic attachment to the Latin Vulgate as similar behaviors, though the two proceed from different assumptions and motivations (*Beyond the Written Word*, p. 85).

97. See Graham's remarks on the role of the sounded Scripture in what he calls "the sensual arena of religion" (*Beyond the Written Word*, 112–115, 162–165).

98. One must, I think, take into account the non-referential expressivity of the "blessed mutter of the Mass" for the uneducated, its capacity to focus, to comfort, and to serve as a centering background of sacred sound for the private prayers and meditations recommended by the *Lay Folks' Mass Book* and similar texts. For those acculturated to it, biblical Latin was a unique referential medium of multiplex expressivity (see Sheerin, *"In media Latinitate,"* 58–59), as was liturgical Latin (60–63). Note, in this regard, the remark of Per Linell, "Linguistics has concentrated on the *what* of communication, where 'what' means 'what is verbally encoded', but a more comprehensive theory of human communication must also consider the *why* of communication, where 'why' has to cover such emotively loaded questions as 'for what reason' and 'to what effect'", in "The Impact of Literacy on the Conception of Language: The Case of Linguistics," in *The Written Word: Studies in Literate Thought and Action,* 41–58.

99. Note, apropos of the following paragraphs, the remarks of Graham about an anecdote concerning an elderly Malay who taught the recitation of the *Qur'an* in Arabic, though neither he nor his students understood that language, because, he maintained, the words are endowed with a "special virtue": "it will simply not do, in dealing with such a case as the Malayan anecdote above, to conclude that it has nothing to tell us about the meaning of the qur'anic text — or even that, as representative of countless similar situations across the Islamic world, it has less to tell us about that meaning historically than do, for example, the great works of Muslim exegesis. We must resolutely avoid dismissing the 'blind' faith of the old teacher in the holiness of the Arabic words and their 'special virtue' as merely uneducated superstition or a quasi-magical understanding of the efficacy of scripture recitation. . . . Any such reductionist analysis of the relationship between the faithful and their scriptural text is an effort to give an easy (and condescending) answer to a difficult problem: that of religious meaning that may exist apart from rational, discursive meaning — and, indeed, apart from mystical and esoteric meaning as well" (*Beyond the Written Word,* 103–104).

100. *Summa de ecclesiasticis officiis* 33b (CCSL, CM 41A:62.13–14): "Dum euangelium legitur, tanquam gladio percutitur diabolus."

101. See Adolph Franz, *Die kirchlichen Benediktionen im Mittelalter* (Freiburg, 1909), 2:582 n. 4, 601.

102. Franz, *Benediktionen,* 2:582 n. 5.

103. W. G. Henderson, ed., *Manuale et processionale ad usum insignis ecclesiae Eboracensis,* Surtees Society 63 (Durham, 1875), 18–19. Note there the dramaturgic rubric on Mark 9:26: "Jesus autem tenens manus ejus elevavit eum, *Hic dicat Sacerdos commatri, ut surgat cum puero,* et surrexit." See also A. Jefferies Collins, ed., *Manuale ad usum percelebris ecclesie Sarisburiensis,* Henry Bradshaw Society 91 (Chichester, 1960), 38.

104. Franz, *Benediktionen,* 2:77 and 58.

105. Franz, *Benediktionen* 2:58 n. 1, 85, 86, 87, 91, 94.

106. Franz, *Benediktionen* 2:58 n. 3, 97, 98. A very different use of the opening pericopes of the four Gospels is to be seen in a stillborn (Roman?) ritual of the catechumenate, the "Expositio evangeliorum in aurium aperitionem ad electos" in the Gelasian Sacramentary, Andrieu's *Ordo Romanus* XI, the Bobbio Missal, and the *Missale Gallicanum Vetus.* See E. C. Whitaker, *Documents of the Baptismal Liturgy* (London, 1970), 172–174, 199–200, and 204–206, for translations from the first three documents, and L. C. Mohlberg, ed., *Missale Gallicanum Vetus* (Roma, 1958), 21–22. The ritual involves a brief explanation of what a Gospel is and a reading of the beginnings of the Gospels, with each followed by an explanation of the symbol of the evangelist.

107. Franz, *Benediktionen* 2:88f; cf. another, similar prayer (97): "Per istos sermones sancti euangelii et per uictoriam uerbi dei saluet et protegat, uisitet ac defendat dominus omnipotens nos et omnia nostra, parochiam hanc cum omnibus terminis et habitacionibus suis, fructus agrorum, camporum cum singulis fructibus arborum, quibus eciam pascimur." There is yet another on 91f. For the similar usage in the Corpus Christi Procession, see Franz, *Benediktionen,* 2:73.

108. Michel Andrieu, ed., *Le Pontifical romain au moyen-âge,* vol. 3, *Le Pontifical de Guillaume Durand,* Studi e testi 88 (Vatican City, 1940), 534.11–16. See also Franz, *Benediktionen* 2:40–42, 70. Note the following inscriptions for bells among those collected by Percival Price, *Bells and Man* (Oxford, 1983), 128: DISSIPO VENTOS; FVLMINA FRANGO; PESTEM FUGO; DAEMONES ANGO; SIGNO DIES; EXCITO LENTOS; COETUM VOCO; and VIVOS VOCO, MORTVOS PLANGO, FVLMINA FRANGO.

109. See Graham's chapter 9, "Voicing the Qur'an: Questions of Meaning," *Beyond the Written Word,* 110–115, esp. the saying ascribed to Ibn Hanbal (110): "I saw God in my sleep, and I asked: 'Lord, what is the best way by which those close to You draw [so] close?' God answered, 'Through My word, Ahmad.' Then I asked, 'O Lord, with or without understanding?' He said: 'With and without understanding.'"

110. Margaret Aston, "Devotional Literacy," 132; Johann Eck, *Enchiridion,* 385–387: "Non est inutilis missae auditio, etiam verbis non intellectis, ob sequentia: 1. Quoniam in missa sacra scriptura in usum recipitur; sed per eam Spiritus sanctus loquitur, eamque cordibus instillat quibuscunque linguis."

111. From *Mons perfectionis, otherwise in Englysshe, the hylle of perfeccyon* (Westminster, 1501), quoted by J. W. Blench, *Preaching in England in the Late Fifteenth and Sixteenth Centuries* (Oxford, 1964), 10.

Peter Lombard as an Exegete of St. Paul

Marcia L. Colish

THERE IS NO DOUBT that medieval Christian thinkers saw the Bible as the book of books and its study as the discipline of disciplines. Nor is there any question of the privileged position they gave to the Pauline Epistles. In the twelfth century, as before, the Epistles of Paul received more sustained attention than did any other part of the New Testament. They now also did so from more than one quarter. The twelfth century continued to witness interest in Paul on the part of monastic exegetes. As had always been the case, their goal remained to inspire unction and compunction in their monastic readers, and their treatment of the text drew on the meditative and homiletic techniques embedded in monastic *lectio divina*. At the same time, the emergence of scholastic theology in the first half of the twelfth century created a demand for a different kind of Pauline exegesis, a systematic study of Paul geared to the needs of doctrinal debate and to the training of professional theologians. The scholastics seized on Paul for these purposes. For them, he was not only a key source of Christian doctrine, but a model theologian and an authority who often needed the help of other resources in his interpretation. Hence, Paul was a test case for the developing hermeneutic strategies which the professionalizing of the liberal arts, no less than the professionalizing of theology, brought to the fore in the reading of the biblical text.[1]

Among these scholastic exegetes of Paul in the first half of the twelfth century, Peter Lombard holds pride of place. Like his well-known *Sentences*, Peter's *Collectanea*, the commentary on Paul he composed between 1139 and 1141, became an instant classic in its own sphere. It at once became the most frequently cited, copied, and studied of the Pauline commentaries produced in the twelfth century. The *Collectanea* was swiftly dubbed the *Magna glossatura*, out-pacing both the earlier *Glossa ordinaria* and the *Media glossatura* of Gilbert of Poitiers, as well as contemporary and immediately subsequent Pauline glosses, whether of Abelardian, Porretan, or Victorine provenance.[2] In grasping why that outcome was the case, the Lombard's handling of Paul as an authority requires investigation, an investigation that will shed light on two important points. First, it will show us how the most authoritative commentator of Paul during the twelfth century went about his work. Then, by comparing Peter with his leading competitors, we will be able to see what most twelfth-century scholastic readers of Paul commentaries wanted out of Pauline exegesis and why they preferred the *Collectanea* to its alternatives. The scholastic exegetes of Paul with whom Peter will be compared are those falling within the target period between about 1120 and about 1160. Where they exist, the printed editions will be used, despite their acknowledged shortcomings. Three main issues will be considered. There is, first, the exegete's address to the text, how he discovers what Paul has said and how he presents the text to his readers. We will consider next the use that the exegete makes of Paul as an authority, whether as an author whose meaning is deemed to be clear and who can be used as the basis for theological reflection, or as an author who needs to be explicated through the exegete's own analysis or that of intervening authorities. Finally, in third place, we will consider the appeal of the *Collectanea* from the standpoint of the exegete's presentation of the material in the physical format of his commentary.

In approaching the exegete's address to the text, it must be stressed that it was the scholastics of the first half of the twelfth century who were chiefly concerned with recovering a literal and historical reading of Paul. This observation may require some insistence, for the prevailing views of this subject still rely heavily on the work of Henri de Lubac and Ceslaus Spicq, who stressed the pervasiveness of the taste for a polysemous reading of the Bible in the twelfth century, as well as on those of Beryl Smalley, who emphasized the centrality of the Victorines in the quest for the literal sense of Scripture.[3] De Lubac and Spicq simply soft-pedaled or ignored those forms of twelfth-century exegesis that did not interest them, while Smalley paid insufficient attention both to the scholastics and to the fact that the Victorines were concerned with erecting a symbolic, contemplative superstructure on the literal foundations they laid.[4] The literalism of the Victorines and their interest in the *hebraica veritas* of the Old Testament did not, for them, extend to a literal study of the Pauline Epistles of the sort required by the twelfth-century scholastics.

A partial corrective to the traditional picture of twelfth-century exegesis has been supplied by Gillian Evans, who accents the ways in which scholastic exegetes imported into their work the technical contributions of their colleagues in the liberal arts.[5] But this style of exegesis might, or might not, associate itself with a primary interest in the literal or historical level of the Pauline text. On the other hand, the scholastics wanted to recover the literal sense of Paul's teaching because they aimed at using it as a basis and a model for dogmatic speculation and construction. Their interest in the historical setting in which Paul had written derived largely from their perception that this background was a help in understanding what he had said, and also from their desire to place Paul in historical perspective as a means of contextualizing his teaching so that its force could be relativized.

With these concerns in mind, let us turn to Peter Lombard's address to Paul in comparison with that of his immediate predecessors and contemporaries. The *Glossa ordinaria* offers a straightforward, no-frills summary of the Pauline text, or of a patristic reader's summary of that text, often accompanied by a polysemous interpretation. For the most part, its contributors are content to rephrase what Paul or the patristic authority says in their own words, and rarely do they go very much farther.[6] When they are literal, then, they could almost be called literalists by default. While in advance of the *Glossa ordinaria* in other ways, the unpublished glosses of Gilbert of Poitiers, dating to about 1130, are much more consistently interested in connecting the literal with the allegorical senses of the text.[7] And, while original, and even idiosyncratic in other respects, Peter Abelard's commentary on Romans, dated provisionally to the years 1135–39, does not depart from the *Glossa ordinaria* tradition on this point.[8] By contrast, in Peter Lombard's gloss there is only one instance in which he reads any event or personage in the text as pointing beyond the literal or historical sense of the text. As we will see below, this sole instance is an explanation of Paul's teaching on the Antichrist, a doctrine that points to the future in any case. But this is the exception that proves the rule. The Lombard's rule is to expound Paul's message, language, style, and emphasis as it was directed to Paul's own audiences in their particular time and place.

The most sustained example of the Lombard's contextualization of Paul is his commentary on the Epistle to the Hebrews. As with previous scholastic commentators on this text, Peter reprises Jerome's brief introduction, which observes that Paul wrote to a group of converts from Judaism, that he wrote in Hebrew not Greek, and that he attacked the vice of pride. The *Glossa ordinaria* stops there, and it is only at verse 7:9, where the apostle refers to Melchisedech and the Levites, that the glossator makes any effort to connect Paul's actual argument to this stated agenda.[9]

For his part, Peter takes the argument of Jerome found in the *Glossa ordinaria* as his starting point, but he goes on from there to a full and detailed introduction of his own, in which he emphasizes the point that Paul's whole strategy in Hebrews is to remind the Jewish converts of the Old Testament events and prophecies which have been fulfilled in the revelation of Christ. Peter urges that Paul is, indeed, the author of Hebrews even though his salutation in this epistle differs in style from those prefacing his other epistles, notably by omitting reference to his name and his status as an apostle. This tactic, according to Peter, is a deliberate omission on Paul's part. Following Jerome, he observes that Paul was sensitive to the fact that his name was hateful to the Jews. Hence, he does not identify himself, lest this opinion prevent his readers from profiting from his message. Likewise, Paul's omission of his status as an apostle is designed to teach a lesson in humility, since the major thrust of the epistle is that faith is sufficient, and that the Jewish converts cannot pride themselves on their former status as the chosen people or on their observance of the ceremonial law. Peter notes as well that Paul has written this epistle in Hebrew, and that it displays a style more eloquent than in his other epistles, "et longe splendidiore et facundiore stylo quam aliae resplendeat." This fluency is attributable to the fact that Hebrew is his native language. As Peter observes, the apostle's overall strategy in Hebrews is to emphasize the connections between the truths adumbrated in the Old Testament and perfected in the New, "quasi ibi umbra, hic veritas."[10]

This preface sets the stage for Peter's thoroughly typological analysis of Paul's Old Testament references. Conscious of the fact that this is Paul's own tactic, he amplifies on it himself. At Hebrews 1:8–12 and again at 1:12–14, he weaves additional quotations from the Psalms into the main body of Paul's text and combines them with other Old Testament passages that bolster the apostle's own technique of argument.[11] At chapters 7 and 8, Peter explores in detail the parallels between Melchisedech and Christ and between the Levitical and the Christian priesthood, accenting as well the superiority of the latter in that it is not confined to any one tribe or group. Moreover, the sacrifice of Christ is greater than the sacrifices offered by the Old Testament priests in that it is the sacrifice of God's own son for the whole human race, rather than the sacrifice of a purely created being for a limited community.[12] Throughout, and in response to Paul's intentions, Peter preserves a balance between the continuities linking the old and new covenants and the consummation of the former in the latter. For its part, the *Glossa ordinaria* makes no comment on why Paul interlards his argument with references to the Psalms and other passages from the Old Testament, and it tends to emphasize the differences between the two covenants while omitting their continuities.

There are two coevals of Peter who, although they paraphrase his introductory remarks, ignore in their actual handlings of the text the Pauline agenda which those remarks announce. The Abelardian author of a commentary on the Pauline Epistles called the *Commentarius Cantabrigiensis,* produced between 1141 and 1153, alludes to Paul's main theme in passing only twice. The gloss is otherwise notable primarily for the heavy attention it pays to dogmatic matters and to its unusual number of digressions and irrelevancies. Glossing Hebrews 5, the author asks how the Old Testament sacrifices remitted sin. On Abelard's authority, he responds that they did so only partially, saving their practitioners from Hell and assigning them to Purgatory instead. What he really wants to talk about are the differences between these two posthumous states. Similarly, he argues that circumcision, even in its own time, was less efficacious than baptism in the Christian dispensation. The author goes on to note that Christ received both rites even though he needed neither. In these two passages, the relations between the Old and New Testaments stressed by Paul slip away into discussion of Last Things and Christology which are not germane to Paul's argument in this context.[13]

The author's only other effort to respond to Paul's agenda is also found in his gloss on the same chapter. How, he asks, are we to understand the idea that Abraham is our father in faith? The question suggests to him the idea that faith, not circumcision, was salvific in Old Testament times since some men, like Abraham, were saved by their faith before circumcision was instituted. So far, so good. But he moves from this point to an idea that Paul could not have addressed, a critique of monks who devote their wits to the praise of poverty, from which he segues to a recapitulation of the *aut liberi aut libri* topos as treated by Jerome and Theophrastus. This batch of apparent *non sequiturs* is loosely strung together and connected to Paul by the thought that people should do whatever they do for the right moral reasons, not for reasons that may be externally applauded or condemned. The glossator caps this conclusion with a quotation from 'Jerome' which is actually a citation of Gregory the Great.[14] As this passage illustrates, Abelard was not always fortunate in his disciples. Nor, in this case, are Paul or the reader seeking to discover his concerns in Hebrews.

Another exegete of Hebrews in our target group is Robert of Melun, whose commentary on Paul dates to between *c.* 1145–1155 and who draws on both the Lombard and Abelard. Robert strays even farther from Paul's text than does the Cambridge commentator. He raises only two questions that even touch on it: the comparison between Melchisedech and Christ and the sense in which Abraham is our father in faith. His treatment of the first question is extremely abbreviated, both as a comparison and as a contrast. He fails to take Paul's point about the second. Discussing how various *figurae* can be understood as descent from the loins of Abraham, Robert treats the connection between Abraham and the rest of humanity physically, not in terms of faith. Robert's chief concern here is how this connection can be true of Christ since Christ lacked original sin, which is transmitted physically through the loins of the parents.[15] With this problem we drift perilously far from both Paul's subject matter and his meaning. While Robert's commentary is replete with other debates and questions, none of them bears any particular relationship to the text of Hebrews.

In these extended examples drawn from Hebrews commentaries, what stands out in the Lombard's handling of Paul as an authority is his respect for Paul, in the first instance, as an *auctor.* He holds that Paul must be understood as such because he composed a text that needs to be read according to the same principles embodied in the *accessus ad auctores,* that is, according to a method used for approaching texts more generally in the twelfth-century schools.[16] As we have seen, Peter is not content to repeat the potted introduction to Paul's epistles given by Jerome and repeated in the *Glossa ordinaria.* Instead, he supplies an elaborate *accessus* of his own. In this respect, his treatment of Hebrews is thoroughly typical of his handling of all the Pauline Epistles. In each case he outlines the author's situation, when he wrote, the nature of his audience and its problems, the issues which Paul, in consequence, has emphasized, his overall strategy of argument, the subdivisions into which the text falls, and how Paul deals with this assignment in each part.

We should note that Peter was not the only exegete of his time to move to this kind of full-blown *accessus ad Paulem*. Abelard, for instance, supplies a detailed *accessus* of much the same type in his commentary on Romans. But, having given it, Abelard proceeds to ignore the rhetorical program developed in his introduction to the text, and he goes off instead on a host of peculiarly Abelardian theological tangents, which often have little to do with Paul's concerns as Abelard himself has outlined them. His chief interest in this work is rather to treat Paul, *ex post facto,* as a prop for some of the highly idiosyncratic positions that he had taken in his own earlier works or that he was planning to expound separately. He does not use his elaborate *accessus* to Romans in any real sense as a guide to, or a control on, his commentary.[17] Both the Cambridge commentator and Robert of Melun postdate the Lombard and both make shorthand use of his *accessus* to each epistle. But, following Abelard, each proceeds immediately to ignore the *accessus,* moving to pursue his own theological excursions.

Within this group, then, Peter is the only Pauline exegete who takes Paul's agenda seriously and who uses it to direct what he actually discusses in his commentary. This overriding commitment to the literal and historical contextualizing of Paul sets the *Collectanea* apart from the other Pauline commentaries of the day. It clearly displays the Lombard as an exegete who sees his first responsibility as the elucidation of the mind of Paul himself. Whatever theological reflection is then to be based on Paul, it must, for Peter, be grounded in an accurate and contextually sensitive grasp of the authority as he is, *in situ.*

This consistent interest in contextualizing Paul and in allowing Paul's goals and rhetorical strategies to control his own interpretation does not mean that Peter regards a literal and historical reconstruction of Paul as his sole obligation. There is another dimension to Peter's handling of Paul as an authority that must also be appreciated, the application of historical criticism to Paul as a biblical writer. As is well known, both canonists and theologians in the early twelfth century were developing modes of criticism for patristic and other post-biblical authorities in the effort to ascertain how weighty their authority was, how generally their teaching had been intended, and the degree to which it could be magnified or relativized in aid of contemporary needs and debates. What is less well known is the fact that exegetes such as the Lombard were willing to extend the same kind of criticism to Paul himself. In so doing, they show a keen sense of the changes which the Church had undergone over the centuries, changes in its beliefs, its doctrinal emphases, and its institutions. Like others in this group, Peter accepts this phenomenon of change, not necessarily as a sad departure from the apostolic age held up as a timeless norm, but rather as a natural development. It permits one to see that what made sense in the *ecclesia primitiva* may not be appropriate here and now. Peter's historical criticism of Paul, in this sense, partakes more of the contemporary theologians' "moderns versus ancients" conception of the primitive church than it reflects the canonists' desire to modernize or reinvent the primitive church as an ideal.[18] A few examples will serve to illustrate this point.

To begin with, there are cases in which Peter treats developments in church history simply as facts we need to know in order to understand what Paul is saying. He treats these neutrally with respect to Paul's authority. Thus, in commenting on the apostle's warning against building doctrine on false foundations (Romans 15:15–22), Peter observes that Paul was referring to the pseudo-apostolic tradition and to the apocrypha, which had not yet been weeded out of the biblical tradition, since Paul wrote before the canon of Scripture was established.[19] Another comparatively neutral historical *scholium*, but one suggesting the transitoriness of the Church's institutional arrangements, is Peter's discussion of the women whom Paul addresses or refers to in his epistles as exercising a leadership role in the Church, and his reaction to Paul's countervailing rule that women should remain silent in church. In commenting on this apparent contradiction at 1 Corinthians 14:34–40, Peter sees the injunction to silence as conditioned, for this particular community, by the apostle's desire to correct moral and doctrinal error which had been spread by the teaching of women immediately before his composition of the epistle. Here, then, Paul's rule is a tactic designed to correct a local abuse and not a general prohibition. Customs of this type, Peter concludes, are not fixed, as is the substance of the Gospels.[20]

The silence of women recurs in 1 Timothy 2:12–15, and here Peter orchestrates the theme rather differently. In this passage, he accounts for Paul's rule as a corollary of the subjection of wives to their husbands in punishment for original sin. But his main point is to criticize Paul, who goes on to say that women can nonetheless be saved through childbearing. Peter regards this claim as ludicrous. He does not hesitate to explain why. Like men, he observes, women will be saved by their faith, their love, and their persistence in virtue, whether they are married or single, fruitful or barren. Childbearing cannot be regarded as salvific, since it is a natural biological function found among all women regardless of their beliefs. At 1 Timothy 3:5–6, Peter notes that Paul himself had no objection to the then-current practice of ordaining women as deacons, a fact that Peter then uses to undercut the apostle's apparent relegation of women to purely domestic roles.[21]

It might be noted, by way of a footnote to the Lombard's exegesis of 1 Timothy, that the Cambridge commentator enthusiastically endorses his critique of Paul on women. Yoking it with an opinion of Abelard's, he amplifies Peter's point about female leadership in the Church by observing that abbesses nowadays perform functions similar to those of the female deacons of Paul's time. Furthermore, abbesses fitly exercise the teaching office in the Church.[22] This argument, like Peter's, uses historical criticism to point up Paul's apparent inconsistency, as well as to underscore the exegete's own preference for one aspect of Paul's teaching over another, bringing to bear on the text the fact that institutions and the rules governing women, in this case, do change with the times, and do so appropriately.

There are two other contexts, marriage and the coming of Antichrist, in which Peter imposes a much more stringent mode of historical criticism upon Paul in an effort to limit Pauline authority. In his commentary on 1 Corinthians, where Paul concedes marriage while urging those who can to remain celibate like himself, Peter pointedly dismisses the apostle's preference for celibacy. He uses the occasion to develop a treatise on marriage that highlights the essentials of the position on marriage which he later develops in his *Sentences*. Peter insists that marriage is a good thing and a sacrament that was instituted before the Fall. Marriage is grounded in the present consent of the spouses. Their sexual relations, when ordered to the ends of marriage, are either not sinful at all or at most minimally sinful and so excusable. Customs regarding marriage have changed over time. This being the case, Paul was mistaken in regarding marriage, not as a requirement, but as an indulgence. In truth, Peter states, the reverse is the case: it is continence that is the indulgence. Marriage, after all, is the calling followed by the many. Theologians and preachers, from Paul to the present, he implies, have a duty to address the realities in the lives of most believers. After all, continence requires a special grace that God concedes to very few—something that Paul ought to have kept in mind. Peter hastens to add that marital chastity and fidelity are also charisms and gifts of God, though they are distributed more widely. Given the fact that the apostle was aware of all this, Peter finds Paul both logically and theologically inconsistent in his advocacy of the celibate life.[23]

How is it then, Peter asks, that the apostle has arrived at these misguided conclusions? It is at this point that Peter detonates the exegetical time-bomb that he has dropped. Paul's counsel on all of these matters, he points out, was predicated on his belief that the Second Coming was imminent, a belief that encouraged him to advise against marital entanglements for those who were single. Now this belief about the impending end of the *saeculum* is, to be sure, a historical datum about Paul and his times. But, Peter continues, as we are well aware, this world is still very much with us. Thus we can and should adjust our perspectives on marriage and celibacy accordingly. Not even Paul deprived married people of future glory, he observes, implying that Paul's teaching is not wholly consistent even judged in terms of its now superseded eschatological expectations. But the full force of Peter's historical criticism of Paul on marriage in 1 Corinthians is to use it to qualify Paul's theological authority on this subject to the point of dismissing it, and so to legitimate his own sharp departures from Paul on the theology of marriage.[24]

In addition to misguiding his views of marriage, Paul's teaching on the imminent end of the age also yields some other difficulties that Peter seeks to iron out by means of historical criticism, with the effect of scaling down Paul's authority. The problem is located in the discrepancies between Paul's handling of the Antichrist in 1 and 2 Thessalonians. In his *accessus* to these epistles, Peter acknowledges that Paul was responding to the Thessalonians' curiosity about Last Things and to the errors that they had embraced on the subject. The content of the two epistles, he notes, is quite similar, even redundant. Whence, "licet obscure" why Paul felt the need to repeat himself.[25] This is especially obscure given the inconsistent descriptions of Antichrist in the two epistles.

The difficulties involved lead Peter to depart from his usual exegetical practice. This is the one place in his commentary on Paul where he adds to a strictly literal reading of the text a spiritual dimension, for reasons that will now be apparent. In 1 Thessalonians, Paul depicts the Antichrist as a supernatural being who will reign for three years before being killed by the Archangel Michael. On the other hand, in 2 Thessalonians, he identifies the Antichrist with the Roman Empire of his own time. The fall of the Antichrist is thus equated with the downfall of the Roman Empire as a world power. This discrepancy had been noticed in the *Glossa ordinaria*. The glossator had amplified on the account in 1 Thessalonians, drawing on Daniel for additional information on the Antichrist and the Apocalypse, but he had repeated the Roman imperial version of the story in glossing 2 Thessalonians without trying to square the two accounts. [26]

Peter seconds the glossator's strategy on 1 Thessalonians, bringing additional Old Testament prophetic material to bear on Paul's scenario in that epistle. [27] But he takes a rather different tack on 2 Thessalonians. Warming to his task, he advises his readers that Paul was not forecasting the fall of Rome as an actual historical event. Paul was, no doubt, upset by the persecution inflicted on Christians by the emperors during his time. Still, Peter notes, we know that the Roman Empire later declared Christianity its official religion and protected the Church. So a different understanding of Rome must be supplied in order to remedy the limitations of Paul's view read literally.

Peter's solution is to associate Rome, in 2 Thessalonians, not with the political imperium of Nero, but with the spiritual imperium of the Roman Church. He thus turns Paul's argument around by 180 degrees. The fall of Rome cannot mean the future political collapse of an empire that has not been in existence for centuries. It must rather mean the falling away of the churches from the Christian faith and from obedience to Rome. Paul's sense in 2 Thessalonians thus would be that Christ will not return to judge the world until all Christians have apostasized and all churches have fallen into schism. Peter has recourse to Augustine and Haimo of Auxerre for this interpretation. He depoliticizes the account in 2 Thessalonians still further by refusing to identify Antichrist with any human leader, whether of church or state. The Antichrist, he says, will be the son of the devil, though by imitation, not strict filiation. He will arise in Babylon out of the tribe of Dan, as the Old Testament foretold. But 'tribe' must be read broadly to include the Greeks as well as the Jews. For just as Christ possesses a fullness of divinity, so the Antichrist possesses a fullness of malice, and his activities embrace all the sons of pride of whatever nation. The key point Peter makes is that the reign of Antichrist represents a negative spiritual condition, which humans will help to bring about by allowing faith to wane and charity to grow cold. In so arguing, Peter rejects Paul's equation of the Antichrist and the historical Nero. By spiritualizing the idea of Antichrist, Peter can treat Nero, not as the literal Antichrist, but as a type of the Antichrist to come. To be sure, Nero's activities, like those of the other persecuting emperors, were evil and can be seen as having been motivated by the devil. Peter concludes, even so, "et sunt Nero et alii umbra futurae, scilicet Antichristus, sicut Abel et David fuerunt figura Christi."[28] This resolution of the problem of Nero as Antichrist found warm support from Peter's immediate successors.[29]

In developing this theology of the Antichrist, Peter does not confine himself to contextualizing and relativizing Paul's belief in the light of superseded apostolic expectations and the warping experience of persecution. He goes on from there to reinterpret the whole subject as pointing to a more general, and less institutional, mystery of evil in which the infidelity of the churches is paralleled by the falling away from faith and charity on the part of individual Christians. He thus finds a way of handling Paul's treatment of Antichrist in 2 Thessalonians that is compatible with the account in 1 Thessalonians, while he expands Paul's more historically limited position into a universal moral doctrine. Peter can thus yoke his historical critique of Paul with a constructive theology of Antichrist, one which draws on other postbiblical authorities and his own ingenuity in the interest of clarification.

This leads us to another striking feature of Peter's *Collectanea* in comparison with other commentaries of Paul dating to our target period — his use of patristic and more recent authorities, both to provide a running commentary on the text and to assist in the unravelling of problematic passages. His recourse to such authorities for the light they shed on Paul as an authority is both deft and apposite. In particular, Peter is more concerned than are other scholastic exegetes of Paul during his time with confronting the fact that the authorities may not agree in their interpretation of Paul. When this is the case, Peter seizes on the fact as an opportunity to explain, by his own word and example, how theological reasoning can be brought to bear on conflicts among the authorities. We can thus see in his Pauline exegesis the same kinds of methodological concerns that surface more systematically in his *Sentences*. In Peter's case, there is an organic relationship between his study of the *sacra pagina* and the teaching of systematic theology, from the standpoint of methodology no less than from the standpoint of doctrinal development.[30]

Consistent with his handling of conflicting authorities on all subjects in the *Sentences*, Peter's exegetical treatment of this problem accents two important methodological principles, ones often ignored by his contemporaries. In the first place, he finds it insufficient to resolve conflicts by the naked tactic of countercitation. The inadequacy of that method is plainly visible in the *Glossa ordinaria*. The glossator responsible for the Gospels of Matthew and Mark takes exception to Origen on salvation and on angels; he seeks to neutralize him by citing Augustine or Bede against him. But the commentary does not stop to explain why Origen's position is unacceptable or why Augustine and Bede are preferable.[31] Peter does explain the reasoning that leads his authorities to the conclusions they adopt, thus giving his reader the capacity to judge the merits of their conclusions. At the same time, he is aware of the fact that the same authority sometimes contradicts himself. This circumstance may result from the rhetorical requirements of the arguments made by the authority at various points in his *oeuvre*. It may result from the fact that he has genuinely changed his mind. But these considerations need to be taken into account in deciding whether the authority's views in one case cancel out his views in another, or whether the problem in Paul's text on which one is seeking help from the authority can be resolved within the framework of that authority's thought more generally. Some examples will illustrate how Peter handles issues of this type.

At Romans 2:3–6, for instance, Peter grapples with the question of whether the sin against the Holy Spirit can be remitted. Some say, he observes, that this sin cannot be remitted because the souls of such sinners are so hardened by despair that they cannot feel the need or desire for penance. Others say that the sin cannot be remitted because such sinners do not actually do penance even though they are capable of it. Peter adduces Augustine on Matthew in support of the first position, Augustine on Mark in support of the second. Peter has yet another resolution of the question that he wants to advance. He rests his own case on a third argument, made by Augustine on John. There, Peter notes, the sin against the Holy Spirit is held to be irremissible, not because the sinner cannot or does not repent, but because he repents so rarely and with great difficulty. This conclusion Peter finds the most persuasive of the three. He also finds it compatible with the broader outlines of both Augustinian and Pauline theology. To say that this type of sinner could not repent would be to undercut his own freedom to respond to the grace of repentance. Equally, if not more importantly, it would limit the freedom and power of God to extend mercy in converting the sinner. This example shows nicely that the Lombard knows that Augustine is not a monolithic source. It also shows that he thinks that one can discover, through an analysis of the reason-

ing in assorted *loci,* which Augustinian position is not only characteristic, as being consistent with his *idées maîtresses,* but also which Augustinian position sheds the most light on Paul.[32]

Another case of conflicting authorities is one that requires far
more of a virtuoso turn to resolve. This is the vexed debate between
Augustine and Jerome, arising from the text of Galatians, over whether
the apostle Peter had dissimulated his beliefs as a missionary tactic
and whether Paul had been right in criticizing him on that account.
The issue had been a sticky one from the patristic period on, not only
because it raised the question of whether apostles can lie or err, but
because Porphyry had seized on this text, and the clash it provoked,
as a means of taxing the Christians for immorality and inconsistency.
Jerome stated that Peter had dissimulated his faith in complying with
Jewish dietary practices. Augustine had rejected that possibility out
of hand.

The Lombard's first line of attack is to bring the Acts of the
Apostles to bear on Galatians. Acts, as he notes, shows that, on another occasion, Peter ate the flesh of animals used in pagan sacrifices,
but without having participated in those sacrifices or having approved
of them. This kind of dietary practice, he continues, is permitted elsewhere by Paul if it does not give scandal. By analogy, then, Peter was
fully aware of the suspension of the Jewish dietary laws by the new
dispensation, but he followed them in the instance mentioned in Galatians so as not to alienate those he sought to convert. Peter was here
acting out a species of Paul's own advice, to become all things to all
men for the sake of winning souls.

With this reasoning in mind, the Lombard argues that we can
say that Jerome is literally correct in stating that the apostle Peter behaved like a Jew when he was a Christian. But Augustine is even more
correct in stating that Peter's behavior was not mendacious. In the
Lombard's view, Peter's actions were "honesta" because they were guided
by good intentions. For his part, Paul was misinformed. His own intention to preach the Gospel vehemently was a good intention, but
on this occasion it had prevented him from grasping what Peter was
really up to. Paul was wrong to attack Peter. Peter's missionary zeal
was also good, but it too had prevented him from seeing that, in the
new dispensation, Jewish and Gentile practices are not matters of in-
difference and that his missionary tactics might therefore be counter-
productive. The Lombard treats both apostles as well intentioned, but
he holds that neither apostle translated his intentions into appropri-

ate action in the case at issue. He also sees the merits of the positions of both Augustine and Jerome, although with a preference for Augustine's. [33]

A comparison between the Lombard and other contemporary exegetes of Galatians shows how much his analysis of the patristic authorities on this passage helped to clear the air. The Cambridge commentator thinks that Peter can be excused because he was not truly lying and because of the difficulties attached to evangelizing the Jews. His gloss on this text gives no indication that there is a patristic debate about it. [34] But Robert of Melun has clearly profited from the Lombard's exegesis. After reviewing his reasoning, Robert supplies an elegant refinement of it. He concludes that both apostles behaved in ways that can be thought of as wrong externally. Both can be excused, however, by mitigating factors in each case. [35] Robert thus retains the balance between correct intention and appropriate action central to the Lombard's analysis, but he invokes the principles of dispensation and the lesser of the two evils as a way of reconciling Jerome and Augustine. And, like the Lombard, Robert shows how Paul's authority can be weighed, judged, and relativized in the light of post-biblical authority and the ingenuity of the expositor.

While it is most typically the confrontation of conflicting authorities or the effort to extract theological principles from the time-bound perspectives of the apostolic age that engender these displays of ratiocination, there are also cases in which the Lombard draws on the disciplines of the *trivium* as tools of analysis in his Pauline exegesis. As we have already seen, his *accessus* to each epistle exerts a firm control over the handling of each commentary, suggesting the centrality of the discipline of rhetoric for him as a source of hermeneutical principles. Less pronounced, but also present, are his appeals to logic, although it has to be said that they are sparing in comparison with those in works by Abelardians or Porretans. Both metaphor and logical analysis help Peter to gloss Romans 8:20–23, where Paul describes the entire creation as groaning and travailing as it awaits salvation. The proper subject of salvation is man, not the rest of creation, says Peter. So what does the phrase "all creation" mean here? It can be regarded, he observes, as a "universale locutione." It is a universal not in the sense that it collects the individual traits of all beings, but rather in the sense that it collects all the traits of the singular beings, namely human beings, who are to be saved. For all aspects of human nature — mind, body, and spirit — are saved. At the same time, since he is composed of mind, body, and spirit, the human is a microcosm of the rest of creation, and it is saved in him metaphorically.[36] There are two passages in the same epistle where the Lombard rephrases the text at issue in the language of cause-effect relationships. In commenting on the point that one man brought sin into the world and one man redeemed it, he argues that the roles of Adam and Christ as causes are not isomorphic. While Christ is the sole cause of the redemption he effects, Adam is not the sole cause of damnation when it occurs, since the actual as well as the original sins of Adam's posterity are involved. Also, the potentiality for damnation does not always get actualized, since God's grace can overcome sin and does in some people.[37] Similarly, in glossing the point that the law gives rise to sin because of human inability to adhere to it, Peter also treats the topic in the language of cause-effect relationships. The law, he notes, is not the efficient cause of sin, but rather the occasion of sin.[38]

Both the substantive explanations Peter gives in these examples and the terminology from the disciplines on which he draws are clear, unexceptionable, and easy to understand. Therein lies much of their success, especially in an age when other masters were using a bizarre and rebarbative lexicon or were invoking the language of the *artes* in defense of highly problematic conclusions. This may well have been one reason for Peter's contemporary popularity as a guide to Paul. There are some other reasons which may also be mentioned, in addition to his rigorous commitment to the *accessus* method, noted above, which controls his exegesis of each epistle and gives the reader a clear road map so that he always knows where he is in Paul's itinerary. There is, further, Peter's balanced combination of the continuous commentary, the gloss on particular words and phrases that require more explanation, and the development of theological *quaestiones* on a more extended basis.[39] Peter gives more attention to questions and to theological speculation than his immediate predecessors. At the same time, in comparison with his immediate successors, his questions are related more integrally to the continuous commentary, and he never loses sight of the text from which the questions are derived. However long an excursus he may make, Peter always returns the reader to Paul's argument. And however much he may disagree with Paul's emphasis or take stands on controversial issues in his questions, they never become *non sequiturs* or theological Flying Dutchmen. Peter adduces more authorities in resolving vexed questions than either his predecessors or contemporaries. He chooses them aptly and he analyzes

and deploys them perceptively. He is concerned with showing the reader
how to evaluate the authorities when they conflict.

There is also another advantage that the *Collectanea* has over all
of its twelfth-century scholastic competitors — the advantage of a physical format that makes it far easier to use. The other commentators
confine themselves to lemmatizing individual words or phrases extracted from Paul's text, often quite selectively, without indicating their
literary context within the epistle. Peter quotes the text of each epistle
in full, subdividing it into units of coherent length. He gives a general
summary of the apostle's argument in each of these units. Only then
does he proceed to his more specialized glosses on particular words
or lines within that unit or to questions on larger theological problems
which it may contain. Hence the larger literary frame of the text is
never lost, and the reader does not have to have a text of Paul in one
hand, alongside of the *Collectanea,* in order to follow the sense of Peter's
commentary. Similarly, in citing authorities, Peter provides a full quotation or paraphrase of the passage cited, unlike other twelfth-century
exegetes who, following the Carolingian exegete, Florus of Lyons, tend
to give only the first and last few words of the citation, with the phrase
"usque ad" linking them. This method makes their citations mere
finding tools that would be usable only in a library as extensive as
that used by the glossator himself. The format that Peter gives to his
Pauline commentaries makes his *Collectanea* a one-stop operation, supplying the reader both with Paul's text, the text or full sense of the
authorities, and Peter's commentary, all laid out on the page in an
immediately comprehensible visual format. This physical organization of the *Collectanea* is a feature of the work from the very beginning;
it is witnessed in the earliest twelfth-century manuscripts.[40] Ease and
convenience of use, not to mention its other strengths, help to explain
why Peter Lombard's commentary on Paul should have been the commentary of choice for his century.

In facilitating the study of Paul, the Lombard also left his own
distinctive legacy to the twelfth-century understanding of Paul as an
authority. Leaving aside the doctrinal conclusions that he derives from
Paul's text, some of which are traditional, some of which are avant-
garde, and some of which articulate the mid-century theological consensus, we may summarize that legacy under three main headings.
First, Paul is and remains for Peter a privileged source of theological
truth. But his authority has to be appropriated in relation to that of
other biblical authors. Writers from the Old Testament and from other

parts of the New Testament need to be brought to bear on Paul to explain what he means and to shed light on his rhetorical strategy. Most important, in positioning Paul within the larger framework of biblical authority, Peter regards him as less weighty than the Gospels. The Gospels report Christ's teaching, whose authority reigns *semper et ubique*. On the other hand, Paul adapted Christ's teachings to the needs of the several communities to which he wrote.

This point leads to Peter's second major legacy as an expositor of Paul, his insistence on the need to understand Paul in context. This requires both a sensitivity to the literal and historical sense of the text, which enables the exegete to avoid an erroneous or anachronistic reading of it. It also enables the exegete to recognize what was timely for Paul, but what has since been superseded in later chapters of church history. Paul thus provides not only a dossier of theological truths on which the systematic theologian may expatiate, he also supplies a model for the ongoing task of theological development, even at Paul's expense when necessary.

Third, and last, Peter's sense of Paul as an authority who lived in time leads him to draw Paul into focus through the insights of post-biblical authorities. These authorities include the arts masters, most notably the rhetoricians, but they are primarily the Church Fathers and more recent Christian writers. Paul, to be sure, plays the senior partner in his association with these later writers, but he does so within an organically conceived system of authority in which he is regarded as a major interpreter of the Christian message and not just as a source of it. The coherence with which the Lombard links these insights on Paul to the theological enterprise of his century, and the exegetical and critical skills he honed in developing them, thus help us to appreciate Peter Lombard's appeal as a guide to Paul as an authority for his own age.

NOTES

1. The best introduction to this subject is Jean Châtillon, "La Bible dans les écoles du XIIe siècle," in *Le moyen âge et la Bible,* ed. Pierre Riché and Guy Lobrichon (Paris, 1984), 163–197. See also Heinrich Denifle, "Quel livre servait de base à l'enseignement des maîtres en théologie dans l'Université de Paris?" *Revue thomiste* 2 (1898): 149–161; Arthur Michael Landgraf, *Introduction à l'histoire de la littérature théologique de la scholastique naissante,* ed.

Albert-M. Landry, trans. Louis-B. Geiger (Montréal, 1973), 47; Beryl Smalley, *The Study of the Bible in the Middle Ages,* 2nd rev. ed. (New York, 1952), chap. 1–4, and more recently, Smalley, "L'exégèse biblique du XIIe siècle," in *Entretiens sur la renaissance du XIIe siècle,* ed. Maurice de Gandillac and Édouard Jeauneau (Paris, 1968), 273–283; Smalley, "The Bible in the Medieval Schools," in *The Cambridge History of the Bible: The West from the Fathers to the Reformation,* ed. G. W. H. Lampe (Cambridge, 1969), 2:197–220; Gillian R. Evans, *The Language and Logic of the Bible: The Earlier Middle Ages* (Cambridge, 1984). A good summary of monastic exegesis is provided by Jean Leclercq, "Écrits monastiques sur la Bible aux IXe–XIIe siècles," *Medieval Studies* 15 (1953): 95–106. Older but still useful guides include Arthur Michael Landgraf, "Der Methode der biblischen Textkritik im 12. Jahrhundert," *Biblica* 10 (1929): 445–474; Landgraf, "Familienbildung bei Paulinenkommentaren des 12. Jahrhundert," *Biblica* 13 (1932): 61–72, 164–193; Landgraf, "Untersuchungen zu den Paulinenkommentaren des 12. Jahrhundert," *Recherches de théologie ancienne et médiévale* 8 (1936): 253–281, 345–268.

2. H. H. Glunz, *History of the Vulgate in England from Alcuin to Roger Bacon: Being an Inquiry into the Text of Some English Manuscripts of the Vulgate Gospels* (Cambridge, 1933), 219–224; Châtillon, "La Bible dans les écoles," 192–193; Jacques-Guy Bougerol, *La théologie de l'espérence aux XIIe et XIIIe siècles* (Paris, 1985) 1:9; Werner Affeldt, *Die weltliche Gewalt in der Paulus-Exegese: Röm. 13.1–7 in den Römerbriefkommentaren der lateinischen Kirche bis zum Ende des 13. Jahrhunderts* (Göttingen, 1969), 138; Z. Alszeghy, *Nova creatura: La nozione della grazia nei commentari medievali di S. Paolo* (Roma, 1956), 8–11, 23–24; Guy Lobrichon, "Une nouveauté: Les gloses de la Bible," in *Le moyen âge et la Bible,* ed. Pierre Riché and Guy Lobrichon (Paris, 1984), 109–110. These authors correct the position stated by Smalley (*Study,* 51, 64–65) and by Margaret Gibson (*Lanfranc of Bec* [Oxford, 1978], 54–61), who stress the continuities between the *Glossa ordinaria* and Peter Lombard's exegesis to the point of obscuring his differences from his predecessors.

3. Henri de Lubac, *Exégèse médiévale: Les quatre sens de l'écriture* (Paris, 1961–64), vol. 2, parts 1–2; Ceslaus Spicq, *Esquisse d'une histoire de l'exégèse latine au moyen âge* (Paris, 1944), 70–71; Spicq, "Pourquoi le moyen âge n'a-t-il pas davantage pratiqué l'exégèse littérale?" *Recherches des sciences philosophiques et théologiques* 30 (1941–42): 169–179; Smalley, *Study,* xvii, xxi, 83–195.

4. Grover A. Zinn, *"Historia fundamentum est:* The Role of History in the Contemplative Life According to Hugh of St. Victor," in *Contemporary Reflections on the Medieval Christian Tradition: Essays in Honor of Ray C. Petry,* ed. George H. Schriver (Durham, 1974), 138–144, 146–158. See also Châtillon, "La Bible dans les écoles," 186–188, 194.

5. Evans, *Language and Logic, passim.*

6. On the authorship of the *Glossa ordinaria,* see the essay in this volume by Margaret Gibson.

7. Vincenzo Miano, "Il Commento alle Lettere de S. Paolo di Gilberto Porretano," *Scholastica: Ratione historico-critica instauranda, Acta congressus scholastici internationalis, Romae, 1950* (Rome, 1951), 171–178; Maurice Simon, "La Glose de l'épître aux Romains de Gilbert de la Porrée," *Revue d'histoire écclesiastique* 52 (1957): 68–70. I have not inspected these manuscripts myself. On the dating, see H. C. van Elswijk, *Gilbert Porreta: Sa vie, son oeuvre, sa pensée* (Leuven, 1966), 57–58; Bruno Maioli, *Gilberto Porretano: Della grammatica speculativa alla metafisica del concreto* (Rome, 1979), xxiii.

8. Damien Van den Eynde, "Les écrits perdus d'Abélard," *Antonianum* 37 (1962): 468; confirmed by Eligius M. Buytaert, ed., Peter Abelard, *Opera theologica,* CCCM 11–12 (Turnholt, 1969), 11:16; Rolf Peppermüller, *Abaelards Auslegung des Römerbriefes,* BGPTMA NS 10 (Münster, 1972), 10; Peppermüller, "Exegetische Traditionen und theologische Neuansätze in Abaelards Kommentar zum Römerbrief," *Peter Abelard (Proceedings of the International Conference, Louvain, 10–12 May 1971),* ed. E. M. Buytaert (Leuven, 1974), 117–119.

9. *Epistola ad Hebraeos, Glossa ordinaria,* PL 114:643A, 655A–B.

10. Lombard, *In Epistolam ad Hebraeos,* argument and 1:1–7, PL 192: 399A–401A. The quotations are at 400B and 401A respectively.

11. Lombard, *Ad Hebraeos,* PL 410C–414A.

12. Lombard, *Ad Hebraeos,* PL 447B–460C.

13. Anonymous, *In Epistolam ad Hebraeos,* as in *Commentarius Cantabrigiensis in Epistolas Pauli e schola Petri Abaelardi,* ed. Arthur Michael Landgraf, 4 vols. (Notre Dame, 1937–45) 4:724–735, 734. On the dating of this commentary, see Landgraf's analysis (1:xv).

14. Anonymous, *Ad Hebraeos* 4:738–741.

15. Robert of Melun, *In Epistola ad Hebraeos,* as in *Quaestiones de Epistolis Pauli,* ed. Raymond M. Martin, Spicilegium sacrum lovaniense 18 (Louvain, 1938), 302–304. For the date, see Martin's analysis, pp. lvi–lvii.

16. On this development see, in general, Edwin A. Quain, "The Medieval *Accessus ad auctores,*" *Traditio* 3 (1945): 215–264, who makes passing reference to exegetes (p. 261, nn. 1, 2). More recent treatments, which include discussion of *accessus* to books of the Bible in the twelfth century, are A. J. Minnis, *Medieval Theory of Authorship: Scholastic Literary Attitudes in the Later Middle Ages* (London, 1984), chaps. 1–2, and A. J. Minnis and A. B. Scott, eds., *Medieval Literary Theory and Criticism, c. 1100–c. 1375* (Oxford, 1988), 69–71, although the latter work misdates Peter's exegetical works. Both confine themselves to his commentary on the Psalms, and do not comment on his Pauline glosses.

17. Peter Abelard, *Commentaria in Epistolam Pauli ad Romanos,* prologus 1:1, ed. Buytaert, CCCM 11:43–55, for the *accessus* and Abelard's introductory remarks. His departure from this agenda in the body of the work has been noted by Buytaert (17–20) and Peppermüller (*Abaelards Auslegung,* 10–24). An analogy to this full *accessus* followed by an extremely narrow exegeti-

cal focus is also found in the monastic exegete Hervaeus of Bourg-Dieu (*c.* 1080–*c.* 1150) in his *Commentaria in Epistolas divi Pauli, praefatio,* PL 181:591D–596C and ff., although his concern is with the moral edification of his monastic readers.

18. On the prevailing attitude of the canonists here, see Glenn Olsen, "The Idea of the *Ecclesia Primitiva* in the Writings of the Twelfth-Century Canonists," *Traditio* 25 (1969): 61–86. For the countervailing attitude of the theologians, see Marcia L. Colish, "Another Look at the School of Laon," *Archives d'histoire doctrinale et littéraire du môyen age* 61 (1986): 12–17.

19. Lombard, *In Epistolam ad Romanos,* PL 191:1524C.

20. Lombard, *In I Epistolam ad Corinthos,* PL 191:1672B–C.

21. Lombard, *In I Epistolam ad Timothaeum* 2:12–15, 3:5–6, PL 192:340A–342C, 345C–346A.

22. Anonymous, *In primam Epistolam ad Timotheum, Commentarius Cantabrigiensis* 3:251.

23. Lombard, *In I Epistolam ad Corinthos* 7:1–28, PL 191:1585D–1597A.

24. Lombard, *In I Epistolam ad Corinthos* 7:29–35, PL 191:1597B–1598D. For Peter's fuller views on marriage, see *Sententiae in IV libros distinctae* 4.26–42.

25. Lombard, *In Epistolam I ad Thessalonicenses,* argument; Lombard, *In Epistolam II ad Thessalonicenses,* argument, PL 192:287D–290A, 311A–312C. The quotation is at 311A.

26. *Epistola I ad Thessalonicenses* 4:15, 5:3; *Epistola II ad Thessalonicenses* 2:3, 2:6–7; *Glossa ordinaria,* PL 114:618D–619B, 622A–D.

27. Lombard, *In Epistolam I ad Thessalonicenses* 5:1–11, PL 192:306A–308A.

28. Lombard, *In Epistolam II ad Thessalonicenses* 2:1–16, PL 192:317B–321D. The quotation is at 318C.

29. Anonymous, *In secundam Epistolam ad Thessalonicenses* 2:1–16, *Commentarius Cantabrigiensis* 3:539–541; Robert of Melun, *De Epistola ad Thessalonicenses prima* 2:7, p. 296.

30. The most important studies of these interrelations have been made by Ignatius C. Brady, in his prolegomenon to Bks. 3 and 4 of the *Sentences* (Grottaferrata, 1971–1981) 2:8*–52*. Compare his edition of three texts reflecting Peter's earlier exegetically derived positions on the Incarnation, the Eucharist, and marriage (pp. 53*–87*), which can be collated with Peter's handling of these themes in his reworking of Romans and 1 Corinthians and in the *Sentences*. This material supplements Brady's earlier discussions of Peter's life and works in "Peter Lombard: Canon of Notre Dame," *Recherches de théologie ancienne et médiévale* 32 (1965): 277–295 and "Peter Lombard," *The New Catholic Encyclopedia* (New York, 1967) 11:221–22. On the double redaction of the *Collectanea,* see also Jean Leclercq, "Les deux rédactions du prologue de Pierre Lombard sur les Épîtres de S. Paul," *Miscellanea lombardiana* (Novara, 1957), 109–112; Ermenegildo Bertola, "I commentari paolini

di Pietro Lombardo e la loro duplice redazione," *Pier Lombardo* 3:2–3 (1959): 75–90. On the connection between exegesis and theology in Peter, see also Glunz, *History of the Vulgate,* 232–258 and Gillian R. Evans, *Old Arts and New Theology: The Beginnings of Theology as an Academic Discipline* (Oxford, 1980), 42. These treatments of the point supersede that of Smalley (*Study,* 75).

31. Matthew 25:48; Mark 1:2, 3:29; *Glossa ordinaria,* PL 114:166D, 179C, 193C.

32. Lombard, *In Epistolam ad Romanos* 2:3–6, PL 191:1340A–D.

33. Lombard, *In Epistolam ad Galatas* 2;14, PL 192:109D–114A.

34. Anonymous, *In Epistolam ad Galatas, Commentarius Cantabrigiensis* 2:351.

35. Robert of Melun, *In Epistola ad Galatas* 2:11, pp. 245–246.

36. Lombard, *In Epistolam ad Romanos* 8:20–23, PL 191:1444C–D.

37. Lombard, *In Epistolam ad Romanos* 5:15–16, PL 191:1392D–1394B.

38. Lombard, *In Epistolam ad Romanos* 7:12–13, PL 191:1420B.

39. On the mix between the gloss, the question, the continuous commentary, and the sources for each, as well as the shift in taste toward the question by the end of the twelfth century, see Smalley, *Study,* 42–86; Lobrichon, "Une nouveauté," 93–114; Gustave Bardy, "La littérature patristique des 'Quaestiones et responses' sur l'Écriture sainte," *Revue biblique* 41 (1932): 210–236, 341–369, 515–537, and 42 (1934): 14–30.

40. Lobrichon, "Une nouveauté," 109–110. The only other contemporary exegete who quotes entire chunks of the Pauline text before glossing individual words and phrases is Hervaeus of Bourg-Dieu. But he is not interested in developing theological *quaestiones* on the basis of the text.

Exegesis and Authority
in the Thirteenth Century

G. R. Evans

WE MIGHT REASONABLY ask whether the thirteenth century
had anything substantially new to say about so well-worn a topic as
that of the use of authority in establishing theological truth. I want
to try to set in context what I suspect was the most significant shift
not only of the thirteenth century, but perhaps of the whole medieval
period, in habits of thought about authority to determine what is
authoritative.

The old hierarchy of Scripture, Fathers, and secular authors was
already beginning to give way in the twelfth century to a more complex structure in which the *moderni* themselves had a place as authorities; there lurked already the *éminence grise* of church authority to determine controversies in matters of faith, and we see that authority in
action in the trials of Peter Abelard and of Gilbert of Poitiers. But
in 1215, the second Canon of the Fourth Lateran Council goes further. After the great affirmation of faith in the "firmiter credimus et
simpliciter confitemur" of Canon 1, Innocent III condemns the heresy
of Joachim of Fiore. He refers to the faith "which the Roman Church
holds, who under the Lord's dispensation (*disponente Domino*), is mother
and teacher (*mater et magistra*) of all the faithful."[1] He goes on in Canon
3 to excommunicate and anathematize all heretics and heresies which
may rise up against "this holy, orthodox, catholic faith." He thus gives,
in the context of what he went to some lengths to establish as a general council,[2] a new, formal character to a position about what we may
call the "magisterial" authority of the Church in matters of faith, an
authority in which "teaching" and "deciding," the "study" and the "governance" senses of *magister* and *magisterium* combine in the epithet *magistra.*[3] The shift I have in mind is that which made it possible for the

reformers to complain with some justification in the sixteenth century that the Church set herself above Scripture, as having a greater authority even than the Word of the Lord.

It is possible to trace the parallel tracks of the use of *magister* and *magisterium* with reference to study, and to mastery or dominion, from patristic usage; it is in Tertullian and Augustine as well as Aquinas and Bonaventure.[4] The two are not wholly conflated in Aquinas's mind. He distinguishes a pastoral *magisterium,* by which a prelate has jurisdiction, from the *magisterium* of the scholar. "The teaching of the Scripture is twofold. In one way it pertains to the office of the priest, just as he who preaches, teaches. No one has licence to preach unless he has the office of a priest, or has permission from a priest (Rom 10:15). The other way pertains to the office of a Master, just as the Masters of Theology teach."[5] "Those who teach are in spiritual danger. But the dangers of pastoral *magisterium* may be avoided by knowledge with clarity; those of the teaching *magisterium* by learning."[6] But distinguishable though the two remained into the thirteenth century, it is apparent that there was significant interplay between them already in the thinking of Pope Alexander III. He was already speaking of the *magisterium* of the Roman Church in terms which give the pope doctrinal authority.[7] In December 1195, Celestine III wrote of the Holy Roman Church which receives, "through the merits of the blessed Peter," *magisterium* and *principatum* over all churches (PL 206:1127). Ironically, Joachim of Fiore uses the term much as Innocent III himself does.[8] But we need not confine ourselves to the terms *magister, magistra, magisterium* to encounter a consciousness of this duality, which is at the same time a unity of determining and teaching authority. Innocent III wrote to Peter of Compostella, who had asked for advice on a christological question, offering him a view *scholastico more.* Were he answering "as Pope" (*more apostolico*), he confesses, he would reply "more simply but more cautiously" (*simplicius quidem sed cautius respondemus,* PL 216: 1178).

It is instructive to compare this kind of talk with the preoccupations of the eleventh century, when the academic milieu was barely beginning to come into being in any sense that a twelfth- or thirteenth-century scholar would have found recognizable, and it had not yet become clear to bishops of Rome that pastoral *magisterium* vested in the *ecclesia Romana* had just in itself a teaching aspect that was also an authority to make decisions in matters of faith. The debate over Berengar's Eucharistic teaching contained much about the danger of

allowing ancient testimonies to be set at naught, and the agreed view
of the faithful through the ages to be overturned, but not the assertion
that we need look only to the leadership of the Roman Church to discover where the truth lies, because that *magisterium* lies with her or
with her bishop.

Lanfranc's *De corpore et sanguine Domini* begins with a tirade accus-
ing Berengar of going against the consensus of the faithful in his teaching. He speaks of the "auctoritas totius sanctae Ecclesiae" (PL 150:
407). He accuses Berengar of opposing the *vetus doctrina,* the ancient
teaching of the Church, and the *catholica veritas* and the "opinion of
all the Churches" (*opinio omnium Ecclesiarum,* PL 150:409). Berengar
challenges him. Is he saying that what are *usitatiora* must be *probabiliora?*[9]
He resents Lanfranc's imputation that what he thinks is opposed to
the common faith.[10] On the contrary, Lanfranc is giving the name
of "the Church" to a crowd of the inept, and is himself going against
the sense of the majority and also their writings.[11] At issue here are
profound assumptions about the nature of the *consensus fidelium.* Lanfranc reminds Berengar that he has sworn his allegiance to the common faith of the Church (PL 150:413), and he warns him that "a member of the Church ought not to differ from the Church" (419). That
is Gilbert Crispin's view, too. He speaks of the bowed neck ("sum-
missa cervice") of faith with which the Christian ought to believe as
"catholic faith believes and dogmatises."[12] When Berengar fails to do
so, he is saying that what the Church everywhere believes is false ("quod
ab Ecclesia ubique gentium . . . creditur," PL 150:440).

The test is that of Vincent of Lérins's dictum, but there is added
to it here the principle that what the Church has always and everywhere unanimously believed is binding upon all the faithful, and that
no individual can declare it false. "Perish the thought that we should
say anything less than what the catholic Church preaches throughout
the world," says Durandus, condemning this "profanae novitatis dogma"
(PL 149:1377). Innocent III's *De Sacrificio Missae* opens with a reference to the Roman Church as *mater* and *magistra* that has a significantly different emphasis from that in the Lateran IV text. In the
Lateran IV Canon, it is described as "mater et magistra ceterarum
Ecclesiarum" (PL 217:714). It is this last emphasis which is taken up
by Honorius III in a letter of 1216. He speaks of the Roman Church
as "caput omnium ecclesiarum . . . et magistra."[13] At the time of the
Council of Constance in 1415, the distinction was blurred: "domina
et magistra omnium."[14] The canon lawyers' glosses are singularly un-

helpful here. Johannes Teutonicus, Vincent of Spain, Damasus, the *Casus Parisienses,* and the *Casus Fuldenses* are all silent on *magistra,*[15] but there is plentiful evidence elsewhere that the Church of Rome was consciously standing as supreme authority in matters of faith. At issue here is unity in matters of faith, the "holy unicity" of which Peter the Chanter speaks.[16] Aquinas stresses that *unitas fidei* is one of the causes of unity in the Church, although he places it alongside hope and love.[17]

The difficulty was to know exactly how the Roman Church could act as *magistra* in determining questions of faith if it were patently not expressing the consensus of all the churches. In the Byzantine view, for example, the second Council of Lyons in 1274 was a local synod of the Roman Church, not an ecumenical council. As they saw it, a form of words affecting fundamentals of the faith had simply been imposed there upon a small Byzantine delegation, without discussion, and certainly without their consent.[18] Here the canonists have something to say. They see the matter as one of jurisdiction. Hostiensis, for example, explains that in a diversity of bodies there is liable to be a diversity of souls. The fullness of ecclesiastical jurisdiction grows feeble and cheap if it is dissipated thus; gathered into one place, it is strong. That is why the Lord bestowed *magisterium* on the Roman Church, over "all the Churches and all the faithful."[19] Even commentators who would not grant that the Roman Church was *univeralis ecclesia,* seeing it rather as *pars universalis ecclesiae,* thought of it still as "head of the body," bearing the Lord's *magisterium.*[20]

The concept of universality was crucial—and it should not be forgotten that *universitas* has connotations of a special sort in the high Middle Ages in reference to the guild system and the universities. The master of such a corporation was the officer in charge. Rainerius Pomposianus defines the "universal Church" as that which "contains all the others" (*sub se continet universas*). It is, as it were, "one general Church" in which there are many particular churches.[21] What is "universal" is, arguably, binding on all simply because it is universal. Stephen of Tournai, one of the canonists working on Gratian, points out that the canons of general councils have force "universally."[22] But an earlier author, in a *Summa* of about 1169, stresses that the authority of the general councils is such that even the Roman Church cannot alter their decrees one jot.[23]

Behind such reflections, the key question of the last medieval centuries was whether a "universal" authority residing in the Roman Church was vested in the community as a whole, in councils, or in the person of the pope. Hostiensis considers whether the pope "is" the Church, whether cardinals are a part of the "body of the Lord Pope," a body that is above all and is subject to no one's judgment. He certainly believes that the plenitude of power vested in the pope enables him to dispense even against the ruling of an apostle, but with the provision that he cannot alter the faith ("sine lesione tamen fidei") or go against the universal decision of the Church ("non potest tamen contra universalem statum ecclesie dispensare").[24] Aquinas argues that since only a pope can call a general council, and a general council may draw up a creed, it belongs to the authority of a pope to draw up a creed. This he sees as the practical means of ensuring that there is one faith throughout the Church. That could not be secured unless any question of faith arising could be decided by the individual who presides over the whole Church. Therefore we may say that it belongs to the authority of the pope alone to publish a revised creed.[25]

Against this sort of thinking, the conciliarists were to press the view that sovereignty in the Church in matters of faith resides in the community taken as a whole.[26] This is an immensely complex debate and there is no space to go into it here. But we need to touch on it in passing because it forms the context for the question of the teaching authority of the Church with which we are concerned. When it is claimed that the universal Church cannot go astray ("ecclesia universalis deviare . . . non potest"),[27] that cannot be said without a multitude of qualifications about the sense in which "universal Church" is to be taken. Innocent III's *magistra* is variously seen by different schools and factions as speaking through the pope alone, through councils alone, through the *consensus fidelium,* as the voice of the Roman Church, as the voice of all the churches speaking through Rome.

It would be too much to say that the Berengarian controversy marked a wholly new departure. Preoccupations over decision-making in matters of faith can be found everywhere in the Church's history when orthodoxy seems threatened. But there was perhaps something new from the eleventh century (it is no coincidence that a formal statement of the doctrine of transubstantiation is included by Innocent in *Firmiter credimus*). From 1215, it became possible to set an official teaching of the *magistra* over against other "authorities" on this particular issue and to ask whether they agree. (The question was asked remorselessly well into the seventeenth century.[28]) We are seeing, in short, the emergence of a "teaching authority" that proceeds from an authority to make definitions in matters of faith, vested in the Roman Church and speaking for the consensus of all other authorities. Once that exists, the possibility arises of challenging it, by showing that one or more of the authorities for which it claims to speak are not in fact on its side. Aquinas thus defends *ecclesiastica traditio* against any contention that it is against the word of the Lord.[29] We have the beginnings of a pattern or habit of thinking about authorities that is familiar in the later Middle Ages and in the debates of the sixteenth century that divided the Church in the West, in which debates the Church as *magistra* who speaks for the consensus of other authorities comes to be seen as possessing just in itself a higher authority than any other.

We see in discussions among the canon lawyers in the early thirteenth century a reflection of some uncertainties about what constitutes an official statement by the Church as *magistra*. Johannes Teutonicus, in the apparatus to the *Compilatio tertia*, remarks that if something is not in the compilation, but is a bull or something publicly proclaimed, then it is "received" (*recipitur*).[30] In the section on "witnesses," he goes in great detail into the status of, for example, a bishop's letters (which create a presumption but are not a full proof), a judge's seal,[31] and so on. But the legal dimension — whose history would be another story to trace — complex though it already was by 1215, does not encompass the theological. (Canon law glosses tend to be conservative and less theologically sophisticated than contemporary theological work.) The development which seems to be visible during the period between the eleventh century and the thirteenth is of another order altogether. It is ecclesiological, and at the same time it reappraises the whole ancient complex of ideas about revelation, witness, and the authority of authors.[32]

At issue was the way in which authorities might be used, judged, tested, even bent to particular purposes. At the end of the twelfth century, Alan of Lille says that "authority has a nose of wax."[33] Honorable criticism allowed the authorities to speak for the truth; in the hands of heretics, they might be made to prove heterodox opinions. It was the Church's responsibility as *magistra* to judge the work of exegetes and to test, by referring to the consensus of the Church through the ages, whether a correct interpretation was being put upon the authorities. But that responsibility could become a right, and deference to consensus could turn into high-handedness. The theologians of the University of Paris in 1544 produced a list of articles, in the context of the Reformation debates, in which they argued that certainly "Scripture has a nose of wax," and that it is for precisely this reason that the Church is entrusted with an authority higher than that of Scripture, so that she may declare authoritatively how Scripture's teaching is to be understood.[34]

The vast bulk of synodical and conciliar legislation throughout the earlier Middle Ages is concerned with matters of discipline, not of doctrine. There are penitential codes and instructions about the behavior of the clergy, points of law within the sphere of ecclesiastical courts in general, and matters where the jurisdiction of the secular and the spiritual powers touch or overlap. This concern remained true even for councils that claimed to be "general"—the four Lateran Councils of the twelfth and early thirteenth centuries, for example.[35] It is only when a question was raised in a manner which seemed to set some point of faith at risk, or to be leading the faithful astray, that it became necessary for some magisterial ruling to be attempted.

For the most part, the Church expected relatively little learning in parish clergy. Grosseteste's Lincoln Statutes require every shepherd of souls to know the Ten Commandments, the seven deadly sins, the seven sacraments with special emphasis on penance, and to have a simple understanding of the faith as contained in the creeds. But there was increasingly urgent need for a body of theological expertise to deal with the proliferation of questions of which Aquinas (for example) complains in the Preface to his *Summa theologiae*. From the days of Berengar onwards, there was an interested scholarly market for new ideas and intriguingly fresh questions about matters of faith. It is striking how many treatises were produced in response to the Berengarian emergency: those of Lanfranc, Guitmund of Aversa, and Durandus, then the work of Gilbert Crispin and the many *Sentences* of the "school" of Laon that touch on the matter, followed soon after the turn of the century by Rupert of Deutz's comments and the responses of Alger of Liège and William of St. Thierry. Some of these were written in genuine fear that the faithful would be led astray, but there was a tendency for all to pause and turn aside when an interesting problem presented itself. How could the same Christ who was risen and in heaven be present on earth in the Host? How could the one historical body of Jesus make so many Hosts? If a mouse nibbled the consecrated bread, would it be partaking of the body of Christ?

This taste for questions showed itself increasingly throughout the twelfth century in the enlarging glosses on Scripture. It eventually became necessary to set aside separate sessions to deal with questions that could not conveniently be dealt with in the run of the lecture. We see this process already quite advanced in Peter Abelard's commentary on Romans, with its long excursus on disputed questions. Simon of Tournai was running *Disputationes*. Peter Lombard's *Sentences* were in part an attempt to marshal authorities systematically in topical order, so as to make it easier to find a reference on a particular issue. The end of the century saw a number of *Sententiae* and proto-*Summae*. One need not labor the point, for this is familiar ground. But it is clear enough that a theological world, which in Gerbert of Aurillac's day was relatively settled, was two centuries later astir with fresh curiosity. The problem Berengar had posed, which at the time had seemed one of a recognizable sort, a heresy to be silenced, now appeared in retrospect the beginning of a fashion for questioning by individuals who had no intention of being unorthodox, but who were driven by something closer to scholarly enquiry than to dissidency. For the most part no "magisterial" ruling was called for. The questions were asked and answered in the course of theological studies in the schools. They were not being put before the faithful as articles of faith.

Of course, that limitation could not hold for long. Already in Abelard's day we find Bernard of Clairvaux profoundly concerned that the controversial lecturer may be leading simple believers astray, beyond the confines of the schools. It was the fear of serious and widespread consequences for the security of the faith that led to the trials of Abelard himself and of Gilbert of Poitiers. The new questioning in the schools threatened at the very least to add complexity and refinement, if not innovations, to established understanding of that consensus of Christians through the ages to which Lanfranc had confidently pointed. The thirteenth century faced, to a quantitatively unprecedented extent, the task of reconciling authorities by the application of formal reasoning. So various and multiplex were the questions that they force what is perhaps not only a quantitative, but also a qualitative change, a need for a means of ruling on disputed matters here and now, which Scripture could not directly provide, because it was itself involved among the authorities in use. Within the schools, a system evolved for settling disputed questions in which the issue was, as it were, put on trial. Evidence was marshalled for and against a particular view, and the master as judge resolved the matter. But that same question could be, and was, opened up again by others. Its very topicality ensured that for a time, each of the favorite questions of the day was taken up by master after master. Commentaries on the

Sentences in the last medieval centuries reflect such changing fashions clearly in their preoccupation with particular points at certain periods. So the schools could advise, but ultimately they could not settle questions. Only a recognizably higher authority could do that. Innocent III saw, at the beginning of the thirteenth century, a clear need to establish in a general council the magistracy of the Roman Church in matters of faith — to make her *magistra ecclesia* and her bishop the spokesman.

We must now come down from the heights on which it is possible to take some sort of overview of these changes and move about in the undergrowth of the actual treatment of the authorities in thirteenth-century interpretation. There we find a good deal of self-consciousness in the handling of authorities and much discussion of their nature and force. The sublimity of the teaching of the Gospel consists, says Aquinas, at the beginning of the *Catena aurea*, quoting the Gloss: "first and foremost in its supreme authority."[36] That is because it is Christ's authority. "The sublimity of the Gospels' authority depends on Christ."[37] The apostles were its first preachers and they saw Christ in the flesh.[38] In the dedicatory epistle to the *Catena aurea*, written at the request of Urban IV in 1261, and sent to him when it was completed, Aquinas explains that his intention was "to do away with error and to confirm catholic truth."[39] So these *auctores* are valuable for the help they can give in clarifying the meaning of the Gospel text, in providing ammunition with which to attack heretics, and in both these ways, in confirming a "catholic truth" whose defense is the object of Christian scholarship. But there are now modern glossators as well as Fathers and classical authors[40] to be reckoned among "authorities" in connection with Scripture's authority and that of the Church speaking as *magistra*. They, too, are spoken of as "teaching."[41] And there are now many styles of exegesis: that of *lectio divina*, that used by preachers, that of the academic.[42] The scene has become vastly more crowded than it had been in the earlier twelfth century, and it has become correspondingly harder to see one's way clearly in the handling of "authorities" as it had in settling questions. Thirteenth-century exegesis of Scripture had the *Glossa ordinaria*, which was used in much the same way as it had been done in the later twelfth century, as a starting-point from which references could be followed up and considered in full in their original context.[43] Simon of Hinton, for example, Dominican successor of Fishacre in the chair of theology at Oxford from 1248, looked up the *Rhetorica ad Herennium* which is referred to by Jerome on the prophet Joel, and more fully by Gilbert the Universal in his contribution to the *Glossa,* and quoted it at some length in his own comment.[44] Thirteenth-century commentators were thus able, in some cases, to take the *Glossa* a good deal further than their predecessors had done—indeed, they were obliged to do so, if they were to make a contribution of their own. From the end of the twelfth century, there were dictionaries of biblical terms and other aids to study.[45] Skills in the arts of language were still more sophisticated in the thirteenth century than in the twelfth, and the nascent speculative and systematic theology of the twelfth century was consolidated into *Summae* and copiously developed in the analysis of Peter Lombard's *Sentences* as that became the standard textbook it was to remain for the rest of the Middle Ages.

The relationship of authority to reason was a classic issue of medieval exegesis. We find Gilbert Crispin discussing it in the *Disputation with a Gentile,* in which the "gentile" is a hypothetical pagan philosopher who will accept only proof by reason, and also in the *Disputation with a Jew,* where the Jew will, of course, accept the authority of the Old Testament but not of the New.[46] From these texts of the 1090s, we move through a succession of twelfth-century treatises against unbelievers, including Jews, Cathars who take the New Testament but not the Old to be authoritative, and another debate with a philosopher by Abelard.[47] Beryl Smalley suggests that in the thirteenth and fourteenth centuries lectures on Scripture "generally kept off speculative theology, which had its own place in the syllabus."[48] That is true only up to a point. A master such as Aquinas, who was himself a speculative theologian (perhaps first and foremost), did not leave such matters out of his biblical exegesis, although he treats them less extensively than he would in their proper context of the *Summa.*

Aquinas's scriptural commentaries survive from the mid-1250s to the mid-1270s: on Isaiah (1256–9), on the Song of Songs, Lamentations and Jeremiah (1259–68), Job (1269–72), the Psalms (1272–3); and for the New Testament, on Matthew (1256–9), the Pauline Epistles and the *Catena aurea* on the four Gospels (1259–68), John's Gospel (1269–72), and a second exposition of St. Paul (1272–3).[49] Some come down to us in better *reportationes* than others. The lectures on Matthew were recorded by an inept reporter, but those on John were put together by the competent and faithful Raynald, who seems to have had some of his master's notes to hand.[50] For the Old Testament commentaries, except that on the Psalms, and for the second exposition of Paul's Epistles, there is a text deriving from writings of Aquinas himself.[51]

It had been increasingly the case since the twelfth century that the discussion of particular passages of Scripture had prompted lengthy disquisitions. By Aquinas's time, the disquisitions could be done with some polish and sophistication. The opening of the lectures on John gives him scope to examine a number of philosophical and theological questions. We must first ask, he says, what is meant by "The Word," then what is meant by "in the beginning," and thirdly what is meant by "The Word was in the beginning." The object of inquiry is "quid sit quod dicitur." In discussing the Word, he explains that if we want to know what the inner word of the mind is, we must always look at what the outward word points to. In our minds there are three things: the power or capacity to understand, the idea or form of the thing to be understood, and the operation of the understanding. The word we hear does not signify any of those things, but rather what is "formed and stated" (*formatum et expressum*) by the operation of the understanding as it "defines or puts into words" (*definientis vel enunciantis*).[52] So a "word" is always something that proceeds from understanding in act, just as a "word" is always like the thing understood, its *ratio et similitudo*. It is necessary for rational natures to think in words. Intellectual natures are of three kinds: angelic, human, and divine. Words are accordingly of three sorts. When the Evangelist speaks of the Word, he does not mean a human or angelic word, which comes to be, but rather the uncreated divine Word, which is the Word by which all things were made.[53] Aquinas can now point out various differences between the divine Word and other words. The human mind darts about when it is trying to put a word to something. Even when it succeeds, its words are imperfect; our words are not part of our very nature. God's Word is sure, perfect, his very self. The thrust of all this is that we can learn much about God's Word by reflecting on what we know of the nature and behavior of language.[54]

Four questions arise about this problem of what it is that we mean by the Word, says Aquinas. The first is in Chrysostom: Why does John begin straightaway with the Son, and not mention the Father first? The second is also Chrysostom's: Why does John not speak plainly of the Son, but refer to the Word? The third question comes from Augustine. The Greek for *verbum* is *logos*. *Logos* means both "word" and "reason." Why does the translation render one sense and not the other? The fourth question is from Origen. Frequently in Scripture

Christ is referred to not simply as *Verbum* but as *Verbum dei*. Why does the text here omit *dei*?[55]

In his lectures on John, Aquinas provides his listeners with three openings: his own Prologue, his remarks on Jerome's Prologue, and his comments on the first verses of the Gospel. In all three he is anxious to make it clear what the thrust of the argument is and how the text is divided. This is no merely mechanical use of the technique of division, but a recognition that, in a physical sense, it was still not easy to find one's way about a written text, that the student needed to be helped to get a picture of the deployment of the material and the arguments.

He begins his own Prologue with a quotation from Isaiah: "I saw the Lord sitting on a throne, high and lifted up" (6:1). "If these words are taken as if John the Evangelist had said them," Thomas suggests, they describe his Gospel well enough.[56] It is, as Augustine says, different from the other Gospels. While they tell us about the active life, John tells us about the contemplative life too. Thomas uses this opening as the starting-point for a discussion of a threefold "contemplation." It addresses itself to the sublimity of Jesus, to the breadth of his majesty, which fills the whole earth, and to its completeness, for those over whom he has dominion "filled the temple."[57] The first aspect of contemplation, which sets before it the Lord's *altitudo et sublimitas,* is treated in four ways by John. There is the height of his authority (*vidi Dominum*), of his eternity (*sedentem*), of his nature (*super solium excelsum*), and his truth which is beyond understanding (*et elevatum*). It was in these four ways that the ancient philosophers came to the knowledge of God.[58] Aquinas now rehearses four proofs for the existence of God. They proceed from the observation in the natural world of the effects of these four aspects of the divine *altitudo.* Created things are ordered and purposeful, and that argues that something higher is guiding and governing them by its authority. Things in the created world are changeable; what stands higher in the order of things is the less changeable. For example, bodies on earth are mutable and can move about; the heavenly bodies move but do not change. It is inferred that there is a first Principle of things, that neither moves nor changes. Thus we have the proof of God's existence from his eternity. The Platonists argued that everything which exists by participation is derived from something that exists *per se* and absolutely, and that gives us the proof from the dignity of the divine nature. All truths that human intellects can know are finite. There must be a truth that stands behind them, which is infinite and which cannot be known.

That is the truth beyond understanding, the divine Truth which is called "elevatum" in our text.[59]

When contemplation is directed towards the breadth of the divine, it sees the multitudinous effects of the First Cause.[60] When contemplation is "perfected," it is itself lifted up to the height of that which it contemplates and it inheres through love and understanding in the truth it beholds.[61] Thus, Aquinas explains, John not only shows us that Jesus Christ, the Word of God, is himself God, and how all things were made by him, but also that we are sanctified by him and that we "inhere" in him through the grace he pours out upon us.[62] It must be admitted that the text has had to be forced a little to yield these results. Still Aquinas wanted his listeners or readers to come away with a sense of delighted recognition of the orderly way in which everything fitted together, their memory fortified by recollection of the way he had pulled rabbits out of hats.

This leads naturally into an *accessus:* "sic ergo ex praemissio colligitur." The subject matter of this Gospel (the *materia*) has already been covered, for while the other evangelists deal principally with the mystery of Christ's humanity, John deals specially and principally with his divinity.[63] He does so because in the interval after the completion of the other three Gospels, there arose a number of heresies about the divinity of Christ, notably that Christ was simply a man (*purus homo*). So, at the request of the faithful (*ad preces fidelium*), John wrote his Gospel, in which he hands down to us his teaching about the divinity of Christ and confutes all the heresies.[64] What has already been said gives us the order (*ordo*) of the Gospel; its three parts correspond to the three aspects of contemplation. Its end (*finis*) is that the number of the faithful should be increased. The author is called John. The name means "in whom is grace," for without grace it is impossible to see into the divine mysteries. John was a virgin, and so, being pure in heart, he was able to see the Lord enthroned in power. His symbol is an eagle, in token that he flies above the preoccupation of the other three Evangelists with those things which Christ did in the flesh. Fourthly, John was the beloved disciple.

The Prologue of Jerome is dealt with more briefly, and Aquinas seeks especially to draw out of it the emphasis on John's virginity with its implications for his special vocation as an Evangelist. "Common grace" calls the married, but the grace of special and single-minded contemplation calls those for whom the "wine of the wedding feast" is lacking.[65]

John 20:23 is the occasion for a short disquisition on absolution.

It is asked why the text says "Those sins you remit," when only God can forgive sins. Some say that only God remits the guilt; the priest absolves only from the penalty, while declaring that the penitent is free of the stain of guilt. That is not right, says Aquinas. The case is parallel with that of baptism, where the priest baptises instrumentally "and yet confers grace" (*et tamen confert gratiam*). In absolution the priest also acts instrumentally and may say that he "absolves" from both guilt and penalty. It remains true that only God absolves, just as only God baptises; the priest does so as his minister (*ministerio*). Thus it is "true by authority" (*verum est auctoritate*) to say that God alone forgives sins, without that implying a contradiction in the text "Whose sins you remit."[66]

As all this makes plain, "true by authority" is not a straightforward notion. The noses of authorities could be bent by critical evaluation of the truth of what they said. Simon of Hinton tests his quotations from Aristotle against experience. Aristotle agrees with experience on sleep, the fertility of sheep, and the malodorousness of goats. "If this is true," Simon warns, when he describes the special properties of the amethyst.[67] Selective use of authors condemned by the Church for some but not all of their opinions is common: Origen, Berengar, Joachim of Fiore are treated in this way, for example.[68] Some freedom was allowed to editors. Aquinas explains at some length the procedure he has followed in the *Catena aurea*. He has not only made extracts and been selective, taking "something out of the middle so as to avoid prolixity,"[69] he has ensured that in doing so he has made the sense clearer. He has felt free to alter the order so as to fit the needs of serial exposition. Sometimes he has just given the sense, not the actual words (*sensum posui, verba dimisi*).[70] In all this, he has had purposes which make him as much an apologist as a compiler: "not only to pursue the literal, but also the mystical sense"; "to put down errors and confirm catholic truth."[71]

There is work to do here and there to save the faces of authority. Aquinas considers why Matthew quotes Jeremiah, when Jeremiah cannot be his source (see Mt 27:9). Jerome suggested that perhaps the prophets wrote some books which were not "canonizati . . . apud Judaeos," and that Matthew is citing one of those. Augustine thinks that it might have been a slip of the pen for Zachariah. But if that was so, why did the Jews, who would have known the correct source, not emend him? Alternatively, says Augustine, perhaps Matthew was referring correctly to Jeremiah, but to some parallel or similar passage.

Aquinas points out that in Jerome's view, the task of the best sort of interpretation is to consider not the words but the sense. He takes courage from that to draw a parallel with a passage in Mark where the Evangelist attributes to Isaiah what is partly Isaiah and partly Malachi.[72] Nose-bending is more robust in the case of recent authorities. Peter Comestor, discussing the point at which the bread and wine of the Eucharist are changed into the body and blood of Christ, had said that it must be when the last word had been uttered and the prayer of consecration was complete for both bread and wine. Simon of Hinton replies that the host is elevated for the people to see before the words of consecration are said for the wine. Christ must already then be "perfectus sub specie panis." So Peter Comestor must be wrong.[73]

One can do no more in such an ambitious survey as this than indicate lines of inquiry. If we try to bring together the experience of the scholars who were weighing authorities in detail in their works as theologians, and that of the Church as a whole facing the need to decide what had to be defined as a matter of faith among the proliferating mass of theological topics under consideration in the schools, we shall find no statements of policy about authority and exegesis in the thirteenth century that recognize the new difficulties clearly. The academic world was doing its job, and in part that was creating the problem. The *ecclesia Romana* made a magisterial pronouncement from time to time in a general council, as at Lateran IV and at Lyons in 1274, but it did not yet spell out a theology of decision making in matters of faith, still less of reception. Nor did it prove necessary, as it would be at Trent, to marshal a defense on the subject of the supremacy of the Church over Scripture and other authorities. The developments we see in the thirteenth century have a natural, an organic quality; they are responses to need. They do not represent a deliberate change of direction on the part of the medieval Church.

Indeed it is striking how hard it is to find statements that indicate contemporary awareness of the way things were moving. Aquinas's *Summa theologiae* opens, like other works of the age, with a preoccupation over the intellectual respectability of theological science, whether it is a true discipline, whether its principles are self-evident truths or derived from self-evident truths. There is very little indeed in the whole *Summa* about the manner in which truths of faith are arrived at, received, passed on, and maintained in the Church. But despite this habit of missing what seems to modern eyes the obvious questions, scholars and the ecclesiastical hierarchy alike were moving inexorably to a position which was to divide the Church in the sixteenth century and from which we are only now beginning ecumenically to recover. The cooperation between professional theologians and those with a primarily pastoral responsibility that was so promising a feature of the last medieval centuries depended on the maintenance of some duality between the *magisterium* of governance and that of learning. Innocent III's *magistra ecclesia* combined both functions without due analysis of their proper spheres, and that way lay the danger of a tyranny in matters of faith. The resentment and fear of that tyranny which drove the Reformers to secede is proving hard to cure four hundred years later, when there is no longer any truth in the accusation that the *Romana ecclesia* claims a supremacy of authority over that of Scripture.

NOTES

1. On the authorship of the Lateran IV Canons, see the edition of A. García y García, ed., *Constitutiones concilii quarti Lateranensis una cum commentariis glossatorum,* Monumenta iuris canonici 2 (Vatican, 1981).

2. Innocent called to his council more than four hundred bishops, the Eastern Patriarchs, eight hundred priors and abbots, over seventy primates and metropolitans, and the crowned heads of Europe and the crusader kingdoms.

3. Yves Congar, "Pour une histoire sémantique du terme 'magisterium,'" *Revue des sciences philosophiques et théologiques* 60 (1976): 88–98, with the appended "Bref historique des formes du 'Magistère' et de ses relations avec les docteurs," 99–112.

4. Ibid., 85–86.

5. Aquinas, *Scriptum super Sent.* 4.19.2.2.2. ad 4.

6. Aquinas, *Quodlibetales* 3.9 ad 3.

7. See Yves Congar, *L'église de S. Augustin à l'époque moderne* (Paris, 1970), 191, and Alexander III, Letter 1447bis.

8. See a series of references in Congar, "Pour une histoire," p. 92, notes 16–20.

9. *Berengarius Turonensis Rescriptum contra Lanfrancum,* ed. R. B. C. Huygens, CCCM 84 (Turnhout, 1988), 41.

10. *Berengarius* (Huygens, p. 43): "communi fidei adversa."

11. *Berengarius* (Huygens, p. 55): "multitudo ineptorum," "sensa maiorum."

12. *The Works of Gilbert Crispin,* ed. A. Abulafia and G. R. Evans (Oxford, 1986), 126.

13. As in *Thesaurus Novum Anecdotorum,* ed. Edmond Martène and Ursin Durand (Paris, 1717), 1:85.

14. *Thesaurus Novum,* 2:1596.

15. All as in *Constitutiones,* ed. García y García.

16. Peter the Chanter, *Verbum abbreviatum* 33, PL 205:118, where that unity is linked with "unicitas sacramentorum et morum."

17. Aquinas, *Symbolorum Apostolorum expositio* 9, as in *Opuscula Theologica,* ed. R. M. Spiazzi (Rome, 1954–1972), 2.211.

18. D. M. Nicol, "The Second Council of Lyons, 1274," *Studies in Church History* 7 (1971): 145.

19. J. A. Watt, "The Use of the Term 'Plenitudo Potestatis' by Hostiensis," Monumenta Iuris Canonici, Series C, Subsidia 1 (Vatican, 1965), 161–188, at pp. 176–177, from *Compilatio* III, 3.8.2.

20. Ibid., 177, from *Collectio Rainerii Pomposiani* 3.1 and 5.2 (as in PL 216).

21. "Generalis Ecclesia," "particulares Ecclesiae," PL 216:1190. Compare the notion of *studium generale.*

22. *Summa des Stephanus Tournacensis,* ed. F. Von Schulte (Giessen, 1891), 2: "vim suam universaliter extundunt."

23. *Summa "Elegantius in iure divino," seu Coloniensis,* ed. G. Fransen and S. Kuttner, Monumenta Iuris Canonici, Series A, Corpus Glossatorum 1 (New York, 1961), 1:15.

24. Watt, "'Plenitudo Potestatis,'" 183–184, and Aquinas, *Super Sent.* prol.1.

25. Aquinas, *Summa theologiae* 2–2.1.10 sed contra and corpus, and Gratian, *Decretum* 1.17.4–5.

26. A. J. Black, "The Council of Basle and the Second Vatican Council," *Studies in Church History* 7 (1971): 229–234.

27. Conrad of Gelnhausen, *Tractatus de congregando concilio tempore schismatis,* in *Thesaurus Novum,* 2:1209.

28. See, for example, the *Historia transubstantiationis papalis* of John Cosin, as in his *Works* 4 (Oxford, 1851). The text was written in the 1640s.

29. Aquinas, *Contra gentiles* 4.68., ed. P. Marc (Rome, 1961) 3:370, nos. 4037–4038.

30. Johannes Teutonicus, *Apparatus glossarum in Compilationem Tertiam,* ed. K. Pennington, Monumenta Iuris Canonici, Series A, Corpus Glossatorum 4 (Vatican, 1981), 1, 9.

31. Johannes Teutonicus, *Apparatus glossarum,* 242–243.

32. See on the subject in general, A. J. Minnis, *Mediaeval Theory of Authorship* (London, 1984), which, however, omits the Fathers from consideration.

33. *Contra haereticos,* as in PL 332–333. Alan's point, in this context, is that the variable meanings of authorities can be pinned down only by

reasoning. Therefore, he says, authority-proofs must always be backed by proofs from reason.

34. As in *Corpus Reformatorum* 35, cols. 31–32.

35. See the essay by W. Ullman in *Studies in Church History* 7 (1971): 3–37.

36. *Glossa continua super Evangelia (Catena aurea)* praefatio (Turin, 1925), p. xxxiii: "primo in eius excellentissima auctoriate."

37. *Catena aurea,* proemium, p. xxxiv: "a Christo dependet."

38. Augustine, *De consensu evangelistarum* 1.1, quoted in *Catena aurea* praefatio, pp. xxxiii–xxxiv.

39. *Catena aurea* epist. ded., p. xxix: "errores destruere, necnon confirmare catholicam veritatem."

40. The use of classical authors is explored by Beryl Smalley in *English Friars and Antiquity* (Oxford, 1970).

41. "For just as Hugh teaches on the Apocalypse. . . ," "For Alexander teaches on the Song of Songs . . ." See Beryl Smalley, "John Russel O.F.M.," *Recherches de théologie ancienne et médiévale* 23 (1956): 283.

42. For an example of Francis of Assisi's exegesis, see the *Expositio in Pater Noster,* as in *Die Opuscula,* edited by K. Esser, Spicilegium Bonaventurianum 13 (Rome, 1976), 292. See as well D. L. d'Avray, *The Preaching of the Friars* (Oxford, 1985). Smalley notes that the lecture-commentary, once published, could be a source for sermon-making (*English Friars,* 34).

43. See Beryl Smalley, *The Study of the Bible in the Middle Ages,* 3rd ed. (Oxford, 1984), especially 184–188, and her "Two Biblical Commentaries of Simon of Hinton," *Recherches de théologie ancienne et médiévale* 13 (1946): 69 and note 32, for an instance where Simon comments, of a quotation, "but this is not in the original, at least not here." Aquinas went to the originals in assembling the texts for his *Catena aurea.*

44. Smalley, "Simon of Hinton," 70.

45. See my *Alan of Lille* (Cambridge, 1983) on these.

46. *The Works of Gilbert Crispin,* ed. Anna Sapir Abulafia and G. R. Evans (London and New York, 1986).

47. It is in this context that Alan of Lille makes his comment about the nose of wax.

48. Smalley, *English Friars,* 30.

49. On the date and order of Aquinas's works on Scripture, see *Super Evangelium S. Ioannis Lectura,* ed. R. Cai (Rome and Turin, 1951), p. viii, and P. Glorieux, "Essai sur les commentaires scripturaires de Saint Thomas et leur chronologie," *Recherches de théologie ancienne et médiévale* 17 (1950): 237–266.

50. See Cai, p. vii, on the problems with the Matthew commentary.

51. See Cai, p. ix, on the differences between *lectura* and *expositio.*

52. *S. Ioannis lectura* 1.1, Cai no. 25.

53. *S. Ioannis lectura* 1.1, Cai no. 25.

54. *S. Ioannis lectura* 1.1, Cai nos. 26–28.

55. *S. Ioannis lectura* 1.1, Cai nos. 30–33.

56. *S. Ioannis lectura* prologus Thomae 1.

57. *S. Ioannis lectura* prologus Thomae 1.

58. *S. Ioannis lectura* prologus Thomae 2.

59. *S. Ioannis lectura* prologus Thomae 3–6.

60. *S. Ioannis lectura* prologus Thomae 7.

61. *S. Ioannis lectura* prologus Thomae 8.

62. *S. Ioannis lectura* prologus Thomae 8. Thomas notes that it is also possible to interpret the height, the breadth, and the perfection in a different way: the breadth as referring to natural science, the perfection to ethics, and the height to metaphysics (9).

63. *S. Ioannis lectura* prologus Thomae 10.

64. *S. Ioannis lectura* prologus Thomae 10.

65. *S. Ioannis lectura* in prologum Hieronymi 18.

66. *S. Ioannis lectura* 4.5, Cai no. 2542.

67. Smalley, "Simon of Hinton," 73.

68. Smalley, "John Russel," 304.

69. Aquinas, *Catena aurea* epistola dedicatoria.

70. He has done so particularly in the case of Chrysostom, where he has had only a "translatio vitiosa" to work with. See *Catena aurea* epistola dedicatoria.

71. *Catena aurea* epistola dedicatoria.

72. Aquinas, *Super evangelium s. Matthaei lectura* 27.9, ed. R. Cai (Turin and Rome, 1951), no. 2321.

73. Smalley, "Simon of Hinton," 83.

Ordinatio and *Compilatio* Revisited

R. H. ROUSE AND M. A. ROUSE

THE CONTENT, value, and interpretation of authoritative texts were constantly reexamined and discussed by medieval writers and thinkers in the disciplines of theology, law, medicine, natural history, poetics, astronomy, and physics, among others. They addressed the matter of authoritative texts from many different perspectives: What constitutes authority? How is it to be recognized? Who is to define it? How far does it extend? What sort of deference is due it, and how much? In turn, modern scholars from many disciplines ask these same, or similar, questions in an attempt to understand medieval society.

In examining the role of the authoritative text in the Middle Ages, those who work specifically in manuscript studies, such as paleography and codicology or archaeology of the book, enjoy one advantage peculiar to their discipline — namely, that they can literally *see* medieval treatments of authoritative texts. They can see and touch the evidence, on the written page, of medieval copyists rearranging and reworking the words of people who have authority, of their finding significant ways to enhance that authority physically by means of its presentation to the eye. As an example, consider, on the one hand, the splendor of a codex filled with letters of gold written on purple parchment and, on the other, a meticulously alphabetical concordance to thousands of words, compiled through the concerted industry of teams of learned men. Each of these objects, in ways appropriate and specific to its time and place, bears visible witness to the authority of the text of Scripture. Yet the differences between them — in matter, in manner, in purpose — are almost beyond measure. What causes such significant change in texts and in presentation? Simply put, this is the focus of our essay. What motivates changes in the purposes of texts, in their structure and organization, in their appearance, in their production?

1.

The terms *ordinatio* and *compilatio* owe their present currency to an attempt to address these questions, an attempt to explain the causes of change in the physical management and manipulation of texts. The terms were introduced into the lexicon of paleography and codicology by Malcolm Parkes in his 1976 article, "The Influence of the Concepts of *Ordinatio* and *Compilatio* on the Development of the Book."[1] Subsequently, this terminology was presented to a wider audience as a result of its use in 1978 in an influential essay that Parkes wrote with Ian Doyle, "The Production of Copies of the Canterbury Tales and the *Confessio amantis* in the Early Fifteenth Century."[2] Their study of commercial scribes in London, quickly recognized as a new insight into the transmission of Chaucer's works, had the unintended side-effect of setting the terms *ordinatio* and *compilatio* loose among the Chaucerians. These terms have since achieved wide currency in the medieval literary criticism of the last dozen years or so, concentrated almost exclusively in Middle English studies. One of the most recent uses, in fact, occurs in the title of a conference paper that is almost an exact contemporary with our essay: "The Towneley Plays Manuscript (HM 1): *Compilatio* and *Ordinatio*," by Martin Stevens. As he says in the published version, he finds the terms "useful because they have become so widely employed."[3]

Despite the frequency of use, however, there seems to be no clearly delineated or broadly shared definition of these words on the part of those who employ them casually. For instance, one influential body of modern criticism defines *ordinatio* as a literary term that refers to the organization of ideas in a text.[4] Erwin Rauner, however, in a book published in 1989 equates *ordinatio* with "searchability" (*Auffindbarkeit*),[5] which implies that an organization is not an *ordinatio* unless it is searchable. The example he gives is alphabetical order. Norman Blake's *Textual Tradition of the Canterbury Tales* (1985) gives a quite different definition: "*ordinatio* [means] the way in which the text was presented on the page."[6] Blake is thereafter consistent in using *ordinatio* as a fashionable substitute for "layout," following our time-honored academic tradition of calling a spade a *pala rustica*. Judith Tschann, writing in *Chaucer Review* in the same year, takes it for granted that the English and Latin terms are synonymous: "layout, or *ordinatio*."[7] However, when A. S. G. Edwards and Derek Pearsall write that "such exigencies of economy and space [viz., "uniformity or standardisation in matters of layout"] doubtless affected the *ordinatio* of poetic texts," they obviously are not saying that the layout affected the layout — and so *ordinatio* to them means something different.[8] The list of proposed session-topics circulated by the Early Book Society in advance of its 1989 conference, "The Reader and the Book in England, 1400–1575," offered as separate sessions Page Format, Apparatus, *Ordinatio,* Illustration, and so on. Obviously, these proposed session topics all have to do with physical aspects of the book. Which particular aspect, then, is *ordinatio?* Is it distinct from the others on the list? Does it subsume some of them? All of them? Does *ordinatio* have any core of meaning left at all? If so, what is it? "'When *I* use a word,' Humpty Dumpty said . . . , 'it means just what I choose it to mean — neither more nor less.' 'The question is,' said Alice, 'whether you *can* make words mean so many different things.'"[9]

If *ordinatio* seems to have too many meanings simultaneously, the term *compilatio* seems almost devoid of meaning in its current usage. Alastair Minnis defines what he calls "the [medieval] genre of *compilatio*" in this way: "Compilations, with their various methods of subdividing and organising material and their elaborate systems of cross-reference, presented excerpts from important works in a convenient and predigested way."[10] Whether or not one concurs that *compilatio* is a "genre," Minnis's explanation seems reasonably clear, until he muddies the water by labeling Chaucer a compiler. (Does this mean that the Canterbury Tales are "excerpts," "convenient," "predigested"?) Tschann writes of an "editor's attempt to make a unified whole or *compilatio* out of separate parts."[11] If a *compilatio* is just "a unified whole," or a "unified whole [made] out of separate parts," then is any *summa* also a *compilatio?* In contrast, Martin Stevens says, concerning the York Plays in London BL Additional 35290, that "this manuscript is manifestly a *compilatio,*" and then proceeds to emphasize the manuscript's total absence of unity (lack of title, of proemium, of headings, of page-by-page continuity — with a play added out of sequence). He adds that "the *ordinatio* of the book is . . . unmistakably that of a collection of works," indicating that a *compilatio* may have virtually no structure at all.[12] M. C. Seymour, in a 1981 edition of Hoccleve, says, "The Canterbury Tales is a *compilatio* in the technical medieval sense,"[13] without saying what this might be, or substantiating the unlikely assumption that the Middle Ages had a technical sense of *compilatio.* Quite possibly the sense Seymour has in mind is neither technical nor medieval. And C. P. Christianson, in an article published in 1989, calls the Canterbury Tales "a pilgrimage *compilatio,*"[14] by which he means neither a "compilation of pilgrimages" nor "a compilation to take on pilgrimage," but rather "a collection of materials organized within the framework of a story about a pilgrimage." Now and again, scholars dutifully adduce St. Bonaventure's definition of the compiler (in comparison or contrast with the definitions of scribe, commentator, and author).[15] But they are vague when it comes to describing a connection between a mid-thirteenth–century Latin *Sentences*-commentary and the world of Chaucer and Hoccleve.

In sum, the introduction of *ordinatio* and *compilatio* to the literature of Middle English criticism has not contributed to clarity, either of thought or expression, but quite the reverse. And the adoption of both terms by Rauner, evidently the first time this terminology has crossed the English Channel, marks the start of a Continental usage that is sure to take one (through the perils of translation) a step further away from consensus.

So perhaps the time has come to pose the question, just what do *ordinatio* and *compilatio* mean? In truth, to elicit a useful response we must rather ask, what do these words mean in specific times and places? Since contemporary use of these terms was initiated in articles by Malcolm Parkes, let us focus on his usage to begin with.

Parkes gives no general-purpose definition of the term *compilatio*, referring to it as a "principle,"[16] a "genre,"[17] or "a literary form,"[18] as "a form of writing and a kind of book,"[19] and as "both a form of writing and a means of making material easily accessible."[20] The shifts in terminology suggest an indecision as to whether *compilatio* is a form, a process, or a principle. In practice, if one sets aside what Parkes says about the term and instead considers how he uses it in context, it becomes clear enough what it means. Whether he is referring to the Canterbury Tales or Vincent of Beauvais's *Speculum*, whenever Parkes calls something a *compilatio* he just means that it is a compilation, a structured collection.

As one can see from the previous quotations, subsequent writers have grasped one or another aspect of Parkes's terminology, without necessarily grasping his intent. Minnis, for example, seems to have elevated *compilatio* into a literary theory of the thirteenth and later centuries,[21] an interpretation that could derive from Parkes's language but not, we think, one that Parkes himself intended. Many students of Chaucer, on the other hand, seem to have seized upon the term *compilatio* gratefully to express the fact that the Canterbury Tales is a novel collection of tales quite different in structure from either Jean de Meung's or Boccaccio's. This usage, far from illuminating Chaucer's genius, merely says in effect, "The definition of *compilatio* is Canterbury Tales."

Parkes's conception of *ordinatio* likewise has occasioned some confusion. Minnis (in *The Medieval Theory of Authorship,* for example) parts company with Parkes on this term. Minnis recognizes that when medieval writers used the word *ordinatio* (which they did very seldom), they employed it to describe literary structure, the grouping of arguments, the logical marshalling of thoughts into chapters and paragraphs — what was more often called the *modus tractatus* or *forma tractatus* of a text. Parkes, in contrast, has moved *ordinatio* from the field of literature to that of codicology in order to refer to aspects of page layout and manuscript design. For example, when Parkes considers the differences "between the ways in which scribe B handled the *ordinatio*" in two manuscripts of the Canterbury Tales, he demonstrates the distinction through a detailed comparison of physical aspects such as ruling, bounding lines, size of margins, placement of glosses, paragraph marks, hierarchy of scripts, and apparatus such as running heads and marginal titles. Elsewhere, he speaks of "all the trappings of *ordinatio:* [namely,] sources and topics indicated in the margins, . . . text well-disposed in sections, . . . each section carefully labelled by means of rubrics, . . . running titles, and . . . pictures of each of the pilgrims."[22] Ultimately, Parkes implies (unintentionally, perhaps) that *ordinatio* is just another name for *mise-en-page* or layout. This implication, as we noted above, has not been lost on Chaucer scholars, many of whom have taken Parkes to mean that "layout" and *ordinatio* are synonymous.

2.

After this brief look at the source of contemporary uses of *ordinatio* and *compilatio,* we might next inquire what the terms *ordinatio* and *compilatio* meant in the Middle Ages — that is to say, what each of these terms meant to specific people or groups at specific times and contexts in the Middle Ages.

Ordinatio, from classical antiquity, meant "a setting in order, regulating, arranging," and by extension "an order, arrangement, regulation." In the English word "order," different families of connotations branch off from twin nuclei of meaning: an arrangement ("Everything is in order") and a command ("Soldiers obey orders"). The Latin word *ordinatio* in antiquity ran essentially the same gamut, from its application to features of architecture (by Vitruvius), to its use as a virtual synonym for "ordinance" or "decree," and then by extension to the act of appointing to office by decree. This last mentioned use of *ordinatio* passed directly into ecclesiastical Latin with the sense its cognate retains in English, "ordination." This and the other classical meanings were transmitted to, and embellished by, the Middle Ages.

The term apparently does not occur in a literary context until the middle of the thirteenth century. Modern literary critics cite a handful of medieval examples. Robert Kilwardby in the 1240s, in his *notule* on *Priscianus minor,* remarks that "the 'form' of a work consists in its manner of procedure, and in the order of the parts of its subject-matter (*ordinatio partium doctrine*)."[23] At virtually the same time, Bonaventure explains in a commentary (written just after 1248) that the "form" of St. Luke's Gospel consists, on the one hand, of its manner of proceeding (namely, narrative) and, on the other, of the order of its parts and chapters ("ordinatio partium et capitulorum").[24] At about the same date, Vincent of Beauvais employs the term at least once, in the prologue of the *Speculum maius* (completed between 1244 and 1260). In making the modest disclaimer that had been customary to compilers since the seventh century or before, Vincent states that the *Speculum*'s authority derives from those whose words he quotes, since he has added little or nothing of his own. He concludes, "Theirs is the authority, mine just the organization of the parts (*partium ordinatio*)."[25] And Nicholas of Paris (late thirteenth century), in commenting on Aristotle's *Perihermeneias,* says "the 'form' of a treatise . . . is the order of its books, parts, and chapters (*ordinatio librorum partialium et capitulorum*)."[26]

This is a disconcertingly early group of writers—mostly mid-thirteenth century—from whom to derive the principles of Middle English manuscript production in the fifteenth. And it is a worrisomely small group—four—concentrated in a surprisingly brief span of time—thirty years? merely twenty?—on which to erect a literary theory for the end of the Middle Ages. It is, moreover, an unexpectedly Latin and scholastic group from whom to draw principles of vernacular poetics.

Doubtless this list is not exhaustive. Since these same four examples are adduced time and again by modern critics, however, the odds are long that one could not enlarge either the numbers or the timespan very much, at least not enough to alter the clear implication that the magnitude is insignificant. The unvarying combination of *ordinatio* with *partium/partialium* might make one wonder, in fact, whether this coupling was just an ephemeral catch-phrase which, at a narrowly restricted time and place, temporarily joined the familiar terms *forma tractatus* and *modus tractatus* in the *accessus* literature of the day. At any rate, the examples of medieval uses of *ordinatio* quoted by modern critics having nothing to do with the layout of the manuscript page, even though most modern Chaucer scholars use the word in that sense only.

One last aspect of the medieval usage of *ordinatio* should be acknowledged. Among the four medieval occurrences of *ordinatio* cited, only one is in any way connected with a compilation, that of Vincent of Beauvais. Three of the four occur in another kind of literature entirely, in some form of *accessus* or commentary. The present-day linking of *ordinatio* with *compilatio* must therefore seem strained. And it must seem odd, for example, to suggest as Minnis does that "Chaucer derived certain principles of order from compilations and from the explanations of *ordinatio* which accompanied them,"[27] when, in fact, such explanations did not accompany them.

A survey of *ordinatio* in the context of medieval literature is necessarily brief, because of the limited use of this term in the sources. To survey the medieval fortunes of *compilatio* is another matter. When we inquire about the medieval history of *compilatio*, we are really asking a question on two levels, (1) about the word and (2) about the thing it represents — or, rather, about whether what we English-speakers call a "compilation" is the thing that was meant by *compilatio*. Modern critics who assert that "the *compilatio* was developed as a genre . . . during the course of the thirteenth century"[28] are taking it for granted that the name and the thing it names are inseparable. To the contrary, (1) the term *compilatio*, and the related forms *compilare* and *compilator*, were employed in literary contexts long before the thirteenth century, but they often did not mean "compilation, compiling, compiler." And (2) compilations existed for hundreds of years before the thirteenth century, but they often were not called *compilationes*.

In investigating the history of the word itself, one can trace the shifting meanings of *compilatio* from late antiquity onward.[29] As an outgrowth of its core meaning, "to rob" or "to plunder," the word long had deliberately pejorative connotations when applied to literature and to writers. A *compilator* was a plagiarist. This implication, found in the writings of Jerome and Macrobius, among others, remained the principal meaning of the word in the ninth and tenth centuries — and, indeed, it remained one of the possible meanings much later. Beginning in the tenth century or perhaps a little before, however, a neutral value was introduced alongside the negative one. *Compilare* in the proper literary context could mean (neutrally) "to borrow" or, to quote an even more positive formulation by Paul the Deacon, "to bring together or to put together into one."[30] These meanings occurred along with the common, negative meaning "to pilfer" or "to plagiarize." In the course of the twelfth century, *compilatio* normally meant something similar to what we mean by the English word "compilation."

Of course, the meanings of *compilare, compilator, compilatio* were not set in stone in the thirteenth century; they continued to evolve. In some contexts these words came close to losing their identity entirely, becoming indistinguishable synonyms for other terms that pertained to writing. Thus, for example, a mid-thirteenth–century manuscript collection of passages for preaching against the Cathars says in its title, "Incipit *compilatio* auctoritatum contra hereticos et manicheos. . . ." But the wording is changed, as if casually, in the colophon: "Explicit *summa* breviata contra manicheos et hereticos."[31] To take another example, contemporary manuscripts of the *Manipulus florum*, a *florilegium* written by Thomas Hibernicus at Paris in 1306, say indifferently in their incipits and colophons that the work was *compilatus, collectus, compositus, editus,* or *factus* by Thomas. Quite clearly they all mean the same thing: Thomas made this work.[32] In the Middle English of Chaucer and Lydgate, indeed, a primary meaning of the verb *compilen* was simply "to compose." Thus, Lydgate speaks of a certain poet who "compiled" many a new song, and he even says that the Pater Noster was "compiled of our lord Iesu."[33] By this stage the meaning of "compile" has come a long way from its origins, untidily adding new meanings while not necessarily discarding the old. "To plunder" became, in literary contexts, "to steal ideas or plagiarize," then "to borrow ideas openly," next "to arrange or structure borrowed ideas," and at length "to structure one's own ideas," that is, "to compose." We can see, then, that the term *compilatio* is neither new, nor permanently fixed, in the thirteenth century, as some have suggested.

The thing itself — the activity of compiling, the creation of something that we today would readily recognize as a compilation — likewise did not begin with the thirteenth century. The archetypal medieval compilation no doubt was the *florilegium. Florilegia* — whether collections of authoritative, sententious statements from patristic and ecclesiastical writers, or anthologies of extracts from classical prose or poetry, or even combinations of the patristic and the pagan — were compiled throughout the Middle Ages. Consider the oldest to be widely circulated, the seventh-century *Liber scintillarum.* It groups its extracts into eighty-one chapters according to subject-matter, and within each chapter it arranges the extracts in descending order of the authority of their sources. Thus it begins with extracts from the Gospels, which are followed in order by extracts from the words of St. Peter, St. Paul, other apostles, Solomon, then other books of the Bible, the Four Doctors (Augustine, Jerome, Ambrose, Gregory), and so on.[34] To be sure, the *Liber scintillarum* is not called a *compilatio,* nor does its compiler "Defensor" call himself a *compilator* — still terms of opprobrium at that date. Defensor labels the work simply a *libellum,* describes his actions with the verbs *colligere* and *congregare,* and calls himself just *scriptor.* Nevertheless, in the *Liber scintillarum,* passages that have been removed from their original contexts are made to conform to a new structure and to serve a new purpose — which meets most definitions of a compilation.

While *florilegia* were the most commonplace examples, there were other types of pre-thirteenth–century compilations as well: the collections of sentences before Peter Lombard, for instance; histories and chronicles; various *De viris illustribus;* and canon law collections, both Gratian's and those of his predecessors, such as Ivo of Chartres (d. 1115). The compiling activities of the canonists, in fact, must have influenced the acceptance of *compilator* and *compilatio* as neutral or even positive terms. Gratian was referred to approvingly as a *compilator* in the mid-twelfth century, while as early as a century before, Peter Damian speaks of his thematic collection of excerpts from papal decrees as "a new *compilatio.*"[35] Long before *compilare* and *compilatio,* however, compilers made do with such terms as *mutuor, excerpere, conflare, coaptare, componere, adnotare, edere,* and particularly *colligere,* together with the corresponding nouns.

We can see, thus, that it is neither the word *compilatio* nor the thing, a compilation, that is new in the thirteenth century. What does it mean, then, when Doyle and Parkes says that "the *compilatio* was developed as a genre in academic and legal circles during the course of the thirteenth century to make inherited material excerpted from the writings of established *auctores* accessible in more systematic and convenient form"?[36] Or when Minnis writes, "By the end of the thirteenth century, the new genre [of *compilatio*] was well-established"?[37] Parkes offers this explanation: "What was new was the amount of thought and industry that was put into [compilation], and the refinement that this thought and industry produced."[38] We would surely agree that compilations organized by schoolmen, supplied with scholarly apparatus, and produced by the university book trade to meet the demands of scholars, did keep pace with the growing institutionalization and sophistication of the universities in the thirteenth century. As we have seen, however, these thirteenth-century compilations were not created ex nihilo, but were the logical outgrowth of a long prior tradition. Thirteenth-century compilers had predecessors and precedents.

Papias is a choice example of a sophisticated early compilation with complex apparatus. He explains this in the prologue of his dictionary, which he compiled in the mid-eleventh century.

> Regarding gender, declension, and tense we shall add something in the nature of guides in all cases . . . we shall designate masculine with an *m*, feminine with an *f*, neuter with an *n*, words of two or three common genders with a *c* or an *o*. . . . The declension of a noun will be distinguished by other letters: the first declension by *p*, the second by *s*, the third by *t*, the fourth by *q*, the fifth by *v*. . . . The conjugation of verbs will be designated by the first and second person or by the infinitive, indications by which conjugation is always recognized. . . . In cases of uncertain quantity, a syllable will be marked with a virgule if it is long, by a point if it is short. . . .[39]

Papias goes on to give a thorough (if not entirely clear) description of how he has distinguished with marginal letters each of the stages in his form of alphabetization, commenting upon the problems of alphabetical arrangement when spelling is in a state of flux. He concludes his prologue with a "list of abbreviations": fourteen two- and three-letter abbreviations of the names of the authorities most commonly cited in the dictionary (on the style of "aug = Augustinus, amb = Ambrosius," and so on).

Ambitious and complicated earlier compilations of this sort were the progenitors of the thirteenth-century university compilations. Moreover, it does an injustice to such innovative compilers as Papias to call the "amount of thought and industry" supplied by thirteenth-century compilers "new" by comparison. Subsequent copyists often omitted or overlooked elements of Papias's intricate apparatus, as though his symbols were invisible.[40] In a sense, they actually were invisible to the perceptions of eleventh- and twelfth-century scribes and readers. The thirteenth-century compilers' advantage over their predecessors, the new ingredient in the mix, was the presence of a different audience, a body of school-trained readers who not only understood but valued an orderly arrangement and a helpful apparatus.

3.

Let us suppose, just for the sake of argument, that we have demonstrated that *ordinatio* and *compilatio* as used by twentieth-century scholars of Middle English would have perplexed, if not confounded, readers and writers who lived in the Middle Ages. This raises the question: What does it matter? It is not unheard of, and may even be useful, to create new Latin words in order to refer to medieval phenomena that the Middle Ages never bothered to name, such as the Early Modern coinage of *florilegia*. *Ordinatio* and *compilatio* do not quite fit into that category, though, because we are told that the modern interpretation is equivalent to how medieval writers used and thought of them. That simply is not the case. More pernicious is the fact that, among modern scholars, the words *ordinatio* and *compilatio* are employed to convey two or more different, even incompatible, concepts; not infrequently, they are used to no particular purpose at all.[41]

Often they serve as pompous but fairly harmless substitutes for more precise English words. Yet when the terms *ordinatio* and *compilatio* are used not merely to name, but to explain, the physical form of texts, the issue goes beyond imprecise or ambiguous language to a basic misunderstanding about the causes of change. When one speaks of the "influence of the concepts" of *ordinatio* and *compilatio* on the development of the book, it implies — and many have assumed — that physical changes in the medieval book were somehow imported from above and outside, governed by theoretical considerations and scholarly discussions. Such an assumption is contrary to what is known about the circumstances of medieval book production. In the Middle Ages, authors seldom determine, and never long control, the physical appearance of their texts. (Papias tried, but was unsuccessful.)

Let us make ourselves clear here. Literary texts are produced by authors and, thus, changes in literary form over centuries are due to authorial decision. Authors do respond to the interests or even the requests of patrons. But those who were touched by the gods — a Chrétien, a Dante, a Chaucer — knew in "responding" to their audience how to teach that audience to want a kind of literature that had not existed until it was created by authorial art and craft. If one were to say, "Authorship belongs to intellectual history and book production to social and economic history," it would be a gross oversimplification. The authors themselves are part of social and, often, economic history. Yet this axiom still contains enough truth at its core to bear remembering.

Take the example of Geoffrey Chaucer, to whom critics have most zealously and least carefully applied the language of *ordinatio* and *compilatio.* "Chaucer the compiler," he has been called.[42] Modern students of the Canterbury Tales speak of "Chaucer's exploitation of the principles of *compilatio,*"[43] saying that "Chaucer 'ordinated' materials in relation to tales and tellers."[44] Again, "the Ellesmere copy is the first manuscript to present the Canterbury Tales in the *ordinatio* of the *compilatio.*"[45] This language harmfully blurs the distinction between what an author composed, and the physical form in which that composition is presented in any manuscript. The physical appearance is the combined result of a patron's desire and a bookproducer's capacities, taking shape most often after the author's death and (in the case, for example, of a Gregory the Great or a Seneca) even changing shape over the centuries as needs, conventions, tastes, and abilities change.[46]

Literary creation and the physical layout of surviving manuscripts are not results of the same actions. One may ignore the distinction and continue to call both of them *ordinatio,* but it will not help. They are still not the same thing. They are not brought into being by the same agents; their presence or absence is not under the control of the same persons; and it is imprudent even to take for granted that their purposes are identical, without a case-by-case inquiry.

There are, as we would acknowledge, exceptions and qualifications to be made to this characterization. We are aware that most authors of the thirteenth and later centuries had a working knowledge of how books were produced. For example, Dante in *Paradiso* 33.85–90 rings the changes on the metaphor of binding up loose leaves into a single volume.[47] There is no suggestion, however, that he had any control or even influence over the physical appearance of manuscripts of the *Commedia,* the final installment of which was only circulated after his death. Some authors, though, did take a lively interest in how their texts would be presented physically. And a few—a small proportion of the whole number of late medieval vernacular authors—even took steps to ensure that the physical appearance of their texts conformed to their wishes. One thinks specifically of those authors who were also professional copyists or who oversaw production of their works, such as Hoccleve or Christine de Pizan. The authors who made such efforts surely influenced the physical appearance even of manuscripts copied outside of their immediate oversight. Instructions from employer or patron, as well as scribal inertia, could ensure that a later copy reflected to some extent the layout of its exemplar — to the extent, for example, that the copyist found it less trouble to follow the layout than to ignore it and substitute instead the conventions of his own time and place.

Still, an exemplar's influence on subsequent copies was severely limited, as manuscripts of the very popular history of Martin of Troppau (d. 1278) demonstrate. This Dominican laid out his Chronicle of the popes and emperors in tabular form, summaries of the reigns of popes on the left-hand page, facing summaries of the reigns of contemporary emperors on the right. Martin explains the system in his introduction. But a recent study of some 400 surviving manuscripts of the Chronicle found that only about 10 percent retain the tabular correspondence, almost certainly because copyists or their patrons were too thrifty to leave the blank spaces necessary to balance the tables.[48] Latin chronicler or vernacular poet, no authors in any way controlled the physical presentation of their texts once those texts had escaped from under their thumbs into the wider world of commercial, amateur, or (especially in the fifteenth century) monastic book production. Indeed, in countless instances the largest collections and the best-known surviving manuscripts of a vernacular poet's works were written after, frequently long after, the poet's death.[49]

Medieval book production is largely a bespoke trade. A book is not made until someone decides, in advance, that he wants that book.[50] Change in book form is thus not to be explained primarily as the result of authorial concepts or theories; rather, such change is a response to the demands of the audience, to the changing needs of those who use books. To cite one example: The *Moralia* on Job, composed by Gregory the Great at the end of the sixth century, undergoes successive remodelings in both structure and format in the manuscripts of the twelfth and thirteenth centuries. A sprawling work in six volumes divided into thirty-five books, the *Moralia* acquires by the late twelfth century running headlines to distinguish the books, while its quotations from the Book of Job are set off from Gregory's commentary by color or underscoring. By the mid-thirteenth century, a chapter structure has been created. Tables of chapters appear at the heads of the thirty-five books, and annotations of this new chapter structure are added in the margins of older manuscripts of the *Moralia.* As a final touch, by the end of the thirteenth century the *Moralia* is usually copied in a single codex, rather than the two or three of earlier times.[51] This sequence of changes was not the result of authorial theory, but was created to meet the needs of those who used this text.

To cite another well-known example: During the first twelve centuries of Christianity, the Christian Scriptures were written in several parts — several scrolls, in the earliest centuries, and thereafter several codices — including a separate volume for the Pentateuch, one for the histories, one for the sapiential books, one for the Gospels, one for the Pauline Epistles, and so on. In the first half of the thirteenth century, this situation changed dramatically with the production of small, one-volume Bibles, which is to say Bibles written in a deliberately reduced and abbreviated script on thin parchment. The layout included running titles at the top and chapter numbers in the margins, while the accompanying apparatus included a dictionary of Hebrew names and, in some cases, a *Summa contra manicheos.* The change in size and presentation embodied in these so-called "pocket Bibles" was not prompted by new theories, however. It was a direct response to the needs of Mendicant preachers, especially the Dominican missionaries preaching against heresy in the south of France.[52]

A different kind of change is exemplified by the form of the great glossed pages of the twelfth-century Bible, which Christopher de Hamel has identified as being in existence by 1140. The words of the text are written in large letters and short lines, flanked by the gloss written in a highly abbreviated half-sized script.[53] Although de Hamel's study does not mention where the idea of this new layout came from, it can be seen that the masters of theology simply adapted the layout that had been used in glossed Virgils, Lucans, and Horaces since the ninth century, a layout familiar to the masters from their training in the *artes.*[54] The concept did not create the glossed scriptures, because the form had long been in existence. Rather, the needs of a community of scholars involved in teaching the sacred page moved them to adapt and tailor a known form to new purposes.

The widespread adoption of the alphabetical subject index, beginning in the 1240s to 1260s, was, again, the application of a known device — alphabetical order — to meet the need for a new kind of access to the authoritative text — the kind of alternative access required for constructing sermons and lectures. This same alphabetical principle, when applied to the text of the scriptures, produced the con-

cordance to the Bible in the 1230s and 1240s. Alphabetization was
not new; the Bible was not new; the practice of concording (a staple
of the gloss) was not new. The new factors in the equation were, first,
the need for such a tool, so essential to the Bible-based preaching and
teaching of the Mendicants and, second, the university-trained Mendicant manpower capable of producing this tool.[55]

As with changes in the form of the book, so also changes in the
manner of book production should be seen as resulting from the changing needs of those who use books. Need for manuscripts of the works
of Thomas — because of their importance to the Dominicans and the
demand for them by other Paris theologians — probably brought the
Parisian version of university stationers into existence in the 1260s
and 1270s.[56] Just so, the needs of the growing class of literate nobility
in France were responsible for bringing into existence a class of writers like Guiart des Moulins and Jean de Vignay, who made a good
living at translating and adapting Latin works into Old French, and
a class of commercial producers of illustrated Latin and vernacular
books for noble household and court.

To sum up: The physical presentation of texts in the manuscripts
of the Middle Ages was determined and perpetually redefined by the
changing needs of their medieval readers — much more so than by the
desires of their medieval authors. The modern introduction of the terms
ordinatio and *compilatio* has done manuscript studies a useful service
in emphasizing physical presentation, in focusing on the development
of scholarly apparatus in medieval manuscripts, and in drawing attention to the connection between how a text is perceived by its audience and the apparatus with which it is equipped. The imprecise
use of these two words, however, has done more harm than good. Let
us take one final example from the Chaucerian heart of the problem:
It would be harmful to imply something like "Chaucer ordinated his
Canterbury Tales like a *compilatio*," because that near-talismanic language would mislead both writer and reader into thinking that something had been said. If instead one were to abandon *ordinatio* and *compilatio* and say simply, "Chaucer arranged his Canterbury Tales like
a scholarly compilation," there is a good chance both writer and reader
at that juncture would recognize the flaw in the logic. Chaucer did
not himself commission or write the Ellesmere manuscript or any other
surviving copy of the Tales, and the physical aspects of arrangement
and scholarly apparatus, varying from one manuscript to another, were
not subject to his control.

We do not purport to be "Paleography Police" empowered to determine which words may be used in the field of manuscript studies and how one may use them.[57] To the contrary, we have no power save persuasion. We are just asking for a bit more clarity of thought and expression. We wish students of medieval vernacular literature might more frequently pause to wonder, "What do the words *compilatio* and *ordinatio* mean, anyhow?" More important still, they might ask, "Do the concepts that these terms represent have any relation at all to the way real people made real books in the fourteenth and fifteenth centuries?"

NOTES

We wish to thank the people who read earlier versions of this essay and offered many helpful suggestions: Consuelo Dutschke, Dennis Dutschke, Ralph Hanna, Neil Hathaway, Anne Hudson, Alan Piper, and Martin Stevens. We are grateful, in addition, to those whose comments enlivened the discussion of the essay at the "Ad litteram" conference in particular Rita Copeland and Martin Irvine. Finally, we appreciate the generosity of Ian Doyle, Alastair Minnis, and Malcolm Parkes, who read and commented on an earlier version of this piece.

    1. M. B. Parkes, "The Influence of the Concepts of *Ordinatio* and *Compilatio* on the Development of the Book," in *Medieval Learning and Literature: Essays Presented to Richard William Hunt*, ed. J. J. G. Alexander and M. T. Gibson (Oxford, 1976), 115–141; reprinted in M. B. Parkes, *Scribes, Scripts, and Readers: Studies in the Communication, Presentation, and Dissemination of Medieval Texts* (London, 1991), 35–70. We cite here the original pagination.

    2. A. I. Doyle and M. B. Parkes, "The Production of Copies of the *Canterbury Tales* and the *Confessio amantis* in the Early Fifteenth Century," in *Medieval Scribes, Manuscripts, and Libraries: Essays Presented to N. R. Ker,* ed. Malcolm B. Parkes and Andrew G. Watson (London, 1978), 163–210; reprinted in Parkes, *Studies,* 201–248. We cite here the original pagination.

    3. A paper delivered at the Society for Textual Scholarship: 5th Biennial International Conference, New York, April 6–8, 1989, as reported by the *Gazette du livre médiévale* 14 (Spring 1989): 46. The paper is now printed as Martin Stevens, "The Towneley Plays Manuscript (HM1): *Compilatio* and *Ordinatio*," in *Text: Transactions of the Society for Textual Scholarship* 5 (1991): 157–173, ed. D. C. Greetham and W. S. Hill; see esp. p. 171.

    4. This is the consistent position of Alastair J. Minnis; see for example, his *Medieval Theory of Authorship: Scholastic Literary Attitudes in the Later Middle Ages* (London, 1984).

    5. Erwin Rauner, *Konrads von Halberstadt, O.P., "Tripartitus moralium":*

Studien zum Nachleben antiker Literatur im späteren Mittelalter (Frankfurt-am-Main, 1989) 1:37–40.

    6. Norman Blake, *The Textual Tradition of the Canterbury Tales* (London, 1985), 55.

    7. Judith Tschann, "The Layout of *Sir Thopas* in the Ellesmere, Hengwrt, Cambridge Dd.4.24, and Cambridge Gg.4.27 Manuscripts," *Chaucer Review* 20 (1985): 1–13, at p. 1.

    8. A. S. G. Edwards and D. Pearsall, "The Manuscripts of the Major English Poetic Texts," in *Book Production and Publishing in Britain 1375–1475,* ed. J. Griffiths and D. Pearsall (Cambridge, 1989), 257–278, at p. 264. Edwards and Pearsall typify a growing tendency to leave these terms undefined on the assumption that they convey meaning—"using them because they are widely used." Thus, for example, Vincent Gillespie writes, without foreshadow or follow-up, "The development of the concept of *ordinatio* greatly increased the usefulness of Latin compilations, and similar techniques were applied to the design of some vernacular compilations." See Gillespie, "Vernacular Books of Religion," in *Book Production and Publishing,* 317–344, at 329–330. This reveals that Gillespie considers *ordinatio* to be a technique, but not what that technique might be. Most recently, George R. Keiser ("*Ordinatio* in the Manuscripts of John Lydgate's *Lyf of our Lady:* Its Value for the Reader, Its Challenge for the Modern Editor," in *Medieval Literature: Texts and Interpretation,* ed. T. W. Machan, Medieval and Renaissance Texts and Studies 79 [Binghamton, 1991], 137–157) takes *ordinatio* to mean the (usually non-authorial) division of a text into chapters or books; cf., e.g., p. 149, "[a revisor] undertook to impose a four-book structure, that is, a new *ordinatio*" on a text formerly divided into eighty-seven chapters, while other manuscripts divide the same text into seventy chapters, fifty-eight chapters, thirty-six chapters, etc.

    9. Lewis Carroll, *Through the Looking Glass,* chapter 6.

    10. Alastair J. Minnis, "Late Medieval Discussions of *Compilatio* and the Role of the *Compilator*," *Beiträge zur Geschichte der deutschen Sprache und Literatur* 101 (1979): 385–421, at pp. 386f.

    11. Tschann, "Layout," p. 5.

    12. Stevens, "Towneley," 159. A. S. G. Edwards, considering four manuscripts that contain works of Chaucer and Lydgate together, in fashion partly haphazard and partly deliberate, concludes that "a study of the *compilatio* of manuscripts containing the works of the two might prove an illuminating exercise." See his "Lydgate Manuscripts: Some Directions for Future Research," in *Manuscripts and Readers in Fifteenth-Century England,* ed. D. Pearsall (Cambridge, 1983), 15–26. It is not clear in this case whether *compilatio* means structure, purpose, or something else.

    13. M. C. Seymour, *Selections from Hoccleve* (Oxford, 1981), p. xxv.

    14. C. Paul Christianson, "A Community of Book Artisans in Chaucer's London," *Viator* 20 (1989): 207–218, at p. 217.

15. The passage in question, which appears in Bonaventure's commentary on the first book of the *Sentences,* is quoted in full by Parkes, "Influence," 127–128, from *Opera omnia* 1 (Quaracchi, 1882), p. 14, col. 2.

16. Parkes, "Influence," 128: "the principle of *compilatio* which emerged in the thirteenth century, 'divide and subordinate.'"

17. Doyle and Parkes, "Production of Copies," 190: "The *compilatio* was developed as a genre in academic and legal circles during the course of the thirteenth century to make inherited material excerpted from the writings of established *auctores* accessible in a more systematic and convenient form."

18. Parkes, "Influence," 130: "As a literary form *compilatio* influenced works in vernacular literature."

19. Ibid., 138: "The notion of *compilatio* both as a form of writing and as a kind of book was disseminated [along with the dissemination of the compilations themselves]."

20. Ibid., 127: "This [i.e., "imposing a new *ordinatio* on the material"] led to the development of the notion of *compilatio* both as a form of writing and as a means of making material easily accessible." Again (p. 137): "The definition of *ordinatio* led to the development of the notion of *compilatio* both as a form of writing and as a means of making material easily accessible."

21. See Minnis, "Discussions," throughout, and especially *Theory,* 191–210.

22. Parkes, "Influence," 134. In the introduction to his collected studies (1991) Parkes has expressed it quite differently when he speaks of "the practice of analysing the *ordinatio* (or structure) of a text in the lecture room"; Parkes, Studies, xviii. Too late, alas, to put the Middle English genie back into the bottle.

23. Cited in Parkes, "Influence," 121. See also Minnis, *Theory,* p. 147 and the notes there.

24. Cited by Minnis, *Theory,* 148.

25. Cited by Minnis, "Discussions," 387, and *Theory,* 155, and by Parkes, "Influence," 128.

26. Cited by Parkes, "Influence," 121, n. 2, and by Minnis, *Theory,* 147 and n. 123. They refer in turn to B. Sandkühler, *Die frühen Dantekommentare und ihr Verhältnis zur mittelalterlichen Kommentartradition,* Münchener romantische Arbeiten 19 (Munich, 1967), 41 and n. 92, who quotes this passage from Munich, Clm 14460, fol. 62rb: "causa formalis tractatus que est ordinatio librorum partialium et capitulorum."

27. Minnis, *Theory,* 201.

28. Doyle and Parkes, "Production," 190.

29. This paragraph is based on the evidence set forth by Neil Hathaway, *"Compilatio:* From Plagiarism to Compiling," *Viator* 20 (1988): 19–44. We thank Mr. Hathaway for permitting us to consult his article in typescript. In addition to the works cited there, see also Bernard Guenée, "L'historien et la compilation au XIIIe siècle," *Journal des savants* (1985): 119–135.

30. Quoted from Hathaway, "Compilatio," 35, who explains that while scholars are not certain of the origin of this remark, at any event it appears in a surviving tenth-century manuscript.

31. For a list of surviving manuscripts, see Laura Light, "The New Thirteenth-Century Bible and the Challenge of Heresy," *Viator* 18 (1987): 275–288, at p. 287.

32. See, for example, Paris, Bibliothèque de l'Université 215, fol. 241 ("Manipulus florum compilatus a magistro Thoma de Hybernia"); Bibliothèque nationale, lat. 15986, fol. 224v ("Manipulus florum collectus a magistro Thoma de Ybernia"); lat. 15985, fol. 1v ("Manipulus florum quem composuit magister Thomas Ibernicus"); lat. 3336, fol. 2 ("tabula . . . qui vocatur Manipulus florum edita a magistro Thomas de Ybernia"); lat. 15986, fol. 1v ("Manipulus florum quem facit magister Thomas Hybernicus"). All these manuscripts were copied in Paris within ten years of the date when the *Manipulus florum* was completed.

33. The Lydgate citations come, respectively, from *Fall of Princes* 1.352 (ed. H. Bergen, EETS e.s. 121–123 [1924]) and from the *Expositio* of the *Pater Noster* 83 (in *Minor Poems*, ed. H. N. McCracken, EETS 107 and 192 [1911, 1934], 60–71). Both are cited here from the *Middle English Dictionary*, 2.1, ed. Hans Kurath et al. (Ann Arbor, 1959), 464.

34. See M. A. Rouse and R. H. Rouse, "*Florilegia* of Patristic Texts," in *Les genres littéraires dans les sources théologiques et philosophiques médiévales* (Louvain-la-Neuve, 1982), 167 and n. 2.

35. See Hathaway, "*Compilatio,*" 38, nn. 81–82 (Gratian, in the words of the future Alexander III) and n. 80 (Peter Damian).

36. Doyle and Parkes, "Production," 190.

37. Minnis, "Discussions," 413.

38. Parkes, "Influences," 127.

39. The translation follows for the most part Lloyd and Betty Daly, "Some Techniques in Mediaeval Latin Lexicography," *Speculum* 39 (1964): 229–239, at pp. 232–233. For a recent consideration of Papias's role in the evolution of lexicography, see Olga Weijers, "Lexicography in the Middle Ages," *Viator* 20 (1989): 139–153, especially pp. 140–141.

40. This was first remarked upon by Daly and Daly, "Latin Lexicography."

41. See, for example, L. F. Sandler, "*Omne bonum: Compilatio* and *Ordinatio* in an English Illustrated Encyclopedia of the Fourteenth Century," in *Medieval Book Production: Assessing the Evidence*, ed. L. L. Brownrigg (Los Altos Hills, Calif., 1990), 183–200. By *compilatio* (a word that, curiously, does not seem to be employed in the text), Sandler means that *Omne bonum* is "a work of compilation," and by *ordinatio*, that its compiler applies "the alphabetical principle to the heterogenous contents of an entire encyclopedia" (p. 184). Except for the title and a token appearance of *ordinatio*, these terms seem not to recur in the article, nor to have any connection with it.

42. See, for example, Minnis, *Medieval Theory,* 202. Scholars often remind us that Chaucer calls himself a "compilator." And so he does; but not
of course with reference to the *Canterbury Tales:* "But considre wel that I ne
usurpe not to have founden this werk of my labour or of myn engyn. I n'am
but a lewd compilator of the labour of olde astrologiens, and have it trans-
latid in myn Englissh oonly for thy doctrine"; *A Treatise on the Astrolabe,* prologue, lines 59–64, in *The Works of Geoffrey Chaucer,* ed. F. N. Robinson (Boston, 1957), 546. In this particular context, Chaucer seems to have meant
by "compilator" a combination of compiler, editor, and translator.

43. Minnis, *Theory,* 202.

44. Ibid., 201.

45. Doyle and Parkes, "Production," 191, n. 61.

46. Stevens, "Towneley," wrestles unsuccessfully with the problem of
responsibility for the layout of HM 1 (the Towneley Plays). He attributes
its appearance in turn to the *compilator* (p. 162, "manuscript . . . with its hand-
some scrolled capitals in red . . . well laid-out pages . . . [and] evident planning as a book is clearly the work of a *compilator,*" "its *ordinatio* is dictated
entirely by the *compilator's* interpretation"), to the illuminator (p. 164, "the
illuminator served as supervisor of the volume," his work serving "as an organizing and guiding device"—curious in a manuscript without illumination), and then to the rubricator (p. 167, "narrative being told in this manuscript is highlighted by the rubricator/supervisor"). However, Stevens might
rather have used the fact that two pages (fols. 5v, 6r) were written out of
sequence, and the prominent appearance of a four-line-high, display-script
rubric containing the wrong title, to demonstrate how easily the presentation of a manuscript escapes the control of author, patron, planner, or supervisor (see his pp. 162, 167, and fig. 1). Stevens also invests great significance
in the scribal commonplace "Assit principio . . ." (pp. 164–166), a conventional invocation for divine help at the start of a copying job with which
many a medieval manuscript begins, including HM 1. He asserts that this
invocation, along with titles of other plays, will "help us understand more
directly the *ordinatio* [= layout? apparatus? organization?] of this volume."
Stevens calls it "the rubric . . . that introduces the contents of the entire
cycle." He implies that it is some sort of title ("the title, if indeed it can even
be called that, of Play 1," "the first play has no other title"), but he twice
refers to it as a "colophon" (the inscription at the end of a book). And, without questioning, Stevens assumes that the presence of this chestnut in HM 1
was the deliberate choice of the collection's compiler ("the compiler asks for
help at the *beginning* of his work," emphasis in original), and therefore that
it associates the compiler with God as maker. Stevens does all this without
facing the question of whose invocation it was.

47. See the exegesis of this passage by John Ahern, "Binding the Book:
Hermeneutics and Manuscript Production in *Paradiso* 33," *PMLA* 97 (1982):
800–809.

48. See Anna-Dorothee von den Brincken, *"In una pagina ponendo pontifices, in alia pagina imperatores:* Das Kopieren der tabellarischen Papst-Kaiser-Chronik des Martin von Troppau OP (+ 1278)," *Revue d'histoire des textes* 18 (1988): 109–136.

49. Examples are the Liederhandschriften of Heidelberg Universitäts-bibliothek. See *Codex Manesse: Die Grosse Heidelberger Liederhandschrift. Kommentar zum Faksimile des cpg. 848 der UB Heidelberg,* ed. W. Koschorreck and W. Werner (Kassel, 1981), and the bibliography cited there.

50. We would by no means deny that there are exceptions to this rule. In some circumstances of production, specifically in the late Middle Ages in those urban centers that boasted a concentration of the wealthy literate, commercial book producers occasionally produced books containing the sort of texts that were in continued demand (run-of-the-mill books of hours, for example) "on speculation"—that is, books which found a buyer after and not before they were copied. We think no one would deny, as well, that these cases are indeed exceptions, and not the rule.

51. See N. R. Ker, "The English Manuscripts of the *Moralia* of Gregory the Great," in *Kunsthistorische Forschungen Otto Pächt* (Salzburg, 1972), 77–89.

52. See Light, "Bible," throughout.

53. C. de Hamel, *Glossed Books of the Bible and the Origins of the Paris Booktrade* (Woodbridge, Suffolk, 1984).

54. On this point, see the review of de Hamel's book by Patricia Stirnemann in *Bulletin monumental* 143 (1985): 363–367.

55. See R. H. Rouse and M. A. Rouse, "The Verbal Concordance to the Scriptures," *Archivum Fratrum Praedicatorum* 44 (1974): 5–30 and bibliography cited there. Here rests the basic difference between two approaches. Parkes attributes change in the attitude to texts, and in specific the emergence of subject indexes and scholarly apparatus, to the influence of the concepts of *ordinatio* and *compilatio.* We attribute the emergence of such tools to changing audiences who place new demands on their books, adapting them to new needs. See R. H. Rouse and M. A. Rouse, *Preachers, Florilegia and Sermons: Studies on the Manipulus florum of Thomas of Ireland,* PIMS Studies and Texts 47 (Toronto, 1979), esp. chapters 1 and 2.

56. See R. H. Rouse and M. A. Rouse, "The Book Trade at the University of Paris, *ca.* 1250–*ca.* 1350," in *La production du livre universitaire au moyen âge: Exemplar et pecia,* ed. L. J. Bataillon, B. G. Guyot, and R. H. Rouse (Paris, 1988), 41–114.

57. Martin Stevens, in a curious interpretation of the present article ("Towneley," p. 171), concludes that our concern with *ordinatio* and *compilatio* is essentially that of etymological crusaders who have vowed to see that the terms are not "used inauthentically," whatever that may mean, while in contrast his own "interest in them is primarily for the concepts they represent and not in their etymology or historical usage." Two problems with his state-

ment are, first, its unwarranted assumption that these terms in today's usage represent definable concepts and, second, its acquiescence in the employ-ment of these protean "concepts" that distort historical perception of medie-val written culture. We leave it to others to judge whether or not Stevens has mischaracterized our argument in his first footnote (p. 171), simply ob-serving that our article is misquoted in both quotation marks *and* italics!

The Continuing Life of
William Peraldus's *Summa vitiorum*

Siegfried Wenzel

THOUGH IT IS well known that the *Summa vitiorum* by the French Dominican William Peraldus or Guillaume Peyraut enjoyed an enormous popularity and exerted a wide-ranging influence on later medieval homiletic and pastoral literature, the changes that the work underwent in the course of its life have hardly been examined in detail. We know from modern studies that occasionally it was combined with another *summa,* and we know — mostly from titles in the manuscripts — that occasionally it was abbreviated. But exactly what forms such adaptations, especially of the latter kind, took remains uninvestigated. It is this aspect of the continued life of the work on which the following observations are intended to throw some light.

To look for treatises on the vices that can be genetically linked to Peraldus's *Summa vitiorum* may at first glance seem a rather foolish enterprise because, as a fifteenth-century writer sighed, "There are so many books and treatises on the vices and virtues . . . that any man's life, which is so short, would end before he could either study or read them."[1] My anonymous predecessor's sigh would surely turn into blank despair were he to see the evidence gathered by Morton Bloomfield and his collaborators, whose list of incipits, even when reduced to works on the vices only and shorn of redundancies, still offers hundreds of treatises for inspection.[2] Beyond the sheer number of works that claim attention, this field is beset by other and more excruciating difficulties, ranging from insufficient and inaccurate cataloging of relevant works and manuscripts to problems of dating and specific ascription. My analysis can thus claim to be no more than a morning's walk through a dense and occasionally very muddy forest. I have undoubtedly missed a number of very important trees and looked too superfi-

cially at others. Yet I hope that this investigation will make some suggestions about the shape of the forest itself, place some of its trees
more accurately than has hitherto been the case, and perhaps even
furnish a tentative field guide to them.

William Peraldus's *Summa vitiorum* or *de vitiis* (written perhaps
before 1236), with its companion piece on the virtues (written before
1248), clearly enjoyed authoritative standing in the field of pastoral
literature through the later Middle Ages and beyond. One *exemplar*
from which Paris scribes made their authorized copies still survives,[3]
and the sheer number of extant copies made from about 1250 until
the end of the fifteenth century, together with a number of early printed
editions, reflects the enormous esteem in which Peraldus's work was
held. In his basic study published in 1948, Father Antoine Dondaine
listed more than 500 manuscripts for the two *summae,* a number that
continues to increase as modern and medieval library holdings are
examined more closely.[4] Peraldus himself was a Dominican friar, and
his *summae* quickly gained an authoritative position within his own
order.[5] But near-contemporary Franciscans as well respected his work
very highly[6] and soon are found copying material from it.[7] In the
fourteenth and fifteenth centuries both *summae* could be found in
practically any major library all over Europe, whether monastic or
secular or eventually lay, often even in multiple copies. In addition
to being copied, Peraldus — or rather "Guillelmus Parisiensis" or simply "Parisiensis" — was also widely quoted in sermons, in manuals,
and even in the theological treatises of John Wyclif, certainly no friend
of the friars.[8] Yet his *summae* were not simply copied and quoted
but, in addition, became changed and recast and adapted in a variety
of ways.

In order to discuss such changes and to relate subsequent works
to the *Summa vitiorum,* some descriptive remarks about it are necessary.[9] Though Peraldus does not give us a formal prologue or introduction that would set out the intentions and order of his *Summa vitiorum,*
it is clear that his concern was primarily practical and ascetical: Christians are asked to avoid sins and vices "studio et summa diligentia,"
but they cannot do so unless they get to know them, and Peraldus
aims to give them this knowledge, together with the urge to apply it.[10]
After an opening paragraph that actually introduces gluttony,[11] he begins his *summa* with a relatively brief section on vices in general (*Summa
vitiorum* 1, pp. 1–3) and then launches into a very long discussion of
the seven chief vices or "deadly sins," in the order of gluttony, lechery,

avarice, accidia, pride, envy, and wrath (*Summa vitiorum* 2–8). By the
early thirteenth century, the seven vices had, in moral theology as well
as in its practical applications, become the standard topic of discussing the major inclinations to evil in human behavior. What was not
standard, and hence surprises us, is the order in which Peraldus presents the seven, which contrasts with the normal one, derived from
Gregory the Great, that begins with pride and ends with lechery.[12]
Though Peraldus does not justify his choice, he tells us that he will
begin with gluttony because this sin is the first to combat since Christ's
first temptation in the desert was to gluttony.[13] This remark establishes an ascetic orientation for the *Summa vitiorum* and betrays its in-
debtedness to John Cassian, for whom also the struggle against sin
had to start with controlling one's bodily desires.[14] Of the following
vices in the *Summa vitiorum,* several are concatenated: a vice is said
to spring from or be born of the preceding one (thus lechery, *accidia,*
envy, wrath). The position of avarice, however, is rationalized by rhetorical purposes ("for the treatment of this vice is more useful to
preaching than the treatment of the other vices," 4.1.1, p. 51), and the
tractate on pride begins with a full scholastic rationale for all seven
capital vices. To devise such an explanation why there are seven vices,
how they are linked, and what fundamental principle they derive from,
was a standard feature in scholastic teaching during Peraldus's lifetime and later; but his particular rationale is, to the best of my knowledge, quite unique, even though it was later to be used by Dante.[15]
Another peculiarity is the place at which Peraldus's rationale appears:
not, as one might expect, at the beginning of his section on vices in
general, but instead much later at the head of his *tractatus* on pride
(6.1, p. 213).

    Another feature that sets the *Summa vitiorum* distinctly apart from
twelfth-century lists of the seven chief vices and from contemporary
as well as later treatments is the addition of an eighth to the seven
deadly sins, the *peccatum linguae,* under which Peraldus lists and discusses twenty-four sins of the tongue (9, pp. 371–420). This unique
element in the *Summa vitiorum* probably grew out of the Schoolmen's
analysis of "sin" and their discussing various patterns of dividing "sin,"
one of which is that of sins of heart, mouth, and deed (*peccatum cordis,
oris, et operis*), drawn from the Augustinian definition of sin as "anything said or done or desired that contradicts the law of God."[16] In
the 1230s Parisian masters assembled long lists of sins of the tongue
together with elaborate logical rationales,[17] though the division of "sin"

into the triad of mouth, heart, and deed usually remained separate from the division into seven chief vices. In Peraldus, the *peccatum linguae* is not included in the rationale he gives for the chief vices, at the beginning of pride. Its tractate begins with the statement that "lastly among the sins we must speak of the sin of the tongue, because this vice remains after the other sins" (9.1, p. 371), which once again reveals what I have called the practical-ascetic orientation of the *Summa vitiorum.*

In dealing with these individual vices, Peraldus consistently proceeds, first, by advancing reasons that should teach us to detest the respective vice; second, by listing and discussing the vice's species or offspring; and third, by suggesting remedies of it. This pattern may occasionally be obscured by additional topics; thus, the section on gluttony adds a part on the vice's "satellites" (2.3, p. 12). In several cases the listing of species goes through a more elaborate process of division, as in the part on pride. Nonetheless, the basic pattern of *detestatio–species–remedia* always remains discernible and furnishes the essential structure for his discussion of individual vices. There are other patterns that appear frequently throughout the *Summa vitiorum,* though not with the same prominence and regularity, which can be considered characteristic of Peraldus. Among these are proving that a vice is detestable because it displeases God, pleases the devil, and does injury to man (the last point being occasionally split into doing injury to the person who practices the vice, and doing harm to others). This *modus tractandi* of the detestability of vices will assume greater importance in my later discussion of particular treatises.

Further characteristics of the *Summa vitiorum* reside in the topics that Peraldus treats. Since he pays little if any attention to the definition of the seven chief vices, nothing can be said about his own conception of their nature. But the picture changes when one turns to the offspring or species of the vices, for here Peraldus played a major role in the history of the vices by creating and "fixing" the series of vices that spring from the seven capital ones. I have elsewhere analyzed Peraldus's innovation in respect to the offspring of *accidia,*[18] and what holds for that capital sin also seems to be true of the other six. Besides the members of the vices' offspring, the *Summa vitiorum* is further characterized by some other topics that were new in works on the sins and afterwards tended to appear again and again in the same places. Some examples are: the discussion of major vices according to status (for instance, avarice in merchants, lawyers, priests, and diceplayers: 4.2.4 and 4.2.6–15, pp. 97–98 and 103–157; lechery in lay-people, clerics, and religious, 3.2.8–9, pp. 24–28), or beginning the discussion of the species of pride with a distinction of the vice within and in outward appearances (6.3.1, p. 235).

Finally, the *Summa vitiorum* is characterized by and indeed well known by the vast amount of "homiletic material" it gathers in order to develop its major topics and to illustrate the evil effects of the vices and their offspring: primarily biblical, patristic, and some classical quotations (the latter mostly from Seneca, but also some verses from Ovid and Horace), as well as a great number of proverbs, similes, and comparisons, and even short narratives (though without moralization). Much of this was common material by the 1230s. Collecting it — rather than making a penetrating conceptual analysis of sin and the vices — constitutes Peraldus's major achievement and ensured his works a permanent place on the reference shelves of medieval preachers.

The vastness of Peraldus's *Summa vitiorum* did not prevent successors from expanding it further. Thus, in his *Destructorium vitiorum*, the fifteenth-century Englishman Alexander Carpenter discussed the vices in the Peraldian order and generally followed the topical patterns noted earlier. He also greatly increased the *Summa vitiorum*'s homiletic material with further substance taken from post-Peraldian authors, including John of Wales, Nicholas of Lyre, Holcot, Bromyard, Rolle, John de Burgh, and others.[19] Perhaps more interesting to note is that Carpenter omitted the sins of the tongue and that he moved the Peraldian rationale for the chief vices from its curious position under pride to the opening part on sin in general, where it logically ought to stand.[20] Except for the sins of the tongue, Peraldus's work is almost entirely preserved in the *Destructorium,* but has undergone extensive substantive expansion as well as some theological deepening or rationalization and reordering.

A different kind of expansion appears in a late fourteenth-century work from Vienna, *Erchantnuzz der Sund (Knowledge of Sin)* by Heinrich von Langenstein, which combines Peraldus's *Summa vitiorum* with Peñafort's *Summa de poenitentia,* much as Chaucer's Parson's Tale does on a smaller scale. The Peraldian part actually shortens Peraldus's text by omitting much homiletic material as well as the sins of the tongue and the rationale for the vices. On the other hand, it adds some new material, which its modern editor has traced to Thomas Aquinas and Bonaventure.[21] *Erchantnuzz der Sund* thus definitely forms part of the

continuing life of Peraldus because it retains the order of the seven
deadly sins, the repeated topical pattern of *detestatio, species,* and *remedia,*
and the bulk of the homiletic material.

In contrast to expanding Peraldus and integrating the *Summa
vitiorum* into a larger work, other treatises go the opposite way and
abbreviate. A number of them simply omit blocks of material from
the parent *summa.* Thus, one fourteenth-century copy of the *Summa
vitiorum* stops at the end of the part on wrath (which in Peraldus precedes the sins of the tongue) with a double *explicit.*[22] In other words,
this copy drops the tractate on *peccatum linguae,* even though the tractate was listed in the summary or discursive table of contents, which
stands here, as it normally does, before the proper beginning of the
summa. A similar cut often affects the other extremity of the *Summa
vitiorum,* its beginning, though in this case only a small paragraph is
eliminated. For instance, instead of starting with Peraldus's "Dicturi
de singulis vitiis," another work begins with the sentence: "Triplici ratione potest ostendi vicia summa diligencia esse uitanda" ("By a threefold reason can it be shown that the vices must be shunned with maxi-
mum diligence"). The three reasons are that the vices please the devil,
displease God, and do harm to man. Otherwise, this work preserves
Peraldus fairly intact, including his order of sins, their rationale, the
sins of the tongue, and his characteristic patterns of treatment. What
has happened here is no more than the simple omission of Peraldus's
very first paragraph.[23]

Omission leads to farther-reaching results when the *Summa vitiorum* has not merely some of its limbs lopped off, but is subjected to
a more general bloodletting. Several works on the vices introduce
themselves precisely as extracts — *Tractatus extractus de tractatu moralium
de septem viciis capitalibus secundum Parisiensem,* as one of them has it.[24]
This work actually is a very generous extract, preserving Peraldus's
incipit as well as the sins of the tongue and omitting only the rationale
and other passages here and there, such as the chapter on lechery among
nuns. Another abbreviation, offering "quedam notabilia a *Summa viciorum* extracta," is very similar in its coverage compared to Peraldus,
though here the sins of the tongue are only listed and not developed
at greater length — the text in fact states, "it is enough to enumerate"
them.[25] But this abbreviation also omits the Peraldian incipit, "Dicturi . . . ," and the first paragraph, and it begins instead directly with
one of the main topics on detesting vices in general: "Ualde placent
vicia demonibus" ("Vices please the devils very much"). Such abbre-

viation is carried even further in another *Summula de vitiis,* which opens
with the same topic as the two works just mentioned: "Uicia uitanda
sunt quia demonibus valde placent." It omits the rationale for the seven
vices but not the sins of the tongue, simplifies several treatments of
the species, and in general offers a text that is Peraldian in substance
but shows stylistic changes throughout.[26]

The treatises so far considered undoubtedly represent redactions
of the *Summa vitiorum* rather than independent works because they
preserve the *Summa vitiorum*'s main features outlined above, including
its homiletic material (even where it has been abbreviated) and in many
cases even its *incipit.* However, several of them lack some of the *Summa
vitiorum*'s characteristic features, notably the sins of the tongue and
the rationale for the capital vices — or they preserve only one of these.
Some works simply omit one or both of these, others shift them to
different positions from where they were found in the *Summa vitiorum.*
Evidently, these features, both of them unique to Peraldus, were quite
unstable in the subsequent history of the work. It would seem that
redactors of the *Summa vitiorum* felt free to omit Peraldus's most
characteristic features, thereby bringing his work in line with more
traditional ways of treating the seven chief vices. This freedom touches
another key feature of the *Summa vitiorum,* its peculiar order of the
vices. Here, again, the oddity of Peraldus's treatment was "rectified"
by changing his order to the standard Gregorian one, from pride to
lechery. A *Summa viciorum* written about 1400 and now at Graz, for
example, begins with the Peraldian opening for the section on vices
in general: "Dicturi de singulis viciis primo ostendemus triplici racione vicia summa diligencia esse vitanda."[27] But instead of following
the section with gluttony, this copy moves into pride (without Peraldus's
rationale) and goes through the standard Gregorian order to lechery.
The sins of the tongue have been preserved and appear in the normal
Peraldian place, after the vice of wrath (fols. 79r–82r). Their position
is handled differently in another treatise preserved in the same library
and written in the second half of the thirteenth century.[28] This work,
too, adopts the Gregorian order, but it reverses the order of gluttony
and lechery at its end, so that the last vice treated here is gluttony,
which is then followed by the Peraldian sins of the tongue. Such
reshuffling makes excellent sense, because (as we are told) both sins
of eating and sins of speaking belong to gluttony.[29]

Investigation of abbreviated versions of the *Summa vitiorum* thus
reveals the instability of several of its main features in the early trans-

mission, including the rationale for the vices[30] and the sins of the tongue (which could be simply omitted) as well as the order of the vices (which could be changed to the more conventional one). Peraldus's homiletic material, too, was of course susceptible to more or less drastic changes, especially in abbreviations of his *Summa vitiorum*. One may at this point well ask what elements from the parent *Summa vitiorum*, if any, remained stable and can therefore be utilized in our attempt to relate later treatises genetically to the parent. The answer is: major topics treated (such as, species of the vices, particular topics such as internal vs. external pride or avarice in diceplayers) and Peraldus's repeated mode of discussing the vices by treating their *detestatio, species,* and *remedia,* and by showing their detestability because they displease God, please the devil, and so on. These features provide a reasonably trustworthy tool that we can now apply to other treatises on the vices which at first sight bear little resemblance to the *Summa vitiorum*.

A good transition to this group of treatises, which do not simply expand or abbreviate the *Summa vitiorum* but restructure its text in more fundamental ways, is provided by a shorter work on the capital vices whose initial words are very reminiscent of two or three abbreviations just mentioned: "Sin must be shunned for six reasons. First because it is injurious to God. Which is shown first by examples in nature. . . ." The other reasons are that sin is hateful to the angels, obedient to the devil, harmful to one's neighbor, hurtful to its practitioner, and lastly disturbing to the whole Church.[31] Though *Peccatum est vitandum* has sometimes been attributed to Grosseteste,[32] it bears no significant resemblance to the bishop's genuine writings. In one important codex it is ascribed to John of Wales and further characterized as "ex Parisiensi confectus," that is, compiled or extracted from William Peraldus.[33] But in actuality *Peccatum est vitandum* represents an abbreviation of a very long treatise entitled *Summa iustitiae.*[34] The latter begins with a substantial prologue, which names the work's title and declares that, since justice as a way to God consists in fleeing evil and pursuing good, this treatise will deal with sin and the vices, in ten parts, and then with the good and the reward for both evil and good, in two final parts. The ten parts devoted to evil deal successively with sin in general, the seven chief vices, the five senses, and several causes of sin, such as ignorance, weakness, and so on. The prologue further tells us that the work's *modus procedendi* is "by examples in nature, examples in art, and examples in *figura* or sacred Scripture," which is then explained and rationalized with references to Aristotle and Augustine.[35] (See Appendix.)

All this may seem far removed from Peraldus. Here the order of the seven chief vices is the traditional, non-Peraldian one from pride to lechery; his rationale for them is not given (even though the *Summa iustitiae* gives several others[36]); and no section on the sins of the tongue is included. But the absence of the latter compels us to take a closer look, because the author of the *Summa iustitiae* states in his prologue that here he repeats the *modus procedendi* he had already employed "in tractatu nostro de lingua," and further references to his work on the tongue occur in at least six other places in the *Summa iustitiae*.[37] The work referred to, *De lingua,* is a fairly popular treatise by this title which indeed uses the triple schema of proof with examples from nature, art, and Scripture and, even more importantly, discusses twenty-five sins of the tongue which, despite some changes in order and terminology, correspond exactly to Peraldus's twenty-four (the added one being "preaching of sin").[38]

If in following this suggestion of a Peraldian presence we return to the *Summa iustitiae* for closer inspection, we find that a good deal of its actual homiletic material also occurs in Peraldus. More significantly, the two patterns used throughout *Summa iustitiae*—that vices are injurious to God, pleasing to the devil, etc., and second that they are shown to be detestable by examples from nature, art, and Scripture—can be traced back to Peraldus as well. The first schema recurs throughout his *Summa vitiorum* and is applied to the chief vices as well as to some of their species.[39] But in contrast to *Summa iustitiae* Peraldus does not give the schema the same exclusive prominence, nor does he use it as consistently with the same number of members or with the same terminology.[40] The second structural schema, which adduces reasons from nature, art (that is, human activity), and Scripture, likewise occurs in Peraldus, though admittedly with even less clarity and prominence than the first.[41]

One can, therefore, see the *Summa iustitiae* as a drastic reworking of Peraldus's *Summa vitiorum.* Besides reordering the chief vices in the traditional Gregorian sequence, as well as omitting much Peraldian and adding a great deal of new homiletic material, its anonymous author has reorganized his extensive subject matter according to organizational principles that were obscurely present in Peraldus but now become clarified, rationalized, or applied with rigor and consistency. Among various reasons one might suggest for his doing so, the most convincing one lies in Peraldus's text itself. At first sight, the latter strikes its readers as very "scholastic" because it progresses by divisions and numbered parts. For example,

> About the vice of gluttony we shall first speak of those things
> that cause us to detest the vice; second, of its species; third, of
> its satellites which the vice uses; and fourth, about the remedies
> against this vice. There are fourteen things that cause us to detest
> the vice. The first is. . . .[42]

But a closer look at this seemingly well-ordered structure quickly reveals several shortcomings. They begin at the very start, when without a prologue Peraldus sets out bluntly: "Being about to speak of
the individual vices as the opportunity offers itself, we shall begin
with gluttony." Yet this is not what he does. Instead, he changes his
subject to vices in general and launches into discussing them with
the new paragraph whose first words I quoted earlier ("By a threefold
reason can it be shown that the vices must be shunned with maxi-
mum diligence") without properly announcing the following topics.
Moreover, as already mentioned, his structural schemata that might
be used in discussing the individual vices or their species vary a good
deal in terminology, completeness, and prominence. And further, he
often presents a number of items for a given topic and then, after
treating them, continues to add some further ones. For instance, in
discussing reasons for detesting *accidia,* Peraldus first lists several things
in nature that give us a good example for being active; then he adduces Scriptural passages that do the same; and thirdly he shows how
the vice displeases God, pleases the devil, and harms man. At that
point he then adds "another five reasons that may be helpful in detesting" the vice, reasons that could have easily been accommodated
under the preceding ones.[43] One gains the impression that in struc-
turing the *Summa vitiorum,* parataxis or juxtaposition prevailed over
hypotaxis or logical subordination, leading occasionally to afterthoughts
or the repetition of a subject already dealt with.[44] I suggest that it
was the resulting slightly bumbling nature of his work that accounts
for subsequent efforts to restructure and to streamline it which we
noticed in *Summa iustitiae.*

The *Summa vitiorum* bears still another aspect that is less than
satisfactory from a stylistic point of view: it lacks a satisfactory prologue or introduction. Its opening is very blunt: "Being about to speak
of the individual vices as the opportunity offers itself, we shall begin
with gluttony." This blunt manner is retained in the various abbreviations of the *Summa vitiorum* that were discussed earlier, which start
equally directly without announcing the contents of the entire work or

at least its first part, on vices in general. In marked contrast, Peraldus's
summa on the virtues begins with considerably greater elegance. It has
a regular prologue, which begins: "As we should also teach about useful things, following the example of Solomon who said, 'I thought in
my heart to withhold my flesh from wine, so that I might lead my
soul to Wisdom'" and so on.[45] The text then goes on to give the author's reason for writing the work, his identity ("minimus de ordine
fratrum praedicatorum"), the work's title ("Tractatus virtutum"), and
its five major divisions. The main part similarly does not at once jump
into its first topic, but instead approaches it with delicate steps. It starts
with a scriptural quotation from Jeremiah, "If you separate the precious from the vile, you shall be like my mouth" (Jeremiah 15:19).
The three terms "precious," "vile," and "separate" are then explained,
and this leads Peraldus to his general subject, the virtues. The use
of such a rhetorical introduction is not surprising; it seems to have
been a convention that can be found in many pastoral and spiritual
treatises from at least shortly after 1200. What does surprise is that
Peraldus did not use it in his *Summa vitiorum*, which demonstrably was
written several years before the *Summa virtutum*. Did he perhaps learn
to write more elegantly in the meantime? Or was the art of introducing one's work, as I sometimes think, influenced by new ways in preaching which had the "scholastic" or "modern" sermon begin with a short
biblical *thema* that was then divided, an influence that might have made
itself felt in Peraldus's case only after the *Summa vitiorum* had been
written?[46]

Whatever might explain the lack of an artistic introduction, let
alone of a prologue to the *Summa vitiorum*, in its subsequent life the
handling of its introduction becomes another interesting factor. The
various abbreviations I have cited are equally devoid of artistry. But
several reworkings made during later generations give evidence that
redactors considered a more rhetorical opening to be highly desirable.
There are even cases in which Peraldus's own, relatively unchanged
text is provided with just such an introduction. One of them begins
with a quotation of Ezechiel 1:7: "Their feet were straight, and the
sole of their foot like the footsole of a calf."[47] This initial foot image
is developed at some length, with considerations about what must be
done when one's feet are hot, cold, dirty, stubbed against a rock, and
so forth, all of which leads to a longer section on justice. Then the
author quotes another biblical verse, this time from Ecclesiasticus 3:32:
"A wise and intelligent heart will abstain from sins." He continues:

> Since Augustine says that evil cannot be avoided unless it is known, therefore, in order to have knowledge of the vices and for the benefit of readers a treatise or *summa* on the vices is to be compiled from the authorities, reasons, and words of the holy fathers and masters.[48]

And with this he launches into the text of Peraldus, somewhat streamlined stylistically, but still unmistakable. Unfortunately the copy of the work, which seems to be unique, breaks off in the part on avarice and thus does not tell us whether such standard Peraldian elements as the rationale and the sins of the tongue were included. What text has been preserved reproduces the *Summa vitiorum* almost verbatim.

This process of introducing a treatise on the vices with greater rhetorical elegance also affected *Summa iustitiae,* which has a full prologue beginning with a biblical quotation that is introduced in the opening sentence:

> The sum of justice of Christ's faithful is to decline from evil and do good, which the Psalmist indicates when he says: "Decline from evil and do good."[49]

And other pastoral works that, like *Summa iustitiae,* cover matters beyond the seven chief vices similarly make use of an initial biblical quotation to lead into their subject matter. The *Dieta salutis* is a good example, as is Chaucer's Parson's Tale and a host of similar handbooks.[50]

The process of restructuring the *Summa vitiorum* apparently also led to two treatises on the vices that stand between Peraldus and Chaucer's Parson's Tale, *Primo videndum est* and *Quoniam ut ait Sapiens.*[51] Once again, at first sight *Primo* seems to have no close relation to the *Summa vitiorum* at all. It arranges the seven chief vices in the traditional order, from pride to lechery; it does not have a separate part on sins of the tongue; and it does not offer Peraldus's rationale for the seven, though it offers a rationale that is equally unique.[52] Though the major topics that Peraldus discusses regularly for each vice — its detestability, species, and remedies — are present in *Primo* as well, the remedies occur as a separate section only in two of the seven vices, *accidia* and gluttony.[53] Further, whereas Peraldus usually begins the tractate on each vice directly with its *detestatio, Primo* regularly opens the discussion with a statement about how this vice is born of its predecessor and then adduces one or several definitions. Though one can find both elements occasionally in the *Summa vitiorum,* they are not employed there with the same regularity as in *Primo.* Using such elements more consistently than the *Summa vitiorum,* or grafting them onto Peraldus's text, is a phenomenon one can observe in other treatises that definitely derive from the *Summa vitiorum.* [54] Moreover, Peraldus's recurrent structural pattern of showing a vice's detestability by point- ing out how it displeases or is injurious to God, pleasing or obedient to the devil, and so forth, also is present in *Primo.* In contrast to Peraldus, where it forms at best one of several topics of treatment, in *Primo* it even yields the major approach in discussing a vice's detestability; but it is so used only in three of the seven vices (*accidia,* avarice, lechery), in contrast to Peraldus, where it occurs more frequently. Lastly, *Primo's* catalogs of species for the individual vices differ considerably from those given by Peraldus. For example, instead of Peraldus's sixteen species of *accidia, Primo* has only nine, and while there is a good deal of overlap and some possible collapsing of three species into one, it is also the case that *Primo* introduces a new one, *timor servilis,* and omits what was a major aspect of spiritual sloth, *indevotio.* [55] Conversely, the spare offspring of envy in Peraldus, who mentions only the two basic tendencies of rejoicing at someone else's adversity and grieving at his good luck (7.2, p. 349), is here increased by another eleven specific branches of the capital vice. [56]

All this may suggest anything but a close genetic relation of *Primo* to Peraldus, and this impression is strengthened by a close examina- tion of *Primo's* homiletic matter, which similarly differs a great deal from the *Summa vitiorum. Primo* lays a heavier stress than does the *Summa vitiorum* on comparisons and similes, many of them taken from nature and everyday life, such as the notorious dog that lifts its leg at every rosebush. [57] It also includes a good deal of canonical material together with precise references, which are almost completely lacking in Pe- raldus. And yet, in reading along one every so often meets an old ac- quaintance. These survivors from the *Summa vitiorum* usually occur in the same sequence or else are taken from a thematically related section and used here where they fit well and sometimes even better than in Peraldus.

This hint of a Peraldian presence gains strength when one ex- amines the topics that *Primo* deals with in its discussion of the vices, as a comparison of the discussion of lechery in the two works will show. Peraldus begins with a clear, summary preview of what he will discuss under *luxuria:*

> First we shall speak of what causes us to detest this vice; second, of its species; third, of what gives occasion for this sin; fourth, of the remedies against it; fifth, why God has forbidden simple fornication; . . . and sixth, we shall touch upon the inability of continence that many people allege.[58]

Although *Primo* lacks such a neat preview—a feature that is characteristic of the treatise's style as a whole—it nonetheless contains all six points, though in a very different arrangement. Under the first major topic—reasons for detesting lechery—Peraldus first discusses six evil effects (such as anxiety, shame, infamy, and so forth), then adds another five (the vice displeases the angels, pleases the devil, and so on), and after those adds another four reasons (the vice captures, retains, defiles, and enslaves its victim—considerations that seem to be extensions of the earlier point that the vice does harm to the person who practices it). This essentially additive schema is in *Primo* replaced by the pattern of the vice displeasing God, doing harm to its practitioner, injuring his neighbor, and pleasing the devil. In other words, *Primo* tightens the *detestatio* discussion by choosing the second of Peraldus's three sections as the overarching scheme into which other material is fitted.

In the second major topic, the species of lechery, Peraldus again places three different divisions side by side: first, a distinction between impurity of heart and of body; then, the traditional five species of fornication, violating a virgin, adultery, incest, and sodomy (which Peraldus then discusses in reverse order); and lastly another division according to one's status, where he dwells at some length on lechery among clerics and among religious persons, including nuns. *Primo,* however, does not call attention to there being different ways of dividing lechery and instead discusses the five species (in the order in which it had listed them, from fornication to sodomy, in contrast to Peraldus) and then adds sections on lechery among clerics, religious, and nuns, slipping in a new, non-Peraldian section on priests' concubines.

In the following part Peraldus turns to the occasions or causes for lechery, of which he finds eight: idleness, indulgence in food and drink, old women go-betweens, bad example, the sight of women, talking with women, listening to love songs, music, or bawdy talk, and touching women. This part is totally reorganized in *Primo,* which expands the sections on how dangerous it is to look at, talk to, and touch women into a pattern of five members that are listed in a popular memory verse: "Visus, colloquium, contactus, oscula, factum." In this, students of medieval and Ovidian love literature will recognize the five *lineae amoris*. [59] *Primo* makes this commonplace into the five fingers of the devil's hand with which he draws people into sin. The image of the devil's hand with five fingers, incidentally, also occurs in Peraldus, but there the five fingers stand for the five species, not occasions, of lechery (as well as of gluttony: 3.2.2, p. 20, with reference to gluttony). Establishing the occasions as the devil's fingers enables *Primo* further to link this section on the occasions of lechery neatly with his earlier point that the sin pleases the devil, under the major topic of *detestatio*.

A similar redistribution affects Peraldus's next topic of remedies for lechery. Again, Peraldus's approach is additive. He first shows that, since lechery is like a fire, in order to protect oneself against it one can pour water on it (the medieval equivalent of taking cold showers), or remove the fuel, or simply run away. The last point leads to fleeing from women, which is expanded by consideration of three features that have deceived many through a false sense of security: relying on a woman's holy life, or on her being a relative, or on one's own chastity. Next Peraldus singles out dances (*choreae*), the avoidance of which is a major and absolutely necessary remedy against the vice. This is discussed at surprising length. And lastly there are several other and more general remedies, such as prayer, keeping oneself occupied, almsgiving, and meditation on death. Now, *Primo* at first sight differs greatly from Peraldus on this major topic, especially since it has no separate section devoted to the remedies of lechery. But we do in fact find a great deal of material from Peraldus's remedies incorporated in *Primo*'s section on incest, particularly but not exclusively the long condemnation of dancing. The linking is effected in a straightforward way:

> And since many people fall not only into fornication and adultery but also into incest by being together with women, therefore they are forbidden to have familiar contact with them. [60]

This leads our author into quoting the relevant and indeed much cited canons from the *Decretum* forbidding the clergy to have close contacts with women. [61] Since avoiding women was the main trend of Peraldus's recommendations against lechery, it is at this point that his entire fourth part on remedies, including staying away from dances, finds its natural home in *Primo*. [62]

Peraldus's next major topic, simple fornication, becomes simi-

larly integrated at a point in *Primo* that is entirely natural and logical,
namely in its discussion of fornication as a species of lechery. What
would need explanation is, rather, why Peraldus devotes a separate
section to a species that he had already discussed among lechery's offspring. I believe the reason is that in taking up the topic of simple
fornication[63] towards the end of his tractate on lechery, Peraldus responds to a major theological and pastoral *quaestio* of his time: Since
God created men male and female and gave them the commandment
to wax and multiply, can it be sin to follow one's natural urge?[64] Consequently, Peraldus's discussion of simple fornication is more argumentative than other sections of his *Summa vitiorum,* even if it does
not have quite the flair of the Parisian classroom.

The same can be said about his last major topic, the excuse some
people make that they are unable to abstain from sex. In *Primo,* this
part is given its own place, after the discussion of lechery among the
clergy and religious, and in fact it is followed by an added section,
not in Peraldus, on people who return to their sin.

This detailed comparison demonstrates not only that the main
topics of Peraldus's discussion of a representative vice are present in
Primo, but also that his text has undergone a process of reordering
that is quite logical. This process is carried out with varying degrees
of intensity, and it produces differing results, in the other chief vices
besides lechery, but it can be shown to run through the entire treatise
and is discernible to an extent that allows one to speak of *Primo* as
a reworking of Peraldus's *Summa vitiorum.* This reworking affects also
another major feature of the *Summa vitiorum* not yet commented on.
In order to discuss it, we must glance at yet another treatise on the
vices.

This is the work beginning with the words *Quoniam ut ait Sapiens:*
"Since, as the Wise Man says, a snare shall bind the sinner, Proverbs
29, the wretches that are reserved for the gallows in hell are bound
with as many ropes as are the sins they have committed."[65] In essence,
this work is an expansion of *Primo,* whose text it preserves substantially intact with only occasional and minor stylistic changes. But it
adds to it a fairly long prologue and introduction; and throughout
it constantly adds to the text taken from *Primo* a good deal of new
material that comes from at least two different sources. One must be
a hitherto unidentified pastoral work of English provenance, for the
respective passages contain sayings and proverbs and the like in Middle English, a situation increasingly common in handbooks and ser-

mons from the second half of the thirteenth century on.[66] One such section, incidentally, brings an analogue to the famous description of Christ's love found in *Ancrene Wisse*. The second source for the added material is — Peraldus's *Summa vitiorum!* It seems that after copying *Primo* the compiler of *Quoniam* went to the *Summa vitiorum* and extracted material he deemed interesting or useful. That this occasionally led to topical and even material repetition either escaped his attention or did not bother him.[67]

The image of binding and of ropes used at the beginning of *Quoniam* leads its author to speak of seven fetters of the devil, i.e., the seven chief vices.[68] But before he launches into their discussion, he adds a very long section on sin in general. Here he quotes the standard Augustinian definition that sin is "anything said, done, or desired against God's law," which causes him to discuss sins of heart, mouth, and deed. It is the sins of the mouth that have some special interest for us in light of the *peccatum linguae* which Peraldus had added to the standard seven chief vices. For in its introductory part on sin in general, *Quoniam* provides a lengthy treatment of evils of the tongue, which it breaks down into *multiloquium, damniloquium,* and *maliloquium.* In discussing the third vice, the author gives the following surprising catalog:

> *Maliloquium* is manifold, according to the manifold sin of the tongue: Contumely, contention, and defending one's sin — which will be discussed below under the sin of pride; perjury, lying, evil counsel — on which see under the sin of avarice; detraction, flattery, murmuring, sowing discord, the sin of the double tongue, making fun of the good, false accusation, and quarreling — see under the sin of envy; strife, contumely, haughty answers, outcry, blasphemy, taunts, threats, cursing, and revealing secrets — on these more will be said below under the sin of wrath.[69]

In this listing, most of Peraldus's sins of the tongue reappear distributed among four of the traditional seven chief vices.[70] Now, *Primo,* the shorter (and apparently earlier) treatise taken over by *Quoniam,* does not contain *Quoniam*'s reference to *peccatum linguae* nor the explicit distributional pattern just quoted. Nevertheless, most of the sins of the tongue listed in the quoted schema do appear incorporated in *Primo*'s own species of the respective chief vices (as they do in *Quoniam*).[71] It would therefore seem that the authors of both *Primo* and *Quoniam* wrestled with the problem posed by Peraldus's establishing the "sins of the tongue"

and giving them a separate place beside the traditional seven chief
vices. This problem they solved, not by simply omitting the sins of
the tongue (as did many other treatises) but instead by integrating
them into the traditional sequence of seven vices. *Primo* does so quietly,
whereas the author of *Quoniam* calls attention to the fact that his work
contains the sins of the tongue either under the chief vices or else under
other branches of sins of the mouth (such as *turpiloquium* and *multiloquium*). It seems that similar attempts to integrate Peraldus's sins of
the tongue into the traditional seven vices occupied other makers of
handbooks during the thirteenth and fourteenth centuries and even
left a trace in the Parson's Tale.[72] The whole topic of the *peccatum linguae* in the later Middle Ages calls for further detailed investigation.[73]

My examination of treatises on the vices which I claim are adaptations of the *Summa vitiorum* has led me, through expansions, abbreviations, and restructuring, a long way from Peraldus's work, to a
point where the characteristic features of the *Summa vitiorum* described
at the beginning of this essay are hardly present any more. One may
reasonably question whether the common ground between especially
the third group of treatises ("restructuring") and the *Summa vitiorum*
is so slim that it becomes possible to prove any treatise on the vices
to be derived from the *Summa vitiorum*. In reply I would point out
that the reduction of characteristic Peraldian elements in these "re-
structured" treatises does not come in sharp distinction to the abbreviations that are unquestionably Peraldian, but rather as the final
point in a continuum of treatises that gradually eliminate more and
more uniquely Peraldian elements. Further, there are of course thirteenth-century works on the vices that are not adaptations of the
Summa vitiorum and differ in essence from it and its offspring. One
is the discussion of the capital vices in speculative theology; here, certain traditional questions are raised and answered, such as, what is
the nature of a given vice, is it a vice, is it a sin, is it a capital vice,
and why does it have the species conventionally assigned to it. This
is the typical pattern found in scholastic *quaestiones* and *summae theologiae*.[74] Peraldus differs from them radically by his concern to help
his readers overcome sin by making the vices known to them and fur-
nishing reasons to detest evil as well as remedies against it. His final
cause, therefore, is not theological clarification but rhetorical persuasion. At the same time, his *Summa vitiorum* also differs from more narrowly pastoral treatments of the vices produced in his time, such as
the *Summa brevis* by Richard of Wetheringsette[75] or the *Speculum iunio-*

rum by Simon of Hinton,[76] which are content with giving the doctrinal bare bones concerning the vices without the rhetorical muscle
assembled by Peraldus.

Does, then, Peraldus dominate the entire field of treatises that
share his fundamental concerns, or should one think it possible that
such treatises as the *Summa iustitiae* and *Primo* are not genetically related to the *Summa vitiorum* but rather independent works whose structural and material similarities to the *Summa vitiorum* derived from a
common source? It seems that in the 1220s and 1230s the ongoing
study of the Bible had led to collections of homiletic material organized by such topics as the vices and virtues; and I can think of one
or two short treatises preserved from the first half of the thirteenth
century that outline major topics on the vices that are very similar
to what we have found in Peraldus.[77] Could it therefore not be the
case that Peraldus, *Primo, Summa iustitiae,* and other works on the vices
are but separate attempts to weave this material together in different
ways? This area admittedly needs further study, especially a closer
investigation of the development of the vices in biblical exegesis just
before and after 1200. Nonetheless, I remain confident that my argument for a genetic relation holds, for two main reasons. First the hypothetical common-source view would mean that a number of large *summae* were developed independently from what amounts to a model too
slim as to be their likely source. And second, in two of the works I
have discussed we found an indication that their authors were conscious of an obligation to deal with the sins of the tongue. In *Quoniam*
they are integrated into the traditional pattern of chief vices, whereas
the author of *Summa iustitiae* had dealt with them in a separate treatise
De lingua, which he refers to several times. It would seem that this
authorial consciousness posits an intermediate stage in the literature
on the vices between those slim models and the long developed *summae,* an intermediate stage which included the sins of the tongue. That
stage is Peraldus's *Summa vitiorum.*

His *Summa vitiorum,* thus, was an authoritative text that continued to be alive in many varied and complicated ways. In addition to
being abbreviated and expanded in different forms—a fate that commonly befell popular works of moral or devotional theology during
the later Middle Ages—Peraldus's *Summa vitiorum* was also subjected
to processes of a more drastic reworking that left the parent *Summa*
almost unrecognizable. These involve both large-scale omission and
addition of homiletic material, but more interestingly also a far-reaching

restructuring and reorganization of familiar matter into more tightly controlled and consistently used patterns. In this process, Peraldus's unique features (order of the seven chief vices, rationale, sins of the tongue) and even a large part of his homiletic material were given up; what remained are certain topics and patterns of treatment. This reduction of Peraldus, incidentally, seems to have been carried to the point where his topics form the *structure* of works whose *contents* owe practically nothing to his *Summa vitiorum*.[78] What motivated Peraldus's successors in this process of restructuring surely was the desire to produce handbooks that were in line with conservative discussions of the seven chief vices (Gregorian order, no separate sins of the tongue, a more common scholastic rationale if required) and that present their material in a more logical[79] and tightly organized form. In addition, these adaptations also show a rhetorical concern. This often goes hand in hand with logical considerations, as is the case in simplifying or streamlining parts derived from a higher concept. But other aspects of post-Peraldian works seem to stem rather from a desire to decorate, found especially in the prologues and introductions I have spoken of. The continuing life of Peraldus's *Summa vitiorum* was, thus, complex and variegated. His successors mixed a good deal of new wine with part of the old, and they poured it into leather bottles that had been cut up and sewn together again into new patterns, in a process that forms a most intriguing *imitatio Peraldi*.

APPENDIX

Prologue, *Summa iusticie*
Cambridge, Jesus College 36, fols. 1r–4r

Summa iusticie Christi fidelium est declinare a malo et facere bonum, quod et Psalmista designat cum dicit: "Declina a malo et fac bonum." Augustinus libro *Sentenciarum Prosperi* 86: "Non sufficit abstinere a malo nisi fiat quod bonum est, et parum est neminem nocere nisi studeas et multis prodesse." Quia ut dicit beatus Bernardus in quibusdam sentenciis: "Iusticia in duobus consistit, in innocencia et in beneficencia. Innocencia iusticiam inchoat, beneficencia consummat." De hac autem iusticia loquitur Crisostomus omelia 10 in *Imperfecto* exponens illud Mathei 6, "Querite primum regnum Dei et iusticiam eius": "Regnum, inquit, Dei est retribucio bonorum operum et malorum. Iusticia autem est via pietatis per quam intratur ad

regnum. Si ergo die ac nocte cogites qualis erit interitus peccatorum, necesse
est ut propter timorem pene territus recedas a malo aut propter desiderium
glorie excitatus festines ad bonum. Et si cotidie cogitaueris que sit iusticia
Dei, quid odit, quid amat — iusticia ipsa ostendet tibi vias suas. Nam iusticia sua, sicut fugientes se fugit, sic amantes se sequitur. Nec enim daturi
sumus racionem vtrum pauperes fuimus aut diuites, quia nec fuit hoc in
nostra potestate, set si bene egimus aut male, quod in nostro iacet arbitrio."
De hac igitur iusticia, ad quam annunciandam populo [MS populus] ac
edisserandam ad honorem Dei et salutem proximi re simul ac nomine predi-
catores celitus instituti sunt, in hoc opere quod nuncupari poterit *Summa
iusticie* disserendum est. Modus autem procedendi seu propositum ostendendi
vt [b] plurimum sicut eciam in tractatu nostro *De lingua,* vbi multa reperiun-
tur que hic ideo transiguntur, triplex est. Primo per exemplum in natura,
quia ut dicit Ambrosius in *Exameron* omelia ultima melior magistra veritatis
natura est. Secundo per exemplum in arte. Tercio per exemplum in figura
siue sacra scriptura. "Funiculus enim triplex difficile rumpitur," Ecclesiastici
4. Natura confertur Patri, tum quia natura habet racionem principii, tum
quia producit similem ex simili. Ars autem confertur Filio, tum quia ars
imitatur naturam, ut dicit Philosophus, libro 2 *Phisicorum,* tum quia Dei sa-
piencia est ars increata, ut dicit Augustinus *De 83 questionibus* 78 et alibi.
Sacra scriptura confertur Spiritui Sancto, a quo inspiratur, Petri 1 in fine:
"Spiritu Sancto inspirati," etc. Ars autem in proposito large siue communiter sumatur, videlicet quod ars est principium humanorum actuum qui ex
recta racione et voluntate procedunt. Philosophus libro 6 *Ethicorum:* "Ars est
habitus cum vera racione factiuus. Est autem omnia ars circa generacionem,"
idest circa alicuius operis constitucionem, "et artificiare et speculari qualiter
vtique fiat aliquid contingencium et esse et non esse, et quorum principium
est in faciente et non in facto. Neque enim ex hiis que ex necessitate vel
fiunt ars enim [*read* est] neque de hiis que sunt secundum naturam." Item 6
Metafisice: "Principium rerum actiuarum est in agente, intellectus videlicet
aut ars aut virtus similis arti; in artificialibus voluntas; artificiatum autem
et voluntarium idem." Sic ergo patet quod que procedunt ex racione et voluntate humana siue in constituendo siue in destituendo ad artem reducun-
tur. Habet autem hoc [fol. 1va] opus 12 partes, que ut patet hic per capitula
infra distinguntur. Prima pars huius operis est de malo culpe siue de peccato
in generali, et habet decem et septem capitula . . . [*Only ten parts are then listed,
with a blank space following*]. [fol. 4ra] Ivsticia, que via est ad regnum, ut supra
dictum est, in duobus consistit, scilicet in fugiendo malum et in eligendo
siue prosequendo bonum. Primum iusticiam inchoat, secundum eam consummat. Primo igitur dicendum est de malo quod est fugiendum; secundo
de bono quod est eligendum, parte vndecima; tercio de utriusque premio,
parte duodecima et ultima. Malum autem secundum Augustinum *De libero
arbitrio* libro 1 et alibi duplex est.

NOTES

1. Quoted in S. Wenzel, *The Sin of Sloth: Acedia in Medieval Thought and Literature* (Chapel Hill, 1967), 69.

2. Morton W. Bloomfield, Bertrand-Georges Guyot, Donald R. Howard, and Thyra B. Kabealo, *Incipits of Latin Works on the Virtues and Vices, 1100–1500 A.D., including a Section of Incipits of Works on the Pater Noster* (Cambridge, Mass., 1979). Henceforth referred to as "Bloomfield."

3. Paris, B.N. lat. 3238C.

4. Antoine Dondaine, "Guillaume Peyraut, vie et oeuvres," *Archivum Fratrum Praedicatorum* 18 (1948): 162–236.

5. Humbert of Romans, Master General of the Dominicans, ordered that a copy of the two *summae* should be among the reference books lying on a *pulpitus*. See K. W. Humphreys, *The Book Provisions of the Medieval Friars, 1215–1400* (Amsterdam, 1964), 136 and note 33.

6. The Franciscan chronicler Adam Salimbene met Peraldus and knew of his *summae* in 1248/49. See the text reproduced in Dondaine, "Guillaume Peyraut," 165.

7. See, for example, the Franciscan *Liber exemplorum*, written between about 1275 and 1279, as edited by A. G. Little (Aberdeen, 1908).

8. See Johann Loserth, *Johann von Wiclif und Guilelmus Peraldus: Studien zur Geschichte der Entstehung von Wiclifs Summa Theologiae*, Sitzungsberichte Akad. Wissen. Wien 180/3 (1916).

9. The *Summa vitiorum* contains nine *tractatus*, each subdivided into parts (*partes*) and chapters. In referring to particular passages, I cite these divisions as well as the page number from the Lyon edition of 1668. For example, "3.2.1, p. 19" refers to the third *tractatus* (on lechery), the second part (its species), the first chapter (lechery of heart and work), found on p. 19 of the edition.

10. The full text is reproduced in the following note. The companion *Summa virtutum*, in its more formal prologue, makes this intention even more explicit.

11. *Summa vitiorum* 1, p. 1: "Dicturi de singulis vitiis cum opportunitas se offert, incipiemus a vitio gulae, et quia locus se offert et propter hoc quod dicit Glossa super Matthaei 4 in pugna Christi prius contra gulam agitur, quia nisi haec prius refrenetur, frustra contra alia vitia laboratur. Et alia glossa dicit ibi quod diabolus victus de gula non tentat de libidine. Ante omnia tamen ostendemus doctrinam vitiorum perutilem esse per hoc quod vitia studio et summa diligentia sunt vitanda. Vitari autem non possunt nisi prius cognoscantur." The text then goes on directly to discuss the capital vices: "Triplici autem ratione potest ostendi vitia summa diligentia esse vitanda, scilicet quia daemonibus valde placent, Deo summe displicent, homini vero summe nocent. Quod valde placent vitia daemonibus ostenditur. . . ." In

quoting Peraldus, I have omitted the modern rubrics and introduced some slight alterations in the punctuation and spelling.

12. See Morton W. Bloomfield, *The Seven Deadly Sins* (East Lansing, 1952; rptd. 1967).

13. *Summa vitiorum* 1 (p. 1), repeated at 9.2.2 (p. 385). This commonplace was formulated in the *Glossa ordinaria* on Matthew 4.

14. In *Collationes* 5, Cassian not only lists gluttony as the first of the principal vices (5.2), he also explains its primary importance in the struggle against the vices as undertaken by the desert hermits (5.17–21) and in the temptations of Adam and Christ (5.5–6). Gregory the Great similarly stresses the fundamental importance of overcoming gluttony in *Moralia in Iob* 30.18.58–59 (PL 76:555).

15. Concerning rationales for the seven chief vices, see Wenzel, *Sins of Sloth*, 38–46, and "The Seven Deadly Sins: Some Problems of Research," *Speculum* 43 (1968): 3–10. For Dante's use of Peraldus, see Wenzel, "Dante's Rationale for the Seven Deadly Sins (*Purgatorio* XVII)," *Modern Language Review* 60 (1965): 529–533, and the more comprehensive study by Franco Mancini, "Un'*auctoritas* di Dante," *Studi danteschi* 45 (1968): 95–119.

16. Augustine, *Contra Faustum* 22.27 (PL 42:418): "Omne dictum vel factum vel concupitum quod fit contra legem Dei." The phrase is quoted in Peter Lombard, *Sententiae* 2.35.1. But see also Carla Casagrande and Silvana Vecchio, *I peccati della lingua. Disciplina ed etica della parola nella cultura medievale* (Rome, 1987), 110–122, who suggest that the creation of this eighth sin developed from a heightened awareness of the evils of speech in thirteenth-century society, especially on the part of Dominican preachers. This excellent study came to my attention after the present essay was written.

17. A good example is John de la Rochelle, *De malo*, in Cambridge, Pembroke College 21, fols. 73v–88r.

18. Wenzel, *Sin of Sloth*, 79–83.

19. G. R. Owst, *The Destructorium Viciorum of Alexander Carpenter: A Fifteenth-Century Sequel to "Literature and Pulpit in Medieval England"* (London, 1952).

20. Alexander Carpenter, *Destructorium vitiorum* (Paris, 1516) fol. a.iiii recto; Cambridge, Peterhouse 41, fol. 3v.

21. Rainer Rudolf, "Heinrichs von Langenstein 'Erchantnuzz der Sund' und ihre Quellen," in *Fachliteratur des Mittelalters: Festschrift für Gerhard Eis*, ed. Gundolf Keil et al. (Stuttgart, 1968), 53–82. See also Rainer Rudolf, ed., *Heinrich von Langenstein, "Erchantnuzz der Sund," nach österreichischen Handschriften herausgegeben*, Texte des späten Mittelalters und der frühen Neuzeit 22 (Berlin, 1969).

22. London, BL Harley 1036, fol. 262r: "Explicit de ira. Gloria Christo, qui est benedictus in secula seculorum. Amen. Explicit tractatus de VII viciis capitalibus secundum Parisiensem."

23. Oxford, Bodleian Library Bodley 848 (late thirteenth century). Notice that the scribe of this copy also consciously omitted some other topics. For example, the chapter on the "satellites" of gluttony (*Summa vitiorum* 2.3, p. 12) is announced at the beginning of the part of gluttony, but later on bypassed with the remark, "De satellitibus gule nichil dicemus" (fol. 52r).

24. Oxford, Bodleian Library Bodley 803, fol. 1r.

25. Oxford, Bodleian Library Bodley 41 (Bloomfield no. 6318), fol. 143r: "Enumerare sufficit xiiii [*read* xxiiii] peccata."

26. Oxford, Bodleian Library lat. theol. e. 12 (Bloomfield no. 6524).

27. Graz, Universitätsbibliothek 607, fol. 66r.

28. Graz, Universitätsbibliothek 1095 (Bloomfield no. 0809), fols. 201r–232v: "Circa tractatum de uiciis nota duo."

29. Graz, Universitätsbibliothek 1095, fol. 229r: "Sequitur de peccato gule, et secundum gustum et secundum loquelam." The same pattern was also used in the *Somme le roi* written in 1279 by Friar Lorens of Orleans.

30. Some examples of the *Summa vitiorum* without the rationale are: London, Lambeth Palace Library 390, fols. 1r–102v (according to the old foliation; manuscript perhaps from the third quarter of the thirteenth century); Oxford, Bodleian Library Laud Misc. 369 (end of thirteenth century); New Haven, Yale University, Beinecke Library 374; Munich, Bayerische Staatsbibliothek, Clm 5899; Philadelphia, University of Pennsylvania, 140.

31. Oxford, Bodleian Library Laud Misc. 206 (Bloomfield no. 3787), fol. 1v: "Peccatum est vitandum sextiplici de causa. Prima quia est De[o] iniuriosum. Quod patet primo per exemplum in natura."

32. See S. Harrison Thomson, *The Writings of Robert Grosseteste, Bishop of Lincoln, 1235–1253* (Cambridge, 1940), 268 and 253.

33. Oxford, Exeter College 7.

34. Bloomfield nos. 5845 and 2881. I quote from Cambridge, Jesus College 36, written about 1300. The work is discussed in some detail by Thomson, *Writings*, 263–265.

35. Cambridge, Jesus College 36, fols. 1r–4r. See Appendix.

36. First the one proposed by Hugh of St. Victor, and then three different scholastic ones; at the beginning of the section on pride, Cambridge, Jesus College 36, fols. 23v–24rb.

37. Cambridge, Jesus College 36, at 2.20 (two references, fol. 55ra), 8.15 and 16 (fol. 191ra-b), 9.5 (fol. 202va), 9.7 (fol. 204va).

38. For *De lingua*, see Thomson, *Writings*, 252–253, and, more recently, Casagrande and Vecchio, *I peccati della lingua*, 141–174. Jenny Swanson counts *Summa iustitiae* among the works of John of Wales without discussion and does not mention *De lingua* at all; see her *John of Wales: A Study of the Works and Ideas of a Thirteenth-Century Friar* (Cambridge, 1989). *De lingua* was used extensively in an alphabetical collection of commonplaces on moral topics, *Accidia aduersatur hominis saluti*. See Cambridge, University Library Ii.1.30

(Bloomfield no. 0166), where *De lingua* is attributed to "Lincolniensis" and cited by part and chapter.

39. For example, in the long tractate on avarice, it appears in the *detestatio* of avarice itself (*Summa vitiorum*, pp. 52–53 and 63), its species of usury and *rapina* (pp. 82, 89), avarice among religious (p. 147), avarice of knowledge (p. 152), and avarice of diceplayers (p. 155).

40. Thus, the examples mentioned in the preceding note use the following members and terms: *iniquus in Deum, in seipsum, in proximum (Summa vitiorum*, pp. 52–53); *Deo exosa, proximo iniuriosa, proprio subiecto nociva* (p. 63); *Deum offendit, diabolum servit* (p. 82); *Deo odiosa, sanctis hominibus exosa* (p. 89); *Deo displicet, diabolo placet* (p. 147); *Deo damnosus, odibilis hominibus, iniuriosus proximo* (p. 152); *Deo contumeliosum, proximo scandalosum, sibi damnosum* (p. 155).

41. For instance, *accidia* is condemned by examples from nature (*Summa vitiorum* 5.1.1), words of Holy Scripture (5.1.2), and finally by what would amount to "reasons," though the term is not used (5.1.3–4, pp. 165–174). Among the "reasons" is the notion that the vice "Deo displicet, diabolo placet, et hominibus nocet" (5.1.3, pp. 168–173).

42. *Summa vitiorum* 2.1, pp. 3–4: "Hoc ordine dicemus de vitio gulae. Primo dicemus de his quae faciunt ad detestationem huius vitii; secundo, de speciebus eius; tertio, de satellitibus quibus utitur vitium istud; quarto, de remediis contra hoc vitium. Quatuordecim autem sunt quae faciunt ad detestationem huius vitii. Primum est. . . ."

43. *Summa vitiorum* 5.1.4, p. 174. For a similar case in the tractate on lechery, see below.

44. An example is his discussion of simple fornication. See further below at note 63.

45. *Summa virtutum* prologue (ed. Lyon 1668): "Cum circa utilia etiam docere debeamus, exemplo Salomonis dicenti: 'Cogitavi in corde meo abstrahere a vino carnem meam ut animam meam transferrem ad sapientiam devitaremque stultitiam donec viderem quid esset utile filiis hominum, Ecclesiaste 2."

46. Such an influence of the scholastic-sermon form on prologues to biblical commentaries has been suggested by Beryl Smalley, "Peter Comestor on the Gospels and His Sources," *Recherches de théologie ancienne et médiévale* 46 (1979): 109–110.

47. London, BL Additional 15123 (Bloomfield no. 3798), fol. 52r: "Pedes eorum pedes recti, et planta pedis eorum quasi planta pedis uituli, Ezechielis 1. Loquitur Ezechiel de quatuor animalibus. . . ."

48. London, BL Additional 15123, fol. 52v: "Quoniam sicut dicit Ecclesiasticus III: 'Cor sapiens est intelligibile abstinebit se a peccatis,' et quia sicut dicit Augustinus, 'Non uitatur malum nisi cognitum,' ideo ad habendam noticiam uiciorum et ad utilitatem legencium compilandus est tractatus tractatus [*sic*] uel summa de uiciis de sanctorum patrum et magistro-

rum auctoritatibus, racionibus, ac uerbis. Incipiemus autem hoc modo. Primo dicemus aliqua de peccato in generali, secundo prosequemur de quolibet in speciali. Dicturi igitur de uiciis in generali duo tangemus. . . ."

49. See above, note 35.

50. See Wenzel, "Notes on the *Parson's Tale,*" *Chaucer Review* 16 (1982): 248–251.

51. See Wenzel, "The Source of Chaucer's Seven Deadly Sins," *Traditio* 30 (1974): 351–378.

52. For a brief account, see Wenzel, "The Seven Deadly Sins," 8.

53. The reason for this reduction may well be that *Primo's* author had already planned to follow his work on the vices with one on the remedial virtues, namely the work *Postquam dictum est.* See *Summa virtutum de remediis anime,* ed. Wenzel (Athens, Ga., 1984). It must also be noted, however, that in some cases the remedies are in fact present and have been integrated with different topics. For one example, the remedies against lechery, see below at note 60.

54. A particularly interesting case is a *Summa viciorum* beginning "Cum nostri prothoplasti suggestiva prevaricacione reducti omnes in uicium inciderimus," in Graz, Universitätsbibliothek 1395 (written about 1400; not in Bloomfield). The treatise is divided into nine parts and has the Peraldian order and topics, including the sins of the tongue, but not his rationale for the capital vices. Yet the discussion of each vice is consistently divided into five parts: the vice's definition *(notificacio),* its effects, its *detestatio,* its remedies, and its species ("vel filie vel satellites"). The *notificatio* contains both a statement linking the vice to its predecessors and several definitions. The work also has a prologue and an introduction that sets forth the order of the work (somewhat garbled in the Graz manuscript).

55. For the species of *accidia* in Peraldus, see Wenzel, *Sin of Sloth,* 195–196; for those in *Primo,* Wenzel, "Source of Chaucer's Seven," 365–366 (note that the asterisked sentences there occur only in *Quoniam*).

56. They are: *Dolor de alieno bono, gaudium de malo proximi, detractio, susurrum idest occultum murmur, odium occultum, amaritudo, discordia, derisio, accusatio, depravatio, malitia, nequitia, malignitas.* Note that many of these species correspond to Peraldus's sins of the tongue, on which see further below.

57. Chaucer, The Parson's Tale, line 858.

58. *Summa vitiorum* 3.1.1 (p. 14): "Primo dicemus de his quae faciunt ad detestationem huius vitii; secundo, de speciebus eius; tertio, de his quae praestant occasionem huic peccato; quarto, de remediis contra vitium istud; quinto, quare Deus prohibuit simplicem fornicationem; . . . sexto, tangemus aliquid de impotentia continendi quam multi allegant."

59. See Hans Walther, *Proverbia sententiaeque latinitatis medii aevi* (Göttingen, 1963–1967), nos. 33816, 33818–19, and so on.

60. I quote from the manuscript used in my edition of the *Summa vir-*

tutum, Einsiedeln, Stiftsbibliothek 275 (latter half of thirteenth century), fol. 82rb: "Et quia solent multi incidere non solum in fornicacionem et adulterium sed eciam in incestum per cohabitacionem mulierum, ideo prohibetur familiaris communicacio earum."

61. *Decretum* 18.2.21, ed. E. Friedberg, *Corpus iuris canonici* (Leipzig, 1879; rptd. Graz, 1959), 1:835. See also 32.17 (p. 121) and 81.25 (p. 287).

62. *Summa vitiorum* 3.4.1–3 (pp. 33–43), reappearing condensed in *Primo,* fols. 82rb–84vb.

63. "Simple fornication" refers to extramarital sex between partners who are not separately married, or related to each other (whether naturally or spiritually), or bound by a religious vow. If one of these conditions held, they would commit adultery or incest.

64. See Thomas of Chobham, *Summa confessorum,* ed. F. Broomfield, Analecta mediaevalia namurcensia 25 (Louvain and Paris, 1968), 341–344; and, more briefly, Robert of Flamborough, *Liber poenitentialis,* ed. J. J. F. Firth (Toronto, 1971), 231.

65. Durham, Cathedral Library B.I.18, fol. 14r: "Quoniam ut ait Sapiens 'peccantem uirum inuoluet laqueus,' Prouerbiorum XXIX, miseri patibulo inferni reseruati tot funibus uincti sunt quot sunt peccata que committunt." Further citations to *Quoniam* are to this manuscript. To the two manuscripts listed in my "Source of Chaucer's Seven," 352–353, should be added Dublin, Trinity College Library 306, fols. 1r–121v (defective at beginning and throughout).

66. See Wenzel, *Verses in Sermons* (Cambridge, Mass., 1978), 94–95.

67. For instance, in discussing the topic of excusing sexual incontinence by claiming inability to abstain, *Primo* condenses and rephrases Peraldus's text (*Summa vitiorum* 3.6.2, pp. 47–50) by selectively drawing on his reasons 1, 3–7, 10, and 12 (fols. 90rb–91rb). *Quoniam* (fols. 133vb–135va) follows *Primo* in this, but also adds several long expansions, including a passage on why God has allowed man to do evil that it has already used earlier under adultery (fol. 119rb). At the point where *Primo* reaches the end of this topic (with Peraldus's reason 12), *Quoniam* returns to Peraldus's reason 10 and recapitulates reasons 10–12 in a style that is much closer to Peraldus than *Primo*'s had been.

68. The text quoted in note 65 continues: "Prouerbiorum II [i.e., 5:22]: 'Iniquitates sue capiunt impium, et funibus peccatorum suorum quisque constringitur,' quia nimirum custos carceris inferni VII principalia habet uincula, secundum quod VII sunt mortalia peccata, quorum quodlibet diuersorum diuersimode ligat sicut in ordine uiciorum patet" (*Quoniam,* fol. 14r).

69. *Quoniam,* fol. 15r: "Est autem multiplex maliloquium, secundum quod est lingue peccatum multiplex: contumelia, contencio, peccandi defensio—de quibus dicetur infra in peccato superbie; periurium, mendacium, pravum consilium—de quibus in peccato avaricie; detractio, adulacio, mur-

mur, seminacio, peccatum bilingue, bonorum derisio, accusacio, convicium
— de quibus in peccato invidie; rixa, contumelia, proterva eciam responsio,
clamor, blasphemia, obprobium, comminacio, maledictum, secretorum re-
velacio— de quibus infra de peccato ire plenius dicetur."

70. If one takes into consideration *Quoniam's* discussion of *multiloquium*
and *damniloquium* (or *turpiloquium*) that precedes the quoted passage, as well
as the following discussion of *taciturnitas,* all twenty-four Peraldian sins of
the tongue are accounted for, except *amor rumorum inter claustrales.* On the
other hand, *Quoniam* adds further sins.

71. The correspondence between the treatment of *peccatum linguae* in
Quoniam and its later discussion (or that in *Primo*) of the species of the seven
chief vices is actually more complicated than space allows me to set forth
here. Briefly, it seems that the entire section on *peccatum linguae* in *Quoniam,*
including the quoted listing, is an attempt to combine or reconcile Peraldus's
sins of the tongue with relevant branches of the chief vices that *Quoniam's*
author found in *Primo.*

72. Chaucer, The Parson's Tale, line 653.

73. A firm base for such a study is now available in Casagrande and
Vecchio, *I peccati della lingua.*

74. For example, John de la Rochelle, *Summa vitiorum;* 'Alexander of
Hales,' *Summa theologica* 2-2; Thomas Aquinas, *Quaestiones disputatae de malo*
and *Summa theologiae* 2-2.

75. Brief descriptions and sample passages may be found in Wenzel,
Sin of Sloth, 73-74, and *Verses in Sermons,* 64-65.

76. My remark is based on London, BL Additional 30508. On the
work, and on this manuscript, see Leonard E. Boyle, "Notes on the Education of the *Fratres communes* in the Dominican Order in the Thirteenth Century," in *Xenia medii aevi historiam illustrantia oblata Thomae Kaeppeli, O.P.* (Rome,
1978), reprinted in Boyle, *Pastoral Care, Clerical Education and Canon Law,
1200-1400* (London, 1981), 259-262.

77. Notably several pieces (sermons?) in Oxford, Bodleian Library
Laud Misc. 544 (a manuscript from the mid-thirteenth century), including
Vidi de mari (fol. 4v, Bloomfield nos. 6452, 6450; *Hec sunt que generaliter de
VII uiciis possunt dici* (fols. 5r-8r, not in Bloomfield); and *Superbia est elacio
uiciosa* (fols. 8r-16r, Bloomfield no. 5905).

78. Two examples are of interest. A *Summa de viciis* beginning "Quis
dives libenter transiret per viam" treats in 73 of its 115 chapters the seven
chief vices in the Gregorian order followed by *peccatum linguae.* Other Peraldian topics furnish the structure of these chapters. But the homiletic material in them — biblical and patristic authorities, and a large number of similes
and stories — is certainly non-Peraldian. See Bloomfield no. 4840. The work
is also preserved in Oxford, Bodleian Library Lyell 16. In addition, a table
of the chapters of this (unidentified) work, written in a hand from the end

of the thirteenth century, appears in Cambridge, Jesus College 41, fols. 45rb–46r. Even more interesting is a work beginning "Presens opusculum . . . ," which in five parts (on *aversio, revocatio, conversio, meritum et sacramenta,* and *premium*) collects only biblical authorities on specified topics in the order of the biblical books. The seven chief vices are dealt with in part 1 on *aversio.* The author uses the Gregorian order, but with *vicia lingue* at the end. Other Peraldian topics occur throughout. See Bloomfield no. 4047, referring to no. 4071; add Salisbury, Cathedral Library 60, and London, Lambeth Palace Library 490. The work is listed as the *Collectarium* by the Franciscan John Peckham in Glorieux, *Répertoire des maitres en théologie au XIIIe siècle,* no. 316g, and Stegmüller, *Repertorium biblicum,* no. 4841. Neither author includes the Lambeth manuscript. Notice that in it, written in a hand of approximately the third quarter of the thirteenth century, *Presens opusculum* bears the explicit (fol. 269r, old foliation), "Expliciunt concordancie autoris fratrum predicatorum"!

79. Another fine example of the process of rationalization in the Peraldian tradition concerns the sins of the tongue. *De lingua* is clearly derived from *Summa vitiorum,* but its individual sins of the tongue have been rearranged in a new and elaborate logical scheme.

Early Scholastic and Mendicant Preaching as Exegesis of Scripture

L.-J. Bataillon, O.P.

THE LINK BETWEEN the teaching of the Bible and preaching is a constant characteristic of Christian literature.[1] The duty that Christ left to his Apostles was to preach the Gospel to all creatures, and to preach the Gospel presupposes knowledge of the whole of revelation. Thus Jesus before sending his disciples to preach opened to them the meaning of Scripture. And the same was done by Apostles and bishops from the beginning of the Church. To preach is nothing but to explain the Scripture to the people. Conversely, to comment on Scripture naturally culminates in preaching. Important scriptural commentaries by Origen, Chrysostom, and Augustine, for example, were first preached to the faithful.

About the end of the twelfth century, this intimate relation between exegesis and preaching was reformulated as a norm for university teachers. It was condensed in Peter the Chanter's famous motto: *legere, disputare, predicare,* in which *disputare* is only a necessary transition between the two principal duties. Thus the Bible was taught to university students as the foundation of their culture. This was done, according to the original intention, in order to have many priests able to hand down this knowledge to their parishioners by teaching and preaching. So the main question that I want to examine here is what knowledge of Scripture was available to the average Christian layman of the thirteenth century from the preaching he typically heard.

The question would be very different if we were to take the cases of monks or canons. These categories of the faithful had a direct and personal contact with the Bible, which they read or heard read daily. The situation of laymen was entirely distinct. A large majority of them was unable to read and had the opportunity of learning only what clerics taught them. It is this situation of dependence on oral teaching that I wish particularly to examine.

A difficulty with this type of inquiry is the lack of editions of medieval Sunday sermons. We do have, of course, some fifteenth-, sixteenth-, and even seventeenth-century printed editions of a few model sermon collections, such as those of Peraldus or Voragine, but they are few and generally of rather low quality. In modern times, with the exception of some authors, such as Anthony of Padua,[2] Bonaventure,[3] and Ranulph of La Houblonnière,[4] the greater number of scholars have worked to publish, not collections, but sermons on themes of particular interest to them. Generally speaking, this led them to edit sermons on saints of their religious orders or on devotions that they cultivated. Thus we have a good number of edited sermons on St. Dominic, St. Francis, and the Virgin's feasts. But this is not very helpful for our question. How many laymen were able to leave their labors in order to hear a sermon about the holy founder of the neighboring mendicant church? And even if each of the four feasts of Mary were probably a holiday, the themes of the sermons preached for these solemnities gave few occasions for scriptural instruction of the unlearned.

In patristic times, there were two main kinds of preaching: sermons about a feast, a liturgical occasion, or some important event, on the one hand, and, on the other, series of homilies on some book of the Bible. Thus, to stay with the great names I mentioned above: Origen preached on a large part of Scripture, Chrysostom on Genesis, the Psalms, Matthew, John, and Paul, and Augustine on the Psalms and on John's Gospel and first Epistle. Later, Gregory the Great gave homilies not only on liturgical Gospels, but also on Kings and Ezekiel. Most of these works were actually preached to laymen, as is clear in the cases of Chrysostom, Augustine, and Gregory. In this way a rather profound knowledge of at least some of the more important books of the Scripture was provided to the laity.

This custom was observed in monasteries, and Bernard was not an exception when he preached both discrete liturgical sermons and running commentaries, such as his famous collection on the Song of Songs. We also have this type of commentary during the thirteenth century with the sermons on the Psalms by Philip the Chancellor and some similar collections, but it is highly probable that these sermons were not made to be preached, at least to laymen. They were more likely written in the manner of concordances, distinctions, and model collections in order to provide material for other preachers.

What then about the biblical training of laymen? If we take the disciplinary texts from the beginning of the thirteenth century, such as conciliar and synodal decrees, we see that what is asked of parish priests in the way of popular preaching is generally limited to elementary catechesis: the Lord's Prayer, the Creed, the Ten Commandments, Sacraments, vices and virtues.[5] There is no question of interpreting the Bible as such.

At the end of the twelfth century, however, when we look at model sermons clearly made to be preached in parish churches, we may note that they generally are prepared as sermons on the liturgical pericopes used for Sundays and feast-day masses, normally on the Epistles and Gospels, and more rarely, on the Introits. If we take these biblical passages used in liturgical readings, which were usually the subject of preaching, we can see that the proportions of the different books of Scripture which were commented on for the hearers were dramatically unequal.

Normally, in Sunday preaching, the theme of the sermon was taken from the liturgy of the day and principally from the Epistle or the Gospel. If we take the pericopes used in the Dominican missal,[6] we see that the Old Testament is practically absent, with a reading of only four verses from Jeremiah on the twenty-fifth Sunday after Trinity Sunday, which is celebrated only about once every two years. Moreover this passage was not even used in the liturgy of the Roman Curia nor in the Franciscan rite. As regards the New Testament, most of the readings were of course from the Gospels, but there were only three pericopes taken from Mark, with a total of twenty-three verses. Matthew was read nineteen times with 314 verses (but 141 were read on Palm Sunday alone); Luke eighteen times with 166 verses; John fourteen times with 151 verses. As for the Epistles, we note the preponderance of Romans (ten times), 1 Corinthians (eight times), Galatians (six times), followed by 2 Corinthians, Ephesians, and 1 Peter — each with five readings.[7] There was only one reading each from Hebrews and the Acts of the Apostles, and none from Revelations or the Pastoral Epistles.[8]

To complete these data, we must add the other important liturgical days, namely Christmas (midnight and morning), Epiphany, the Purification, Ash Wednesday, the Annunciation, Maundy Thursday, Good Friday, the Ascension, St. John the Baptist, St. Peter, the Assumption, Mary's Nativity, All Saints, and All Souls.[9] These were probably the feasts when the greatest number of laymen went to church. For these solemn weekdays, the picture is slightly different. The Old

Testament is better represented, chiefly by Isaiah, with five readings, but also by Exodus, Proverbs, Ecclesiastes, Hosea, Joel, and Malachi, with one reading for each.[10] For the New Testament, we have still the preeminence of the Gospels, this time with John — because of the Passion account read on Good Friday — in first place with four readings and a total of 116 verses, then Luke and Matthew each with five readings, and finally Mark with only one. For the Epistles we have only two readings from 1 Corinthians, one each from Titus and Hebrews, one from the Apocalypse, and two from Acts.[11]

We thus arrive at the very modest total of 1366 verses from the whole of Scripture read in one liturgical year. If we consider that Luke and John, which form about a twentieth of the Bible, together provide a little more than 2000 verses, it must seem that preaching presented to its hearers only a ridiculously small part of the Bible. Moreover, even for the Gospels, some passages of great importance for Christian teaching, such as the parable of the Prodigal Son or Jesus' conversation with the Samaritan woman, were read only on Lenten weekdays, when very few lay people could have attended Mass. But it must be replied to this statistical conclusion that the rhetorical structure of medieval sermons did make room for a somewhat richer teaching about the Bible.

We must first recall that at the beginning of the thirteenth century, there were two different schools on sermon-making. There was an older one according to which the whole pericope was to be explained; this style was closely related to the homilies of the high Middle Ages. Then there was the "modern" style, in which a single verse was chosen as a thema, to be divided and developed by means of distinctions often taken from other biblical verses. The old system survived chiefly in Italy, but we can also find in France some preachers whose sermons use both patterns.

In the modern style, the system of distinctions used to explain a passage by the study of the different senses of a word, with examples taken from elsewhere in Scripture, allowed for not only explanation of the thema, but also of other passages of the Bible. To take an example from the third quarter of the century, when the "modern" model had generally superseded the old one, we may choose a sermon for Christmas by the regular canon of the Val des Ecoliers, Evrard of Villaines,[12] the thema of which was taken from Habacuc 3:13: "Egressus es in salutem populi tui."[13] After a very short division of the thema into two parts, Jesus' birth (*Egressus es*) and the utility of this birth (*In salutem populi tui*), Evrard shows that Jesus had "gone forth" in four manners: as a ray goes forth from the sun, by his eternal generation from God the Father; as honey goes forth from the honeycomb, by his temporal birth; as power goes forth from a strong man, by his victory over his enemies; and as a flower goes forth from a tree, by the consolation he gives us. Jesus' eternal generation is explained according to a verse taken from Hosea, "Quasi diluculum preparatus est egressus eius," with the help of two quotations from the Psalms and a passage of Augustine. The temporal nativity of Christ is expounded first by Job's remark, "Ab infantia crevit mecum misericordia," then by the episode of 1 Samuel 14:27, where Jonathan sees better after having eaten honey. Three other biblical verses and quotations from Bernard and Augustine complete the exegesis. The third sense of *egredi*, the going-forth of power from a strong man, is briefly related to David's war against the Philistines. The fourth sense, the going-forth of a flower from a tree, is naturally treated according to Isaiah's prophecy of the rod of Jesse. The second part is similarly, but more succinctly, explained according to four meanings of *salus*, with a short interpretation of four other biblical quotations. Thus we have small commentaries on eight passages of the Scriptures, which are not, in general, treated according to the literal sense. [14]

To begin with, I shall examine sermons from the old, homiletic, system intended for the catechesis of laymen. Among the earlier collections of this type is the one published by Maurice of Sully, bishop of Paris, at the end of the twelfth century, for the use of the priests of his diocese. [15] In these sermons, the bishop begins by telling the whole story of the liturgical Gospel and then gives a short moral application. This was a very simple kind of preaching but probably rather well adapted to the psychology of the hearers. It gave them a solid, if limited, view of some important passages of the Gospel, but left unexplained the remaining parts of the Bible. [16]

At about the same time, in a parish of Poitou, Raoul Ardens was giving his people a much wider knowledge of Scripture. [17] His collection of *sermones de tempore* has two sermons for each Sunday — one on the Epistle, another on the Gospel. [18] They are always composed according to the homiletic scheme, with a rather developed exposition of the literal sense and sometimes with other parts treating the pericope *moraliter* or *allegorice*. If we take Sermon 40 for the second Sunday of Lent on the thema "Erat Iesus eiciens demonium," we find a long and careful explanation of the whole Gospel with two references to parallel passages in other Gospels, an allusion to Ephesians, and another to the *Magnificat* in Luke. In the moral part, allusions to other books are more numerous, but generally rather vaguely indicated as "Sapiens" or even simply "dicitur." Quotations from the Psalms, Isaiah, Ecclesiastes, Ecclesiasticus, and Matthew[19] occur in this way.

A follower of the old method during the thirteenth century was Thomas of Lentini, a Dominican who ended his life as Latin Patriarch of Jerusalem after having exercised many offices within his order and the Church.[20] He left a model collection of *Sermones festivi*. We shall consider as an example one of his themes for the feast of St. Peter's Chair, which is taken from the opening lines of 1 Peter, "Petrus Apostolus Iesu Christi," the Epistle for this feast. It forms a pair with the following sermon, which is based on the continuation of the same text. Actually, the first sermon is twofold. The opening part gives a scheme of Peter's address to his readers; the second part, which is more developed, treats of the whole pericope. So does the entire second sermon. In these three pieces, Thomas gives an analysis of the text with divisions and subdivisions. Nearly always, after having explained a part of the Epistle, he adds a confirmation from another biblical book. There are six quotations from the Old Testament and eleven from the New. In this way, Thomas provides a good exegesis of the liturgical reading while shedding a bit of light on the rest of Scripture.

I shall now take some examples of the "modern" homily from some other early Dominicans whose sermons are preserved. The first is Peter of Rheims, who was provincial of France during the first part of the thirteenth century and who died as bishop of Agen in 1247. His first sermon for the second Sunday after Easter is taken from the Epistle for the day, "Christus passus est pro nobis."[21] The given thema consists of only these five words, but the sermon comments more fully on verse twenty-one of 1 Peter 2, with its ending, ". . . ut sequamini vestigia eius." In the schematic form in which the sermon was written down, the developments are not given as they normally would be when actually preached. Even so we can see there was to be some discussion of twenty-nine verses taken from books ranking from Genesis to Revelations, with emphasis on 1 Peter, Job, the Psalms, and Matthew.[22]

We may turn next to one of Peter's sermons on the Gospels, that for the third Sunday of Lent, on the thema, "Erat Iesus eiciens demonium."[23] There stands at the beginning a short list of the four ways in which God expels the devil. We pass then to a moral interpretation of the spiritual dumbness caused by sin — the dumbness that keeps one from confessing sins, edifying others, and praising God. Next, and despite there being no suggestion of this in the Gospel reading, Peter provides a similar development of the talkative devil. He concludes with a much shorter paragraph on the *spiritus nequiores,* which are the seven kinds of pride. Each step is supported by one or two biblical verses, seven from the New Testament and forty from the Old, among which fourteen are from Ecclesiasticus and nine from other wisdom books — an odd proportion given Ben Sirach's disgust at loquacity.

The second Dominican, certainly an Italian, remains anonymous, although his works were printed under the name of Thomas Aquinas. We may date his collections between 1235 and 1250.[24] From them, we shall take two sermons for the same two dates considered in connection with Peter of Rheims. For the epistle of the second Sunday after Easter,[25] the anonymous preacher makes a fourfold division, showing Christ's innocence, his patience, his charity, and the benefits we derive from them. In the *dilatatio,* we find twenty-four biblical quotations, of which five are from Isaiah and John.[26] But only one quotation is shared with the corresponding sermon of Peter of Rheims, namely, Job 23:11.

For the Gospel of the third Sunday of Lent, our anonymous Dominican has two sermons, the first on the beginning of the pericope, "Erat Iesus eiciens demonium," and the second on its end, "Beatus venter qui te protavit."[27] The first sermon has three parts: the seven expulsions of the devil, the three demonic evils in the soul, and the three benefits of his being expelled. Each division is matched by a biblical verse, seven from each Testament. Three of them also occur in the corresponding sermon by Peter of Rheims. The second anonymous Gospel sermon gives eight reasons to bless the Virgin's womb. It uses only four citations from Scripture.

If we go a little further ahead in the century, between 1250 and 1265, we find many collections of model sermons, which have been carefully studied by David d'Avray.[28] In some of them, like those of Peter of St. Benoît,[29] Nicholas of Biard,[30] and especially William of Mailly,[31] we note an evolution of classical distinctions in the direction of comparisons or chains of comparisons, which develop certain images or metaphors of the liturgical text.[32]

Taking once more the Gospel for the third Sunday of Lent, we see William of Mailly[33] making a division into two topics: God's goodness ("Erat Ihesus eiciens demonium") and the devil's wickedness

("Et illud erat mutum"). For the first part, Mailly shows seven ways of putting out the devil. First, as we drive away a dog from the kitchen by throwing hot water at him, so we drive away the devil by the warm tears of contrition, as did Mary Magdalen. Then, just as a husband goes out of his house to avoid a quarrelsome wife, so the devil goes out when the conscience feels remorse. The preacher goes on in this vein until he reaches the seventh way: as a snake emerges from its hole when it hears singing, so does the devil on hearing the invocation of God's name. At this point, William digresses to treat the seven names of God. Then he passes to the second part, on the devil's wickedness, and shows how the fiend takes a sinner's spiritual senses. Just so a rich man who wants to sleep peacefully eliminates his bodily sensations. The man closes the door and tells his servants to say he is out — this is like the spiritual dumbness that impedes confession. Then the rich man shuts out the light; similarly the devil takes away the sight of the knowledge, which would show the ugliness of sin. Then the rich man seals the windows, just as the ears are shut to avoid the entry of teaching. He tells his family that they may not disturb him, which signifies the cessation of good actions. Finally, as in sleep, the devil takes away the sense of smell so that the sinner cannot detect his spiritual stench.

Each of these similes is attested by some biblical verse, and Mailly is conspicuously generous in this matter. There are sixty-two quotations, fifteen from the Prophets, eleven from the wisdom books, and nine from Luke.[34] But the sermon is clearly made for delivery, and so it employs concrete, vivid, often humorous images and an explanation of the Gospel that is easy to remember.

"Old" and "modern" sermon styles are used together systematically in the beginning of the thirteenth century by a secular master, John Halgrin of Abbeville, who became archbishop of Besançon in 1225 and cardinal in 1227, and died in 1237.[35] When he was at the Curia, he wrote two collections, not of sermons intended for the subtle *prurientibus scolarium auribus,* but rather of *rudes omelias rudibus rudi sermone.* These homilies are models for parish preaching. In the series *de tempore,* let us again take as an example the sermon *de evangelio* for the third Sunday of Lent.[36] In some manuscripts, we have rubrics indicating two sermons on this theme, in others only one that is divided in two parts, one literal, the other entitled "moraliter" or "moralitas."

The first part is a verse-by-verse exegesis of the pericope.[37] It is a very literal periphrasis of the *Glossa ordinaria,* and thus represents the average exegesis of the time. John begins by noting that in the parallel passage of Matthew, the possessed man is not only dumb, but also blind. We are then given an explanation of the name "Beelzebub." After this John shows that Jesus replies "non ad verba sed ad cogitationes," a sign of his power. He goes on to explain Jesus' argument against his adversaries and how the miraculous healing is a sign of the Spirit's work. Next comes the exegesis of the devil's return to the soul. Finally, John of Abbeville shows how the woman's blessing of Mary and the complementary blessing by Christ are a reply both to contemporary Jewish incredulity and to certain future heresies. This literal exegesis takes up a third of the whole sermon.

There follows the reading "moraliter." Here the last passage, the woman's blessing, is entirely omitted and the division is a threefold one: the gravity of the spiritual sickness, the manner of healing, and the danger of relapsing. The three parts are treated very unequally, the third one being as long as the two others combined. The first part shows how the sinner is at the same time blind, possessed, and dumb. The burden of blindness is illustrated by a verse from the Psalms and another from Hosea. The miserable condition of the possessed man is treated at greater length. He is not guided by his own judgment, as is shown by the Psalmist and Isaiah; he does not realize his evil and rejoices at his bad actions, a situation condemned by three passages from Job, one from Matthew, and one from Genesis. Then comes a digression on the necessity of a good remedy, "tyriaca," namely Christ's passion, supported again by two verses from Job and a quotation from Leo the Great. A short paragraph on the sinner's dumbness allegorizes an episode of the first book of Kings where Samuel's actions are commented on according to some Jewish models, which became normal after Rupert of Deutz and Peter Comestor.[38]

The second part of the *moralitas* is about the manner of the healing. But John's first division is a description of the devil's armor, given to him by the world and by the sinner himself. The breast-plate, given by the world, is curiously made of water, according to Ben Sirach's description of the north wind. His sword is the shimmering of worldly glory. His helmet is like a mask, with which he hides the ugliness of sin. Once having known the devil's weapons, we may fight him successfully as David did Goliath.

Then comes the last and longest part of the moral section. It concerns the dangers of recidivism. A repentant sinner may have confessed his faults, but if he lack charity, his cleansed soul stands empty.

It lies open for the return of the wicked spirit with seven of his even more wicked comrades. This shows why it is more and more difficult for sinners who relapse to promise their confessors that they will not sin again. But the seven devils may also be taken as the seven calamities that affect the recidivist: worse sin, the breaking of peace with God, treason, false confidence in God's mercy, lack of mercy to oneself, the Holy Ghost's sorrow, and ingratitude towards God. John concludes that we must be careful not to sin again in order to progress in the virtues and reach the vision of God.

All these developments are illustrated by quotations from the Bible. Curiously, the greatest number are taken from the Old Testament, from which there are twenty-five, as against only five from the New. Among the former, the most often used book is Job (seven times), followed by the Psalms (four times). The wisdom books provide more than half of the Old Testament references. Generally, these quotations are only meant to support an argument without themselves requiring explanation, but some are briefly commented on. Remarks are made, for example, on the description of the devil's watery armor and the roaring of the holy soul, of which the Psalmist and Job speak. We also have a rather vivid narration of that episode of David's life, when he delivers the men of Ceila from the Philistines only to find them prepared to hand him over to Saul. Just so the repentant sinner in falling again betrays Christ. The pattern is familiar to us: a serious literal or moral exegesis of the biblical passage with glimpses of passages in other books.

We find an analogous case in one of the first Dominicans whose sermons are known, Constantine of Orvieto, an Italian friar who was elected bishop of Orvieto in 1250 and who died in 1256. His sermons, recently identified, were certainly composed when he was still a friar.[39] Some of his sermons are in the style of the old homilies, others in "modern" form. For the first case, I will take his *processus,* that is, a short scheme for a sermon, for the second Sunday after Easter on 1 Peter 2:21–25.[40] If the written thema is made up only of the opening phrase of the pericope ("Christus passus est pro nobis, vobis relinquens exemplum"), his division shows clearly that he will comment on the whole text, since the second part begins with the end of the twenty-fourth verse. The first part shows from the text itself how Christ's example is fourfold: innocence, patience, humility, and love, each element being confirmed by another scriptural verse, respectively from Malachi, Wisdom, Isaiah, and Philippians. The second part, still shorter, treats of the four things that constitute man's healing. This division is confirmed by a verse from I Corinthians. Here we actually have attention concentrated on the pericope itself.

If we now take Constantine's three sermons for the third Sunday of Lent,[41] we see that the first is again a short, twofold analysis of the whole liturgical Gospel. The first division concerns the miracle itself: the man's healing from blindness, possession, and dumbness, with a moral application to the recovery of the soul. Next we learn the consequences of the miracle: simple admiration in the crowd, calumny by the scribes and pharisees, and edification of the poor — three attitudes that are still to be seen among hearers of preaching. Six biblical quotations are used to fortify the moralizations: two are taken from Acts, two from 1 Corinthians, one each from Romans and Ecclesiasticus. A second division without any citation ("Item aliter potest procedi summatim in evangelio . . .") shows Jesus' power in healing, his wisdom in confuting his adversaries, his justice when he announces punishment for blasphemers, and his goodness when he corroborates the blessing of the woman.

The second and the third sermons for this third Sunday are wholly different. The second is a development of the five kinds of moral dumbness in bad prelates or preachers and in sinners who refuse to confess. The third is devoted to the blessing of Mary by the anonymous woman of the crowd, and it shows many similarities with the sermon on the same theme by the anonymous Dominican. In these two sermons, each subdivision is illustrated by one or two biblical verses. Seventeen biblical verses are referred to in the second sermon, six in the third, with only one verse in each sermon from the New Testament.

We find a similar case in the widely circulated collections of William Peraldus. To take once more the third Sunday of Lent, we find five sermons on the Gospel in the printed editions.[42] The first sermon is, here again, a simple, mainly literal explanation of the whole liturgical passage, often taken word for word from Hugh of St. Cher's commentary on Luke.[43] The second sermon is a moralization of the miseries of the possessed man. The third treats of the different expulsions of the devil, the fourth of capital sins and confession. The fifth mixes various points, such as neglect of penance, recidivism, and the Holy Virgin's blessed womb. Biblical quotations are very numerous. In the first sermon, we find one from Exodus, five from Kings, two from the Psalms, five from the wisdom books, four from the Prophets, six from Matthew, one from Luke, one from Paul, and two from Peter.

In the second, there are no less than forty-seven quotations, fifteen from the New Testament and thirty-two from the Old, with ten from the Prophets and sixteen from the wisdom books. Peraldus shares many elements with John of Abbeville, though they are rather more expanded. Moreover, there is probably no direct dependence, but only an extensive use of such common sources as the *Glossa ordinaria*.

It would be easy, but probably unnecessary, to go on to examine further individual sermons. We may, however, make some general observations, which additional texts would corroborate. First, we see how generally repetitive the sermons for a Sunday are. Many things are said again and again, even with the same *exempla* and comparisons. Some sermons actually preached are constructed by mixing available models, but rather curiously this does not apply to the quotation of biblical *auctoritates*. The same argument may be illustrated by different biblical verses in different homilies. Thus a sermon by Ranulph of La Houblonnière borrows heavily from Nicholas of Biard and William of Mailly.[44] But of the thirty-two biblical quotations by Ranulph, only two are found in both of his main sources, while three are shared with Mailly alone and another two with Biard alone. It seems, then, that a preacher, even when using some of his predecessors' materials, looked for different biblical *auctoritates*.

We may also note that the famous four senses of Scripture were very differently used. There is nearly always some literal interpretation, but very few allegorical or anagogical ones, a greater amount of space being taken up by the tropological or moral sense. In the case of the Gospel for the third Sunday of Lent, it is notable that the devil is seldom spoken of as a person, but nearly always only as a principle of sin, if not as sin itself. There is no mention of Hell, which would be a normal subject for the anagogical or eschatological sense. This supremacy of the moral sense would appear in the great majority of thirteenth-century sermons.

As might have been foreseen, scriptural instruction was indeed very selective. The liturgical readings, carefully explained in the old homiletical pattern, were, with the "modern" way, more and more cut into small pieces, some of which were very seldom preached. Thus the scriptural culture of laymen was made up of some solid exegesis, in the medieval sense, of a very limited part of Scripture, and of a sprinkling of many verses, generally taken out of context. Exceptions would be some famous biblical *exempla*, such as Jacob deceiving Esau or David fighting with Goliath, which were fairly often told in detail and were probably the parts of Scripture that stayed most firmly in the mind of the layman together with Christ's life and passion.

APPENDIX 1

Iohannes de Abbatisvilla

Sermo in secunda dominica aduentus

Listed in Schneyer, *Repertorium*, 3:514, nos. 61–62. The manuscripts used are Paris, Bibliothèque Nationale, Ms. lat. 15935, ff. 61va–62va (= A) and Ms. lat. 16464, f. 73va (= B); Città del Vaticano, Biblioteca Apostolica Vaticana, Cod. Burghesianus 6 (= V), and Burgh. 199 (= W). The basic text is taken from A and only the more important variants are noted; B and W are very corrupt and their unique variants were not taken into account.

Erat Iesus eiciens demonium,[1] etc.

«Post predicationis uerba que humilibus proposuit etiam miracula operatur ut qui predicanti non credunt, uisis miraculis credant. Matheus hunc demoniacum etiam cecum fuisse dicit,[2] in quo tria miracula a Domino fiunt, uidelicet mutus loquitur, cecus illuminatur,[3] possessus a demonio liberatur; quod tunc in uno carnaliter factum est cotidie fit in conuersione gentium, ut primum expulso demone et omni spurcicia ydolatrie fidei lumen uideant; deinde tacentia prius ora ad laudem Dei laxentur.»[4]

Igitur: *Erat Iesus eiciens demonium et illud erat mutum,* id est mutos faciens, *et cum eiectum esset dominium locutus est mutus et ammirate sunt turbe.*

Quidam autem ex eis, scilicet scribe et pharysey, *dixerunt: In Beelzebub principe demoniorum eicit demonia.*[5] «Ninus rex, conditor Niniue, Belo patri statuam consecrauit eique diuinos honores constituit, cuius simulacri similitudinem Daldei suscipientes Bel uocabant; inde Palestini suscipientes Baal dicebant, Moabite Beelphegor; Iudei autem unius Dei cultores propter derisionem gentilium Beelzebub appellabant: Baal enim uir dicitur, zebub muscha; inde Beelzebub quasi uir muscarum siue habens muscas, propter sordes cruoris qui in templo eius immolabatur. Asserebant etiam Iudei in hoc simulacro

[1] Lucas 11:14
[2] Matthaeus 9:32, 12:14
[3] illuminatur] uidet A
[4] Post predicationem . . . laxentur: *Glossa ordinaria* in Lucam 11:14 (*Biblia sacra cum glossa interlineari ordinaria* . . . Venetiis 1588, 5:154va; PL 114:289A).
[5] Lucas 11:15

principem demoniorum habitare per cuius potestatem dicebant Iesum demonia pellere.»[6]

Et alii temptantes signum de deo querebant ab eo.[7] «Proprium est enim Iudeorum signum quererе.»[8]

Ipse autem ut uidit cogitationes eorum dixit eis: Omne regnum in se ipsum diuisum desolabitur et domus aduersum domum diuisa cadet. Si autem Sathanas in se ipsum diuisus est,[9] secundum uos, quia dicitis me in Beelzebub eicere demonia. «Non ad uerba sed ad cogitationes respondet, in quo dat certum potentie sue signum, qua secreta cordium rimatur. Iuxta litteram patet, quia omne regnum solidum et firmum, si per partes diuiditur, in solitudinem redigitur uacuatum ab habitatoribus, et domus supra domum cadet cum habitatores unius domus ab alterius domus familia uel opprimuntur uel perimuntur. Quo autem hec spiritualiter tendant, exponit cum adiungit: *Si autem et Sathanas in se ipsum diuisus est:* si ego, ut uos dicitis, in principe demoniorum eicio demones, ergo regnum diaboli est diuisum contra se et potestas malicie eius stare non potest. Si autem demon demonem non potest expellere, falso dicitis me in principe demoniorum eicere demonia; si uero potest sicut dicitis, prospicite uobis ut de regno eius quod diuisum est exeatis, ne iniuria eius pariter inuoluamini.»[10] Si autem ego in Beelzebub eicio demonia, *filii uestri in quo eiciunt?* quasi dicat: cur non in eadem potestate creditis me eicere demones in qua filii uestri eiciunt? «Filios Iudeorum Apostolos uocat qui inter alia miracula, que a Domino acceperant, etiam demonia pellebant, quam expulsionem non diabolo sed Domino assignabant, qui sibi conscii erant nichil malarum artium a Domino didicisse; ideo ipsi qui sunt *ignobilia et contemptibilia*[11] huius *mundi,* in quibus nulla malitia artificiosa, sedebunt *super sedes duodecim iudicantes duodecim tribus Israel.*[12] Vel filii, id est exorciste illius gentis qui inuocato nomine Domini demonem expellebant, quasi dicat: si expulsio in illis non diabolo sed Deo deputatur, cur idem opus in me non habeat eandem causam? Ideo ipsi iudices uestri erunt, non potestate sed comparatione, dum illi expulsionem non diabolo sed Deo assignabant.»[13]

Porro si in digito Dei.[14] Postquam ostendit quod non in Beelzebub eicit

---

[6]Ninus . . . pellere: *Glossa ordinaria* in Lucam 11:15 (*Biblia* 5:154va; PL 114:289B).

[7]Lucas 11:16

[8]*Glossa interlinearis* in Lucam 11:16 (*Biblia* 5:154va).

[9]Lucas 11:17–18

[10]Non ad uerba . . . inuoluamini: *Glossa ordinaria* in Lucam 11:17–18 (*Biblia* 154vb; PL 114:289C).

[11]1 ad Corinthios 1:28

[12]Matthaeus 19:28; cf. Lucas 22:30

[13]Filios Iudeorum . . . assignabant: *Glossa ordinaria* in Lucam 11:19 (*Biblia* 5:155ra; PL 114:289D).

[14]Lucas 11:20

demonia, sumit illud quod scilicet in spiritu Dei eadem eicit. Et quid inde sequitur ostendit decens: *Porro si in digito Dei,* id est in Spiritu sancto, nam «Filius dicitur manus uel brachium Patris, Spiritus sanctus dicitur digitus propter differentiam uariorum donorum que propter Spiritum sanctum hominibus dantur,»[15] sicut in digito diuerse iuncture sunt. *Si* inquam *in digito Dei eicio demonia, profecto peruenit,* id est perueniet, *in uos regnum Dei,* scilicet «iudiciaria Dei potestas qua malos a bonis secernet in die iudicii.»[16]

   Cum fortis armatus,[17] etc. Adhuc ostendit quod non in principe demoniorum eicit demones, quia «tunc in aliquo ei consentiret; set ei in nullo consentit set pocius illum superare et eicere festinat a suis fidelibus. Unde dicit: *cum* diabolus *fortis* ad nocendum *armatus* spiritualibus nequiciis *custodit* in sua seruitute *atrium suum,* scilicet mundum in quo usque ad aduentum Christi sine contradictione principabatur,»[18] *in pace sunt ea que possidet; si autem fortior illo superueniens uicerit eum, uniuersa eius arma aufert in quibus confidebat et spolia distribuit.* Iste fortior Christus est qui «fortiori potentia diabolum strauit et uersucias diaboli quibus tanquam armis utebatur abstulit et spolia, scilicet animas seductas quibus eum diabolus spoliauit, distribuit»[19] dum diuersis ministeriis in Ecclesia assignauit.

   Sequitur: *Qui non est mecum aduersum me est et qui non colligit mecum despergit,*[20] quasi dicat: «et uere opera mea non conueniunt cum operibus Sathane quia ego ipse in nullo conuenio cum ipso, set omnino contrarii sumus, quia ego humilis, benignus, animas uolo saluare, ille superbus, inuidus, cupit perdere; ego predicatione mea congrego uirtutes, ille spargit et separat ab unitate Ecclesie.»[21]

   Sequitur: *Cum immundus spiritus exierit ab homine,*[22] etc. «Diabolus exit ab homine cum in baptismo pompis eius abrenuntiat et precedentium peccatorum illecebris; quem deserans *anbulat per loca inaquosa,* quia corda sanctorum ab omni malitia fluxarum cogitationum et humore immunia callidus temptator explorat, si quos ibi sue nequicie gressus figere possit,»[23] unde subditur: *querens requiem et non inueniens,* quia «qui prauis cogitationibus et

<hr>

   [15]Filius dicitur . . . dantur: *Glossa ordinaria* in Lucam 11:20 (*Biblia* 5:155ra; PL 114:290A–B).

   [16]iudiciara . . . iudicii: ibid.

   [17]Lucas 11:21–22

   [18]tunc . . . principabatur: cf. *Glossa ordinaria* in Lucam 11:21 (*Biblia* 5:155ra; PL 114:290B–C).

   [19]fortiori . . . distribuit: cf. *Glossa ordinaria* in Lucam 11:23 (*Biblia* 5:155ra).

   [20]Lucas 11:23

   [21]et uere . . . Ecclesie: cf. *Glossa ordinaria* in Lucam 11:23 (*Biblia* 5:155ra; PL 114:290D).

   [22]Lucas 11:24

   [23]Diabolus . . . possit: *Glossa ordinaria* in Lucam 11:23 (*Biblia* 5:155rb; deest in PL).

actibus pascitur in mentibus fidelium omnia temptamenta sua cessare perpendit.»[24]

Tunc dicit: *reuertar in domum meam unde exiui.*[25] «Reuertar ad illius conscientiam unde in baptismo eiectus fueram et pristinam possessionem consueto dominio michi subiciam»;[26] et *cum uenerit inuenit scopis mundatam et ornatam,* etc., «quia cum huiusmodi reprobum repererit, inuenit conscienciam peccatoris uiciis in baptismo mundatam sed nullo bono opere cumulatam.»[27]

Et *tunc uadit et assumit septem spiritus nequiores se et ingressi habitant ibi,*[28] quia assumit «plenitudinem omnium uitiorum,»[29] et *fiunt nouissima hominis illius peiora prioribus,* etc., quia «melius,» id est minus malum, «erat uiam ueritatis ignorare quam post agnitionem retrorsum conuerti.»[30]

Factum est autem, cum respondens blasphemantibus hoc diceret, *extollens uocem quedam mulier de turba dixit illi: Beatus uenter qui te portauit et ubera que suxisti.*[31] «Hic et Maria laudatur que Dominum portauit, et prauitas tam presentium Iudeorum quam futurorum hereticorum qui ueram Christi humanitatem negant confutatur, quia et uerum Dei filium aduersus blasphemos Iudeos confitetur, et uerum hominis filium testatur matri consubstantialem: nisi enim esset una caro cum matre, frustra uenter ille et ubera beatificarentur. Secundum phisicos ex eadem fonte et lac nutriendis et semen procreandis pueris emanat; ergo de semine Virginis potuit concipi qui lacte eius potuit nutriri.»[32]

At ille dixit: Quinimmo beati qui audiunt uerbum Dei et custodiunt illud,[33] in opere; «quasi non solum laudanda est Maria quia verbum Dei portauit in utero, sed maxime beata est quia precepta Dei seruauit in opere; sic et omnes beati qui Verbum Dei auditu fidei concipiunt et boni operis custodia in suo uel proximorum corde pariunt et nutriunt.»[34]

---

[24]qui prauis . . . perpendit: *Glossa ordinaria* in Lucam 11:23 (*Biblia* 5:155rb; PL 114:291B).

[25]Lucas 11:24–25

[26]Reuertar . . . subiciam: *Glossa ordinaria* in Lucam 11:24 (*Biblia* 5:155rb; PL 114:291B).

[27]quia . . . cumulatum: *Glossa ordinaria* in Lucam 11:25 (*Biblia* 5:155rb; PL 114:291B).

[28]Lucas 11:26

[29]plenitudinem . . . uitiorum: *Glossa ordinaria* in Lucam 11:26 (*Biblia* 5:155rb; PL 114:291C).

[30]melius conuerti: ibid.

[31]Lucas 11:27

[32]Hic et . . . nutriri: *Glossa ordinaria* in Lucam 11:27 (*Biblia* 5:155rb-va; PL 114:291C-D).

[33]Lucas 11:28

[34]quasi . . . nutriunt: *Glossa ordinaria* in Lucam 11:28 (*Biblia* 5:155rb-va; PL 114:291C-D).

Moraliter:[35]

Erat Iesus eiciens demonium et illud erat mutum.

In hodierno euangelio tria docentur: grauitas infirmitatis, modus curationis, periculum recidiuationis.

Grauitas informitatis, quia peccator comparatur infirmo qui hodie legitur in euangelio, qui erat cecus ut legitur in Matheo, demoniacus et mutus ut legitur in Luca.

Cecus est peccator, quia sicut ursus cecatur ad peluim ardentem, sic cecatur peccator ardore desiderii sui, ut non uidet solem, unde in Psalmo:[36] *Supercecidit ignis et non uiderunt solem,* et Osee VII:[37] *Omnes calefacti sunt quasi clibanus et deuorauerunt iudices suos;* ardore etenim praui desiderii calefactus homo estuat intus quasi clibanus, et hoc igne iudices deuorantur, scilicet intellectus et ratio, dum sic prauo absorbantur desiderio quod non iudicant de peccato.

Demoniacus est, quia demoniacum non conducit propria ratio, sed diabolus dominatum habet in ipso, unde peccatori dicitur: *Nolite fieri sicut equs et mulus quibus non est intellectus.*[38] Mulus enim non discernit inter onera nec peccator sarcinam peccatorum, nec credit consilio Ysaie prophete dicentis LVII:[39] *Disrumpe cogitationes iniquitatis, solue fasciculos deprimentes.* Hii sunt fasciculi peccatorum qui per confessionem dissoluuntur. Equs non discernit sessorem; equs est peccator cui insidet diabolus tanquam eques deducens eum sicut uult, nam *ignee habene et currus eius,*[40] sicut dicit propheta Naum II.

Preterea demoniacus gaudet et exultat tanquam non sentiens afflictionem quam portat et tales sunt qui exultant in rebus pessimis et gaudent cum male fecerunt, qui querunt mel in felle, dulcedinem in peccato, de quibus Iob XXX:[41] *Qui letantur in huiuscemodi et esse sub sentibus delicias* reputabant. Peccato quidem nichil amarius. Amarus est cibus quem anima sine morte glutire non potest, sicut dicit Iob VI:[42] *Quis* gustauit *quod gustatum affert mortem?* Sed multi sunt uelud sus, ideo immundum animal secundum Legem quia non ruminat: glutiunt enim peccatum et non masticant, et sicut dicit Iob:[43] *Bibent iniquitatem sicut aquam,* glutientes non dente terentes, quia sicut medicus pillulas amaras inuoluit nebula ut cito gluciantur nec emasti-

---

[35]moraliter] moralitas B *om.* VW
[36]Psalmi 57:9
[37]Osee 7:7
[38]Psalmi 31:9
[39]Isaias 58:6
[40]Nahum 2:3
[41]Iob 30:7
[42]Iob 6:6
[43]Iob 15:16

centur, quia sapor amaritudinis ferri non posset, sic diabolus uenenum peccati inuoluit quadam nebula et non ueritate dulcedinis; sed si illud inuolucrum homo masticaret, sentiret amaritudinem et refugeret a peccato. De hoc Dominus in Euangelio ait:[44] *Nunquid colligent de spinis uuas aut de tribulis ficus?* Certe non. Cum igitur, sicut dicitur in Genesi,[45] terra tua *spinas et tribulos germinabit tibi,* id est maiores et minores aculeos peccati, non potest colligere de spinis uuas leticie nec de tribulis ficus dulcedinis.

Ad hoc facit quod habetur in Iob VI:[46] *Vtinam appenderentur peccata mea quibus iram merui et calamitas quam patior in statera.* Siquidem toxicum magis uenenosum et magis noxium probatur per uirtutem tyriace, quia contra pessimum toxicum oportet haberi tyriacam optimam; scitis autem quod peccatum Ade acutissimum fuit toxicum infectione duplici, scilicet miseria pene et uitio culpe; tyriaca autem est gratia Spiritus sancti, que etsi in uiris sanctis habundauerit ad purgationem culpe, tamen non purgauit miseriam pene; nam etsi in humana Christi natura fuit plenissima diuinitas, non tamen fuit per hanc tyriacam purgata miseria pene sicut dicit Leo papa:[47] portauit enim defectus nostros preter peccatum. Statera est humanitas Christi in qua Christus moriendo calamitatem nostram grauis esse ponderis demonstrauit.

Bene autem subditur de calamitate, id est miseria, uite presentis: *Quasi harena maris hec grauior appareret.*[48] Vita hominis dicitur harena, mare mundus; nam sicut harena maris quanto magis fluctibus maris tunditur, tanto magis salsificatur, sic uita presens, curis et negociis secularibus dum continue tunditur, semper amaricatur.

Mutus quoque est peccator quia bibit de aquis secularium delitiarum in quibus congesta sunt maledicta ueteris et noui testamenti, et compacta sunt labia eius et factus est mutus sicut legitur quod Samuel in Masphat[49] effudit aquas in quibus congesta erant maledicta[50] de quibus, si biberet ydolatra, labia eius inseparabiliter sibi coherebant.

Ecce grauitas infirmitatis quod peccator cecus est, demoniacus et mutus.

Ad hoc facit quod sequitur: *Cum fortis armatus custodit atrium suum,* etc. Diabolus fortis est, potens in subuertendo et antiquitate temporis et subtilitate nature; et preterea est armatus.

Armat enim eum homo contra se ipsum, quia sicut cum aliquis nobilis se reddidit alicui regi, reddit ei gladium suum et propriorum claues castrorum, et ita contra se ipsum roborat aduersarium; sic peccator membris suis

---

[44]Matthaeus 7:16
[45]Genesis 3:18
[46]Iob 6:2
[47]Cf. Leo Magnus, *Tractatus* 63.4 (CCSL 138A:384, 1.58–59; PL 54:355B).
[48]Iob 6:3
[49]Cf. 1 Samuelis 10:8
[50]Cf. Numeri 5:18,23 et 22:6

et naturalibus potentiis suis armat diabolum, sicut dicit Apostolus ad Romanos XVI:[51] *Non regnet peccatum in uestro mortali corpore, ut exhibeamus menbra uestra arma iniquitatis peccato.*

Preterea mundus armat diabolum, de cuius lorica dicit Ecclesiasticus XLIII:[52] *Induet se quasi lorica aquis et deuorabit montes et exuret desertum et extinguet uiride sicut ignem.* Aque sunt terrene et instabiles seculi delitie, quibus diabolus deuorat montes, id est potentes et magnos[53] in seculo qui putant se uorare delitias et ipsi deuorantur a delitiis; sicut stultus putat se bibere uinum set ipse bibitur a uino. Desertum significat uiros religiosos et omnes clericos qui tanquam spirituales imitatores Christi debuerunt desseruisse delicias, set illas amantes exusti sunt, id est concremati, et ad similitudinem olle combuste nigri effecti sunt; unde in Naum II:[54] *Et facies omnium sicut nigredo olle.*

Sequitur: *Et extinguet uiride sicut ignem,* quia aque deliciarum extingunt uirorem fidei et ignem caritatis, cum se homo illis assueuerit.

De gladio diaboli dicit Ezechiel XXI:[55] *Gladius exacutus est et limatus. Vt cedat* acutus *est, ut* fulgeat *limatus est.* Gladius diaboli est nitor glorie secularis que quanto nitidior tanto cedit profundius.

De eius galea in libro Regum loquitur,[56] libro primo, capitulo XVII:[57] *Et cassis erea erat super capud Philostei.* Diabolus habet galeam quia uenit quasi laruatus[58] occultans turpitudinem peccati sub galea erea que mentitur similitudinem auri, quia sub specie boni occultat uenenum.

Contra tot mala unum est remedium, ut ueniat fortior, scilicet gratia Dei et auferet diabolo uniuersa arma in quibus confidit.

Aufertur ei lorica que est ex aquis, nam aque limum habent in fundo: moue aquas et commisce limum: cum aquis deliciarum commisce sordes peccati et non erunt potabiles, et sic spoliabis diabolum lorica. Dauid sumpsit lapidem in torrente quem misit in funda;[59] post percussit Philosteum et deiecit.[60] Fac similiter: in torrente huius seculi est quidam lapis qui nullis deliciarum aquis potest emolliri, scilicet ineuitabilis necessitas moriendi; hoc lapide percussus, fracta galea sua, interficitur diabolus.

Gladius quantuncumque clarissimus missus ad terram rubiginem trahit qua consumitur; sic nitor glorie secularis rubiginem trahit et contemptibilis

[51]ad Romanos 6:12–13
[52]Ecclesiasticus 42:22–23
[53]magnos] malignos A
[54]Nahum 2:10
[55]Ezechiel 21:9–10
[56]legitur] loquitur A
[57]1 Samuelis 17:5
[58]laruatus pA] galeatus sAV laniatus B lauatus W
[59]1 Samuelis 17:40, 49
[60]1 Samuelis 17:50

efficitur si consideres quoniam terra es et in terram ibis.[61] Sic exarmatur
diabolus armis quibus eum armat mundus.

Armatura uero qua ipsum armasti contra te exarmatur si feceris quod
dicit Apostolus ad Rom. VI:[62] *Sicut exhibuistis menbra uestra seruire inmunditie
et iniquitati ad iniquitatem, ita exhibiete menbra uestra seruire iustitie in sanctificationem.*

Sed cum exiuerit anbulat per loca arida, etc. Diabolus est uelud porcus, querit
uolutabrum sordidum, et quia in mentibus uirorum sanctorum non inuenit
lutum uel sterquilinium reuerti desiderat ad uasculum unde exiuit, quia
in uiris bonis non inuenit requiem, in quorum mentibus non est nisi rugitus, sicut habetur in Psalmo:[63] *Rugiebam a gemitu cordis mei.* Rugitus proprie
leonum est, qui tante uirtutis est quod bestie audientes sistunt pedem ut
ultra non moueant gradum;[64] ita gemitus contriti cordis spirituales nequitias sistit ut attendere[65] non audeant ad sic contritum, quia undas sic rugien-
tium ferre non possunt, sicut dicit Iob III:[66] *Quasi inundantes aque, sic rugitus
meus.*

Reuertitur ergo diabolus *in domum unde* exiuit, et *inuenit eam scopis mundatam,* id est confessione, quia domus cordis debet primo mundari cum pala
ut eiciantur modici pulueres peccatorum, *et inuenit eam ornatam,* ieiunio, ora-
tione et elemosina. Et tunc sumit audaciam reuertendi in eam, quia inuenit
eam uacantem, sicut dicit Lucas, id est sine caritate sine qua meritoria non
sunt opera, quia quantum diligis, tantum operaris; et necesse est ut mens
uel habeat caritatem et ita sit plena, uel non habeat caritatem et ita sit uacua.
Si autem fuerit uacua, patet ingressus diabolo, unde Iob XXXVI:[67] *Qui ex-
tendit aquilonem super uacuum.*

Intrans autem diabolus, ducit *alios septem spiritus nequiores se,* quia eandem mentem plenius possidet quam ante, *et fiunt nouissima hominis illius peiora
prioribus.* Frequens enim recidiuatio frequenter aufert locum penitentie. Sicut
enim calceus frequenter reparatus tandem non admittit reparationem set
mittitur in sterquilinium, ita quandoque peccator frequenter reparatus per
penitentiam tandem reparationem non recipit. Non dico quod aliquis sit ter-
minus diuine misericordie uel quod clausa sint uiscera diuine pietatis alicui
penitenti, set cum homo pluries recidiuauerit contingit quandoque quod ex
animi pusillanimitate non audet firmiter[68] promittere confessori quod absti-
neat a peccato consueto, licet liquescet in lacrimis. Vnde Apostolus ad He-

[61]Cf. Genesis 3:19
[62]ad Romanos 6:19
[63]Psalmi 37:9
[64]gradum] gressum A
[65]attendere] accedere VW
[66]Iob 3:24
[67]Iob 26:7
[68]firmiter] plane B *om.* A

breos penultimo[69] dicit de Esau quod *non inuenit locum penitentie licet eum quereret cum lacrimis.* Qui enim peccato non renuntiat quantumcumque fluat in lacrimis ueniam non meretur.

Possumus etiam per septem spiritus nequiores septem intelligere malitias[70] que recidiuidantem ideo nequius possident, quia fortius captiuant et durius[71] ligant.

Et est una malitia ipsum peccatum per quod fit recidiuium, quod grauius dicitur propter effectum nocendi sicut febris recidiua grauat et nocet amplius quam prior.

Secunda malitia est fractura federis uel pacis inite cum Domino in confesssione, que pax nobis figuratur per Ysaac et Iacob in Genesi,[72] ubi legitur[73] quod cum Iacob optulisset patri suo Ysaac duos edos quibus libenter uescebatur, uinum quoque pariter et fragrantiam uestimentorum, pariter petiit pater ab eo et dixit: *Da michi osculum, fili mi.*[74] In duobus edis confessio peccatorum designatur et satisfactio, in uino cordis compunctio, in fragrantia uestimentorum odor significatur uirtutum, set cum hiis omnibus necesse est ut accedat osculum, scilicet federatio pacis ad Deum, ut qui semel penitet, ad rebellandum contra Dominum de cetero non resumat arma uitiorum.

Tertia malitia est proditio,[75] similis illi de qua legitur primo Regum XXIII.[76] Siquidem cum Dauid liberasset uiros Ceyle de manu Philistinorum et moraretur in Ceyla, uenit Saul ut oppugnaret Ceylam, dixitque Dauid ad Dominum: *Si tradent me uiri Ceyle? Et dixit Dominus: Tradent.* Quid per Dauid nisi Christus? Quid per Philosteos nisi maligni spiritus? Quid per uiros Ceyle nisi peccatores quos maligni spiritus inpugnant designatur? Set Dauid percussis Philisteis saluat uiros Ceyle. Cum Christus noster Dauid, superata maligni hostis uersucia, peccatores liberat et in eisdem habitat[77] per inspiratam gratiam, uenit autem Saul aduersarius Dauid ut oppugnet Ceylam in qua Dauid habitat, cum hostis antiqus mentem quam Christus inhabitat uitiis inhabitare festinat; similes autem uiris Ceyle sunt proditores qui temptationibus nolentes resistere expulso Christo castrum[78] mentis sue tradunt eius aduersario.

Quarta malitia est adulatio diuine misericordie, nam sicut scortator scortum suum non timet offendere, set eo liberius offendit quo facilius re-

---

[69] ad Hebraeos 12:17
[70] malitias] nequitias uel *add.* A
[71] durius] fortius AB
[72] Genesis 27:8–28
[73] legitur] dicitur A
[74] Genesis 27:26
[75] proditio] perditio A
[76] 1 Samuelis 23:1–12
[77] habitat] inhabitat A
[78] castrum] castellum A

uocatur ad pacem, sic multi contra misericordem Deum peccare non formidant quia placabilis est et pronus ad ueniam. Qui Dei misericordiam frequenter irritant per culpam et placare nolunt per penitentiam sicut mechus adulteram sicut dicit Ambrosius: sunt qui frequenter agendam putant penitentiam qui luxuriantur in Christo.

Quinta malitia est inmisericordia sui, scilicet crudelitas hominis in se ipsum in reuocatione preteritorum uulnerum; maxima enim crudelitas est cum quis in se ipsum contorto iaculo uulnerum renouat cicatrices et hausto ueneno curatas renouat egritudines; unde exclamat Ecclesiasticus X:[79] *Peccantem in animam suam quis iustificabit et quis honorificabit exhonorantem animam suam.*

Sexta malitia est contristatio Spiritus sancti et maligni spiritus legifacatio, unde Apostolus ad Ephesios IIII:[80] *Nolite contristare Spiritum sanctum in quo signati estis,* cuius contristatio est nostra recidiuatio, et Osee VII:[81] *In malitia sua letificauerunt regem et in mendaciis principes;* nam qui post emendationem proximam ad uomitum reuertitur leticiam facit diabolo et ministris eius quos prius cum penituerit contristauerat.

Septima malitia est ingratitudo in Deum datorem libertatis qui penitentem de seruo fecerat liberum, et hec ingratitudo meretur reditum seruitutis, ut quicquid pene ipsi dimissum fuerat per penitentiam totum ab ipso repetat Dominus propter ingratitudinem quam commisit.

Hee sunt igitur septem malitie designate per septem spritus nequiores, que quoniam recidiuantem arripiunt, cum a triplici infirmitate que nobis in hodierno euangelio de[82] demoniaco demonstrata est,[83] per Dei gratiam curati fuerimus, uitantes recidiuium, in accepta gratia proficiamus euntes *de uirtute in uirtutem*[84] donec *Deus* uideatur *in Syon,* prestante Domino nostro, etc.

APPENDIX 2

Petrus de Remis

Dominica III in Quadragesima

Listed in Schneyer, *Repertorium,* 4:727, no. 32. The manuscripts used are Assisi, Biblioteca comunale, 452, ff. 28ra–29rb (= A), and Roma, Archivum Generale Fratrum Praedicatorum XIV 38a, ff. 28v and 17r (= R).

[79] Ecclesiasticus 10:32
[80] ad Ephesios 4:30
[81] Osee 7:3
[82] de SV] *om.* ABW
[83] demonstrata est] demonstrante sunt BVW
[84] Psalmi 83:8

Erat Iesus eiciens demonium et illud erat mutum.[1]

Non dicit: *eicit,* sed *erat eiciens,* notans continuitatem eicientis. Primo enim eiecit de celo, Eze. XXVIII:[2] *Cherub peccasti et eieci te.* Secundo, de mundo, Io XII:[3] *Nunc princeps mundi huius eiditur foras.* Tercio uero, de corporibus obsessis, ut hic. Quarto spiritualiter, cotidie de animabus peccatricibus, et hoc in digito Dei, ut hic: Cum fortis armatus custodit atrium,[4] etc., id est diabolus peccatorem, sed diaboli multi, id est scientes multi, eiciuntur hodie a studio, in Beelzebub, qui interpretatur deus muscarum,[5] quia non spiritus sanctus aut zelus animarum sed magis musce, id est sollicitudines et cure temporales[6] eos eiciunt, et postea pungunt se et sordidant et inquietant.

Hoc demonium mutum[7] dicitur ab effectu quia mutum efficit[8] tripliciter: a peccatorum confessione, a proximorum[9] edificatione, a Dei laudatione. De hoc Prou. XXVII:[10] *Qui abscondit scelera sua non dirigetur.* Iob XXXI:[11] *Si abscondi ut*[12] *homo peccatum meum,* scilicet per rationes uel excusationes.[13] I Mach. V[14] habetur quod obstruentes portas Effron non sinebant Iudam transire. Effron interpretatur puluis meroris uel uisio iniquitatis[15] et significat animam contritam cuius portas, id est confessionem, obstruant demones duobus uectibus, scilicet confitendi uerecundia et persistendi diffidentia, de quibus Eccli. III:[16] *Ne confundaris pro anima tua dicere uerum,* etc., et post: *nec accipias faciem tuam,* scilicet erubescendo sacerdotem, *nec aduersus faciem tuam mendacium,* ut dicas in corde tuo quoniam non possem perseuerare. Hos uectes

---

[1] Lucas 11:14

[2] Ezechiel 28:16

[3] Ioannes 12:31

[4] Lucas 11:21

[5] Cf. Stephanus Langton (?), *Interpretationes hebraicorum nominum:* "Belzebub uir muscarum uel princeps muscarum seu uetustus deus habens muscas aut uetustus deuorans muscas" (Paris, BN, Ms. lat. 15467, f. 586ra; Torino, Biblioteca Nazionale, D V 32, f. 525ra). Cf. Hieronymus, *Liber interpretationum hebraicorum nominum,* in Ioannem (CCSL 72:142, 1.10).

[6] et cure temporales] curarum temporalium R

[7] mutum] *om.* A

[8] mutum efficit] mutus efficitur R

[9] proximorum] proximi A

[10] Revera Proverbia 28:13

[11] Iob 31:33

[12] abscondi ut] absconderit A

[13] excusationes] per accusationes A

[14] 1 Machabaeorum 5:47

[15] Cf. Langton, *Interpretationes:* "Effron puluis meroris uel puluis inutilis seu puluis eorum aut uisio [Torino: ultio] iniquitatis" (Paris, f. 593rb; Torino, f. 530rb). Cf. Hieronymus, *Liber interpretationum,* Genesis E (CCSL 72:65, 1.22).

[16] Revera Ecclesiasticus 4:24,26

confregit Dominus, Ys. XLV:[17] *Ego ante eum ibo et gloriosos terre humiliabo, portas ereas conteram,* etc. Ps.:[18] *vestes ferreos confregit, quia Spiritus* Domini *quasi turbo impellens parietem.*[19]

Item facit mutum a proximorum edificatione, maxime prelatum. Quandoque enim proicit in os eius aliquid *et quasi mutus in ore auertit interpretationem,* Eccl. XX.[20] Mutus dicitur quedam ranuncula que proiecta in os canis eum latrare non sinit, ideo quia ipsa[21] semper nititur exire et ipse eam nititur deglutire. Hec sunt dona et munera que semper ad linguam redeunt cum illis dici debeat, Ys. LVI:[22] *Canes muti non ualentes latrare.*

Item ab increpando et predicando facit eos[23] obmutescere peccatum proinde quasi calculus in ore proiectus, Prou. XX:[24] *Suauis est homini panis mendacii,* id est delectatio peccati. Sed postea cum increpare uel predicare aliquibus[25] debet[26] implebitur os eius calculo, id est uermes consciencie qua timet ne dicatur ei: *Medice*[27] *cura te ipsum,* et illud Luce VI:[28] *Eice trabem de oculis tuis,* et Tren. III:[29] *Conclusit uias meas lapidibus quadris.* Lapides quadri peccati cordis, oris, operis, consuetudinis, uel ideo quadri dicuntur quia[30] a quatuor que loqui deberent eorum ora obstruuntur, scilicet a correctione,[31] consolatione, consilio et instructione, unde II Cor. XIII:[32] *Si uenero ad uos linguis loquens nisi aut in reuelatione* oculorum consolando *aut in scientia* corrigendo et inter malos bene uiuere docendo *aut in prophetia* per futurorum manifestationem consulendo, scilicet quomodo aggredienda sunt ardua et fugienda pericula *aut in doctrina* instruendo *quid uobis* proderit, etc.

Item facit mutum a Dei laude. Ponit enim *frenum erroris in maxillis populorum,* de quo Ys. XXX:[33] *Et frenum erroris,* etc. Videns enim tota die

[17]Isaias 45:2
[18]etc. Ps.] et post R. Psalmi 106:16 (cf. Isaias 45:2)
[19]Isaias 25:4
[20]XX] *om.* A. Ecclesiasticus 20:31: "et quasi mutus in ore auertit correptiones eorum."
[21]ipsa] *om.* A
[22]Isaias 56:16
[23]eos] *om.* A
[24]Proverbia 20:17
[25]aliquibus] aliquos A
[26]debet] *om. (lacuna)* pA erudierit sA
[27]Lucas 4:23
[28]Lucas 6:42
[29]III] IIII R (Lamentationes 3:9)
[30]quia] *om.* A
[31]correctione] correptione R
[32]Revera 1 ad Corinthios 14:6
[33]Isaias 30:28

multos qui sicut equus frenum non cessant rodere, ita et ipsi quin de mundo loquantur non possunt tacere. E contra dicit Donimus, Ysa. XLVIII:[34] *Laude mea infrenabo te ne intereas;* quod petimus cum dicimus: *Domine, labia mea aperies;* Ps.:[35] *Semper laus eius in ore meo.* Ecce aliud frenum; isto infrenatur homo qui mutus permanet sicut Zacharias ex quo Iohannes concipitur,[36] id est Dei gratia inspiratur.

In huius autem contrarium intelligitur demonium garrulum similiter ab effectu, quod Apostolus in hodierna epistola[37] innuit dicens: *fornicatio aut immundicia aut stulticia aut scurrilitas.* Quod demonium similiter tripliciter uexat, scilicet contra seipsum, contra proximum, contra Deum. De primo, Eccles. V:[38] *Ne temere quid loquaris,* precipue in quatuor: in consiliis dandis, in iudiciis faciendis, in testimoniis ferendis, et in uotis emittendis. Est enim multiplex loquendi temeritas. Prima est incertitudo eius quod asseritur, Ia. I:[39] *Sit omnis homo uelox ad audiendum,* etc. Secunda temporis consideratio, Eccli. XX:[40] *Ex ore fatui reprobabitur parabola.* Tercia importunitas, Eccli. XXII:[41] *Musica in luctu,* etc. Quarta usurpatio, scilicet cum aliquis imprudenter se iungit ad loquendum quod ad alium pertinet, Eccli. XXIII:[42] *Loquere maior natu,* etc. Quinta presumptio, cum scilicet iuuenis cum senibus loquitur, Eccli. XXX:[43] *In medio magnatorum,* etc. Sexta inutilitas locutionis ex defectu audientium, Eccli. XXXII:[44] *Vbi non est auditus non effundas loquelam,* etc. Septima audacia loquendi ultra proprium intellectum, Eccli. III:[45] *Altiora te ne quesieris,* etc. Octaua loquendi inanitas, scilicet cum pro humano fauore quis loquitur, Eccli. XXXII:[46] *Ne impedias musicam.* Nona est uituperandi intentio, Eccli. X:[47] *Antequam interroges, ne uituperes quemquam.* Decima est precipitata responsio, Eccli. XX:[48] *Antequam audias ne respondeas.* Vndecima mutua laudatio, Prou. XXVII:[49] *Quomodo probatur in conflatorio argentum,* etc.

[34] Isaias 48:9
[35] Psalmi 33:2
[36] Lucas 1:20–22
[37] ad Ephesios 5:3
[38] Ecclesiastes 5:1
[39] Iacobus 1:19
[40] Ecclesiasticus 20:22
[41] Ecclesiasticus 22:6
[42] Ecclesiasticus 32:4
[43] Ecclesiasticus 32:13
[44] Ecclesiasticus 32:6 (Vulgata: sermonem)
[45] Ecclesiasticus 3:22
[46] Ecclesiasticus 32:5
[47] Ecclesiasticus 11:16
[48] Ecclesiasticus 11:8 (Vulgata: Priusquam)
[49] Proverbia 27:21

Item est demonium garrulum contra proximum in adulatione et detractione, de qua dicit Eccli.:[50] *Cum detractore ne commiscearis.* Quare? Quia fetet et mordet. De primo Ps.:[51] *Sepulcrum patens est guttur eorum.* De secundo, Eccli. IX:[52] *Quomodo mordeat serpens,* etc. De adulatione, Eccli. VIII:[53] *Melius est a sapiente corripi quam stultorum adulatione decipi.* Adulantes enim sunt syrene incantatrices, diaboli nutrices, Tren. IIII:[54] *Lamie nudauerunt mammam, lactauerunt catulos.* Lamie sunt quia habent faciem hominis et lac uenenosum. Item ipsi sunt sacerdotes Baal, ioculatores diaboli, rane Egypti, pseudo prophete: omnes enim clamant: *Ascende in Ramoth, ascende, preualebis.*[55] Vlule sunt quia non cantant nisi rostro malefacto. Item proditores ut Iudas. Item aucupes diaboli. Item latrones qui interficiunt homines occulte, Osee VI:[56] *Participes latronum,* etc. Item fornarii diaboli succedentes clibanum eius et coci parantes cibos, Abacuc:[57] *Cibus eius electus.*

Item est demonium garrulum contra Deum in blasphemiis, periuriis et mendaciis, Ps.:[58] *Posuerunt in celum os suum,* etc. Apo.:[59] *Datum est ei os loquens grandia,* quia si os tale datum est a diabolo, ergo non potest repeti in morte ut rehabeatur per confessionem faciendam quia sine penitentia sunt dona Dei.

De hiis tribus garrulantibus dicitur Apo. XVI:[60] *Vidi tres spritus immundos in modum ranarum,* etc., et nota quod immundus spiritus est spiritus luxurie et nequam de quo hic: *Cum immundus spiritus exierit;* sed spiritus nequior est spiritus superbie. *Deinde assumit septem spiritus nequiores se,* qui sunt septem filii superbie, de quibus Prou. XXX:[61] *Generatio cuius excelsi sunt oculi,* propter quam Lucifer de celo corruit, Ysa. XIIII,[62] Adam de paradiso eiectus est, Gen. III,[63] phariseus a Domino reprobatus, Luce XVII,[64] linguarum facta est diuisio, Gen. XI,[65] Nabugodonosor in bestiam mutatus, Dan. III,[66] Saul

---

[50] Revera Proverbia 24:21
[51] Psalmi 5:11
[52] Ecclesiastes 10:11
[53] Ecclesiastes 7:6
[54] Lamentationes 4:3
[55] Cf. 3 Regum 22:12,15,22
[56] Osee 6:9: "Participes sacerdotum, in uia interficentium. . . ."
[57] Habacuc 1:16
[58] Psalmi 72:9
[59] Apocalypsis 13:5
[60] Apocalypsis 16:13
[61] Proverbia 30:13
[62] Isaias 14:12
[63] Genesis 3:6–24
[64] Lucas 18:9–14
[65] Genesis 11:1–9
[66] Daniel 4:25–34

a regno deiectus, I Reg. XV.[67] Huius prima filia est cum quis bonum quod non habet se dicit uel putat habere, et dicitur arrogantia. Secunda est quando de bono quod habet laudes querit, et dicitur inanis gloria. Tercia quando bonum quod habet se dicit super alios uel putat habere, et dicitur singularitas. Quarta quando bonum quod habet pro suis meritis se putat habere, et dicitur presumptio. Quinta quando pro bono quod habet se eleuat et alios condempnat, et dicitur elatio uel indignatio. Sexta[68] quando pro bono quod habet se ipsum laudat, et dicitur iactancia. Septima[69] est appetitus honoris uel dignitatis et dicitur ambitio. De hiis septem Amos II[70] dicitur: *Super tribus sceleribus Moab et super quatuor non conuertam eum eo quod incenderit ossa regis Ydumee.* Rex Ydumee Christus, ossa eius sunt uirtutes.

APPENDIX 3

Constantinus Urbevetanus

Sermo in tertia dominica quadragesime

The manuscript used is München, Bayerische Staatsbibliothek, Clm 7794 (= M). The first section is taken from ff. 34vb–35ra, the second from f. 35ra–va, the third from ff. 35vb–36ra.

(1) *Erat Iesus eiciens demonium.* Lu. XI.[1]

Duo in summa quantum ad litteram notantur in hoc ewangelio: scilicet miraculum factum a Iesu in eiectione demonii, et id quod secutum est miraculum.

Sicut dicit Glossa:[2] «Eicitur demonium, uidet cecus, quia Matheus[3] etiam hunc cecum fuisse dicit, et mutus loquitur. Quod spiritualiter adhuc agitur in unoquoque liberato a peccato per gratiam.» Liberatur enim anima a peccato per purgationem affectus, uidet per illuminationem intellectus, loquitur postmodum per oris confessionem, et hec sunt tria que operatur fides infusa. Que purgat enim affectum, Act. XV:[4] *Fide purificans corda.* Il-

---

[67]1 Samuelis 15:13–31
[68]quando pro bono . . . Sexta] *om.* R
[69]Septima] sexta R
[70]Amos 2:1
[1]Lucas 11:14
[2]*Glossa ordinaria* in Lucam 11:14 (*Biblia* 5:154va).
[3]Matheus *scrip.*] Marcus M
[4]Actus 15:9

luminat intellectum, Eccli. XV:[5] *Dulce lumen et delectabile oculis uidere solem,* id est Christum per fidem; *In lumine tuo uidebimus lumen,*[6] id est in fide tua. Aperit os, Ps.:[7] *Credidi propter quod locutus sum;* Ro. XII:[8] *Corde creditur ad iustitiam.*

Circa secundum nota etiam tria que secuta sunt ex miraculo, scilicet: turbe mirantur: unde *ammirate sunt turbe,* alii scandalizantur et emulantur quidam blasphemant, quidam temptant, unde: *Quidam ex hiis dicebant,*[9] et post: *alii temptantes,*[10] quos confutat dominus multipliciter, et forte erant scribe et Pharisei qui consueuerunt talia facere. Muliercule edificantur et laudant, unde: *Factum est autem cum.*[11]

Hec diuisio fit in uerbo Dei et in opere bono. Quidam enim de uerbo Dei quod audiunt et de opere bono quod uident non reportant nisi ammirationem: quam bene dixit, quam bene fecit. Hii sunt Attenienses qui *ad nichil aliud uacabant nisi aut dicere aut audire,* Act. XV.[12]

Quidam reportant emulationem et blasfemationem; hii sunt scribe et pharisei qui calumpniantes in omnibus operibus et dictis Iesu, Cor. 1:[13] *verbum crucis,* etc.

Quidam reportant edificationem et hii sunt maxime simplices et ydiote, Cor. primo:[14] *Non multi sapientes secundum carnem,* et ibidem:[15] *Christum predicamus,* etc.

Item aliter potest procedi summatim in ewangelio ut notantur in eo quatuor circa Iesum, scilicet potentia, sapientia, iustitia, bonitas. Potentia in operatione miraculi et nota sicut supra. Sapientia in confutatione blasphemantium et temptantium et confutat eos arguendo primo per positionem similitudinis, ibi: *Omne regnum in;*[16] secundum per locum a minori, ibi: *Si autem in Belzebub;*[17] tercio per contrarietatem operum suorum ad opera dy-

[5]Revera Ecclesiastes 11:7
[6]Psalmi 35:10
[7]Psalmi 115:10
[8]ad Romanos 10:10
[9]Lucas 11:15
[10]Lucas 11:17
[11]cum] tur *add.* M. Lucas 11:27: "Factum est autem cum haec diceret, extollens uocem quaedam mulier de turba dixit illi: Beati uenter qui te portauit."
[12]Actus 15:21
[13]1 ad Corinthios 1:18: "Verbum autem crucis pereuntibus quidem stultitia est."
[14]1 ad Corinthios 1:26
[15]1 ad Corinthios: "Nos autem praedicamus Christum crucifixum, Iudaeis quidem scandalum, gentibus autem stultitiam."
[16]Lucas 11:17
[17]Lucas 11:19

aboli, ibi: *Cum fortis armatus.* [18] Iusticia uero in descriptione penitencie debite blasphemantibus et peccantibus et hoc ibi: *Cum immundus spiritus.* [19] Bonitas autem in confirmatione uerbi mulieris et promissione quam fecit conuersis ad uerbum Dei, ibi: *Beati qui audiunt,* [20] etc.

(2) *Erat Iesus eiciens,* etc.

Demonium mutum est prelatus uel predicator non predicans et non arguens peccata aliena. Item demonium mutum est peccator non confitens peccata sua.

Nota quinque casus ex quibus mutitas prouenit. Aliquando enim mutitas prouenit ex incisione lingue. Aliquando paralitici amittunt linguam, id est loquelam. Aliquando ex carnositate excrescente in lingua. Aliquando ex eiectione calamiti in os canis. [21] Aliquando ex stupefactione inmoderati timoris. Secundum hec, accipe quinque casus mutitatis in prelato uel predicatore muto.

Prima est incisio lingue per malam uitam que incidit linguam mali prelati uel predicatoris ut audeat arguere aliquos. Gregorius: [22] «Diuino iudicio agitur ut non habeat linguam qui non habet uitam.»

Secunda est infrigidatio negligencie, Eccli. XX: [23] *Est autem tacens et non habens sensum loqui.* Incautio priuat menbrum sensu, Iere. XLVIII: *Maledictus qui facit opus.* [24]

Tercia est callositas consanguineorum, Reg. II [25] de Hely: *Magis honorasti filios tuos quam me,* et ibidem III: *Nouerat agere indigne filios.* [26]

Quarta est calamitum munerum et temporalium proiectum in os eius; propterea similis factus est cani, Ys. LVI: [27] *Canes muti,* et post: *Canes inpudentissimi.* Mich. III: [28] *Et si quis non dederit in ore eorum.*

[18] Lucas 11:21
[19] Lucas 11:24
[20] Lucas 11:28
[21] Cf. Vincentius Bellovacensis, *Speculum naturale* 19.19 (ed. Duaci, 1624, col. 1394): "Auctor. Est etiam ranunculus uiridis modicus qui calamitates dicitur, de quo dici solet quod se proiciatur in os canis reddit eum mutum, unde ab effectu mutus dicitur."
[22] Gregorius Magnus, *Moralia in Iob* 11.15 (CCSL 143A:599; PL 75:964B).
[23] Ecclesiasticus 20:6
[24] Ieremias 48:10: "Maledictus qui facit opus Domini fraudulenter."
[25] 1 Samuelis 2:29
[26] 1 Samuelis 3:13
[27] Isaias 56:10–11: "Canes muti non ualentes latrare, uidentes uana, dormientes et amantes somnia. Et canes impudentissimi nescierunt saturitatem."
[28] Michaeas 3:5: "Et si quis non dederit in ore eorum quippiam, sanctificant super eum praelium."

Quinta est obstupefactio timoris potentum et tyrannorum, Io. X:[29] *Mercennarius,* etc. Eccli. VII:[30] *Noli querere fieri iudex,* etc.

Item secundum hec, accipe quinque casus mutitatis in peccatore nolente confiteri.

Primum est enormitas uicii et maxime sodomie, unde Sodoma interpretatur pecus silens.[31] Sed certe quanto magis illud absconditur ab aure hominis, tanto magis clamat ad aures Dei, Gen. XVIII: *Clamor Sodome.*[32] Hoc fit <in>cisione lingue.

Secunda, insaciabilitas temporalium ut est usura que uix aut nunquam permittit usurarium uenire ad confessionem quia non est paratus ad confessionem, Osee III:[33] *Colligata est iniquitas Effraym,* id est usura, *absconditum est peccatum.* Effraym interpretatur fructificans,[34] id est usurarius. Sed certe diuicias quas sua uoluntate non extrahit de bursa, extrahet Deus noster de uentre, Iob XX:[35] *Diuicias quas deuorauit,* unde sequitur in predicta auctoritate: *Dolores parturientis.*[36] Hec est mutitas ex <in>iectione calamiti.

Tercia est promissio longioris uite procrastinans confessionem, Soph. II:[37] *Vox cantantis in fenestra,*[38] id est in ore, unde sequitur: *et corui in superliminari,* id est in ratione. Sed certe uiri inpii *non dimidiabunt dies,*[39] scilicet quos sibi promittunt. Hec est mutitas ex supercrescente carnositate.

Quarta est presumptio diuine bonitatis, Prou. XVIII:[40] *Inpius cum in profundum uenerit contempnit,* scilicet conuerti, presumens male de bonitate. Psalmista:[41] *Propter quid irritauit inpius Deum, dixit enim,* etc. hec est mutitas ex frigiditate menbrorum, id est uirium anime.

Quinta est desperatio; hec est massa plumbea que proicitur in os anphore in qua clauditur inpietas, Zach. V.[42] Hec est mutitas ex stupefactione timoris de iusticia diuina. Sed ab omnibus omnibus liberat Dominus cum conuertitur et confitetur.

---

[29]Iob 10:12–13

[30]Ecclesiasticus 7:6

[31]Hieronymus, *Liber interpretationum,* Genesis S (CCSL 72:71, 1.18–19).

[32]Genesis 18:20

[33]Revera Osee 13:12

[34]Hieronymus, *Liber interpretationum,* Genesis E (CCSL 72:65, 1.20; cf. 81.25, 142.15, 161.12).

[35]Iob 20:15: "Diuitias quas deuorauit euomet et de uentre eius extrahet eas Deus."

[36]Revera Psalmi 47:7

[37]Sophonias 2:14

[38]fenestra] corui in fenestra *add.* M

[39]Psalmi 54:24: "Viri sanguinum et dolosi non dimidiabunt dies suos."

[40]Proverbia 18:3: "Impius, cum in profundum uenerit peccatorem, contemnit."

[41]Psalmi 10:13: "Propter quid irritauit impius Deum? Dixit enim in corde suo: Non requiret."

[42]Zacharias 5:6–9

(3) *Beatus uenter qui te.*[43]

Beatus sibi et beatus nobis. Beatus sibi, quia non solum a beatitudine mentis que erat gratia plena, sed etiam respectu uentris ipsius. Beatitudo autem, ut dicit Boetius,[44] < est > «status omnium bonorum congregatione perfectus.» Status autem qui habent aliquid boni respectu uentris sunt tres, uirginum, coniugatorum et continencium.

Bonum respectu uentris in statu uirginum est integritas, in statu coniugatorum fecunditas, in statu continencium castitas. Beata autem Virgo de statu uirginum habuit summam integritatem, de statu coniugatorum summam fecunditatem, de statu continencium summam castitatem, et sic habuit statum omnium bonorum que sunt respectu uentris congregatione perfecta.

Fuit enim beata Virgo < integra > cum uirginibus, fecunda cum coniugatis, casta cum continentibus, unde Eccli. XXIIII:[45] *In Iacob inhabita,* per quem intelliguntur coniugati, quia semper sunt in lucta huius seculi, *et in Israel hereditare,* per quem intelliguntur continentes, quia quando hoc nomen in lucta accepit cum angelo, emarcuit neruus femoris eius, in quo continencia, *et in electis meis mitte radices;* electi sunt uirgines.

Item fuit beatus uenter Virginis propter summam beatitudinem, id est Trinitatem que habitauit in ea specialiter ratione uentris. Fuit enim sponsa Patris, mater Filii, sacrarium Spiritus sancti.

Fuit enim beatus uenter Virginis propter tria alia que sunt inpossibilia in alio uentre. Venter enim eius concepit sine corruptione, gestauit sine labore, peperit sine lesione, Luce I:[46] *Spiritus sanctus superueniet,* et ideo concipies sine corruptione, *uirtus Altissimi obumbrabit,* et ideo gestabis sine dolore, *quod nascetur uocabitur Filius,* et ideo paries sine lesione.

Item fuit beatus nobis quia portauit nostram beatitudinem. Ipse enim fuit thesaurus qui portauit precium nostre redemptionis, Numeri. XX:[47] *Domine Deus, audi clamorem populi tui et aperi,* id est produc et ostende beatam uirginem. Item fuit apoteca et domus aromatum nobis, de qua processit medicina nostre curationis, Eccli. XXXVIII:[48] *Altissimus de terra,* id est de beata Virgine de qua Psalmista: *Et terra nostra dabit fructum suum,*[49] id est *creauit* medicinam. Item fuit ager plenus qui protulit nostre refectionis odorem, Gen. XXVIII: *Ecce odor.*[50]

[43]Lucas 11:27: "Beatus uenter qui te portauit."
[44]Boethius, *De consolatione philosophiae* 3 prosa 2 (CCSL 94:38, 1.10; PL 63:724A).
[45]Ecclesiasticus 24:13
[46]Lucas 1:35
[47]Numeri 20:6: "Domine Deus, audi clamorem huius populi et aperi eis thesaurum tuum fontem aquae uiuae."
[48]Ecclesiasticus 38:4: "Altissimus creauit de terra medicamenta."
[49]Psalmi 24:13
[50]Genesis 27:27: "Ecce odor filii mei sicut odor agri pleni."

NOTES

1. See L.-J. Bataillon, "De la lectio à la predicatio: Commentaires bibliques et sermons au XIII^c siècle," *Revue des sciences philosophiques et théologiques* 70 (1986): 559–564.

2. Anthony of Padua, *Sermones dominicales et festivi* (Padua, 1974).

3. Bonaventure, *Opera omnia* 9 (Quaracchi, 1901). Superseded in part by Bonaventure, *Sermones dominicales,* ed. J.-G. Bougerol, Bibliotheca franciscana scholastica medii aevi 27 (Grottaferrata, 1977).

4. N. Beriou, *La prédication de Ranulphe de la Houblonnière: Sermons aux clercs et aux simples gens à Paris au XIIIe siècle,* 2 vols., Études augustiniennes (Paris, 1987).

5. J. Longère, *La prédication médiévale* (Paris, 1983), 82–84; F. Morenzoni, "La promotion de la prédication dans les paroisses au début du XIII^c siècle: La *Summa de arte predicandi* de Thomas de Chobham, étude et édition critique du texte "(Thesis, University of Geneva, 1989) 1:206–212; O. Pontal, "Les statuts de Paris et le Synodal de l'Ouest," *Les statuts synodaux français du XIIIe siècle* (Paris, 1971), 72 n. 62; 84 n. 83; 226.

6. Maura O'Carroll, "The Lectionnary for the Proper of the Year in the Dominican and Franciscan Rites of the Thirteenth Century," *Archivum Fratrum Praedicatorum* 49 (1979): 79–103.

7. Romans, 5 verses; 1 Corinthians, 61; Galatians, 50; Ephesians, 38; 2 Corinthians, 43; Philippians, 25; 1 Peter, 33.

8. To be complete, there were four readings from Philippians (25 verses), three from 1 John (21), two each from Colossians (8) and James (11), and one from 1 Thessalonians (7).

9. I take the days where there was preaching in the Cistercian custom, excepting of course St. Benedict and St. Bernard, and adding Ash Wednesday, Holy Week, and All Souls.

10. Exodus, 11 verses; Proverbs 14; Ecclesiastes, 10; Isaiah, 29; Hosea, 7; Joel 8; Malachi, 4.

11. Matthew, 53 verses; Mark, 7; Luke, 55; 1 Corinthians, 20; Titus, 5; Hebrews, 12; Acts, 23; Revelations, 11.

12. P. Glorieux, *Répertoire des maîtres en théologie de l'université de Paris au XIIIe siècle* (Paris, 1934), 2:279. See also Schneyer, *Repertorium der Lateinischen Sermones des Mittelalters,* BGPTMA 43.1–11 (Münster 1969–90) 2:2–15.

13. Schneyer, *Repertorium* 2:4, n. 28. I am using Tours, Bibliothèque Municipale 483, f. 59vb.

14. The total number of biblical quotations is nineteen, with eleven taken from the Old Testament. In a *reportatio* of this sermon from Laon, Bibliothèque municipale 289, f.54v–55r, etc.), forty-one scriptural verses are used.

15. J. Longère, *Oeuvres oratoires de maîtres parisiens* (Paris, 1975) 1:14–18.

16. As the Latin text is not yet published, the medieval French translation must be used. See C. A. Robson, *Maurice of Sully and the Medieval Vernacular Homily* (Oxford, 1952).

17. A. Solignac, "Raoul Ardent (Radulphus Ardens)," in *Dictionnaire de Spritualité* 13:97–106, and J. Longère, *Oeuvres oratoires* 1:30–31.

18. Radulphus Ardens, *Sermones de tempore*, PL 155:1667–2118. There is also the collection *De sanctis,* PL 155:1301–1626.

19. PL 155:1805–1811.

20. On Thomas of Lentini, see A. Redigonda, "Agni (Thommaso)," in *Diccionario biografico degli Italiani* (Rome, 1960) 1:499–500. An incomplete list of his sermons is given in Schneyer, *Repertorium* 5:642–662 (nos. 162–500), under the mistaken name of Thomas de Lisle. I use Biblioteca Apostolica Vaticana, Vat. lat. 4961, f. 42vb–43rb.

21. See Schneyer, *Repertorium* 4:727 (no. 43). I use Assisi, Bibliotheca communale 452, and Roma, Archivum Generale Fratrum Praedicatorum XIV 38a.

22. 1 Peter, 4 occurrences; Job, Psalms, Matthew, 3 each; Jeremiah, Isaiah, John, 2 each; Genesis, Song of Songs, Wisdom, Lamentations, Ezekiel, Habacuc, 1 Corinthians, 2 Corinthians, 1 John, Revelations, 1 each.

23. Schneyer, *Repertorium* 4:727 (no. 32, Assisi 452, ff. 28ra–29rb; Roma, Arch. Gen. Frat. Praed. XIV 38a, ff. 28v, 17r). See also Appendix II.

24. See L.-J. Bataillon, "Les sermons attribués à saint Thomas: questions d'authenticité," in *Thomas von Aquin,* Miscellanea Mediaevalia 19 (Berlin and New York, 1988), 331.

25. Schneyer, *Repertorium* 5:587 (no. 99). Compare Thomas Aquinas, *Opera omnia* (Parma, 1864) 15:155b–156a, and Thomas, *Opera omnia* (Paris, 1876) 24:234.

26. There are others. Leviticus, Hebrews, and 1 Peter are quoted twice each; Job, Jeremiah, Matthew, Luke, Romans, 2 Corinthians, Philippians, and Titus, once.

27. Schneyer, *Repertorium,* 586 (no. 85). In Thomas Aquinas, *Opera omnia* (Parma), 146b–147a; 148ab; (Paris, 221, 223).

28. D. L. d'Avray, *The Preaching of the Friars: Sermons Diffused From Paris Before 1300* (Oxford, 1985).

29. D. L. d'Avray, "Pierre de Saint Benoît," in *Dictionnaire de Spiritualité* 12:1667–69.

30. C. Schmitt, "Nicholas de Biard," in *Dictionnaire de Spiritualité* 11: 254–255; and T. Kaeppeli, *Scriptores ordinis praedicatorum medii aevi* (Rome, 1970–) 3:148–153.

31. Kaeppeli, *Scriptores* 2:118–121.

32. L.-J. Bataillon, *"Similitudines* et *exempla* dans les sermons du XIIIe siècle," in *The Bible in the Medieval World: Essays in Memory of Beryl Smalley* (Oxford: 1985), 191–205.

33. Sermon "Erat Iesus . . . ," Schneyer, *Repertorium* 2:485 (no. 27); ed. N. Beriou in *La prédication* 2:329–337.

34. The remaining are taken from the Pentateuch (3), the historical books (7), the Psalms (4), Matthew (6), Mark (2), John (2), and Paul (3).

35. Glorieux, *Répertoire des maîtres en théologie* 1:272–273; Schneyer, *Repertorium* 3:510–566.

36. Schneyer, *Repertorium* 3:514 (nos. 61–62, Paris, B.N. MS lat. 15935, ff. 61va–64ra, and MS lat. 16464, ff. 73va–76rb). See Appendix 1.

37. The division into verses was not yet in use in the thirteenth century, but in fact John of Abbeville's divisions correspond exactly to the modern ones.

38. Paris, B.N. MS lat. 15935, ff. 62vb–63ra, and MS lat. 16464, f. 75ra: "Mutus quoque est peccator quia bibet de aquis secularium delitiarum in quibus congesta sunt maledicta veteris et novi testamenti, et compacta sunt labia eius et factus est autus sicut legitur quod Samuel in Mosphat effudit aquas in quibus congesta sunt maledicta, de quibus si biberet ydolatra, labia eius inseparabiliter sibi coherebant." The texts are 1 Kings 7:5–6 conflated with Numbers 5:18–28. Cf. Peter Comester, *Historia scolastica,* 1 Kings 9 (PL 198:1302C): "Cumque ascendissent in Masphath effundens aquam coram Domino in qua maledicta congesta erant, quam si isoloatra bibebat labia eius adhaerebant sibi inseparabiliter."

39. Kaeppeli, *Scriptores* 1:292. For his sermons, see C. Cenci, "Il Commento al Vangelo di S. Luca di Fr. Costantino da Orvieto, O. P., Fonte di S. Bernardino da Siena," in *Archivum Franciscanum Historicum* 74 (1974): 103–145.

40. München, Bayerische Staatsbibliothek Clm 7794, ff. 47v–48r.

41. München, Clm 7794, ff. 34vb–36ra. See Appendix 3.

42. William of Auvergne, *Opera omnia* (1674) 2:225–231.

43. See Hugh of St. Cher, *In Evangelia secundum Matthaeum, Lucam, Marcum et Ioannem Opus admirabile* . . . (Venice, 1754) 6:201r–203r. For one example concerning Luke 11:17, see f. 201vb: "Non ergo hic respondet verbis signa quaerentium, sed blasphemantium. Quibus obviat dupliciter. Primo utitur indirecta ratione, postea directa, sicut ex ipso textu Evangelii patebit. Et est indirecta ratiocinatio, cum pars adversarii sumpta, et ad inconveniens ducta, falsa esse ostenditur, et sic deinceps ad veritatem redditur. . . ." Compare William, 213b–214a: "Primo probat dominus indirecta probatione quod non expellit daemones in principe daemoniorum: deinde probatione directa. Probatio indirecta est, cum parte adversarii sumpta, ad inconveniens ducitur, ut ad veritatem redeatur. . . ."

44. N. Beriou, *La prédication* 1:80–82, 2:85–98 (Ranulph's sermon), 2: 329–337 (Mailly's sermon), and 2:337–342 (Biard's). Both Mailly and Biard have probably made some use of Peraldus.

Abelard and the Medieval Origins of the Distinction between God's Absolute and Ordained Power

Stephen F. Brown

Let me tell you why the maker and producer of the world made the universe. He was good. And no goodness can ever have any jealousy of anything. And being free of jealousy he desired that all things should be as like himself as possible. This is the true beginning of the world, as we shall do well in believing on the teaching of wise men: God, desiring that all things should be good and nothing bad, in so far as this could be accomplished, begot offspring.[1] (Plato, *Timaeus*, 29D–30A)

IF WILLIAM OF ST. THIERRY had written the *Story of Abelard's Calamities,* one of the great calamities he would have included in his account would have been Peter's use of this *Timaeus* text of Plato. For Abelard used this text frequently throughout his career and on different issues. His approach to the *Timaeus,* however, was not that of a *lector.* There is no evidence that he ever wrote a literal commentary on the Platonic text made available in part to medieval Latin thinkers through the translation of Chalcidius. His treatments of this *Timaeus* passage are often in the educational framework of the *quaestio,* so often associated with him and his school.[2] Not only is this true of the *Sic et Non,* where we would expect it, it is also true of the later *Theologies* he authored.[3] In Abelard's works this text of Plato is frequently surrounded by conflicting interpretations of the issues raised by Plato's text. The conflicting authorities — the Scriptures, the Fathers, or other ancient writers — stimulated a *quaestio* that begged for an answer.

We have said that he used the *Timaeus* passage we quoted throughout his career and on different issues. For one, he used it to show that God the Father, being good and not jealous of sharing his

199

goodness, had to produce a Son equal to himself. Although it might be quite shocking, and was shocking to William of St. Thierry, that Abelard would use a pagan to show the coequality of the Father and the Son, still Abelard here could bring Augustine and Jerome to his defense.[4] Certainly they did not quote these words of the *Timaeus* explicitly, but doubtless their argument comes from that source, for Augustine in chapter 64 of his *Book of 83 Questions* declared: "God when he generated could not generate someone better than himself, so he had to generate someone equal to himself. For if he *chose* to generate and could not, he would have been weak. If he *could* generate and chose not to, he would have been jealous."[5] And the anonymous writer who penned the seventeenth letter attributed to Jerome likewise argued: "If the Son were not equal to the Father in all things, then the Father would either be jealous or powerless."[6]

But if William of St. Thierry could not disagree with the argument of Abelard on this point, only to his use of Plato as a support for the characteristically Christian doctrine of the Trinity, he had much more to be upset about in a further application of the *Timaeus* text by Abelard.

In the *Theologia Christiana,* the *Theologia 'Scholarium',* and in the *Expositio in Hexaemeron* Abelard argues from this same *Timaeus* text that God could only create what in fact he did create and could not produce a better universe than he has produced.[7] For Abelard, God had to work in accord with the full nature of his goodness. Goodness is for God not an accidental quality. He is substantial goodness. So, when God creates, he cannot be stingy or miserly. Just as the Father could not spare himself in producing the Son and make the Son less than the Son could be — otherwise he would be miserly (and therefore not substantially good) — so the Creator could not hold back something and not make the world the best that he could make it be. For, in such a case, the Creator would be miserly.

Abelard further argued that whatever God does, he does for the best and wisest reason — even if it be hidden from us. God's nature is such that he has thus to create what is wisest and best. The world he actually created must be the best that the most wise God could create. Otherwise, he could have planned in a more wise manner, which is impossible because of his being most wise. If one rejects this option, one falls back to the previous dilemma — that God planned most wisely, but he held back on the side of his goodness — that is, he was selfish. Or one might say that God is most wise, and most good, but not most powerful—that he planned most wisely, and was generous in his desire to share his goodness, but could not accomplish his will.

As Abelard first set up his reflection on God's will, he saw only two commanding alternatives. One view was suggested by Jerome when he gave his account of Nabuchodonosor's view of God's will. For Nabuchodonosor, God's will is pure will. God chooses to do something and wants to do it just because he chooses it. God's will, in this view of it, is not directed by his goodness, nor by his wisdom. God's freedom is pure choice. According to Abelard, Jerome contrasts this view with his own position in the following words: "'It is not what God wills that he does, but rather it is what is good that he wills,' as if he were to say: God does not act as Nabuchodonosor thinks, namely, after the manner of those who do what they want, and do not pay attention to what is good but rather pursue the satisfaction of their own will, no matter what it might be. Of those who act in this willful manner, it is written: 'This is what I want. This is what I command. My will is its own reason.'"[8] Nabuchodonosor's God is a tyrannical god of pure will.

The other commanding alternative is that which Jerome himself seems to follow in order to avoid Nabuchodonosor's willful God, as also does Augustine in certain writings where he attempts to avoid a world based on fortune or chance.[9] It is the alternative represented by the *Timaeus*. Abelard says it is based on the Platonic principle or *illa Platonis verissima ratio*: "Everything that is caused is caused by a necessary cause. For nothing takes place that is not preceded by a legitimate cause and reason."[10] Now, since God is as good as he can be and cannot lose any goodness, it is necessary for him to choose each thing as well as he can. If he has the will to do something, then he necessarily has to do it, since he does not lack the power to accomplish it. His goodness is so great that it necessarily compels him to do those good things which ought to be done. Nor can he at all abstain from what he does, or do it better, or more quickly.[11]

These are the two commanding alternatives—the *pro* and *contra* that make up the opposing forces of Abelard's *quaestio*, the instruments to stimulate the search for a deeper understanding of the texts cited and the issues involved. Knowing that he would never be accused of Nabuchodonosor's contention that God acts without reason, Abelard is very careful to note that Plato's optimistic thesis (and Jerome and Augustine's use of it) is not his own position: "This position is remote from the truth and also is remote from our opinion."[12]

What, then, is Peter's own position? We have already indicated, in effect, how he would answer the question: "Can God make more things or better things than he does make, or could he in any way cease to make the things he makes, so that he would never make them?" What, however, does Peter mean by his response? We know that he does not want to say with Nabuchodonosor that "God can make and do whatever he wants." Nor does he agree with the interpretation of Plato that would say "God has to make whatever he makes and make them the best that they can be, because his goodness compels him to do what he does."

Abelard's own response needs clarification. Following largely on different texts of Augustine, Peter recognizes that traditionally God has been seen as capable of saving humanity in a different way than he did, that in the Book of Wisdom God's servants hoped that God would (and thus could) bring many more torments on the impious, and that in the Gospel of Matthew Christ ordered his disciple to put his sword back in its sheath with the words "Do you think that I cannot call upon my Father and he will provide me at this moment with more than twelve legions of angels?" In short, Abelard realizes that things could be different. However, the way in which he explains these contingencies never succumbs to placing contingency in God himself. To that extent, and in this manner, he holds to Plato's side:

> And accordingly we have seen that God—who is supremely good, and who can neither increase nor diminish in goodness, since he is naturally and substantially good by his very nature and not good by an accidental quality after our human manner—is always, if I may speak in human terms, incited to such a degree by his own ineffable goodness that what he wills he necessarily wills and what he does he necessarily does. [13]

We must remember, however, if we wish to grasp Peter's position, that he says his own opinion is far from the interpretation of Plato that would go a step further and say: "Therefore, he makes created things as good as they can be." For Abelard, this would be akin to saying: God must save man, therefore he must make it that man cannot not be saved. [14] It wrongly transfers a necessity that belongs to God to a necessity that also belongs to creatures. Keeping to this salvation example, we get a glimpse of the distinction Peter wants to make. Because of his substantial goodness, wisdom, justice, and mercy, God by his nature must necessarily choose the best way to save all human beings; this does not mean that all human beings must necessarily be saved. [15]

In a parallel way, God necessarily does what is the best, and so Peter answers the question by saying God could only create what in fact he did create and could not produce a better universe than he has produced. On his part, the Creator could not hold back something and not make the world the best that he could make it be. He has necessary reasons for what he does, even though these reasons, as we have said, may be hidden from us. [16] Continuing the parallel with human salvation, however, Abelard insists that creatures on their part are not necessarily produced.

> It is, therefore, necessary for God to do that which is not necessary that it be done by him. In the case of 'it is necessary for God to do it,' the force of necessity is applied to the immutable God; in the case of 'it is not necessary that it be done by him' the denial of necessity is applied to the changeable event of his operation, an event that just as equally can happen or not happen. [17]

The contingency of creation, on its side, is not something over which Abelard and his contemporaries disagreed. Where they did disagree was over the necessity involved in God's creating. Abelard, siding with Plato, claims that God had to create the best. His goodness compelled him to do so. Disagreeing with an interpretation of Plato that would make creation in itself necessary and best, Abelard claims that, on its part, creation has no necessity about it. Is his position meant also as a new interpretation of the *Timaeus* text of Plato? Abelard makes no claim that it is, although he has elsewhere pushed to a deeper understanding of Plato's texts and may well be doing so here. [18]

In the other direction, however, William of St. Thierry definitely places the blame of introducing necessity into the manner in which God creates on Peter's reading of Plato: "In this he would rather imitate Plato whom he loves . . . than defer to the things toward which Paul sends us, to the depths of the wisdom and knowledge of God and his inscrutable judgments and incomprehensible ways, . . . for he [Peter] tries to examine and evaluate all things through the power of reason. Does he put his faith in Plato? I know for sure that he does." [19]

Now Abelard knew his position was novel and that he did not have the unambivalent support of Augustine and Jerome to back him up. In the third redaction of the *Theologia 'Scholarium'* he states that "although our opinion has few or none who agree with it, and for the most part goes against what the Fathers have said, and seems to some small degree even to be at odds with reason, yet I think that God can only create what he has in fact created."[20]

One can see immediately that William of St. Thierry and Peter Abelard must have two different views of Plato—if not to say philosophic reason, pagan literature, and even of God's providential directing of history. Tullio Gregory provides us with the best summary appreciation that I could find:

> The use of Platonic texts by Abelard is not the result of a circumstantial choice to underscore some more or less happenstance agreements; on the contrary, this corresponds to a fundamental attitude present in all the theological works of Abelard. It is an attitude that implies a precise conception of *ratio* considered as a means of revelation itself. . . . This is the reason for the particular interpretation of Platonic texts, and the constant effort of reading the *mysteria [Dei]* in the depths of the *littera [Platonis]*. Those who lean more to underline the disagreement between Platonic texts and the teachings of the Bible or St. Augustine—such as William of St. Thierry—will be scandalized by the method of Abelard. This will be because they stop at the letter—Abelard would say—because they've given up on finding a deeper understanding of God hidden in the Platonic text.[21]

William of St. Thierry, however, not only wrote a *Disputatio adversus Petrum Abelardum;* he also wrote a letter—to Bernard of Clairvaux. Yet Bernard did not need much convincing. He already had his own judgment concerning Abelard, so he worked diligently and successfully to get him condemned.[22]

Despite Abelard's condemnation (perhaps even because of it), his thesis concerning the identity of God's power (what he could do) and will (what he does) did not die. It lived on as the opponent's position for another hundred years or more in the works of the systematic theologians. Even though the author of the *Summa sententiarum,* Hugh of St. Victor in his *De sacramentis fidei Christianae,* and Peter Lombard in his *Sentences* might pick up the rhetoric of Bernard, Thomas, and William as they speak of Abelard as "puffed up by his knowledge" or as "glorying in his own powers," it is for grammatical and logical tools that they primarily reach in their efforts to refute the Abelardian arguments derived from the *Timaeus*.[23]

Abelard's Platonic arguments, according to Lombard, are basically these:

1. God can only do what is just and good, and it is only just and good for him to do what he does. For if there were some other just and good things to do, then he did not see and do everything that it was just and good for him to do. And who would dare to say such a thing?

2. Likewise, God can only do what his justice demands, and that justice only demands that he do what he does, so he can only do what he does.[24]

Lombard, who gives the best organized and most detailed analysis of the issue, faces the first argument in this way:

> The first part of the major 'God can only do what is just and good' needs to be distinguished: 'God can only do what, if he would choose to do it, would be just and good' is true, but there are many things which he can do which are neither just nor good, because they neither are nor will be, nor will they become just or good, since they will never happen. If, however, you take the statement to mean God can only do what he actually does and his power to do anything is limited to this, then it is false.
>
> Likewise, the major of the second argument 'God can only do what his justice demands' has a double sense. If you understand it to mean he can only do what his just will demands, that is, only what his just will actually chooses, it's a false statement. If by these words, however, you mean that he can only do that which, if he would choose to do it, would agree with his justice, then you are correct.[25]

In such ways Lombard tries to show why Abelard was wrong in arguing that God could only create what he does create. Peter had failed to see that there is a distinction between God's power and his will.

Furthermore, the author of the *Summa sententiarum* argues that God could also have created a better world. For there is no parallel between arguing that God the Father had to produce God the Son as an equal or he would be jealous and that *a simili* he had to produce the best world or he would have been jealous. Such an *a simili* argument is not justified, for in begetting the Son, God the Father begot of his own substance; if he did not beget an equal he would have been jealous. But, unlike the Son, the created world is not made up of God's substance, so he did not have to create the world equal to himself. Other things, distinct in substance, he can make better than he has made them.[26]

Basically, what Lombard did, following Hugh of St. Victor and the author of the *Summa sententiarum,* and employing explanations found in the Fathers, especially Augustine, and in the exegetes, like Anselm of Laon in the *Glossa interlinearis,* was to introduce a distinction between God's *power* (in the sense of what he could do) and his actual *will* (in the sense of what he chose to do). The more systematic theologians of the thirteenth century will provide this distinction with a technical vocabulary and attempt to clarify its meaning and distinguish this meaning from false interpretations.

Alexander of Hales, who turned Lombard's *Sentences* into the official theology text alongside the Bible at Paris, shows these efforts in his *Glossa in Sententias,* but even more so in his *Summa* where he asks if God's power and will have the same extension:

> If we consider the divine power *absolutely,* and compare it to the divine will, then the power is of greater extension than the will. But if we consider power as ordained (*ordinata*) power—and by this ordination we mean *preordination*—then power and will are of equal extension. Absolute power, therefore, is distinct from ordained power (*Distinguitur ergo potentia absoluta a potentia ordinata*). We speak of absolute power with regard to things or events which God has not foreordained; whereas we speak of ordained power with regard to things or events which have been foreordained or predisposed.[27]

Here we have our distinction with the technical vocabulary: *potentia absoluta* and *potentia ordinata.* Yet, even though Alexander's statement of it has a mark of clarity about it, by stressing that *ordinata* really means *preordinata* (preordained, predisposed, chosen, willed) he lets us know that the distinction is not one of ordered (*ordinata*) power in contrast to disordered or despotic power, but accentuates the chosen or willed order without suggesting any disorder among the non-chosen or non-foreordained alternatives. *Ordinata* means 'ordered', but it does not mean only that; it also means 'ordained'.

However, for some of his readers suggestions of no disorder were not enough. Bonaventure had still some doubts about the meaning of these technical words. In the seventh *dubium* at the end of Distinction 43 of *Book I of the Sentences,* Bonaventure notes:

> Some distinguish at this point the power of God by saying God can do something either by his absolute power or by his ordained power. But this distinction seems unsuitable, for God can do nothing that he does in a disorderly way. To be able to do something in a disorderly manner is weakness. [28]

And Richard of Middleton, but only to clarify, also worries about the meaning of *potestas ordinata.* If one means by *potestas ordinata* the power of God which alone is directed by his wisdom, then it is absurd to say that God can realize by his absolute power what he could not do by his ordained (in the sense of ordered-by-wisdom) power, that is, that he would will what is unreasonably or badly ordered. However, one might understand that he argues the distinction differently: that God can, absolutely speaking, do everything that is not contradictory or contrary to his attributes. For given that God has freely placed a certain order among creatures, it is manifest that there is an infinity of other possible and perfectly good things that could have been chosen by God absolutely speaking. If one understands the expression *potentia ordinata* in this second sense, that is, the power of God insofar as it is related to the order actually realized, the distinction between God's absolute and ordained power is legitimate, and one can say that God can (has the power to) do some things by his absolute power which he cannot do by his ordained power (since he does not will to alter his preordination): For absolutely, he can do what does not include a contradiction. [29]

Richard, in effect, has incorporated Bonaventure's objection and, while expressing himself more clearly than Alexander of Hales, returns to the original meaning Alexander gave to the technical term *ordinata.* It does not mean 'orderly' as opposed to 'disorderly', but 'preordainedly' or 'actually chosen' or 'willed' as opposed to what was not preordained or chosen.

Others, e.g., Peter of Trabes the *vox altera* of Peter John Olivi, see the distinction being misunderstood not only because of the equivocal character hidden in the word *ordinata,* but just as much, if not more, by the meaning of *potentia* in the expressions *potentia absoluta* and *potentia ordinata* and in the verbal forms *potest* and *posse* employed in many propositions dealing with the issue. In the solution to the sixth question of Distinction 43, he tries to steer clear of having his students think there are two powers (in the sense of two wills) in God. He argues:

> Commonly a distinction is made between God's being able to do some things by his absolute power and some things by his ordained power. By his absolute power God is said to be able to do whatever falls under the definition of the term 'possible', because he does not lack the power to realize whatever is capable of being realized. By his ordained power, however, he is said to be able to do only those things which his will commands to be done and which his wisdom dictates and appoints to be done.
>
> If we speak of God's absolute power, it is clear that he can do what he does not do, since God is an agent acting with infinite power, not limited or determined to some specified class of possible things. Also he is an agent acting not by the necessity of his nature but through the freedom of his will. Because of the first (his infinite power) he can do the things he does and many others, since those which he does are finite. Because of the second (his freedom) he can do more or fewer or other things according to the freedom of his will. . . .
>
> If we speak of his ordained power, since that order and number of things is established and foreordained eternally by divine wisdom and will, not otherwise, then although he is able to do other things, yet it could never happen that he would act otherwise. That is why we stressed at times that he is able to do other things or do things differently. For the 'to do' (*facere*) is subject to the preordination of the divine will and the preordination of his wisdom, but this is not the case with the power (*posse*) itself, since it precedes such preordination according to the order of our understanding.[30]

In short, when we speak of God's absolute power and say 'God can do anything possible', we mean that 'God does not lack the power to do whatever is possible'. Maybe, as Gedeon Gál suggests in summing up Peter of Trabes's position, it would help if we followed Peter's advice and used the formula 'does not lack the power to do' instead of 'can do'. For the statement 'does not lack the power to do' does not suggest that some day by his absolute power God might do other things or do things otherwise, the way 'he can do other things' might suggest. For God does nothing by his absolute power; indeed it is absolutely impossible for God to do anything at all *de potentia absoluta*. All divine doing is *de potentia ordinata*.[31]

Peter of Trabes wrote between 1290–1295, and when we first read his treatment of the issue we feel that the Abelard of tradition is the lone opponent. Why not? All the *pro* and *contra* arguments are found in the twelfth-century sources. But a certain phrase stands out indicating that we are dealing with some intruders. It is the phrase "not by the necessity of his nature but through the freedom of his will." This is not an expression that would be used against Abelard. It sends one back to look for it in authors before Peter of Trabes. Already one may observe that with Thomas Aquinas a slight shift of focus is taking place; not, however, in the original meaning of the distinction as found in Alexander of Hales. For although the treatment is more developed in Dist. 43, q. 2 of Book I and in Dist. 1 of Book III of Thomas's *Sentences,* and in article 5 of question 25 of the *Pars prima* of the *Summa theologiae,* and in the *Contra gentiles,* Book II, cc. 23 and 26, and Book III, c. 98, Thomas still holds to Alexander's basic understanding. In article 5 of the first question of the *De potentia,* however, he introduces to the discussion some new associates for Peter Abelard:

> I answer that this error, namely that God can do only what he does, belongs to two sources: first, it was the error of certain phi-losophers declaring that God acts out of the necessity of his na-ture (*ex necessitate naturae*). Which, if this were the case, since a nature is determined to one effect, the divine power could not extend itself to do other things than the ones which it does. Sec-ondly, it was the error of certain theologians . . . and is imputed to Peter Abelard.[32]

A discussion that flourished in the twelfth and early thirteenth century, and a discussion very much set by Abelard's terms and argu-ments, begins to face, in Thomas's era and thereafter, a much greater challenge of necessitarianism. It does not show its face clearly at first, but in Aquinas's *De potentia* and Book III of the *Contra gentiles,* the new challenge is peeking through. It is also there, but very subtly, in the text of Peter of Trabes. However, when one reads Henry of Ghent and Duns Scotus, one finds that Abelard has for the most part gone to the happy oblivion William of St. Thierry and Bernard of Clair-vaux had hoped for him, and Henry and Scotus face these new philo-sophical opponents.[33]

What Abelard and these philosophers had in common was that none of them could find a way to prevent their God from causing nec-essarily. The problem that the distinction between God's absolute and ordained power most fundamentally faced was to explain how God

creates freely, or as Scotus put it more precisely: how God causes everything distinct from himself not necessarily but voluntarily.

Abelard saw some reason on the side of free or voluntary creation,[34] and he admits that to say that God can only create what he
does create is derogatory to God's excellence (*multum derogat divinae
excellentiae*). But Peter saw more reason to follow the Platonic side: "the
deed of him who is the best can never be or have been other than
the fairest." To say that God does not act according to the fullness of
his power would make him jealous of sharing what he could, or in
plain words, it would make him stingy. To admit that God does not
give the absolute best is derogatory to his goodness (*Multum summae
eius bonitate derogabimus*).

Abelard's twelfth-century opponents well knew the authorities
that were contrary to Peter's position, and, supposing the truth of the
position that God could create other things than he did create, they
were able to make the necessary logical distinctions to challenge his
arguments. Lombard, following the *Summa sententiarum* and Hugh of
St. Victor, does this very ably. Nonetheless, they lacked the philosophical basis to refute him directly. In the thirteenth century, as we can
see especially in Thomas Aquinas's *De potentia,* the argumentation
against Abelard's position goes beyond the logical level and becomes
more directly and properly philosophical.

God's goodness, for both Aquinas and Abelard, is really identical with the divine substance. If there are differences between the
two views of God's goodness, one of those differences would be that
for Aquinas God's goodness is self-sufficient, and it alone compels his
will:

> It is necessary that every will have some end that it naturally
> wills, and the contrary of which it cannot will, as a man, for ex-
> ample, naturally and necessarily wills happiness and cannot will
> misery. Along with the will necessarily willing its natural end,
> it also necessarily wills those things without which it cannot at-
> tain its end, if it knows this to be the case, since these means
> are things that are commensurate with its end. If, for example,
> I choose life, then I also will choose the food that sustains this
> life. Those things, however, which are such that the end can be
> attained without them are not commensurate with the will and
> the will does not choose them necessarily.
>
> The natural end of the divine will is his goodness, which
> he cannot not will. Creatures, on the other hand, are not com-

mensurate to this end which is the divine goodness, so the divine goodness can still manifest itself without their existence, even though God intends to manifest his goodness through creatures. Just as the divine goodness is manifested through the created things that now exist and through the present order of things, so also can that goodness be manifested through other creatures and through creatures arranged according to a different order. Thus, the divine will, without any prejudice to the divine goodness, justice, or wisdom can extend itself to things other than the things it has made. Now, the reason why he [Peter Abelard] was led astray was because he thought that the present order of creatures was, as it were, commensurate with the divine goodness, almost as though the divine goodness could not exist without the present order of creatures.[35]

According to Thomas, the self-sufficiency of God's goodness as the final cause of his will entails many corollaries. His goodness is the perfect manifestation of itself to God himself. No further manifestation of this goodness by creatures who participate in it, but add nothing to it, is required. God, therefore, is not compelled to create. If he chooses to create, then, he might be compelled to create whatever might be commensurate to the end he has in creating the created order he has chosen. That compulsion, however, is not absolute, in the sense that it had to be chosen in itself; rather, it is a compulsion *ex suppositione:* a compulsion to choose the necessary means to a freely chosen end.

Another difference between the views of Abelard and Aquinas concerning divine goodness indicated in this *De potentia* text is that for Abelard divine goodness fulfills the role of efficient cause, while for Aquinas it serves as final cause. It is true that when Abelard speaks of creatures, he does speak of God ordering them to himself as final cause, but when he speaks of God's will to create, he speaks of it in a way parallel to God the Father's necessary production of the Son. Aquinas, on the other hand, is very clear in emphasizing that God's goodness is the final cause of his willing. It draws the divine will to it inexorably; but it is the only end capable of doing so, for the divine will does not necessarily will any lesser good. There is no necessary reason, even within God himself, that compels God to create.

The distinction *de potentia Dei absoluta et ordinata,* whether expressed in this technical language or not, was primarily the instrument the twelfth- and thirteenth-century authors used to solve Abelard's dilemma and answer the necessitarianism of the philosophers.[36] God creates freely; his causality is contingent toward creatures. Yet this distinction, meant fundamentally to show the freedom and contingency of God's creative activity of itself or in itself does not pulverize natures or open up the floodgates of whimsicality. Scotus tried to show this at the end of his treatise on God's immutability in distinction 8 of the *Lectura:*

> The relation of a secondary cause to an effect presupposes the relation of the primary cause to a secondary one. Now the relation of the primary cause to any effect (and thus to any secondary cause since it is an effect) is contingent. Thus the relation of a secondary cause to its effect is contingent. And so no cause is *simpliciter* necessary in regard to its effect, but it is *secundum quid* necessary. For example, the relation of fire to burning is not *simpliciter* necessary. If it were *simpliciter* necessary, then in the furnace (spoken of in the Book of Daniel) the fire could not not burn the three boys. . . . But the action of the fire to burn is necessary *secundum quid*, because on the part of the fire itself it will always burn, and it is never in its power not to burn. But it does not cause unless God is causing, and so it does not necessarily cause in some absolute way.[37]

There are many other aspects of this so-called 'two powers distinction'. The *Summa sententiarum,* quoting Augustine, puts us on to the questions "Would it have been fitting for God to have redeemed the world in a different way?" or "Could God have made man to be such that he could not or would not choose to sin?" Albert the Great, going beyond the principle of Abelard's first argument, asks: "Did God do or can he do something which it is not just or good to have happen?" "Can he do unjust things? Or things outside or against justice?" Scotus will wonder whether, if we say God can make all possible things, the primary reason for something to be impossible is on the side of God or on the side of things themselves being impossible. The list of associated puzzles is almost interminable, and the issue is capable of great complications, as developments in the thirteenth and fourteenth century testify. However, until the time of Aquinas it was a simple question focused on Abelard as the opponent. In Henry of Ghent and Scotus, and thereafter, Abelard has disappeared and the philosophers, principally Avicenna, are the opponents. Abelard, nonetheless, provided the scholastics enough of a test that they had gathered and developed the logical, grammatical, and philosophical weapons they needed to meet the new challengers. Even though his name disappears, he still lives in a very real way in the debate that continues.

NOTES

1. Peter Abelard, *Theologia Christiana* 5.35, ed. E. M. Buytaert, CCCM 12 (Turnhout, 1969), 361–362; PL 178:1326. Compare Plato, *Timaeus a Calcidio translatus,* ed. J. H. Waszink (London, 1962), 22E.

2. For example, in the *Theologia Christiana* the discussion occurs within a series of questions, beginning with 5.29, "Quaerendum arbitror utrum plura facere possit Deus vel meliora quam faciat, aut ab his etiam quae facit ullo modo cessare posset, ne ea umquam videlicet faceret." In 5.41, he notes, "His itaque tam rationibus quam auctoritatibus graviter in utraque parte complexionis implicit, quo nos explicare possimus non facile aditum invenio. Quo enim vehementiores sunt *quaestionum* depugnationes, difficiliores profecto necesse est esse solutiones." On the development of the *quaestio,* see B. C. Bazán, "Les questions disputées, principalement dans les Facultés de Théologie," in *Les questions disputées et les questions quolibétiques dans les Facultés de Théologie, de Droit et de Médicine* (Turnhout, 1985), 25–31. Bazán provides a good summary and evaluation of previous studies on the development of the *quaestio.*

3. For the general use of the *Timaeus* in Abelard's works, see L. Moonan, "Abelard's Use of the *Timaeus,*" *Archives d'Histoire Doctrinale et Littéraire du Moyen Age* 57 (1990): 7–90. For specific consideration of the *Timaeus* text that we cite, see pp. 30–32 and 72–74.

4. *Theologia Christiana* 5.35b (Buytaert, 362; PL 178:1326). See also Abelard's *Theologia 'Scholarium'* 3.5 (PL 178:1094).

5. Abelard cites Chapter 64 of the *Book of 83 Questions,* but the reference is rather to Chapter 50 (PL 40:21–32; CCSL 44A:77).

6. Ps-Jerome, *Epist. 17 ad Cyrillum* (PL 30:183).

7. *Theologia Christiana* 5.29–58 (Buytaert, 358–372; PL 178:1324–1330).

8. Abelard, *Theologia Christiana* 5.35a–f (Buytaert, 362–363; PL 178:1324–1330); *Theologia 'Scholarium'* 3.5 (PL 178:1093–1095). Compare Jerome, *Commentariorum in Danielem libri tres* 1.4.32 (PL 25:517–518; CCSL 75A:818). See also the Vulgate renderings of Daniel 4:32 and Psalm 148:5.

9. Compare *Theologia Christiana* 5.35c–d (Buytaert, 362–363; PL 178:1327).

10. *Theologia Christiana* 5.30a, 35c (Buytaert, 359, 362; PL 178:1324, 1327).

11. *Theologia Christiana* 5.43 (Buytaert, 366; PL 178:1330).

12. *Theologia Christiana* 5.36 (Buytaert, 362–363; PL 178:1327): "Quod tam a veritate quam a nostra remotum est opinione."

13. Augustine's influence can be seen in detail in *Theologia Christiana* 5.38–40 (Buytaert, 364–365; PL 178:1328–1329). Our quotation concerning the necessity of God's choice and execution is found in *Theologia Christiana* 5.42 (Buytaert, 366; PL 178:1329–1330). Abelard repeats his position in his final summary, *Theologia Christiana* 6.57 (Buytaert, 371).

14. *Theologia Christiana* 5.37 (Buytaert, 364; PL 178:1328). Compare also 5.57 (Buytaert, 371).

15. *Theologia Christiana* 5.58 (Buytaert, 371–372), to which compare 5.33 (360–361; PL 178:1325–1326).

16. *Theologia Christiana* 5.45 (Buytaert, 367; PL 178:1330), to which compare 5.50 (369).

17. *Theologia Christiana* 5.58 (Buytaert, 371).

18. *Theologia Christiana* 4.138 (Buytaert, 335; PL 178:1310). Rather than giving a new interpretation to the *Timaeus,* however, Abelard might be trying to stress how he differs from Plato and from accusations made against him by stating that one interpretation of Plato is far removed from his own opinion.

19. William of St. Thierry, *Disputatio adversus Abaelardum* 8 (PL 180: 270). See also the critique by Thomas of Morigny, *Disputatio altera adversus Abaelardum* 3 (among the works of William at PL 180:318). Thomas blames Abelard for not studying Augustine more fully. See generally E. M. Buytaert, "Thomas of Morigny and the 'Apologia' of Abelard," *Antonianum* 41 (1966): 413–453, and M. B. Carra de Vaux St. Cyr, "Disputatio catholicorum patrum adversus dogmata Petri Abaelardi," *Revue des Sciences Philosophiques et Théologiques* 47 (1962): 481–495.

20. Abelard, *Theologiae 'Scholarium'* 3.5 (PL 178:1098).

21. Tullio Gregory, "Abélard et Platon," in *Peter Abelard: Proceedings of the International Conference, Louvain, May 10–12, 1971,* ed. E. M. Buytaert (Louvain and The Hague, 1974), 63–64.

22. Compare Peter Abelard, *Apologia contra Bernardum* 11, ed. E. M. Buytaert, CCCM 11 (Turnhout, 1969), 354–355 and 359–368.

23. Compare *Summa sententiarum* 1.14 (PL 171:1094–1096 or PL 176: 68–70); Hugh, *De sacramentis fidei Christianae* 1.2.22 (PL 176:214–215); Peter Lombard, *Sententiae* 1.42–43, ed. I. Brady, Spicilegium Bonaventurianum 4 (Grottaferrata, 1971) 1/2:294–303.

24. Peter Lombard, *Sententiae* 1.43 (Brady, 1/2:298–299). Compare Peter Abelard, *Theologiae 'Scholarium'* 3.5 (PL 178:1095).

25. Peter Lombard, *Sententiae* 1.43 (Brady, 1/2:299).

26. *Summa sententiarum* 1.14 (PL 171:1095 or PL 176:69).

27. Alexander of Hales, *Summa theologica* 1.1.4.1.2, ed. Collegium S. Bonaventurae (Quaracchi, 1924) 1:207. Compare Alexander's *Glossa in qua-*

tuor libros Sententiarum 1.43.8, ed. Collegium S. Bonaventurae (Quaracchi, 1951), 441–442, where, however, the treatment of the same question lacks the *Summa's* formal terminology.

28. Bonaventure, *Commentaria in quatuor libros Sententiarum* 1.43 dub. 7 resp, in *Opera omnia,* ed. Collegium S. Bonaventurae (Quaracchi, 1882–1902) 1:778.

29. Richard of Middleton, *In I Sententiarum* 1.43.7 corp (Venice, 1507), 387.

30. Peter of Trabes, *In I Sententiarum* 43.6 corp, ed. G. Gál in *Studies Honoring Ignatius Charles Brady, Friar Minor* (St. Bonaventure, N.Y., 1976), 290.

31. G. Gál, "Petrus de Trabibus on the Absolute and Ordained Power of God," in *Studies Honoring . . . Brady,* 289, and the passage cited in the preceding note.

32. Thomas Aquinas, *Quaestiones disputatae de potentia* 1.5 corp, in *Opera omnia,* ed. E. Fretté (Paris, 1889) 13:14.

33. Henry of Ghent, *Summa (Quaestiones ordinariae)* 14.5 (Paris, 1516) 2:59va–60vb.

34. Although Abelard does not specify what he means in saying that there is some reason on the side of the position that God can do more than he does, perhaps the Lombard offers a specification when he argues that "sine mutabilitate potentiae vel voluntatis potest Deus et alia velle et alia facere quam vult et facit. Quod etiam ratione probari potest. Non enim vult Deus omnes homines iustificare, et tamen quis dubitat eum posse? Potest ergo Deus aliud facere quam facit; et tamen si aliud faceret, alius ipse non esset. . . ." (*Sententiae* 1.43; Brady, 303).

35. Thomas Aquinas, *De potentia* 1.5 corp, in *Opera omnia* 13:15.

36. For the parallel application to the philosophers, see Thomas Aquinas, *De potentia* 1.5 (p. 15), and also John F. Wippel, "The Latin Avicenna as Source for Thomas Aquinas's Metaphysics," *Freiburger Zeitschrift für Philosophie und Theologie* 37 (1990): 51–90.

37. John Duns Scotus, *Lectura in I Sententiarum* 8.2.1, in *Opera omnia* (Vatican City, 1950–), 17:108, no. 285.

Some Aspects of the Reception of Aristotle's *Physics* and *Metaphysics* in the Thirteenth Century

Albert Zimmermann

DUE TO THE MANY long, patient, and intensive inquiries into the development of philosophy and the sciences in the twelfth and the first decades of the thirteenth century, we are now very well informed about the translation of the works of Aristotle into Latin and about their reception in the most important schools in Europe, above all the universities of Oxford and Paris. Translators as well as places and dates of various translations are known, and one is impressed by the astonishing learnedness contained in many historians' publications.

The phrase "the dark ages" is often still heard, and many otherwise quite well-educated people still have completely false ideas of the scientific and cultural life of the Middle Ages. One cannot help being astonished by these prejudices when one recalls the eagerness with which the medieval masters welcomed, studied, and commented upon the new scientific and philosophical works. Many of the numerous commentaries on Aristotle are the fruit of an extremely careful reading, of constant reflection, of an admirable skill in reasoning and argumentation, and of prudent judgment. The fact that we also meet extreme positions—an excessive veneration of Aristotle as well as an anxious rejection of the works of the "heathen"—does not justify the verdict still repeated by many of our contemporaries.

The writings of Aristotle, it seems, would never have attracted the medieval scholars had they not given rise to many grave questions that are sometimes most difficult to answer. Surely the medieval masters above all learned much from these writings, but at the same time they were stimulated to question, to doubt, and to discuss various opinions and doctrines found in the texts and developed in connection with them.

I would like to draw our attention now to some problems caused by the reception of Aristotle's *Physics* and *Metaphysics* and to the answers given by medieval authors to these problems. The first concerns a consequence this reception has for the faculty of arts. Then I shall speak of two questions arising from texts of the *Metaphysics*.

1. RECEPTION IN THE FACULTY OF ARTS

Thomas Aquinas mentions a very important problem in his *Expositio super librum Boetii de trinitate,* written about 1255. In questions 5 and 6 of this book, he works out his famous theory of the speculative sciences, of the system they form, and of the methods that characterize each of them. Our attention should be given to the third objection in article 1 of question 5: "Philosophy usually is divided into the seven liberal arts, to which neither physics nor metaphysics (*scientia divina*) belong, but only logic and mathematics. Consequently, neither physics nor metaphysics could be regarded as parts of speculative science."[1] In other words, since the new disciplines do not fit into the system of the liberal arts, they cannot receive a place within the approved teaching of the old and highly esteemed schools forming the faculty of liberal arts.

The answer given by Thomas shows that he is very well aware of the consequences that the reception of the new disciplines will have for this faculty. It will become a faculty of philosophy. But this does not mean that there is a rupture with the tradition of learning. As Thomas says at once, the seven liberal arts do not cover speculative philosophy. In fact, they were never regarded as covering the whole of non-theological theoretical knowledge. Hugh of St. Victor, whose *Didascalicon* was written more than a century before and was still an important treatise on what should be learned, gives much credit to the arts of the *trivium* and *quadrivium.* He even deplores a certain negligence in the teaching of them. This imperial authority in matters of teaching and learning characterizes the liberal arts so far as they prepared the student for the secrets of philosophy. In this Hugh agreed with Aristotle, who said that the mode of a science is to be explored before the science itself, and with the Arabic master Averroës, who assigned the first place of learning to logic, that is, to the disciplines of the *trivium*.[2] Furthermore, the very meaning of the word *ars* indicates that physics and metaphysics do not fall within the range of *artes*. The end of an *ars* never is just knowledge for its own sake, but certain products of the human intellect: propositions and syllogisms, speeches, counting, measuring, melodies, and calculating the course of planets.[3] Physics and metaphysics, on the other hand, do not aim at any practical knowledge. Their end is nothing but knowledge, understanding, insight. Consequently, they cannot rightly be called *artes*.[4] But this does not change at all their character as philosophical sciences. On the contrary, if the true perfection of the human—as Thomas holds— is knowledge of the truth, the philosophical disciplines and not the arts determine the real rank of the arts faculty.

There is no doubt that working with school texts like the *Physics* and *Metaphysics* strengthened the self-confidence of the *magistri artium*. Whoever had to comment on these works had to discuss some problems that had been the domain of the theologians—for example, whether the universe has a beginning or is eternal, whether there is blind fate or divine providence, whether there is cosmic determinism or freedom for the human will, whether there is personal immortality or an everlasting, impersonal intellect for the whole of humanity.

This new self-assessment by masters of the arts faculty is shown very clearly in some of the theses condemned by the bishop of Paris in 1277. This first in a series of quarrels between the faculties of philosophy and theology—leading all the way up to Immanuel Kant's "Streit der Fakultäten"—could hardly be avoided when masters and students of the arts thought and talked openly of themselves as being or becoming "the only wise men of the world (*sapientes mundi*)," or when they taught "quod non est excellentior status quam vacare philosophiae."[5]

The *facultas artium* could never again completely come to terms with its earlier status as a mere preparation for higher studies.

2. THE UNITY OF METAPHYSICS

As far as I know, the *Physics* of Aristotle was commented on much more often than the *Metaphysics*. This might be the consequence of the curricula. But one can easily imagine that the medieval masters were more attracted by the problems dealt with in the *Physics,* such as the structure of material being, chance and fate, space and time.

Even natural science and natural philosophy in our days are constantly interested in similar, if not the exact same problems. It might also be that the medieval masters judged the *Physics* less difficult than the *Metaphysics.*

In this respect, then, the *Physics* of Aristotle seems to have exercised a greater influence. But this influence ended quite abruptly with the rise of the modern natural sciences. The *Metaphysics,* on the other hand, continued to be the subject of attacks and controversies. Thomas Hobbes, for example, regarded the *Metaphysics* as part of "the vain philosophy of Aristotle." He wrote: "And indeed, that which is there written, is for the most part so far from the possibility of being understood, and so repugnant to natural reason that whosoever thinketh there is anything to be understood by it, must needs think it supernatural."[6] The German philosopher Thomasius wrote: "Metaphysica est regina, sed inter illas disciplinas quae circa falsa et erronea sunt occupatae."[7] Even in popular pamphlets of the seventeenth century, metaphysics was derided. A German text describes a dialogue between a child and his mother. The child: "Mom, I wanna' get an *ens.*" Mother: "Sure, my darling, but what sort of *ens?*"[8]

Let me try now to illustrate how medieval thinkers dealt with philosophical problems arising from the text of the *Metaphysics.* I have chosen two examples. The first can be found in an unpublished commentary on the *Metaphysics,* extant Oxford, New College MS. 285.[9] The attribution of this work to Richard Rufus of Cornwall is not undisputed. It seems to belong to the early commentaries. My conjecture is based on the structure of the commentary (a literal explanation with inserted short "dubitationes"), on the absence of a discussion of certain questions concerning the subject of metaphysics (which stemmed from the critical remarks directed by Averroës against Avicenna and which was a fixed topic in all later commentaries), and on the fact that some of the ideas the author explains in his introduction (such as his doctrine of the subject of the "prima philosophia") seem to be mentioned and rejected by Roger Bacon in his own commentary on the Aristotelian text, written about 1245. Attention may also be drawn to a curious inclination of the author to a very formalistic argumentation using letters as symbols, as in mathematics. This appears to be a first step towards the so-called *argumentatio in terminis* characteristic of many works of the fourteenth century.

The introduction starts with some extensive considerations of the famous Aristotelian thesis, "Omnes homines natura scire desiderant." Linked with these is the question, whether knowledge is the highest good, and if so, what kind of knowledge might be the best. At the conclusion of his deliberation, the author states that metaphysics is the noblest science, of course with the exception of Christian theology. The reason for this ranking of metaphysics is found in its subject. For even if it is difficult to decide whether this subject is substance (*substantia*) or being as a whole (*ens universum*), there cannot be a nobler subject for any philosophical science. For the time being, I have to set aside any explanation of the author's detailed reasoning within these *quaestiones*.

The author then raises the question left unanswered in the previous part of his introduction: What precisely is the subject of metaphysics? Is it substance or is it being, *substantia* or *ens*? The difficulty now to be taken into account is no longer the place of metaphysics within the sciences, but the unity of the science called metaphysics. Since the unity of a speculative science is based on its subject, only a subject that guarantees the unity of metaphysics can be regarded as appropriate. Now the transcendental unity of *ens* is not sufficient for this unity of subject. *Ens* is no genus and therefore cannot be a *genus subiectum*. The author also refutes the doctrine of some contemporaries, who hold that the unity of metaphysics is rooted in the unity of the first cause. This is nonsense. For accepting this doctrine makes it impossible to distinguish one science from another. The first cause is the principle of all the sciences and consequently does not give just one of them its specific unity. [10]

The solution finally proposed runs as follows. The subject of metaphysics is substance. "Substance" is here to be understood as common to all things that are caused, not as signifying the first cause itself. The first cause is neither the subject nor part of the subject of any philosophical discipline. [11] But how, then, can the unity of metaphysics be explained? This unity has to follow upon the unity of its subject. Now every genus owes its unity to a principle that is in itself indivisible and present in every instance falling under this genus. Evidently the author has in mind as an example the unity of the genus of natural numbers. This unity follows upon the indivisibility of the number "one." Likewise, the *genus subiectum* of metaphysics has to be taken in such a way that it is an indivisible principle of all the various objects considered in metaphysics.

As just mentioned, according to some masters, the indivisible principle that gives unity to metaphysics is the first cause. But against this doctrine there is yet another argument. The principle that gives unity to a science has to belong to the same genus to which the objects of this science belong. Otherwise it could not exercise its function as common measure of these objects. As the genus of numbers shows, there exists a relation between a measure and the things measured by it only if both fall under one and the same genus. But the first cause and the beings it causes do not form one genus.[12] Moreover, the first cause is a principle of the subject of metaphysics, but it is an exterior principle with respect to this science. What we are looking for is rather the interior principle of this subject.

These considerations seem to leave only one answer to the question. The indivisible principle that gives unity to the science of substance is nothing else than the "substance of prime matter (*substantia materiae primae*)."[13] Why does the author regard this answer as the solution of the problem? I think he reasons that the substantiality of prime matter, as the weakest form of being a substance, is the "minimum" in the realm of substantial being. Therefore it can function as the measure of all substances, just as the number "one," the minimum of natural numbers, functions as the measure of all these numbers, giving unity to their genus. To my knowledge, no other medieval commentator of the *Metaphysics* shared this doctrine concerning the subject of this science. Nor do I know of a discussion, critique, or explicit rejection of it.

3. *ENS INQUANTUM ENS*

Describing the task of the prime philosopher in *Metaphysics* Γ.1 (4.1), Aristotle says that he has to search out the first principles and the most ultimate causes. These principles are then called "principles of being *qua* being." Thus the last phrase of this famous chapter states: "Therefore it is of being *qua* being that we too must grasp the first causes (*unde et nobis entis inquantum est ens, primae causae sunt accipiendae*)." The formula "principia et causae entis inquantum ens" appeared very puzzling to many philosophers, beginning with Avicenna,[14] and with good reason. Nearly all medieval commentators try to explain it, and in doing so, some of them are led to remarkable ontological theories. I would like now to draw attention to a text of Siger of Brabant, who also wanted to understand the above-mentioned formula.

No doubt, the metaphysician has to discuss the meaning of the term "principle." For what is called a principle is always something that follows upon being. The extension of the concept of principle is certainly limited in comparison with that of "being." But being a principle is not sufficient to constitute the subject of a particular science. There is no science of principles as such. So the task of understanding being, insofar as it has the character of principle, rightly belongs to metaphysics, and the quest for a first principle goes along with this task.

But it is misleading, even false, to ask for a principle of being *qua* being. For this question implies — as Avicenna already says — the conception that every being has a principle. This, however, is impossible, since it is equivalent to the assumption that there is something that is the principle of itself.

Yet Aristotle speaks of the principles of being *qua* being. What did he intend to say? He cannot have meant that there is a principle or cause of being insofar as it is being. All that belongs to being *qua* being must be found in every being. Now if every being had a cause, no being has a cause, since there would not be a first cause and, consequently, no cause at all.[15]

By using the phrase "principles and causes of being insofar as it is being," Aristotle had another objective in view. In every being having causes, he has to distinguish between causes that are essential and causes that are merely accidental. Asking for principles and causes of being *qua* being thus means searching for the essential causes of every being that is caused.[16] Since the distinction between essential and accidental principles and causes of a thing is a very important one, the phrase not only makes sense, but indicates a major aim of metaphysics.

Siger then tries to explain why the Aristotelian formula has to be understood in this way. Certainly there are beings having causes. But not every being has a cause of its *entitas,* and correspondingly, not every question concerning *esse* and aiming at a cause is meaningful.[17] This can easily be understood by considering the following question: "Why is there something in existence at all rather than just nothing?" No difficulty arises so long as this question concerns the realm of caused beings. Then one merely answers: Because there is an unmoved first mover, an unchangeable first cause. But one cannot give a sensible answer if one asks this question with regard to the whole universe of being. One might utter the question, certainly, but one is in fact uttering words in the form of a question that only appears to make sense. For with respect to the whole universe, this question is equivalent to asking: "Why is it that God exists at all rather than not?" There is no cause or principle for the being of God, and so there is no answer to this question.[18]

I would like to add three comments to Siger's explications, which, by the way, are only partially preserved in the *reportatio* of Cambridge and in the short notes taken by Godfrey of Fontaines.[19]

1. So far as I know, Siger is the only commentator of the *Metaphysics* who probed the formula of the principles and causes of being as being so radically. Through his argument, he shows clearly what conception he has of the subject of metaphysics: Being *qua* being includes the first principle, namely God.

2. Leibniz is usually regarded as the first one to formulate what Heidegger called the "Grundfrage der Metaphysik": "Pourquoi il y a plutôt quelque chose que rien?"[20] But there cannot be any doubt that Siger of Brabant had in mind exactly the same question when commenting the *Metaphysics,* though he rejected the question as senseless. So some of Heidegger's praise of Leibniz should be extended to Siger. This might give many historians of philosophy, who usually ignore the Middle Ages, a higher notion of the efforts of medieval thinkers.[21]

3. The problem arising from the Aristotelian formula, "ens inquantum ens," is still discussed by contemporary philosophers. A very remarkable example is to be found in Fernand van Steenberghen's *Ontology.*[22] Discussing the meaning of being as the object of ontology, van Steenberghen asks whether this object can be thought of as something "relative." The object is, as he puts it, represented by the transcendental concept of being, which brings before our intellect "the totality of reality." So it is possible for me to have in view the totality of being. Van Steenberghen then continues to reflect on this object: Considering any particular being belonging to this totality, one can always ask, whether this particular reality is relative. This is a meaningful question, because there is the possibility of a positive or a negative answer. But to ask the same question with regard to the whole of reality or to the universe of existing things is senseless, since the hypothesis included in the question does not exist. "The whole as such," thus, "cannot depend on anything else, and must in consequence stand in its own right." So the idea of being as the object of ontology represents the totality of what there is, an 'object' that is without condition and uncaused. In other words: "The *raison d'etre* of all that there is, is to be found within the universe." It is impossible for this *raison* to lie beyond the totality of what there is. The proposition, "The totality

is conditioned," is "plainly absurd," since it implies a contradiction.[23]

This doctrine obviously corresponds to the conception of the *subiectum metaphysicae* elaborated by Siger of Brabant.

3. CONCLUSION

I am not enough of an historian to judge whether my understanding of the texts considered is adequate. Nor am I enough of a philosopher to risk the judgment that the questions discussed by medieval thinkers and mentioned in this essay can still raise the interest of philosophers. But it has always been my suspicion that problems considered long ago and answers given long ago do not have the strangeness for us usually presumed in talk about "historicity." Is there no longer a "Streit der Fakultäten?" Do we no longer try to understand the fundamental unity of what there is? Do philosophers no longer ask the question: *Quare est magis aliquid in rerum natura quam nihil?* As long as human beings wonder, they can always learn that their own thinking unites them with their ancestors, whose essential questions retain their value and fecundity.

NOTES

1. *S. Thomae de Aquino Expositio super librum Boethii de trinitate,* ed. B. Decker, Studien und Texte zur Geistesgeschichte des Mittelalters 4 (Leiden, 1965), p. 162, lines 5-6: "communiter dividitur philosophia in septem artes liberales, inter quas neque naturalis neque divina continetur, sed sola rationalis et mathematica. Ergo naturalis et divina non debuerunt poni partes speculativae."

2. Thomas Aquinas, *Super Boethii de trinitate* 5.1 ad 3 (Decker, p. 167, line 22, to p. 168, line 10).

3. Thomas Aquinas, *Super Boethii de trinitate* 5.1 ad 3 (Decker, p. 168, lines 11-14).

4. Thomas Aquinas, *Super Boethii de trinitate* 5.1 ad 3 (Decker, p. 168, lines 14-17).

5. See Roland Hissette, *Enquête sur les 219 articles condamnés à Paris le 7 mars 1277,* Philosophes Médiévaux 22 (Louvain and Paris, 1977), 15-20.

6. Thomas Hobbes, *Leviathan,* Chapter 46, as in his *English Works,* ed. W. Molesworth (London, 1839), 674.

7. Christian Thomasius, *Introductio ad philosophiam aulicam,* chap. 11, sect. 32 (edition of 1702).

8. See Ernst Lewalter, *Spanisch-Jesuitische und Deutsch-Lutherische Metaphysik des 17. Jahrhunderts* (Hamburg, 1935), 82.

9. See Gedeon Gál, *"Commentarius in Metaphysicam Aristotelis,* codex Vat. lat. 4538, Fons Richardi Rufi," *Archivum Franciscanum Historicum* 43 (1950): 209–242. I am grateful to Rega Wood and Stephen Brown for information concerning this work, which is also contained in Vat. lat. 4538, Erfurt Ampl. A 290, and a codex in Prague. It has been the subject of a study by Timothy B. Noone, "An Edition and Study of the *Scriptum super Metaphysicam,* Book 12, Distinction 12, a Work attributed to Richard Rufus of Cornwall," Dissertation, University of Toronto, 1987.

10. Oxford, New College 285, fol. 195rb: "Et si dicatur quod haec scientia . . . est una . . . ab unitate primae causae, idem est. Hoc enim modo essent omnes scientiae una scientia. Prima enim causa est respectu omnium scientiarum et principium earum. Per unum et idem in se non diversificantur. Oportet igitur ut specialius illud a quo procedit unitas scientiae iniquiritur. Et modo quid hic sentiendum?"

11. Oxford, New College 285, fol. 195rb: "Dicendum quod substantia est subiectum huius scientiae. Sed substantia, quae continet omnia causata sicut commune ad ea, quae sunt sub ipso. nec tamen substantia quae hic ponitur esse genus subiectum, est prima causa. Ipsa enim neque est subiectum neque pars subiecti."

12. Oxford, New College 285, fol. 195rb: "Unigenae enim sunt principium in scientia et illa quorum est principium. Ipsum enim principium mensura est illorum, quae sunt in eadem scientia. Mensura autem et mensuratum sunt eiusdem generis. Igitur cum primum non sit unius generis cum causatis, non erit mensura in scientia."

13. Oxford, New College 285, fol. 195rb: "Quid autem sit illud minimum? Forte dicendum quod substantia materiae primae."

14. See Avicenna, *Metaphysica* 1.2 (Venice, 1508), fol. 71ra.

15. Siger of Brabant, *Quaestiones in Metaphysicam* 4 commentary, ed. W. Dunphy, Philosophes Médiévaux 24 (Louvain-La-Neuve, 1981), 169.

16. Siger, *Quaestiones in Metaphysicam* 4 comm. (Dunphy, 169).

17. Siger, *Quaestiones in Metaphysicam* 4 comm. (Dunphy, 169).

18. Siger, *Questiones in Metaphysicam* 4 comm. (Dunphy, 169): "Si enim quaeratur, quare magis est aliquid in rerum natura quam nihil, in rebus causatis loquendo, contingit respondere quia est aliquod Primum Movens immobile et Prima Causa intransmutabilis. Si vero quaeratur de tota universitate entium, quare magis est in eis aliquid quam nihil, non contingit dare causam, quia idem est quaerere hoc et quaerere quare magis est Deus quam non est, et hoc non habet causam. Unde non omnis quaestio habet cuasam nec omne ens."

19. Both of these texts are edited by Armand Maurer in Philosophes Médiévaux 25 (Louvain-La-Neuve, 1983).

20. G. W. Leibniz, *Principes de la nature et de la grace,* in *Die philosophischen Schriften von Gottfried Wilhelm Leibniz,* ed. C. J. Gerhardt, 7 vols. (Berlin, 1875–1890; reprt. Hildesheim, 1960–1961) 6:602, no. 7.

21. See Zimmermann, "Die 'Grundfrage' in der Metaphysik der Hochscholastik," *Archiv für Geschichte der Philosophie* 47 (1966): 141–156.

22. Fernand van Steenberghen, *Ontology,* trans. L. Moonan (Louvain and New York, 1970), 59ff.

23. Ibid., 61.

Aquinas Reading Aristotle's *Ethics*

Mark D. Jordan

THOMAS AQUINAS BELONGS to the first generation of readers who were able to make use of the exegetical aids provided alongside Robert Grosseteste's Latin version of the *Nicomachean Ethics,* which became available in 1246–1247.[1] The *translacio lincolniensis* was a revision of an earlier translation, now largely lost,[2] done with the aid of at least two Greek versions. Its supplements comprised a Latin corpus of Greek commentators and a set of notes (*notulae*) by Grosseteste himself.[3]

When Grosseteste's work began to circulate, Thomas was only twenty or twenty-one, newly arrived in Paris and under the tutelage of Albert the Great.[4] In Paris, or earlier in Italy, Thomas seems to have learned something of the older translations of the *Ethics* and of the styles of commentary on it current in faculties of the arts.[5] Whatever the extent of this early acquaintance, Thomas would soon share in one of the first systematic studies of the *Ethics* to make use of Grosseteste's work. After Thomas moved with Albert to Cologne in 1248, Albert turned from his commentaries on ps-Dionysius to expound the *Nicomachean Ethics* in Grosseteste's translation, already somewhat corrupted, and with the aid of his supplements, already somewhat curtailed. Thomas was set to edit Albert's *Lectura* of the *Ethics,* though his exact editorial task remains uncertain.[6]

Albert's exposition would have given even an ordinary student a thorough and laudably philological familiarity with the Aristotelian text. Thomas was no ordinary student. The impression made on him by Albert's reading of the *Ethics* was remarkably deep. It seems, for example, that Thomas could remember details of the reading well enough after twenty years to cite it without having to reread Albert.[7] But the more striking evidence is provided by Thomas's major works. In the *Scriptum* on the *Sentences,* the *Contra gentiles,* and the *Summa theo-*

logiae, four Aristotelian texts account for more than eighty percent of the citations to Aristotle. These are the *Physics, On the Soul,* the *Metaphysics,* and the *Ethics.* In the *Contra gentiles, On the Soul* is the most frequently cited text, in large part because of the extended treatments of the human soul in book 2. In both the *Scriptum* and the *Summa,* it is the *Ethics* that is most often cited, and by a wide margin. Citations to the *Ethics* make up exactly half of all the citations to Aristotle in the *Summa.* To say this in another way: the *Ethics* is cited in the *Summa* four times for every one citation of the next most frequent text, which is the *Metaphysics.* The figures for the *Scriptum* would be comparable. Thomas's early and thorough acquaintance with the *Ethics* is put to special use throughout his authorship.

It would be odd, however, if a reader of Thomas's gifts would have read so important a book once, at age twenty-five, and never learned anything more from it. To admit this does not authorize the making of psychological fables or the postulation of Hegelian 'developments'. There are indeed some small signs of changed readings — points on which Thomas moves further away from Albert, say. But the interesting changes in Thomas's reading of the *Ethics* come in his relation to the whole of the Aristotelian text. I shall try to show in the balance of this essay what these changes are and how they can be described candidly. In watching Thomas read and reread Aristotle, we learn something of how he understands relations to authoritative teachers who teach through texts.

1. THE *ETHICS* IN THE *SCRIPTUM* ON THE *SENTENCES*

In the version generally received, each of the four books of Thomas's *Scriptum* on the *Sentences* draws on the whole of the *Nicomachean Ethics.*[8] This is not to say that they do so equally or uniformly. The subject-matter of the first book seems least related to that of the *Ethics,* and it is not surprising that this book contains the fewest citations. The second book of the *Scriptum* contains four times as many, the third book eight times. What may be surprising is that the fourth book, in which the subject matter would seem less susceptible to the lessons of pagan ethics, contains many more citations than the second book and almost as many as the third. The explanation for this is connected to the explanation for the lack of uniformity in citation. Thomas's uses of the *Ethics* are clustered around certain specific topics. In each of

books 3 and 4, for example, more than half of the citations are contained in ten percent of the distinctions. A single distinction of the
third book contains 125 citations or thirteen percent of the total for
the whole of the *Scriptum*.[9]

The clustering of citations becomes even more remarkable when
citations are sorted by their specific importance to the construction
of the argument or determination. It is obvious that a citation to Aristotle in an argument to the contrary is rather different from a citation
in a *sed contra* or in the body of an article. Just as obviously, a citation
in the body of an article will often lie on one side of the point at issue.
The citation may support a general maxim or explain a peripheral
matter or provide the other term of an analogy. That is why it would
be misleading to rely on a statistical summary of citations alone. Let
me offer instead a sampling of types of uses, with a few examples for
each taken only from the *Scriptum* on book 1 of the *Sentences*. I can
then turn to the types most important for understanding Thomas's
reading of Aristotle and to more substantive texts in later books.

(1) The first type of citation is merely a learned allusion. For the
most part, Thomas is free of such ornament. There may be some exceptions. For example, in glossing the Lombard's prologue, Thomas
cites both the *Poetics* and the *Metaphysics* to argue that a fable (*fabula*)
is made up of wonders — this in reference to 2 Timothy 4.[10] The single
such ornamental use of the *Ethics* in book 1 might be a reference to
Aristotle's remark that small things cannot be beautiful.[11] The citation is incorporated into a Dionysian and Augustinian justification
of Hilary's appropriation of qualities to the Persons of the Trinity.

(2) A second type of citation is speciously disputative, so far as
it depends on a superficial misreading of a fragment from Aristotle.
This type of citation occurs most often in objections or *dubia* about
the Lombard's letter. The first example comes from the first distinction of the first book. An argument there is buttressed by what Thomas
takes to be a misconstrual of Aristotle's remarks on prudence in book
6 of the *Ethics*.[12] The Aristotelian remarks are being used to construct
an analogy with the Augustinian notion of *uti*. Thomas does not reject the analogy, but he does correct a misunderstanding of the relation of prudence to the will.[13] A similarly disputative example, not
involving analogy, misuses Aristotle's definition of *consilium*.[14]

(3) A third type of citation to the *Ethics* establishes a general point
in no way specific to ethical matter or to Aristotle. An early example
in the *Scriptum* comes when *Ethics* 1 is invoked, after Boethius, to

establish that the mode of each kind of science should proceed according to the consideration of its matter.[15] Other examples would be citations in support of assertions that there is delight in God[16] and that God cannot undo the past.[17] In such citations, Aristotle serves as a convenient but not indispensable authority. He offers a clear or memorable formulation of what could be supported from many other authors.

(4) A fourth type of citation is more specifically Aristotelian, but supports a peripheral point. There is a good example in the first article, which asks whether a teaching beyond "physical bodies of learning" is necessary for humans.[18] In arguing that such a teaching is necessary, Thomas mentions that the incomplete contemplation of God attainable through creatures is said by Aristotle to be the source of contemplative happiness — that is, Thomas explains, the happiness of the wayfarer.[19] The doctrine is specifically (though not exclusively) Aristotelian, but it is not integral to the argument here.

(5) A fifth type of citation supplies a general maxim or rule that can be used in a wide variety of ethical contexts. These are among the most frequent and most interesting of the substantive uses of Aristotle, since they contribute to the lexica and schemata within which Thomas articulates his teaching on almost any point. A good example from the first book of the *Scriptum* is the use of the *Ethics* to support the distinction between *operatio* and *motus*.[20]

(6) The sixth and final type of citation, by far the most important, is both specifically Aristotelian and essential to Thomas's ethical purposes. An example of this kind is found in the *Scriptum*'s second and third citations of the *Ethics*. Here Aristotle's book 6 is used to establish the number of speculative habits and the character of wisdom. Both assertions are integral to the determination of the article, which concerns theology as speculative and practical.[21] Both invoke typically Aristotelian arguments. Similar examples concern the teachings that delight follows upon habitual operation[22] and that a good act requires three things, will or choice, a proper end, and firmness in performance.[23]

The fifth and sixth types, the generally or specifically constructive uses, are obviously most pertinent to assessing Thomas's reading of the *Ethics*. They show his incorporation of Aristotelian terminology and argument into the analysis of traditional theological materials. They also mark an interesting departure from the immediately preceding *Sentences*-commentaries of Albert and Bonaventure, in both the boldness and explicitness of the reliance on the Aristotelian *Ethics*.

Important constructive uses of the *Ethics* are found in those sections of books 2, 3, and 4 that contain the Lombard's scattered remarks on moral matters. Some of the sections are unexpected. Important use of Aristotle on justice is made in the discussion of the adoration of the humanity of Christ.[24] Aristotle's teaching on friendship appears in every discussion of charity,[25] as his definitions of fortitude figure in articles on the Spirit's gifts.[26] But most citations fall where one would expect them, in discussions of sin,[27] grace,[28] free choice and will,[29] the virtues,[30] repentance,[31] contemplation,[32] and happiness.[33]

From this range, I would like to take only a single example, from distinction 33 of book 3. This is the distinction that contains, just by itself, some 125 explicit citations to the *Ethics*. The reason for this is that Thomas here interjects within the Lombard's sequence of topics an examination of moral virtue.[34] The Lombard enumerates the cardinal virtues and provides a few definitions for them, but his main concern is with their survival in the afterlife. Thomas uses the enumeration as an occasion for a fuller doctrine of the moral virtues, including the cardinal virtues and their parts.

In doing so, he goes considerably farther than either Albert or Bonaventure. Albert's commentary on the *Sentences,* which would have been finished before the circulation of Grosseteste's anthology,[35] offers four articles on the number, name, differences, and survival of the cardinal virtues.[36] But the *Nicomachean Ethics* is cited only six times in two of these articles.[37] Only one of these citations could be regarded as programmatic; it concerns the order of treatment of virtues in the *Ethics.*[38] Bonaventure undertakes a more extended discussion, including questions on the unity, locus, sufficiency, origin, and permanence of the cardinal virtues.[39] He also alludes to the *Ethics* somewhat more frequently, though many of the allusions are implicit or anonymous.[40] Bonaventure's manner of citation is also noteworthy. Though his commentary would have been finished at Paris well after the Grosseteste became available, he continues to cite the *Ethics* in the old manner.[41] By contrast to these, his immediate predecessors, Thomas introduces three Questions with thirteen Articles on the moral virtues in common, then the cardinal virtues, then the parts of the cardinal virtues.[42] It is by far the longest distinction in Thomas's *Scriptum* on the third book.[43]

Even in this lengthy discussion, in which references to Aristotle's *Ethics* appear on most pages, it is no easy matter to judge their use.

Many of the citations are convenient authorities for the construction of the dialectic. Thus almost half of the citations figure in objections, and some of them pass back and forth between objections, determinations, and answers to objections.[44] In a few places, an authoritative text from Aristotle is deemed sufficient, by itself, to constitute a *sed contra*.[45] But Aristotle's texts are hardly given unique authority. The last question of this distinction performs a series of alignments among divisions of the cardinal virtues by Aristotle, Cicero, Macrobius, and anonymous Greek philosophers, whom Thomas knows through Grosseteste — that is, through Albert.[46] In these alignments, the Aristotelian terminology is not privileged. In other passages, Thomas remarks on the limited scope of Aristotle's inquiry. The Philosopher speaks, he says, of the acquired virtues that complete human life in the earthly city.[47] Just above, Thomas had invoked Macrobius's three-step transposition of the virtues of the active life into the contemplative life.[48]

The complexity is not simply in the handling of citations. Aristotle figures importantly in the construction of certain doctrines, but not of others. He is the main authority in the arguments that the virtues are found in the mean, as he is when describing the matters of the various cardinal virtues.[49] Aristotle is not an important authority for establishing the number and names of the cardinal virtues, or their locus, or their relation to prudence.[50] Moreover, and decisively, the Aristotelian doctrine about the virtues is being qualified at every turn by theological teaching. Experience establishes the Aristotelian tenet that virtues are acquired by practice; but we also need infused moral virtues to be ordered to our highest end, and these differ in species from the acquired.[51] All the kinds of virtues lie in the mean, except for the theological virtues.[52] Acquired moral virtues, being the virtues of the earthly city, do not remain *in patria;* infused virtues do.[53] Reason appropriately rules over the acquired moral virtues, but the highest infused virtue, namely charity, resides in the will and commands reason.[54] At all these points, the Aristotelian doctrine is subordinated to other teaching and is corrected by them.

Three conclusions can be gathered from the citations to the *Ethics* in the *Sentences*-commentary. First, there is irreducible variety in Thomas's manner of using the citations. The variety covers selectivity and irregularity of use. Second, the Aristotelian citations are mixed in with other authorities of all kinds. Third, the variously used and unevenly distributed Aristotelian *auctoritates* are subsumed within a framework that is not theirs.

2. THE *SENTENTIA LIBRI ETHICORUM*

Thomas's composition of a distilled exposition of the *Ethics* follows the main redaction of the *Sentences*-commentary by at least a decade, making it contemporary with the composition of sections of the *Summa*. The *Sententia libri Ethicorum* is no halfway point chronologically, then, but it is a halfway point exegetically. It represents Thomas's most sustained attempt to read the Aristotelian text whole for the important, if limited truths that it can teach.

Much polemical talent has been exercised over Thomas's intention in writing expositions of Aristotle late in his career and at a time when he was much pressed by other projects. I will not rehearse the polemics, especially because many of them seem to presuppose a misleading formulation of the issue. No single answer can be given to the question about Thomas's intention. His procedure varies from exposition to exposition depending on the earlier commentaries known to him, on the history of reception for the particular Aristotelian work, on his interest in the matters discussed. Setting aside the general question, then, I turn only to the intention in his exposition of the *Ethics*.

Its genre seems plain enough. The work is a literal exposition aimed chiefly at making reflective sense of the Aristotelian text. There are several signs of the genre. One is the unbroken format of *divisio textus* followed by sequential gloss. Another is the limited range of authorities, which is confined to pagan authors and to a very few Christians writing within the realm of pagan arts.[55] The limited range cannot be excused as a concession to the capacities of unaided reason. The first three books of the *Contra gentiles,* which are meant to treat of truths accessible to reason, deploy a much richer range of authorities. The limitation of authorities in the exposition of the *Ethics* is not in view of philosophy, but of Aristotle. In being a literal exposition only, Thomas's commentary is thus unlike Albert's *Lectura,* which combines literal exposition with disputed questions.[56] The generic antecedents for Thomas's commentary would be found rather in Averroës's middle commentary and in some of the sorts of expositions known to Thomas from the arts faculties.

Still, there are literal expositions and literal expositions. Thomas knew well the expository practice of Albert and of the Greek commentators presented by Grosseteste. He chose to write something different. There are a number of glosses in Thomas's exposition — on Greek practices and Greek names, on figures from classical literature and history.[57] Some of the glosses are surprisingly elementary and raise questions about Thomas's intended audience.[58] But for the most part they are notable only in their scarcity. Given the sources at his disposal, Thomas spends little time glossing terms or explaining etymologies. His literal exposition is not a full-dress commentary on the letter done up to the standards of mid-thirteenth-century philology. It seems rather an attempt to extract what is essential in Aristotle's teaching.

Aristotle's teaching in the *Ethics* cannot be presumed to be identical with moral philosophy simply speaking. Thomas does begin the exposition with a fourfold order of things that grounds a fourfold order of sciences. The third of these is "moral philosophy," which is in turn divided into *monastica, economica,* and *politica.*[59] Aristotle's book is subsumed under the first of these — subsumed, not identified. Moreover, once he begins actually to expound the book, Thomas proceeds with his customary devices for textual exegesis. He discovers in a first textual division that Aristotle provides an *accessus* under three headings, *intentio, modus tractandi, qualis debeat esse auditor.*[60] These headings are applied literally to the science, but also and perhaps more importantly to the book in which Aristotle treats the science. One can see this in several ways. First, Thomas in his prefaces not infrequently uses *'scientia'* to mean what is taught in a book. In doing so, he echoes a usage of the Parisian Arts faculty.[61] Second, in speaking about the science rather than the book, Thomas is simply following the manner of speaking in the book itself, which is never far from sight even in these opening pages.[62] Third, Thomas uses terms for textual parts to describe the parts of the science.[63] Fourth, as soon as Thomas moves from Aristotle's *proemium* to the *tractatus* proper, he insists repeatedly on the limits of Aristotle's investigation in this particular book.

There are various ways in which Thomas reminds the reader throughout that the Aristotelian text is an ancient work by a pagan. Even within the exposition of the *proemium,* he qualifies Aristotle's remarks on politics by noting that politics is architectonic only for the active sciences of human life. Divine science is architectonic simply speaking.[64] Elsewhere he notes, against the apparent sense of the Aristotelian text, that virginity cannot be seen as an extreme beyond the virtuous mean.[65] He records that the ancients allowed marriages to be dissolved because of sterility,[66] that they posited semi-divinities known as daemons,[67] that they deified heroes.[68] Throughout the text, Thomas remarks that Aristotle speaks *"more gentium"* in calling the separate substances or the planetary bodies "gods."[69] In most of these instances, the reminders are quiet, but at one point Thomas makes his point patent. Aristotle is speaking of contributions to the maintenance of civic cult by those who have the virtue of magnificence. Thomas says,

> The Philosopher speaks here according to the custom of the Gentiles, which has now been abrogated by revealed truth. So that if someone were now to spend something on the cult of daemons, he would not be magnificent, but sacrilegious.[70]

The careful reader hardly needs any other reminder of the distance between the circumstances of Aristotle's composition and the circumstances of the New Covenant.

If these reminders should prove insufficient, however, Thomas reiterates what seems the most important limitation on the inquiry of Aristotle's *Ethics*. It is a limitation he had learned from Albert and used already in the *Sentences*-commentary.[71] Aristotle's *Ethics* is concerned with the virtues of the present life, that is, with those of the human city.

> The Philosopher speaks in this book of happiness, such as it can be had in this life. Now the happiness of the other life exceeds all investigation of reason.[72]

This limitation allows Thomas to explain many omissions or commissions that might seem to bring Aristotle into conflict with Christian faith. But it is a limitation in the book, not in moral philosophy itself. So Thomas seems sometimes to broach the limit with philosophical reasonings. On the one hand, he asserts that the question of the survival of death does not arise for Aristotle and that the things that belong to the condition of souls after death are not visible to us.[73] He agrees with Aristotle that complete happiness is not possible in the present life.[74] On the other hand, Thomas seems to suggest a philosophical argument for the existence of a complete happiness in the afterlife. And because no desire of nature is in vain, it can rightly be reasoned that complete happiness is reserved for after this life.[75] Moreover, Thomas excuses Aristotle from considering immortality not because the *Ethics* is a philosophical work, but because it is a practical work. Thomas adds an explicit self-reference meant to guide the reader to an adequate speculative treatment of immortality.[76]

Let me end the remarks on the exposition of the *Ethics* by giving their sum. The exposition is literal in the sense that it is governed by

Aristotle's intention as it is discoverable through the letter. Aristotle's intention is worth recovering not as an artifact, but as a perennial contribution to the thinking about ethics. But this does not mean that any literal exposition of Aristotle's *Nicomachean Ethics* could become identical with moral philosophy. Much less could a Christian consider the Aristotelian text to contain an adequate moral teaching. In short, the *Sententia libri Ethicorum* is hardly Thomas's last word on the *Ethics*. It is not even his commentary on it, if one distinguishes commentary from exposition. The commentary is to be found in the second part, the *pars moralis,* of the *Summa.*

3. THE *ETHICS* AND THE SECOND PART OF THE *SUMMA THEOLOGIAE*

Certain large similarities can easily be asserted between the second part of the *Summa* and the *Ethics.* Both begin with a protreptic discussion of happiness, proceed to examine the principles of human action, then consider particular virtues, and end with reflection on particular states of life. But one could just as easily be struck by large differences. It is obvious that certain Christian doctrines make their appearance in the second part, among them the Old and New Law, grace, and the theological virtues of faith, hope, and charity. More pervasively and more subtly, Thomas changes the specificity and confidence of Aristotelian moral teaching. Where Aristotle begins by emphasizing the limitations of moral teaching and raising difficulties about happiness, Thomas offers a rapid ascent to a divine good. Where Aristotle offers a few remarks on the terms for ascribing and mitigating responsibility, Thomas gives a detailed analysis of nine interlocking acts of knowing and willing. Most profoundly, Thomas engages the structure of Aristotle's *Ethics* as a pedagogical analogy for the construction of a Christian moral teaching.

In the *Sententia libri Ethicorum,* Thomas has described three very unequal parts of the *Nicomachean Ethics.* After a procedural introduction, he says, Aristotle "investigates happiness" in the first part, which is most of the first book. At the end of that book, Aristotle turns to what Thomas counts as the second part of the trichotomy, the main matter of the *Ethics,* which is the discussion of virtue. Aristotle begins with the moral virtues. In the second book and part of the third, he defines moral virtue in general and certain principles of moral action.

In the balance of the third book and the fourth, Aristotle treats virtues concerned with interior passions, chiefly fortitude and temperance. In the fifth book, the subject is the virtue of external actions, namely justice. The sixth book of Aristotle considers the intellectual virtues. The seventh, eighth, and ninth books describe things that follow on virtues or accompany them, namely continence and friendship. Aristotle's tenth book, which is the third, short member of Thomas's original trichotomy, completes the treatment of happiness, individually and in the city.[77]

Compare Thomas's own order in the second part of the *Summa*. First, Thomas separates the definitions of virtue and the other principles or elements much more strictly from the treatment of particular virtues. Thomas insists, second, on the sufficiency of the four cardinal virtues as a comprehensive organization for all moral virtue. They are the organizing principles, and such matters as friendship or continence must be subordinated to them. In the *Summa*, friendship becomes a quasi-potential part of justice,[78] while continence appears as a potential part of temperance.[79] Third, Aristotle's separate treatment of the intellectual virtues is suppressed by Thomas. Prudence is combined with the similarly named cardinal virtue. Art is excluded as not pertaining to moral matters. Wisdom, understanding, and knowledge are treated with their related gifts of the Spirit under the appropriate theological virtue.[80] Fourth, Thomas inserts into the investigation of principles a long treatment of the passions, which he thinks Aristotle had relegated to the *Rhetoric*.[81] Fifth, Aristotle's discussion of law is moved from the end of the tenth book, where it forms a bridge to the *Politics*, back to a point just before the consideration of particular virtues. It becomes part of the preliminary review of virtue and choice. Under Thomas's reorganization, then, the *Nicomachean Ethics* would proceed as follows: investigation of happiness; definitions of virtue, choice, passions, and law; the four cardinal virtues; and the personal attainment of happiness, especially in contemplation.

Thomas regards his revision of the order of the *Ethics* as an improvement in clarity and comprehensiveness. Thus far I have only remarked on changes in the philosophical order of teaching; it should be stressed that Thomas differs from Aristotle even on details of that order. Still, what enables him to proceed so much more confidently and clearly through the uncertainties of moral life also requires him to regard a clarified and augmented *Nicomachean Ethics* as still less than adequate to moral life. At the center of the revised Aristotelian pattern, Thomas must insert two things: an eminent external principle for teaching good action—a principle much more powerful than the law of cities; and an eminent set of new virtues—virtues much more important for happiness than the cardinal virtues. The principle is grace, and the new virtues are the theological virtues of faith, hope, and charity. The addition of these topics makes for the greatest structural difference, of course. But its importance for Thomas's reading of Aristotle can only be understood after it has been remembered that Thomas is performing a similar transformation on another set of antecedent texts—I mean the previous theological patterns for moral teaching. In these revisions, lessons learned from the order of Aristotle's *Ethics* help Thomas to correct the prevailing order of instruction.

There are a number of surprises for a medieval reader in the order of both sections of the second part of the *Summa*. For example, the *prima secundae* surprises in at least four ways: in its presentation of the second half of the teaching about the soul's powers as separate from what has already been said in the *prima;* in the position of the treatment of beatitude; in the text on the passions; and in the delayed appearance of law and grace. Each of these surprises owes something to the order of Aristotle's *Ethics.* But a much more satisfying glimpse can be gotten by looking at the order of the *secunda secundae.*

Thomas begins the *secunda secundae* with a relatively lengthy explanation of the order he will adopt, in which he criticizes received patterns. His first step is to remind that moral discourse must be particular if it is to be useful. It must be particular in treating both of individual virtues or vices and in treating the different ways-of-life. Now the risk in particular treatments of the first kind is useless repetition. To understand the commandment, "Thou shalt not commit adultery," the theologian must conduct an inquiry into a sin, adultery, the knowledge of which notion depends on grasping the opposed virtue, continence. Yet the serial or sequential treatment will relegate law, vice, and virtue to three different sections. The treatment would be better done by clustering in one inquiry a virtue, its corresponding gifts, its opposed vices, and the entailed positive and negative commands.

Moreover, the table of the vices should itself be constructed by real differences and not accidental ones. "It has been shown that vices and sins are distinguished by species according to their matter and object, not according to other differences of the sins, such as 'of the heart', 'of the mouth', and 'of the deeds', or according to weakness, ignorance, and malice, and other such differences" (1–2.pro). Now the immediate references are to two traditional classifications, both passed down by Peter Lombard. The first triplet, "of heart, mouth, and deed," is a mnemonic rendering of a division from Jerome.[82] The second triplet, "weakness, ignorance, and malice," derives from Isidore.[83] Both distinctions are used by Thomas in other texts, even within the *Summa*, though he is careful to point out that they are not classifications by genera or essential species.[84] What is more striking is that both triplets represent the sorts of classifications seen in pastoral and casuistical writing, including the *Summae* of Peraldus. The criticism would surely apply to Peraldus's addition of a special section on sins of the tongue. It must also cut against Peraldus's practice of distinguishing sins by their external occasions—as, for example, the multiplication of types of *superbia* by types of ornament or, indeed, by subtypes, such as horse-trappings, buildings, books, singing, and so on.[85] But the main force of Thomas's criticism about the organization of sins must be applied to the main principle of Peraldus's *Summa*, namely the order of the seven chief vices itself.

One of the effects of Thomas's organization of the *secunda secundae* is to push the seven capital vices to the margin.[86] They appear, each in turn, but without obvious connection or special importance. *Acedia* and *invidia* appear together as vices opposed to *gaudium* (1–2.35–36), which is one of the acts or effects of charity. *Avaritia* is one of two vices opposed to liberality (2–2.118), which is itself a quasi-integral part of justice. *Inanis gloria* is one of the vices opposed to magnanimity (2–2.132), itself a part of fortitude. The other three sins are listed among the vices opposed to subjective and potential parts of temperance. *Gula* is opposed to abstinence (2–2.148), *luxuria* and its species to chastity (2–2.153), *iracundia* to mercy (2–2.158). Thomas asks in each case whether the sin is a capital vice.[87] In each case, the *sed contra* is a citation to Gregory's *Moralia*. Thomas is so faithful in following Gregory's list that he refuses to identify *superbia* with *inanis gloria* or to call *superbia* a capital vice (2–2.162.8). He is well aware that there are other authorities with other lists (2–2.36.4), but Thomas is willing to follow Gregory because he regards the listing of capital vices as a listing not of species, but of what are for most people the final causes of other signs. Thomas does defend Gregory's list as a suitable classification of these final causes (1–2.84.3–4), but he explicitly denies that the classification by final causes—or any causes—ought to count as an essential classification (1–2.72.3 corp & ad 3). The essential classification of sins or vices is aligned with the classification of virtues because both are made with an eye to the object (1.72.1).

The structural accomplishment of the *secunda secundae* is not only that it replaces the serial order with a more compendious, 'simultaneous' order according to virtue, but also that it thus shifts the whole consideration from an accidental or causal classification to an essential one. The result is not only clarity by compression, but a theoretically justified form within which to arrange the sprawling matter of the moral *summae*. The *secunda secundae* is a hybrid genre precisely because it uses the conclusions of the most academic moral account to inform what was usually taught in homiletic or pastoral works.

Where is Aristotle's *Ethics* in this hybrid? I have suggested that its structure was tacitly corrected by the order adopted in the *secunda pars*. But it now seems that Aristotelian 'principles' are used in turn to reorder Christian topics in the *secunda* — though that word 'principles' is deceiving, because rules from Aristotle are being used to cover cases never intended by him. Such ambivalences of description bring forward in final form the question that has been lurking throughout my remarks: What categories of intellectual affiliation can be used to describe Thomas's successive readings of Aristotle? How can we speak of the readings without being misled about Thomas's dependence on Aristotle or independence from him? I would like to end by addressing this question, and to do so by remarking on some ways of describing the affiliation.

4. THOMAS'S AFFILIATIONS WITH THE ARISTOTLE OF THE *ETHICS*

There is, first, an easy exclusion. Nothing is to be gained by talking about Thomas's 'Aristotelianism'. 'Aristotelianism' as a descriptive category owes much more to the prejudices of Enlightenment historiography than to the medieval texts in hand. The model of 'critical' historiography, made famous by Jakob Brucker, proceeds by identifying the irreducible, 'natural philosophic' content within a position. This model ought to be clearly distinguished from the ancient and medieval doxographies by school. Thomas speaks frequently of "sects (*sectae*)" of philosophers, and he knows well the various doxographies in Aristotle and the commentators on him. But *sectae* are historical communities constituted by relations of students to teachers, by common practices of ways-of-life, by the tradition of certain texts. *Sectae* are not "-isms." And so we betray Thomas's own understanding of the history of philosophy if we describe his relation to Aristotle as a relation to an "-ism."

A second description to be excluded sees Thomas as defending a set of crucial doctrines or tenets by means of canonical arguments. It is true, of course, that Thomas was willing to defend certain Aristotelian positions and to do so largely with Aristotelian weapons. But these defenses are consequences of readings, not motives for them. Thomas himself makes it a principle of disputative exegesis that salient points are to be read back into the lexica and the contexts from which they emerge. Moreover, the arguments used are often revised— sometimes quite profoundly—and are almost always sharpened for application in a particular dialectic. They are not so much solid units to be borrowed, as suggestions or sources for invention.

A third description, more plausible, would want to speak of Thomas's readings as different ways of adopting the Aristotelian lexica. It is profoundly true that Thomas learns from Aristotle—as we all can—a powerful and supple set of interlocking terminologies by which to talk about so many parts of the world. Thomas takes over large portions of these lexica, as he takes over Aristotle's concern for the ranges of meaning in philosophic argument, for deduction from deep grammar, and so on. But it must immediately be added that there is a plurality of philosophic lexica in Thomas and that these languages form different constellations on different matters. Thomas treats the Aristotelian lexica as one level in a hierarchy of traditions of philosophic speech. It may be the privileged level in many cases, but it is not the only one, and its very conjunction with other levels, other lexica, modifies it in various ways. Thomas's readings of the *Ethics* are appropriations and modifications of the Aristotelian lexica—but the appropriations and modifications are made in view of a hierarchy that extends beyond them.

A fourth description, and a very attractive one, would take Thomas's successive readings of the *Ethics* as his appropriating larger and larger sets of heuristic schemata from Aristotle. By 'heuristic schemata' I mean nothing more than those marvelously useful patterns of distinction in which Aristotle is so rich—act/potency, form/ matter, mean/extreme, intellectual/moral. Thomas's successive readings of the *Ethics* would be described as so many ways of deploying and combining such schemata. He would begin, first, with discrete schemata on small points together with those schemata needed in wide, analogous application at a goodly level of abstraction. Then Thomas would take a whole set of schemata, connected to one another by the progress of the Aristotelian *Ethics* read straight through. Then, finally, he would put these schemata together with others from diverse authors when composing the *Summa*. Surely this description is correct and in part acceptable, and it invites us to understanding in more detail how Thomas analogizes Aristotle's schemata. But this description does not yet capture the central feature of Thomas's successive readings — namely, the progressive engagement with the structure of the *Ethics*.

The description that seems most adequate — that is, least misleading — would seem to me to narrate Thomas's greater and greater engagement with the textual pedagogy of the *Ethics*. Many lasting texts in ethics propose exemplary pedagogies. They set forth — or promise, or prophesy, or attempt to conduct — a pattern of education for the souls of readers. Now Aristotle's *Ethics* is exemplary in just this way. The *Ethics* served medieval pedagogies in many ways — as providing proof texts, terminologies, examples, distinctions, and so on. But it serves pedagogy most importantly by tracing a pedagogy of its own for the reader, by which the reader is brought to convictions about how to live. The whole text of the *Ethics* thus serves to provoke for Thomas the question of pedagogy in morals — and with it the question of whether there ought not to be a more encompassing textual pattern than Aristotle's for the formation of souls.

Thomas's readings of Aristotle rise from the dispersed *auctoritates* of the *Sentences*-commentary, through the single *auctor* of the *Ethics*-commentary, to the Aristotelian voice as full interlocutor in the construction of a moral theology. This is reminiscent in many ways of Albert's eclectic and sometimes ironic relation to Aristotle in the *Lectura*. But Thomas goes further. He recognizes that the only adequate reading of a book like the *Ethics* is a reading in which the reader's own way-of-life is put at stake. The *Ethics* begins by saying that certain sorts of readers cannot properly approach it — a restriction that we never take seriously in academic readings. The reader who does approach it seriously must claim to be a fit candidate for its habituation or to have benefited from a more complete and better habituation. The only serious response to the pedagogy of the *Ethics* is to propose an alternate pedagogy — and the most compelling response is to propose a pedagogy in which the *Ethics* itself is preserved as an organic part. A Christian reader of the *Ethics* can only respond to it in the end by showing how the Aristotelian pedagogy is absorbed into the higher pedagogy of grace. The second part of the *Summa* deserves to be described as Thomas's full reading of the *Ethics* precisely because it transforms the pedagogy of the *Ethics* into an even more encompassing pattern for Christian teaching.

NOTES

1. D. A. Callus, "The Date of Grosseteste's Translation and Commentaries on Pseudo-Dionysius and the *Nicomachean Ethics*," *Recherches de théologie ancienne et médiévale* 14 (1947): 200–209; confirmed by René-Antoine Gauthier in the introduction to his edition of the *Ethics, Aristoteles Latinus* 26:cci.

2. Gauthier, *L'Ethique à Nicomaque*, 2d ed., vol. 1, part 1 (Louvain and Paris, 1970), 121. Compare his introduction to the *Tabula libri Ethicorum*, in the Leonine edition of Thomas Aquinas, *Opera omnia* (Rome, 1882–), 48:B33 (editions hereafter cited as LE).

3. Gauthier, *Ethique à Nicomaque*, 1/1:121–122; and H. Paul F. Mercken, *The Greek Commentaries on the Nicomachean Ethics of Aristotle . . . ,* vol. 1 (Leiden, 1973), 30*–66*.

4. James A. Weishiepl, *Friar Thomas d'Aquino: His Life, Thought, and Works,* rev. ed. (Washington, 1983), 36–38; Simon Tugwell, *Albert and Thomas: Selected Writings* (New York, 1988), 208.

5. Gauthier thinks that Thomas first learned the *Ethics* as a student of arts at Paris; see LE 47:246* and LE 48:xvi–xvii. His evidence shows no more than that Thomas has some acquaintance with the *Ethica vetus* and a few details in the arts commentaries. The materials for constructing Thomas's biography are not continuous enough to support Gauthier's argument that Thomas could only have learned these at Paris.

6. See the remarks by Wilhelm Kübel in Albert the Great, *Super Ethica,* as in the Cologne edition of Albert's *Opera omnia* (Munster, 1951–) 14/1:v–vi.

7. Gauthier in LE 47/1:254*–256*.

8. I must leave aside the complicated questions about subsequent redactions of the text of the *Scriptum.* Hence, I take the Mandonnet-Moos, less the passages omitted by the Parma edition, as substantially reproducing the text of the *Scriptum* at the time of its first public circulation.

9. *Super Sent.* 3.33.

10. *Super Sent.* 1.pro divisio textus (ed. P. Mandonnet and M. F. Moos [Paris, 1929–1947], 1:22 [edition hereafter cited as MM]).

11. *Super Sent.* 1.31.2.1 solutio (MM 1:724).

12. *Super Sent.* 1.1.1.2 obj. 2 (MM 1:35).

13. *Super Sent.* 1.1.1.2 ad 2 (MM 1:36).

14. *Super Sent.* 1.5 expositio textus (MM 1:160).

15. *Super Sent.* 1.pro.1.5 solutio (MM 1:17).

16. *Super Sent.* 1.8 expositio secundae textus (MM 1:235).

17. *Super Sent.* 1.39.1.1 obj. 1 (MM 1:920).

18. *Super Sent.* 1.pro.1.1 titulus: "Utrum praeter physicas disciplinas alia doctrina sit homini necessaria" (MM 1:6).

19. *Super Sent.* 1.pro.1.1 solutio: "Una [*scil.* contemplatio] per creaturas est, ratione jam dicta, in qua contemplatione Philosophus, X *Ethic.,* cap. ix, felicitatem contemplativam posuit, quae tamen est felicitas viae. . ." (MM 1:7–8).

20. *Super Sent.* 1.4.1.1 solutio (MM 1:132), 1.7.1.1 ad 3 (MM 1:177), 1.37.4.1 (MM 1:881). Notice that the three passages cite two different texts in the *Ethics* — 5.4–6 and 10.3 — in support of the same maxim.

21. *Super Sent.* 1.pro.1.3.3 solutio (MM 1:12). Compare the equally integral citations in 1.1.1 solutio & ad 1 (MM 1:33–34).

22. *Super Sent.* 1.17.1.4 solutio (MM 1:403).

23. *Super Sent.* 1.46 expositio textus (MM 1:1060).

24. *Super Sent.* 3.9.1.

25. *Super Sent.* 2.27–29 for the main treatment, but see also 1.17.

26. *Super Sent.* 3.34.

27. *Super Sent.* 2.22, 2.39. 2.42, 2.44.

28. *Super Sent.* 2.24, 2.27.

29. *Super Sent.* 2.25, 2.38–39, 2.44.

30. *Super Sent.* 3.23, 3.33, 3.36, 4.14.

31. *Super Sent.* 4.14–17.

32. *Super Sent.* 3.35.

33. *Super Sent.* 4.49.

34. This is not the first discussion of virtue as such in the *Sentences*-commentary. That has already come at *Super Sent.* 2.27.1–6.

35. Tugwell, *Albert and Thomas,* 11.

36. Albert, *Sent.* 3.33.1–4 (ed. Borgnet in *Opera omnia* [Paris, 1890–1899], 28:606–615).

37. Albert, *Sent.* 3.33.1 objs. 7–8 & ad 7–9 (Borgnet 28:606,608), 3.33.3 obj. 5 & ad 5 (Borgnet 28:610–611).

38. Albert, *Sent.* 3.33.3 ad 5 (Borgnet 28:611).

39. Bonaventure, *Sent.* 3.33.1.1–6 (ed. Collegium S. Bonaventurae in *Opera omnia* [Quaracchi, 1882–1902] 3:712–731 [edition hereafter cited as CSB]).

40. For example, Bonaventure, *Sent.* 3.33.1.2 objs. 3–5 & ad 5 (CSB 3:713–714), 3.33.1.3 sed contra 3 (3:716), 3.33.1.5 sed contra 4 (3:722), 3.33.1.5 dubium 3 (3:729).

41. For example, Bonaventure, *Sent.* 3.33.1.3 sed contra 1: "secundum quod dicit Philosophus in fine Novae Ethicae" (CSB 3:716).

42. *Super Sent.* 3.33.1–3 (MM 3:1015–1104).

43. The next longest are dd. 3 and 34, which are each about two-thirds the length of d. 33.

44. For example, *Ethics* 2.2 (1004b4) is used in *Super Sent.* 3.33.1.2.2 solutio and 3.33.2.2.2 obj. 3 (MM 3:1029 and 1052, respectively). *Ethics* 5.7 (1123b30) is used in 3.33.2.1.4 obj. 2 and 3.33.3.3.4 solutio (3:1044 and 1091). *Ethics* 6.14 (1138a1) is used in 3.33.3.1.1 ad 2 and 3.33.3.4.4 obj. 1 (3:1083 and 1094). *Ethics* 7.13 is used in 3.33.2.3 solutio, 3.33.2.4 solutio, and 3.33.2.5 obj. 6 (3:1057, 1067, and 1068).

45. *Super Sent.* 3.33.1.3.1 sed contra 1, 3.33.2.2.2 sed contra 1, 3.33.2.2.3 sed contra 1 (MM 3:1032 and 1052–1053, respectively).

46. *Super Sent.* 3.33.3.1–4.

47. *Super Sent.* 3.33.1.4 ad 5 (MM 3:1041): "Tamen sciendum est quod Philosophus loquitur de virtutibus acquisitis quae perficiunt hominem in vita civitatis terrenae, in qua vita non habemus aliquam communicationem cum angelis; unde non est simile de illis virtutibus quae perficient in vita civili civitatis quae constitutitur ex angelis et hominibus."

48. *Super Sent.* 3.33.1.4 ad 2 (MM 3:1041).

49. Respectively, *Super Sent.* 3.33.1.3.1–3 and 3.33.2.2.1–3.

50. Respectively, *Super Sent.* 3.33.2.1.1–4, 3.33.2.4.1–4, 3.33.2.5.

51. *Super Sent.* 3.33.1.2.3–4.

52. *Super Sent.* 3.33.1.3.4 solutio.

53. *Super Sent.* 3.33.1.4 solutio.

54. *Super Sent.* 3.33.2.4.2 ad 3.

55. The only Christian authorities cited are ps-Dionysius on the nature of the good in 2.7 (LE 47:98.9–12) and Isidore on the definition of 'ius' in 5.12 (47:304.16–17). The one Christian example is the martyrdom of St. Lawrence, but immediately after mentioning it Thomas attributes another sense to Aristotle's remarks on suffering death in 3.2 (47:122.52–58): "sicut beatus Laurentius sustinuit adustionem craticulae ne idolis immolaret. Et hoc ideo Philosophus dicit vel quia morienti propter virtutem remanet post mortem gloria, vel quia fortiter persistere in bono virtutis est tantum bonum ut ei aequiparari non possit diuturnitas vitae quam homo moriendo perdit."

56. There are a few passages in the *Ethics* commentary where Thomas raises disputes, but these are exegetical. See, for example, the objections against Aristotle's division of mind, which are settled in 6.1 by distinguishing senses of 'contingentia' in various passages (LE 47:333.150–334.214).

57. For example, the Olympic games, 1.12 (LE 47:44.189–196); Solon, 1.5 (47:54.32–33); nudity and the palaestra, 2.6 (47:195.128/131–132); the Scythians, 3.7 (47:139.79–80); the Celts, 3.15 (47:165.134–166.135); Homeric heroes, 3.16 (47:169.57–170.69); and so on.

58. For example, the need to identify the "Peripatetics" as followers of Aristotle in 1.12 (47:42.65) and 1.16 (47:59.138–139).

59. *Sent. Eth.* 1.1 (especially LE 47:4.99–106).

60. *Sent. Eth.* 1.1 (LE 47:5.110–113).

61. For example, in the anonymous commentary on *De anima* edited by R. A. Gauthier, *Lectura in librum de anima* (Grottaferrata: Collegium S. Bonaventurae, 1985), 4: "Diuiditur autem hec sciencia in partes duas, in proemium et executionem, que incipit: 'Intendentes de anima. . . .'" Compare the commentary's alignment of the sciences with the Aristotelian works, pp. 2–4.

62. See, for example, the instruction on how to construe a difficult sentence in 1.1: "Littera autem suspensiva est et sic legenda. . ." (LE 47: 6.259–260).

63. *Sent. Eth.* 1.2: "Horum autem duorum, primum quidem pertinet ad tractatum huius scientiae, quia talis consideratio est circa rem de qua haec scientia considerat, sed secundum pertinet ad prooemium, in quo manifestatur intentio huius doctrinae" (LE 47:8.89–93). Compare 1.1 (LE 47: 14.1–11), where the "tractatus huius scientiae" is divided into the parts that are sections of Aristotle's book.

64. *Sent. Eth.* 1.2 (LE 47:9.193–202).

65. *Sent. Eth.* 2.2 (LE 47:81.124–131). Compare *Super Sent.* 3.33.1.3.1 ad 4 (MM 3:1036).

66. *Sent. Eth.* 8.12 (LE 47:488.285–288).

67. *Super Sent.* 4.7 (LE 47:222.23–26), 9.10 (47:542).

68. *Sent. Eth.* 7.1 (LE 47:381.88–90), though he goes on to stress that Aristotle denies deification in any literal sense (381:118–123).

69. *Sent. Eth.* 1.14 (LE 47:50.66–76), 1.18 (47:65.78–80), 3.13 (47:157. 112–113), 5.12 (47:306.158–160), 8.7 (47:465.130–131), 10.12 (47:591.126, 592.169).

70. *Sent. Eth.* 4.7 (LE 47:222.28–32).

71. For example, Albert, *Super Ethica* 1.3 (*Opera omnia* 14 [Munster 1968–1972]:17.53). Compare Thomas, *Super Sent.* 3.33.1.4 (MM 3:1041).

72. *Sent. Eth.* 1.9 (LE 47:32.162–165). Compare 1.15 (47:54/52–54), 1.17 (47:62.58–60), 3.18 (47:178.103–108).

73. *Sent. Eth.* 1.17 (LE 47:63.142–148), 3.14 (47:161.124–131).

74. *Sent. Eth.* 1.10 (LE 47:37.166–167), 10.11 (47:587.71–73), 10.13 (47:595.141–144).

75. *Sent. Eth.* 1.16 (LE 47:60.222–226).

76. *Sent. Eth.* 1.17 (LE 47:63.148–153).

77. Thomas's understanding of the order of the *Ethics* is drawn from his remarks in *Sent. Eth.* 1.1 (LE 47:4.107–127), 1.3 (47:12.165–170), 1.4 (47:14.1–25), 1.19 (47:67.1–68.22), 2.1 (47:76.1–41), 3.14 (47:160.1–34), 7.1 (47:380.1–24), 10.1 (47:551.1–17).

78. *Summa* 2–2.114. Of course, many of the matters that Aristotle discusses in the books on friendship appear in Thomas under the acts of the theological virtue of charity. See, for example, *Summa* 2–2.28–33.

79. *Summa* 2–2.155.

80. Thomas explains this in the prologue: "Virtutum autem intellectualium una quidem est prudentia, quae inter cardinales virtutes continetur et numeratur; ars vero non pertinet ad moralem, quae circa agibilia versatur, cum ars sit recta ratio factibilium ut supra dictum est; alia vero tres intellectuales virtutes, scilicet sapientia, intellectus et scientia, communicant etiam in nomina cum donis quibusdam Spiritus Sancti, unde simul etiam de eis considerabitur in consideratione donorum virtutibus correspondentium" *(Summa* 2–2.pro).

81. *Sent. Eth.* 4.17 (LE 47:261.137–139). Compare 2.9 (47:109.166–167).

82. Jerome, *Super Ezechielem* 43.23–35 (CCSL 75:642), as in Peter Lombard, *Sententiae* 2.42.4 (CSB [Grottaferrata, 1971–], 1:569).

83. Isidore, *Sentences* 2.17.3–4 (PL 83:620A–B), as in Peter Lombard, *Sententiae* 2.22.4 (CSB 1:445).

84. For the use of the first triplet see, e.g., *Super Sent.* 3.37.1.2.3 solutio (MM 3:1242); *De malo* 9.2 sed contra 3 (LE 23:212.84–85). For its qualification, see *Super Sent.* 2.42.1.2.1 solutio (MM 2:1072–1074), 4.16.1.1.3 ad 1 (MM 4:775); *Summa* 1–2.72.7. For the use of the second triplet, see *De malo* 3.6–12, *Summa* 1–2.76, 1–2.77.3, 1–2.78, where the three are classed among the causes of sin.

85. William Peraldus, *Summa aerea de virtutibus et vitiis* (Venice, 1497), fols. 293ra–299rb and 304ra–306vb, respectively.

86. Yet another instance of a return to old ways after Thomas's innovations is the compiling from the *Summa* of a treatise on the seven capital sins, e.g., Bamberg, Staatliche Bibliothek Patr. 122 (Q. V. 12), ff. 220r–225v, as in H. F. Dondaine and H. V. Shooner, *Codices manuscripti operum Thomae de Aquino,* vol. 1 (Rome, 1967), p. 48, #113.

87. Respectively, *Summa* 2–2.35.4, 36.4, 118.7, 132.4, 148.5, 153.4, 158.6.

Henry of Ghent and Augustine

Raymond Macken, O.F.M.

WITHIN THE WELL-CHOSEN theme of this conference, it was wise to give Augustine a well-merited place. Since he was omnipresent in the medieval thought of the Christian West, it is often forgotten that his thought was in great part the result of a personal pilgrimage to the light of Christian faith, or, to express it with the words of a well-known Dutch poet, "the most individual expression of a most individual emotion."[1] However, Augustine's emotions were those of a universal spirit, so that his writings have the dimension of reflecting the deep feelings of human beings in general.

Nobody, I think, will deny what Johannes Hessen says in the preface of his sympathetic synthesis of the philosophy of Augustine: "Together with the Thomistic direction of Christian philosophical and theological thought, the classical expression of Augustine's thought is equally at home in the Christian tradition; nor when we give to Augustine his legitimate place and audience, does it oppose the intentions of the ecclesiastical authorities."[2]

To all those familiar with the history of Western philosophy, it is well known that Henry of Ghent may be rightly considered, although with some restrictions and in a personal way, as a representative of a Platonic-Augustinian current of thought. In this he represents a venerable tradition, which has always been acknowledged and respected in the Christian world, has never ceased to attract brilliant minds, and continues to exercise a great attraction on several creative thinkers of our time.

The study of the relation between Augustine and Henry of Ghent is useful for a right interpretation of Henry's thought, and also for an understanding of medieval Augustinianism in general. Henry's contacts with Augustine illustrate how astonishingly fresh Augustine's thought remained in the Middle Ages, how it attracted respectable

251

thinkers with different geniuses and animated by different preoccupations. In what follows, we will explain what Henry's principal preoccupations with Augustine's intellectual heritage seem to have been
and how he tried to reach his aim.

As stated, Augustine is omnipresent in Henry's works, the critical edition of which will occupy about forty-six volumes, so that here
only a brief and suggestive survey can be given. Most of my colleagues
are familiar with the world of thought of the "Father of the Christian
Occident," as Augustine was sometimes called, but less familiar with
the thought of Henry of Ghent. They will allow me to reverse the roles
and to explain how in the very extensive oeuvre of Henry of Ghent
Augustine's heritage remained lively and exercised its influence. For
the doctrines of Augustine treated here, I have relied on Hessen's succinct book; for Henry of Ghent, I have relied on my own studies of
several of his doctrines.

HENRY'S ELABORATION OF THE GREAT THESES
OF PLATONISM AND AUGUSTINIANISM

One of the principal preoccupations of Henry's scholarly activity was to expound and prove strictly the major theses of Augustine
and their Platonic underpinnings. From the extensive introduction
of his *Summa,* written in the very first year of his teaching as master
of theology at the University of Paris, it is interesting to see Henry
with his habitual energy at work towards this aim.

Augustine's rethinking of Platonic tradition was more than a
superficial "correction." According to Hessen, "two worlds of thought
meet in the elevated mind of Augustine: the Platonic, and in part Neo-
platonic, and the Biblical-Christian world. Augustine's philosophy can
only be well understood in its final intentions when we try to understand it as a synthesis of Platonism and prophecy."[3] "Platonism is idealism," Hessen claims. "Sensible things are real only insofar as they participate in the supra-sensible world. The starting point of prophecy
is completely different." Not the ideal world, but the reality of this
world is of primary importance. In Augustine's spirit idealism and
realism have struck an alliance. Augustine asserts the existence of an
ideal world; he also maintains the full reality of finite things.[4] Hessen
adds,

From another point of view, we must consider in Augustine's Platonism the entry of the realistic; when we compare the two worlds of thought, which we formerly opposed as idealism and realism, we can characterize the opposition still more accurately if we consider Platonism as a philosophy of the objective spirit, and the prophetic as a philosophy of the subjective spirit. The philosophy of the objective spirit searches the contents of the spirit, in other words, ideas and values. Platonism at its heart is a philosophy of the ideal and values. The world of ideas, the realm of the suprasensible essences, is for Platonism the central object of all philosophy. In face of this the prophetic appears as a philosophy of the subjective spirit, of the spirit as an acting, creative principle. This does not mean that we remain limited to the study of the structure of the human spirit, but that we stand before it with respect as before an active creative force, which is ultimately the image and effect of an absolute and infinite Spirit.[5]

Hessen's remarks concerning Augustine can also be applied to Henry of Ghent's philosophy. Here also is not only a great interest in Platonic ideas as they have been translated and adapted by Augustine, but a very concrete component, which should not be underestimated and which is already manifest in his concern to maintain the metaphysical unity of the concrete being. This is the reason for his well-known preference for an intentional distinction in the creature, instead of the real distinction proposed by Thomas Aquinas. Also like Augustine, Henry is interested in the spirit itself as an acting and creative principle. Characteristic of Henry is his insistence on the active and autonomous character of human spiritual faculties, intelligence and will, which in his philosophy are only two faces of the same spiritual substance: the soul.

Henry enjoyed a long life and academic career. He was convinced of the importance of the task of the master in theology, who had to strive, according to his expression, to be "a major light in the Church."[6] Many aspects of his thought are not up to now well known. The editors of his *Opera omnia,* in addition to their critical editions, are publishing new doctrinal studies. We must beware of all premature conclusions. However, some great lines of Henry's thought are known, and they allow us to present a provisional synthesis. In this spirit we propose that we view Henry of Ghent's work as an extensive and impressive attempt to give a strictly scientific basis to the Platonic-Augustinian tradition of thought by combining with it some other positions coming from Aristotle and Avicenna and other scholastic authors, such as Bonaventure and Thomas Aquinas.

Let us now pass in review some points of similarity and influence between Augustine and Henry and see each time how the spiritual heritage of Augustine has been preserved, and at the same time developed, by Henry of Ghent.

A SPIRITUAL CONCEPTION OF THE HUMAN CREATURE

Henry is not at all pessimistic about human possibilities and expectations. His conception, on the contrary, is optimistic, insofar as with Augustine, Avicenna, and other thinkers he admits in the human soul the possibility of a direct contact with spiritual realities. In the conception of Henry only the human soul gifted with spiritual faculties bears the proper image of God.[7] Also in the natural order God helps human beings to strive to a greater conformity with their model.[8]

DIVINE ILLUMINATION AND DIRECT HUMAN KNOWLEDGE OF SOME SPIRITUAL REALITIES

"In the manner of Plato," says Hessen, "Augustine cast his eyes in the direction of the contents of the spirit. The sphere of the ideal, the realm of the intelligible, became visible to him in its full greatness and elevation, its metaphysical dignity. This sight became for him a valuable foundation for the whole of philosophy, as a warrant for the truth of human knowledge."[9] Once Augustine had founded metaphysically the objective value of human knowledge, he was confronted with a further task: to show how knowledge originates psychologically, how the human spirit acquires the possession of those truths on which all knowledge rests. For the solution of this second question the Father of the Church first followed the traces of Plato and took over his opinion that all knowledge consists in a remembrance by the soul of the ideas contemplated in a former existence before it was incorporated in this world in a body. But because the doctrine of the pre-existence of the soul disagrees with Christian dogma, he was urged to search for another solution. He found this solution in Plotinus, who admitted an illumination of the human spirit by the Nous. Augustine took over this conception and solved the problem of (intellectual) knowledge by the theory of divine illumination. According to this theory the human intellect is in its knowledge illuminated by the light of the divine Truth, so that it contemplates the truths in its light.[10]

The possibility of a direct contact of the human soul with the spiritual realities, which Henry admitted, goes immediately together with the theory of divine illumination, which Henry defended strongly in the introduction to his *Summa* and maintained during the rest of his life. Henry defended Augustine's theory of divine illumination, however, with his customary prudence. In his view divine illumination was only rarely experienced in human life. But what humans have contemplated in these elevated moments they can recall afterwards with the help of memory. Henry limited illumination to a minimum in order to maintain for the human intellect its full inborn activity with its own natural powers. From the senses our knowledge receives the exterior, superficial truth of things (their "declarativum esse," as Hilary says.) This knowledge is not unmixed with errors. Behind the cover of phantasms divine illumination helps to find the ontological truth,[11] which, according to Anselm, consists in the conformity with the original idea corresponding to it ("conformitas ad suum exemplar verissimum"). In the human spiritual soul originates a dynamism of intelligence, which seeks to surmount the superficial truth and to discover the ontological truth. Therefore divine illumination is never to be understood as an invitation to laziness, but as an invitation to penetrate more deeply the proper truth.[12]

AUGUSTINE'S HUMAN DUALITY AND HENRY'S HUMAN DIMORPHISM

"How much the Christian platonist Augustine moves in the ways of the anthropological dualism proposed by Plato," Hessen says, "is shown by how much he stresses the superiority of the soul in comparison with the body. The principal in us is our spirit, Augustine claims. Man is defined as a rational soul possessing a body. In this way man is not to be seen as the psycho-physical composite proposed by Aristotelian philosophy, but more as a soul gifted with intelligence, which possesses a body. This body is seen as the instrument of the soul, to whose rule it is subjected by God. The soul is defined by Augustine as a substance, gifted with intelligence and apt for the regiment of a body."[13] This dualism in the philosophy of Henry of Ghent is technically expressed in his theory of human dimorphism.[14]

THE HUMAN SOUL'S SPIRITUAL FACULTIES
AND SUBSTANCE

With other thinkers in the Platonic-Augustinian tradition, Henry considered the faculties only as "aspects" (*respectus*) of the soul. This shows again his solicitude for the metaphysical unity of the concrete. With regard to the functioning of these faculties, he admits the psychological facts commonly received in his time, but on the metaphysical level he does not conceive the faculties as entities really distinguished from the soul; in his view an "intentional" distinction between these faculties and the substance of the soul suffices.[15]

THE HUMAN BEING *IN VIA* AND *IN PATRIA*[16]

Both Augustine's and Henry's works contain a psychology and an ethics; I shall confine myself to what I call their "metaphysics of man." Because of their spiritual nature, human creatures possess self-consciousness, living in communion with other beings of the same kind. When they try to turn their aptitudes into realizations, they may be judged only by their success in this world.[17] But human beings are open to the infinite in this life and in the next, everlasting life.

According to Henry of Ghent, God is part of the object of metaphysics. This object comprehends being in general as well as the highest being, who causes all created beings. God and creatures are included in the same concept of being, although in an analogical way. In the *Summa,* which is much more than a theodicy, the divinity is examined in itself and in relation to creatures. Although Henry finished only the first part of the *Summa,* devoted to God, he often announced the second part, which would be devoted to creatures. Nevertheless, the completed first part includes many expositions concerning creatures in relation to God.

Henry ascribes a threefold causality of God in relation to creatures: he is their formal, efficient, and final cause. As formal and efficient cause, God is Alpha, the origin of all created beings; as final cause, he is Omega. Thus for intelligent creatures he is not only the first, implicitly known object,[18] he is also the goal towards which they must all strive.[19] Metaphysics must formulate the way all things come from God and return to him.

Treating the going out of creatures from God, Henry regularly warns against the uncritical acceptance of Aristotle, whose doctrines clash with the dogma of creation. In this respect, the doctrines of Plato, whom Henry calls "the most eminent of philosophers" in the *Lectura ordinaria super sacram Scripturam,* had the better insights.[20]

Treating the return of creatures to God, Henry relies most on the authority of Augustine.[21] For those medieval philosophers who were at once influenced by Augustine's doctrine of divine illumination and Avicenna's conception of the agent intellect, Étienne Gilson proposed the term "Avicennasizing Augustinianism."[22] This term applies well to Henry of Ghent, who like Augustine and Avicenna, had a highly spiritual conception of human beings. Henry's preference for Augustine reflects his philosophical preference for Plato over Aristotle, who better than Aristotle understood the extra-temporal object of human life in the possession of the uncreated good, or God himself.

PRIME MATTER

Augustine suggested the possibility that seminal reasons exist in matter.[23] Similarly, Henry of Ghent teaches that prime matter is more than a transcendental relation to the form and has a certain consistency in itself and possibility to subsist alone without further union with a form.[24]

THE SEARCH FOR TRUTH

"Augustine," Hessen claims, "was the most passionate searcher after truth of the ancient world. More than his ancient masters Plato and Plotinus, he struggled with the problem of the truth. For him indeed the question of truth was the vital question. From the solution of this question he expected more than mere intellectual satisfaction: it signified for him the acquisition of a stable conception of the world and of life, which would enable a true development of his personality. In this way we should understand Augustine, when in the beginning of the *Confessions,* speaking of his first wrestlings with the truth, he exclaims: 'O Truth, how intimately the depths of my soul aspired to Thee.'"[25]

According to Henry, the immediate object of the intellect, in its simple perception that sees but does not yet compare, is being.[26] This simple perception usually unites intellectual and sensible perceptions, although sometimes there can be a purely intellectual perception that consists in a direct, brief contemplation of a purely spiritual reality ("intellectus qui est simplicium intelligentia").

As soon as the human intellect begins to compare, it shows the dynamism and initiative of a spiritual faculty, as does the human will at the beginning of its activity. The intellect then tends towards its proper final cause, not its immediate first object. The intellect's proper first object is the true: "in the measure that a thing is more perfect in being," Henry claims, "it becomes more perfect in truth."[27] He quotes here an Aristotelian principle, but he interprets it in the framework of a more spiritual conception, wherein a thing is more true to the measure it has a higher degree of being.

How can the human intellect know the truth of a thing? It can know it through the universal, which is the formal cause of the human intellect. The formal object of the intellect is the universal; the formal object of the senses is the singular.[28]

One must add immediately that for Henry, the singular is also an object of the human intellect, although not its formal object. By means of the species presented to it in concrete circumstances of time and space, it discovers the singular and enriches the knowledge that it had already acquired from it.[29] But the universal is the form that the true takes for the human intellect, and the universal is what it seeks immediately to detect in the things it perceives (sometimes directly in the form of spiritual realities).[30]

Henry tends generally to magnify the spiritual character of the human intellect and will and to demonstrate their creativity and independence: the independence of the intellect from the senses, and the will's independence from the intellect. The intellect is far more than a receptive faculty of sensible impressions; it is a dynamic, initiating faculty.[31] Upon contact with a thing, the intellect begins a conquest of its "truth," until it achieves a complete and profound understanding of it. The intellect is not satisfied until it acquires this ultimate truth. Henry says that a created being has its deep ontological truth only in the measure that it participates in the first truth, which is God.

Therefore, the intellect knows a participated reality perfectly and definitively only when it knows the ground of its being in that which it participates. In this sense, God is the principal object of created spiritual intellects; this is so because he is the formal and final cause of their intellects.[32]

But how can the intellect know the ultimate ground and truth of a thing's participated being? Here we confront Henry's conception of God as the principal object of human intellect from the beginning of its intellectual life. Certainly Henry does not mean that human knowledge of God is the result of a special, divine illumination, so he cannot be reproached with "ontologism." Henry says explicitly that here he treats only the facts of general human knowledge. The apparent duality of the objects of the intellect has nothing to do with an addition of a special knowledge of God by a direct illumination; rather, this duality must be understood in relation to Henry's conception of the analogy between the concepts of being and the good.[33]

In Henry's eyes, the concept of being is not univocal, insofar as it cannot be applied in the same way to two different realities. Nor is it analogical in the Thomistic sense. In a sense, it is equivocal, since in our mind at the same time two different concepts of being are present, one applied to creatures, the other to God. These two concepts, however, are not completely different. There is an intimate connection between the two that can be called analogical, although not in the Thomistic sense.

We must understand that the origins of our concepts of creatures and God are not understood in the same way by Henry and Thomas Aquinas. For Henry, divine illumination is a part of human intellectual experience, even though the direct contact with spiritual realities occurs on earth only rarely. However, Henry does not admit that all of our concepts must pass through perceptions of our senses; rather, more like Plato, he accepts the direct contact of spiritual faculties with spiritual realities.[34] Thus, the connection between the dual objects of the intellect is strengthened by the fact that both can refer in some part to immediate contacts with spiritual realities.

But the connection between the two concepts derives not only from their common origin, but also from the proper character of the concept of being that applies to creatures. As we have seen, the immediate object of the human intellect is being received in a simple intellectual perception before the mind begins to compare. This immediate concept is not univocal, however, in the way Henry understood Avicenna to teach; that is, this concept is not a substratum to which may be added other determinations in order to build the complex structure of a concrete being. Rather, Henry's concept of being is analogical in a pregnant sense; it is determined not by specifying additions, but by limitations that pertain to the whole of being. As long as these determinations are not explicit, the first concept of being that applies to creatures bears a certain likeness to the concept of the infinite being, which is God. In both concepts limiting determinations are wanting: in the first, which applies to creatures, because the limiting determinations are not yet explicit; in the second, which applies to God, because such limiting determinations are denied. This does not mean, however, that God is an undetermined being. As Henry says in *Quodlibeta* 15.9, "determination" can mean two things: (1) a limitation in the degree of being, and in this sense it applies to creatures, or (2) a strict separation from all other beings, and in this sense it applies to God, and exactly defines his divine being.[35]

Thus, according to Henry's understanding, the unity of the concept of being is characterized by a unity to which two different, but ontologically related realities correspond.[36] Of the two objects, that which applies to God has natural priority. As Henry says, for angelic and human minds, the knowledge of God is more essential than the knowledge that they have of themselves. In the *Summa* a. 24, qq. 7–9, Henry argues that God is involved in the first, natural, indistinct knowledge of the human mind before the intellect begins to compare; in other words, the equivocal concept of being includes both the not-yet-determined being of the concrete creature and the indeterminable being of God. Of course, the concept of God is here perceived only confusedly.

Henry distinguishes clearly between natural and rational knowledge of God. Rational knowledge of God is obtained by way of discursive reasoning ("cognitio via ratiocinativae deductionis animadversa").[37] In this knowledge, the nature of God is not the first known object but the last. It is the dynamism of the mind that drives it to proceed from its first undetermined knowledge to understand its object with increasing clarity; it cannot rest until it understands its object in its ultimate reality, in relation to its ultimate cause.[38] This relation has a double aspect: the relation to the origin of all created things, and the relation to their end and purpose.

To understand the essence of a thing, we must understand it not only in itself, but as an image of the divine idea, which is the creature's divine exemplar. The divine exemplar is the creature's formal-extrinsic cause and its ultimate meaning. Knowledge of the divine exemplar is a necessary element of the complete understanding of a creature's essence. But the human mind strives not only to know the origin of each creature, but also its ultimate final cause, to which it tends beyond the limited objects and purposes of temporal life. As the human will tends to reach through created goods to the ultimate subsistent Good, so the intellect tends to reach beyond the limited truths that are its good towards the first subsistent Truth.[39]

God's formal-extrinsic causality and his final causality are the keys to Henry's metaphysical proof for the existence of God by means of his essence. But even without this philosophical proof, the original obscure knowledge of God becomes progressively more detailed by means of a dialectic founded on the fundamental dynamism of the human mind. The first, obscure, confused concept of God is the starting point and impetus of the soul's journey to God.

Henry was always careful to correct expressions that could be the occasion of misinterpretation. In the last quodlibetal question of his career (15.9), Henry does not call God the "first object" of the mind as he had fifteen years earlier in the *Summa*. His fundamental position, however, remains the same. In the mind's first undetermined perception of being, both the yet-to-be determined creature and the indeterminable being of God are involved, the former clearly, the latter only as necessarily connected. But the subsistent being has a natural, if not a temporal, priority, because it has made the intellect and all created things. In this sense subsistent being is the principal object of the intellect. It is the duty of the human intellect, by way of discursive reasoning, to discover ever more clearly what is implied in its first confused perception, to cast more light on its relation to its formal-extrinsic and final cause, and to pursue an ever clearer sight of God, insofar as it can be attained.

THE PRIMACY OF LOVE

Many who follow Augustine assert the primacy of love and judge that the will is a more elevated faculty in the human soul than intelligence. This position occupies an important place in the thought of Henry of Ghent.[40] Not only with respect to creatures but also with respect to God, the question of the primacy of love is posed by Henry.

It is treated in the framework of his monumental *Summa,* and he answers it in the same way: will is also primary in God.[41]

On the question of final beatitude, Henry likewise defends the
primacy of love, despite the position of some thinkers of his time, who
under the influence of Aristotle saw human beatitude as an act of intelligence, the contemplation of the divinity. Against such conceptions,
Henry understands the beatitude of human creatures in heaven as
the satiation of their desire to become one with God. This union is
obtained in the first instance through acts of the will. Not the will
alone, but the whole person becomes blessed, because according to
Henry there is not a real, but only an intentional distinction between
the soul and its faculties.[42] They penetrate one another: the will
makes the intelligence free, and the intelligence makes the will rational.[43] The will however is more free than the intellect.[44] The will is
the proper faculty that enables one to approach God more and more
closely.

THE AFFECTIVE WAY TO GOD

In light of the primacy of love in Henry's philosophy, the profound motives of the affective way to God become clearer. (The affective way provides even a metaphysical proof for God's existence.)[45]
On this point, Henry is evidently close to Augustine.[46] It is in the
Summa, the fruit of the *Quaestiones disputatae ordinariae* that he held during his career as master of theology, that we find Henry's proofs for
the existence of God treated at length.

In the extensive introduction of twenty articles that opens the
Summa, Henry treats first the existence of God and the knowledge that
human minds can have of it (aa.21–22), and then the essence of God
and the knowledge that human minds can have of it (aa.23–24). This
order is logical: Henry admitted some proofs that are of a physical
character, and proceed directly from an initial but imperfect notion
of God toward his existence.

In article 22, questions 4 and 5, Henry examines what knowledge
of the existence of God can be obtained by the human intellect, when
limited to its own powers. The title of question 4 is: "Can the human
intellect demonstrate God's existence from creatures?" The title of question 5 is: "Is there a way for the human intellect to know the existence
of God other than by arguing from creatures?"[47] Question 5 is clearly

raised in contrast to the previous question. Henry also explicitly mentions a source: Avicenna. "It was the opinion of Avicenna," he says, "if, at least, he spoke here as a pure philosopher" (Henry was conscious that Avicenna was an adherent of another monotheistic religion), that there is an *a priori* way possible for showing the existence of God. He announces this way in the first book of his Metaphysics in the following words: "Another way for demonstrating the existence of the First Principle is open to man, besides the way through the testimony of material creatures: namely, the way of universal intelligible propositions, which evidently show that the material creatures must have a First Principle, that this must exist necessarily, and that all creatures must have their existence from it."[48]

After having treated the existence of God in articles 21–22, Henry treats his essence in articles 23–24. In article 24 he treats his essence concretely in regard to the knowledge which human minds can have of it, and in question 6 of his article, whether the human mind can know the essence of God by means of creatures.[49] This question of the *Summa* was written not long after questions 4 and 5 of article 22, but in the meantime Henry's mind seems to have continued working on the question. When we compare question 6 of article 24 to questions 4 and 5 of article 22, we notice that Henry has introduced some new terminology in the later question.

From material substances, Henry says, we can acquire a knowledge of God in two ways: either insofar as they are material and changing and are studied by the philosophy of nature, or insofar as they are beings and substances and are studied by metaphysics. In the first way we can know that God exists, because from caused effects, we can ascend to the cause, and from movement to the mover. The second, metaphysical way is the way of eminence, which abstracts from creatures the intentions which they have in common with the Creator in an analogical way and then applies them to the Creator on a level corresponding to his own way of being. This metaphysical knowledge leads us to the existence of God and a limited knowledge of his essence. Whereas the way of natural philosophy only reveals God as the first mover, the way of eminence reveals God as the first form of creatures and their last aim.[50]

Henry clearly applies to this metaphysical way what he previously stated about Avicenna's way of the concepts of universal propositions, which likewise are analogically common to material creatures and to the Creator. There are also clear allusions to the way of formal causality, together with the way of eminence, with which it practically coincides, spread over four proofs. One should note that, when speaking of the metaphysical way, Henry refers repeatedly to the same passages of Augustine.

Each proof based on eminence supposes a middle term, which can be used for judging what is more or less eminent. Henry says that the human intellect cannot conceive these pure perfections as limited and gradually ordered without having present in the mind the pure subsistent perfection, with respect to which they are limited. Is not the existence of this middle term, which must be known before the other terms, thereby demonstrated?

In Henry's thought there are two, clearly distinguished stages of the knowledge of the essence of God: the first, which we have already at the start of our cognitive life, is an obscure and implicit knowledge; in the second, we are advancing to a distinct knowledge, which is an explicit discursive development of the dialectic already implicit in the first obscure knowledge. As this good or that good, Henry claims, cannot exist or be known except by means of Being and the Good considered simply, so also the Good in itself considered simply cannot exist or be known except by means of the Good in itself existing simply in an unparticipated way. In support of this he quotes Augustine from *De Trinitate* 8: "This good, or that good . . . , try to see the Good itself, if you can: then you will understand something of the essence of God." Indeed, Henry says, if we wish to judge rightly, we cannot judge that this good is better than that good, if we do not have in our mind the notion of the Good in itself."[51]

God's existence is also proved by way of final causality. The ultimate explanation of the finality in human intellectual activity can only be found in God: this is a position which Henry regularly sets out in his works. Only the first truth can completely satisfy human intellectual desire. If the human intellect could know all the essences of creatures in themselves, even this would not satiate the intellectual desire; the mind would go on longing to see them all together in a simple intuition of the divine being.[52] The knowledge which we have of God from his effects is only the first step; precisely because it reaches only an imperfect knowledge of God, it further stimulates our desire to know him better, beyond the limits of our natural capacities.[53]

This desire for the direct intellectual knowledge (or vision) of God, in Henry's view, goes together with the love of God. Because the soul is naturally capable of loving the highest good through the affection and of knowing the highest truth through the intellect, it cannot be satisfied with less. Adding in this way the role of the will to that of the human intellect, Henry comes to a conception similar and complementary to that which he has of the human intellect. At the base of all of the decisions and acts of the human will, he says, lies the love of the highest good, in which alone our heart can repose as Augustine says. Only this fundamental, implicit appetite for the Good itself explains the movement of the human will toward limited goods.[54]

The metaphysics of desire accompanies Henry's conception of God as final cause.[55] God is subsistent being. He knows and loves himself and makes creatures participate in his own perfection and happiness. In Henry's view rational creatures are profoundly marked by attraction to the subsistent being in order to know it and love it. It is characteristic of Henry that he likes to mention the final causality of God with respect to creatures before formal causality and efficient causality. All creatures, he says, are referred to God as to one and the same goal, one form and one efficient cause.[56] By their relation to God as their formal cause, they receive their essential being, which is the created imitation of an uncreated exemplar in God. By their relation to God as their efficient cause, they receive their existential being. The final cause in God should be considered the most noble of the three, because it is the deepest ground for God's giving to creatures their essence and existence.[57] The famous text of Augustine is repeatedly quoted by Henry in this context: "Fecisti nos ad Te, Domine. . . ." The "ad Te" refers to God as final cause, the deepest reason for God's creation. Creatures are made in order to participate in God to the extent that the nature of each allows; having been made, according to the possibilities of their natures, they strive to come ever closer to God.

DIVINE IDEAS, CREATURELY NOTHINGNESS, AND HUMAN DYNAMISM

"The central piece of Christian Platonism," Hessen says, "is the anchoring of the ideal world, the realm of truths and values, in the absolute, in God. Of this central idea," he continues, "one may say that it is present in some form in each more profound philosophy, which searches ultimate grounds of explication. By the attempt to secure the possession of the truth, to reach absoluteness against all relativism and skepticism, all philosophy conceived in a metaphysical sense has until now turned towards the final principle of being, the foundation of the world, and so anchored the truth in the Divinity. It suffices to think in modern times of Nicholas of Cusa, Descartes, Malebranche, Leibniz, German idealism, of Lotze, von Hartmann, Eucken and many others. Something similar," he continues, "applies also to the world of values. That they have also their mystical foundation in God, as Christian Platonism proposes it, is a thought valid for all times: Max Scheler expresses it so: 'All possible values are founded on the value of an infinite personal Spirit and the world of the values which is before him.'"[58]

"When so-called goods already delight us so," says Augustine, "which are not in themselves goods — indeed, all that is changeable is not good in itself — how great then will be the delight of the unchangeable, eternal goods, which remain always the same!"[59]

Henry sees the divine ideas as the examples of the essences of creatures. Creatures are composed by their essence, which is an image of its model, the divine idea in God, and nothingness. This divine idea is only realized when God gives to it existence in a finite image in a creature. The "vanity of the creature" is based on the nothingness which is one of its components: indeed, not only has it been created in the past from nothing, but nothingness remains a permanent component in its being. This nothingness is for Henry of Ghent the basis of a creature's strict temporality. He uses it as an argument in order to prove that the creature, which has nothingness as an essential component, cannot exist from eternity.[60]

On the other hand, the creature's vanity and feebleness is the source, when a reasonable creature remarks it, of its dynamism.[61] We are aware that we could be better human beings and wish to be so. Philosophically, Henry explains that the human essence is indeed a feeble reflection of its divine idea, because it partakes being as well as non-being. Because of this deficiency, however, the divine idea of the human creature becomes an ideal to which all tend and must tend.

Henry's philosophy can in a certain sense be characterized as an "essentialism," under the condition, however, that we are conscious of the fact that such general terms cannot cover the complexity of the philosophy of an important thinker. If we try to designate Henry's philosophy with such a term, it is important to take into account that the essence is not seen in Henry's thought in the same way as in Thomas

Aquinas. In Thomistic philosophy the essence is that which constitutes the limitation of a being, but existence constitutes its riches and is the origin of the dynamism of the creature; in this view the human will is rooted in the actuality of human existence, not in the limitations of the human essence. Henry's "philosophy of essence" can perhaps be seen as an alternative to a "philosophy of existence."

In an essentialistic philosophy the ideas are unchangeably present in God — this Henry claims with Plato and Augustine — but the essence of the creature is only an imperfect representation of the corresponding divine idea. That the proper ontological truth is placed outside creatures is an important philosophical alternative. In God these ideas reign as guiding stars, which expand their light on creatures. Because the ideas are "imitable," creatures can correspond to them in their being. Only if an idea receives additional existence in a creature in concrete circumstances of time and space ("here and now," as Henry expresses it), is it reflected, in an imperfect way, in a created essence.

With respect to the idea to which each creature corresponds, Anselm says that each being has a more profound truth. This more profound truth consists in precisely this, that we know the idea to which a creature corresponds.[62]

Not only in relation to intelligence, but also in relation to the will, the human tendency is clear: to direct itself towards objects higher than the immediate goods of everyday life. Therefore, according to Henry, there is not only an ontological truth for the intelligent creature, but there is also for the will a kind of authenticity, in the measure that, created to the image of God and corresponding to one of his imitable ideas, it develops always more by an "authentic" execution and elaboration of the ontological truth of its being.[63] The intelligent creature will in this way try to approach closer to its higher and more elevated model. When we are conscious of this natural tendency, we have already a natural desire to see God.

Only the divine being is being that exists in itself, and is being itself. The creature is in itself a non-being. Being itself, which is God, possesses the ways of participation, which can bring to existence a being that participates in a limited way in his infinite being. These ways of participation belong to the divine being, and are therefore eternal. God can bring them to existence through his almighty will, which is completely free, and not necessitated, as Avicenna proposed. Henry emphasizes the radical contingency of the creature in opposition to the plenitude of God's being. What the creature possesses by itself is only non-being; what is authentic in it is essence, by which it participates in the eternal divine idea. In this way Henry emphasizes the distance between the Creator and the creature.[64]

Henry of Ghent's metaphysics of man is characterized by Gomez Caffarena as a metaphysics of human "restlessness."[65] This restlessness, however, has nothing unhappy or pessimistic about it. It raises, on the contrary, the slumbering forces of the human soul. It is an invitation to human souls, almost a challenge. It shows them the great possibilities of their spiritual faculties. It exhorts them to approach ever more closely the higher, ontological truth of their being. The response of each human being who has understood this encouragement is the response of Augustine: "You have made us for You, O Lord, and our heart is restless until it rests in You."[66]

THE PLACE OF *SYNDERESIS*

"Whence," says Augustine, "have the atheists the knowledge of moral norms, which they evidently possess? They cannot read them in their own nature, because this is changeable, but these norms are unchangeable. They can hardly have drawn them from their own spirit, because there are general norms of morality that surpass them. Where are written these laws, if not in the book of the light which is called Truth, from which the moral law is copied and impressed in the heart of the moral man, not by descending to it, but by a direct impressions, as the image of the seal-ring imprints itself on the wax and in spite of this does not leave the ring."[67] Henry of Ghent, with Bonaventure, places *synderesis* in the sphere of the human will.[68]

FREEDOM OF THE HUMAN WILL

Besides intelligence, the human soul possesses will. The discovery of the ontological truth concerning the human soul itself implies the dynamism also of the human will, which finds its divine invitation and its task to execute. In each creature there is the being of the essence itself, which derives from and reflects the idea to which it corresponds, but is mixed with the non-being which the creature has from itself.[69] When an intelligent creature commits a sin, to ontological non-being he adds a moral non-being when the will does not execute the task imposed on it by its very essence. The will of the intelligent creature is invited to the test of love. Here it must show, as the most elevated human faculty[70] endowed with the ability to move itself,[71] that it will exercise an imperial power,[72] conforming to the divine idea. One achieves this conformity through "works of justice" (*opera iustitiae*), which must be preferred to "terrestrial works" (*opera terrestria*). (Terrestrial works are all the activities which result from concern for bodily things; these "earthly works" must hold only second place.[73]) According to Henry, the fundamental attitudes which enable one to perform works of justice are received in divinely illumined acts of knowledge, which help the intelligence by bestowing on it a fund of sure knowledge, unmixed with errors. These acts also influence the will, and confer upon it a stock of good and noble basic moral dispositions.[74]

GOD AS THE FINAL CAUSE OF HUMAN DESIRE

That God is above all the final cause is a salient feature of Henry's thought and is closely connected with the text from Augustine he so often cites: "You have made us for yourself, Lord, and our heart is restless until it rests in You." Henry strengthened this sentiment in his optimistic conception of the innate human desire for God.[75]

Until now we have treated strictly philosophical ideas. As long as one does not know through revelation that God has encountered the creatures made for him, one can only speak of the limited knowledge of God that one can reach by natural powers. However, one can state that our nature is open to a supernatural grace, by which God would help one to know himself better.

The question of man's natural desire for God had been raised from the beginning of scholasticism and was in general answered positively, although in different ways. Henry emphasizes that the supernatural order is a completely free gift of God, but he stresses at the same time that the human soul's openness to the supernatural is one of its most profound tendencies.[76] For a long time, Henry says, a supernatural order has actually existed along with a natural order. Those who with the help of divine illumination, including philosophers, prepare themselves for the supernatural order will soon perceive the influence of divine grace, and with its help become aware of God's presence in the world, where full of love, he comes to encounter those he has made for himself.[77]

CONCLUSION

Some authors think that Augustine in his later years became somewhat pessimistic, especially in his doctrine of predestination, and that his pessimism perhaps derived from the impression made on his finely tuned mind by the dissolution of the ancient world as he had known it. We leave to historians to judge if Augustine was truly pessimistic in his later years. Surely Henry of Ghent was not a pessimistic thinker. His activity was above all devoted to strictly scientific study and teaching, without being so frequently occupied as Augustine with direct pastoral work.[78]

It seems to me that one of Henry's great preoccupations was to give a satisfactory scientific foundation to the thought of his beloved Augustine. At the same time he represents a later evolution and a personal appropriation of Augustine's thought, influenced as well by some ideas of Aristotle, Avicenna, and other medieval scholastics. Indeed Henry's development of the Augustinian tradition assumes a personal and daring form, which deserves to be better known. Henry's philosophical thought is valuable and able to inspire thinkers, who like him, find deep inspiration in the insights of Augustine.

NOTES

See Plate 11 (Paris, Bibliothèque Nationale. Ms. lat. 15355, f. 162r.) Henry of Ghent, *Summa,* art. 34, q. 5, authorial corrections on the apograph. The manuscript was later owned by Godfrey of Fontaines. See R. Macken, "Les corrections d'Henri de Gand à sa Somme," *RTAM* 44 (1977): 55–100.

1. Willem Kloos (1859–1938).

2. J. Hessen, *Die Philosophie des heiligen Augustinus,* 2d ed. (Nuremberg, 1958), 9.

3. Ibid., 17.

4. Ibid., 17–18.

5. Ibid., 19–22.

6. Henry of Ghent, *Quodlibet 1,* in *Opera omnia* 5, ed. Macken (Leiden and Leuven, 1979), p. 200, line 21: "luminare maius in Ecclesia." See also Macken, "La personnalité, le caractère et les méthodes de travail d'Henri

de Gand," in *Festschrift für Martin Anton Schmidt zum 70. Geburtstag am ao. Juli 1989* (*Theologische Zeitschrift* 45, 1989), 192–206..

7. Henry of Ghent, *Quodlibet 13*, in *Opera omnia* 18, ed. J. Decorte (Leuven, 1985), p. 35, lines 35–36: ". . . ratio imaginis Dei . . . non est nisi in substantia intellectuali. . . ." We find the same conception in another work attributed with great probability to Henry, the *Lectura ordinaria super Sacram Scripturam Henrico de Gandavo adscripta*, in *Opera omnia* 36, ed. Macken (Leuven, 1980), p. 148, lines 77–81.

8. Macken, "Selbstverwirklichung des Menschen in der Philosophie Heinrich von Gent," in *Renovatio et Reformatio: Wider das Bild vom "finsteren" Mittelalter, Festschrift für Ludwig Hödl zum 60. Geburtstag überreicht von Freunden sowie Kollegen und Schülern*, ed. M. Gerwing and G. Ruppert (Münster, 1985 [issued November, 1984]), 136–137.

9. Hessen, *Die Philosophie*, 20.

10. Ibid., 27–28.

11. Henry of Ghent, *Summa (Quaestiones ordinariae) art. 31–34* 34.5, in *Opera omnia* 27, ed. R. Macken with an Introduction by L. Hödl (Leuven, 1991), p. 527, line 21.

12. Macken, "Selbstverwirklichung," 137. See also Macken, "La théorie de l'illumination divine dans la philosophie d'Henri de Gand," *Recherches de Théologie ancienne et médiévale* 39 (1972): 82–112; and Macken, "Denys the Carthusian, Commentator on Boethius' *De Consolatione Philosophiae*," *Analecta Cartusiana* 118 (1984): 60–65.

13. Hessen, *Die Philosophie*, 49.

14. Macken, "Unité et dymorphisme de l'homme selon Henri de Gand," in *Teoria e Prassi (Atti del Congresso Internazionale Genova — Barcelona, 8–15 settembre 1976)* (Naples, 1979) 1:177–182.

15. Macken, "Les diverses applications de la distinction intentionnelle chez Henri de Gand," in *Sprache und Erkenntnis im Mittelalter (Akten des VI. International Kongresses für mittelalterliche Philosophie, Bonn 29.viii–3.ix.1977)* Miscellanea Mediaevalia 13/2 (Berlin and New York, 1981), 769–776. See also Macken, "La volonté humaine, faculté plus élevée que l'intelligence selon Henri de Gand," *Recherches de Théologie ancienne et médiévale* 42 (1975): 23–31; Macken, "La liberté dans la philosophie d'Henri de Gand" (paper read at the 6th "Congresso Internazionale Scotista," Padua, September 24–29, 1976); Macken, "Heinrich von Gent im Gespräch mit seinen Zeitgenossen über die menschliche Freiheit," *Franziskanische Studien* 39 (1977): 125–182.

16. See J. Gomez Caffarena, "Metafísica de la inquietud humana en Enrique de Gante," in *L'homme et son destin d'après les penseurs du Moyen Age (Actes du premier Congrès international de philosophie médiévale, Louvain-Bruxelles, 28 août–4 septembre, 1958)* (Louvain, 1960), 629.

17. Henry of Ghent, *Quodlibet 1*, Macken, 133; and *Summa (Quaestiones ordinariae), art. 31–34* (Macken, xxi–xxiiib).

18. Macken, "God as "primum cognitum" in the Philosophy of Henry of Ghent," *Franziskanische Studien* 66 (1984): 309–315.

19. Macken, "Lebensziel und Lebensglück in der Philosophie des Heinrich von Gent," *Franziskanische Studien* 61 (1979): 107–123; and Macken, "Deseo natural y vocación sobrenatural del hombre en la filosofía de Enrique de Gante," in *La filosofía del cristiano, hoy* (Cordoba, 1980) 2:839–846.

20. Henry of Ghent, *Lectura ordinaria super Sacram Scripturam . . .* (Macken, xvii–xviii).

21. Macken, "Lebensziel," 213.

22. See Macken, "Henri de Gand et la pénétration d'Avicenne en Occident," in *Philosophie et culture (Actes du VIIe congrès mondial de philosophie), . . . Montréal 21–27.viii.1983)* (Montreal, 1988) 3:845–850.

23. See Macken, "Le statut philosophique de la matière selon Bonaventure," *Recherches de Théologie ancienne et médiévale* 147 (1980): 219–220.

24. See Macken, "La subsistance de la matière première selon Henri de Gand," in *San Bonaventura maestro di vita francescana e di sapienza cristiana (Atti del Congresso Internazionale per il VII centenario di San Bonaventura di Bagnoregio, Roma, 19–26 settembre 1974)* (Rome, 1976) 2:107–115.

25. Augustine, *Confessions* 6.10: "O Veritas, Veritas quam intime etiam tum medullae animi mei suspirabant tibi. . . !" Compare Hessen, *Die Philosophie,* 23.

26. Henry of Ghent, *Summa* 1.2 (1:5rD). Except for articles 31–34, for which there is a critical edition, we must cite the *Summa* in its *editio princeps* by Badius (2 volumes, Paris, 1520), on which the 1646 edition of Ferrara depends. The first edition has been reprinted as Franciscan Institute Publications, Text Series 5 (St. Bonaventure, N.Y., 1953). I have modernized the punctuation. On the two early editions, see Macken, "Les corrections d'Henri de Gand à sa *Somme," Recherches de Théologie ancienne et médiévale* 44 (1977): 55, note 3, and Macken, *Bibliotheca manuscripta Henrici de Gandavo* (Leuven and Leiden, 1979) 2:1018, and Henry of Ghent, *Summa (Quaestiones ordinariae) art. 31–34,* (ix–x).

27. Henry of Ghent, *Summa* 4.6 (1:27vD): "Nunc autem ita est quod veritas rei et esse eius parificantur, secundum quod dicitur 11° Metaphysicae, 'Unumquodque . . . sicut se habet ad esse, sic se habet ad veritatem.' Quanto igitur, ut dicit Commentator ibidem, res quaelibet magis fuerit perfecta in esse, tanto magis erit perfecta in veritate."

28. Henry of Ghent, *Quodlibet 15* q. 9 (581rD): "Universale est per se et primum obiectum intellectus creati, sicut singulare est per se et primum obiectum sensus." The *Quodlibeta* of Henry of Ghent that are not yet edited for the new *Opera omnia* are cited here from the edition of Badius (Paris, 1518; reprinted Louvain, 1961). The later editions of 1608 and 1613, both accompanied by the commentary of Vitalis Zuccolius, depend on Badius. I have modernized the punctuation.

29. Henry of Ghent *Quodlibet 5* q. 15 (182rC–vC): ". . . intellectus noster . . . primo et per se cognoscit in singulari formam sub ratione universalis, hoc est sub ratione esse indeterminati et indesignati. Quod esse, in quantum huiusmodi, in nullo habet esse ut in subiecto, sed solum in intellectu ut in apprehendente et cognoscente. Sed quia eadem ipsa forma ut est in ipso phantasmate aut in ipsa re, est determinata et designata, intellectus secundario apprehendit illam designationem."

30. On Henry's theory of a possible direct perception in human life on earth of some spiritual realities, see Macken, "La théorie d'illumination divine."

31. See Macken, "Heinrich von Gent in Gespräch," 180–181.

32. Henry of Ghent, *Quodlibet 15* q. 9 (581rE).

33. Gomez Caffarena, "Metafísica de la inquietud humana," 633.

34. J. Paulus, "A propos de la théorie de la connaissance d'Henri de Gand," *Revue philosophique de Louvain* 47 (1949): 495.

35. Henry of Ghent, *Quodlibet 15* q. 9 (581rE–vE).

36. Henry of Ghent, *Quodlibet 15* q. 9 (581vF).

37. Henry of Ghent, *Summa* 24.7 (1:144rF).

38. Henry of Ghent, *Summa* 24.7 (1:144rF–H).

39. Henry of Ghent, *Summa* 24.7 (1:145vP).

40. Macken, "La volonté humaine," 4–5; Macken, "La doctrine de S. Thomas concernant la volonté et les critiques d'Henri de Gand," in *Tommaso d'Aquino nella storia del pensiero (Atti del Congresso Internationale Roma — Napoli, 17 — 24 aprile 1974)* (Naples, 1976) 11:84–91; Macken, "Heinrich von Gent im Gespräch," 128–129.

41. Macken, "Will and Intellect in God According to the Philosophy of Henry of Ghent," forthcoming in *Franziskanische Studien*.

42. Macken, "Les diverses applications," 769–776.

43. Macken, "L'interpénétration de l'intelligence et de la volonté dans la philosophie d'Henri de Gand," in *L'homme et son univers au moyen âge (Actes du Septième Congrès International de Philosophie Médiévale, 30 août — 4 septembre 1982)*, ed. C. Wenin, Philosophes Médiévaux 26–27 (Louvain-la-Neuve, 1986) 2:808–814.

44. Henry of Ghent, *Quodlibet 15* q. 5 (565rB). See also Macken, "Heinrich von Gent im Gespräch," 180–181.

45. See Macken, "The Metaphysical Proof for the Existence of God in the Philosophy of Henry of Ghent," *Franziskanische Studien* 68 (1986): 247–260.

46. See Macken, "La personnalité," 176.

47. Henry of Ghent, *Summa* 22.4–5 (1:129vI).

48. Henry of Ghent, *Summa* 22.5 (1:134rB–vB).

49. Henry of Ghent, *Summa* 24.6 (1:136vZ).

50. Henry of Ghent, *Summa* 24.6 (1:141rN–vN).

51. Henry of Ghent, *Summa* 24.8 (1:145vP).

52. Henry of Ghent, *Quodlibet 5* q. 26 (205vQ).

53. Henry of Ghent, *Quodlibet 2* q. 8 (32–33rE).

54. Henry of Ghent, *Quodlibet 3* q. 17 (79rH).

55. Henry of Ghent, *Quodlibet 15* q. 9 (581rD).

56. Henry of Ghent, *Summa* 21.2 (1:124vI).

57. Henry of Ghent, *Summa* 49.51 (2:39vZ).

58. Hessen, *Die Philosophie*, 60.

59. Ibid., 55.

60. Macken, "La temporalité radicale de la créature selon Henri de Gand," *Recherches de Théologie ancienne et médiévale* 38 (1971): 211–272. This is a revised version of "De radicale tijdelijkheild van het schepsel volgens Hendrik van Gent," *Tijdschrift voor Filosofie* 31 (1969): 519–571.

61. Macken, "La théorie de l'illumination divine," 107–110; and Macken, "Selbstverwirklichung," 132–140, especially p. 140.

62. Macken, "La théorie de l'illumination divine," 99.

63. Henry of Ghent, *Summa* (1:219rY). ["Veritas enim creaturae . . .]

64. Macken, "Selbstverwirklichung," 135–136.

65. Gomez Caffarena, "Metafísica," 629.

66. Augustine, *Confessions* 1.1. See also Macken, "Lebensziel," 123.

67. Hessen, *Die Philosophie*, 53.

68. Macken, "Synderesis and Conscience in the Philosophy of Henry of Ghent," *Franziskanische Studien* 70:186–195.

69. Henry of Ghent, *Quodlibet 1* (Macken, 27–46); and Macken, "La temporalité radicale de la créature selon Henri de Gand," 227–230.

70. Macken, "La volonté humaine," 5–51.

71. Henry of Ghent, *Quodlibet 9* q. 5, in *Opera omnia* 13 ed. Macken (Leuven, 1983), 99–139; and Macken, "Heinrich von Gent im Gespräch," 141–147.

72. Henry of Ghent, *Quodlibet 9* q. 6 (Macken, 139–149), and Macken, "Heinrich von Gent im Gespräch," 147–148.

73. Macken, "La théorie de l'illumination," 108.

74. Henry of Ghent, *Summa* 1.2 (1:7rL).

75. Macken, "Lebensziel," 107–123.

76. Henry of Ghent, *Summa* 4.5 (1:33rE–vE); see also Macken, "Lebensziel," 119–120, and Macken, "Selbstverwirklichung," 139–140.

77. Henry of Ghent, *Summa* 4.5 (1:33vI); see also Macken, "Lebensziel," 119–120, and Macken, "Selbstsverwirklichung," 140.

78. Macken, "La personnalité," 10–12.

The *Accessus* Extended:
Henry of Ghent on the Transmission
and Reception of Theology

A. J. MINNIS

THE PURPOSE OF this essay is to explore the way in which Henry
of Ghent amplified and elaborated a standard type of academic introduction to a school text, generally known as the *accessus,* in his examination of the way in which the science of theology had been transmitted from God its ultimate *auctor,* through the authors of the Bible,
the doctors of the Church, and the exegetes who sought to clarify the
meaning of Scripture, to its audience — or, rather, to its different types
of audience.

    The history of the development of the *accessus* is in large measure
the record of the movement of certain analytical methods and vocabulary from the *artes* into theology, as theology came to be defined and
described as a science.[1] The form of *accessus* which attained the greatest popularity and frequency of use in the twelfth-century Renaissance
was the one which Richard Hunt termed the 'type C' prologue.[2] Within
its characteristic framework the intention (*auctoris intentio*), subject-
matter (*materia*), type of style and structure (*modus agendi*), usefulness
(*utilitas*), and relevant part of philosophy (*cui parti philosophiae suppona-
tur*) served by the text in question would be identified.[3] Having been
used for several generations in *accessus* to secular authors, this paradigm began to appear at the head of Bible commentaries in the first
quarter of the twelfth century. The credit for this transference cannot
be given to Anselm of Laon, the begetter of the *Glossa ordinaria,* for
the 'type C' prologues which appear therein are later elaborations of
his work.[4] Two eminent scholars, Richard Hunt and Beryl Smalley,
very much wanted to believe that the great innovator here was Peter
Abelard,[5] but there is no firm evidence for this,[6] though we can be

confident that he was one of the first. Others were Gilbert of Poitiers, also a pupil of Anselm, and Honorius "of Autun," who wrote his *Expositio psalterii* probably between 1115 and 1120.[7]

In the thirteenth century a new paradigm assumed the popularity which the 'type C' prologue had enjoyed during the twelfth century, this one being based on the four major causes—efficient, formal, material, and final—which scholars were finding in newly recovered works by Aristotle. The efficient cause of a text was its author, the formal cause its stylistic and didactic procedure (sometimes specifically termed its *modus agendi* or *modus tractandi*) along with its organization, the material cause its subject-matter, and the final cause its ultimate objective in a Christian society. This type of introductory treatise seems to have made its appearance in the faculties of arts and theology at roughly the same time. Between 1235 and 1245 it came into vogue among lecturers in the Parisian arts faculty. As far as theology is concerned, the paradigm was used in the first instance in scriptural exegesis and subsequently in commentaries on Peter Lombard's *Libri sententiarum*. To the best of my knowledge, the first Bible commentaries to feature it were the expositions of Mark and the Acts of the Apostles which form parts of the voluminous postill on the whole Bible which Hugh of St. Cher and his Dominican research team produced at St. Jacques, Paris, between 1230 and 1236.[8] In all the other thirty-five major prologues in this work, versions of the older 'type C' paradigm are employed. Perhaps this postill marks the point of transition from the old model to the new—though it should be recognized that later exegetes continued to use the older prologue vocabulary, sometimes in conjunction with the jargon of the four causes and sometimes not. A younger contemporary of Hugh at St. Jacques, Guerric of St. Quentin, who held the second chair of theology there between 1233 and 1242, was perhaps the first exegete to apply the four causes in exegesis of the Old Testament; specifically, in his commentary on Isaiah.[9]

Turning now to commentaries on the *Sentences,* it is noteworthy that Alexander of Hales, who between 1223 and 1227 had broken with tradition by substituting the *Sentences* for the Bible in his lectures in the Parisian faculty of theology,[10] had not himself invoked the four causes in his prologue; neither do they appear at the beginning of his commentary on John's Gospel (written before 1236).[11] Perhaps the first *Sentences* commentary thus introduced was also the first *Sentences* commentary to issue from Oxford—the work of Richard Fishacre, produced between *c.* 1241 and 1248.[12] Fishacre describes the *necessitas vel utilitas* of the work as its *causa finalis,* the *auctor* as its *causa efficiens,* the *subiectum* as its *causa materialis* and the *unitas et divisio* as its *causa formalis.*[13] But it is impossible to be exact as to who did what first, given the difficulty of dating precisely the early *Sentences* commentaries. Suffice it to point out that sometime between 1248 and 1261 Robert Kilwardby introduced his *Sentences* commentary with a very elaborate "Aristotelian Prologue"[14] — hardly surprising, given that he had used the paradigm in his lectures on the set texts of grammar and logic during his time as a lecturer in the Parisian arts faculty (*c.* 1237– *c.* 1245) before he joined the Dominican order.[15] Bonaventure's *Sentences* commentary, with its splendid "Aristotelian Prologue," can be dated more precisely between 1250 and 1252.[16] Albert the Great had made merely incidental use of the *causae* in glossing Peter Lombard's own prologue, sometime during the period *c.* 1245–1250.[17] In the great *Summa theologiae* which was attributed to Alexander of Hales and actually finished by his pupils after his death in 1245, large structural use is not made of the four causes in the introductory discussion, but its elaborate analysis of the biblical *formae tractandi* set the standard and provided much of the vocabulary for subsequent discussions of the formal cause of theology considered as a science.[18] Certainly it was a major influence on the theologian who is the subject of this essay, Henry of Ghent — though something of a negative influence, in that Henry profoundly disagreed with many of its contentions and implications. But it is indubitable that the *Summa Alexandri* set much of Henry's agenda in the prologue to his *Summa quaestionum ordinariarum.*

Henry of Ghent, a secular master and one of the key figures in the doctrinal controversies current at the end of the thirteenth century, has been seen, perhaps somewhat condescendingly, as an interestingly eclectic thinker who did not subscribe to the tenets of any single school, the evidence consisting of his attempt to effect a reconciliation between certain strands of Neoplatonism and Aristotelianism. Recent research, however, is revealing him as one of the truly great ideological synthesizers of his day, the creator of a system which in its scope and depth rivals those of the Dominican master Thomas Aquinas and the Franciscan master Bonaventure.[19] Between 1278 and 1280 Henry was principal Archdeacon of Tournai; from 1270 onwards his main sphere of activity was Paris, where he taught first in the university's faculty of arts and subsequently (from *c.* 1275 until 1292) in the faculty of theology. The two works on which his reputation rests, a series of quodlibets and the *Summa quaestionum ordinariarum,* date from that last period.

The *Summa,* which utilizes materials from the quodlibets but is far more comprehensive and often more subtle, to some extent conforms to the standard thirteenth-century type of *Summa theologica,* but only the prologue and the theodicy were completed; doubtless Henry had planned to proceed from God to treat of creation. The prologue (first written *c.* 1275–6 and edited towards the end of his career, in 1289[20]) contains Henry's opinions on those topics which traditionally occupied that position in a *Summa* or *Sentences* commentary:[21] science or knowledge *(scientia)* and the knowable in general, the manner of knowing, and what can be known by humans, the human desire and appetite for knowledge, the attainment of knowledge, theology considered as a science in itself, theology in comparison with the other sciences (these being the subjects of articles I–VII). Articles VIII–XX consider the four causes of theology. After this, Henry proceeds to discuss God in terms of his existence, *quidditas,* unity, nature, essence and knowability, and so forth.

In particular, his consideration of the four causes of theology (which is at the center of our attention) is one of the most elaborate and thoroughgoing to have survived, as this more detailed review will show.[22] Article VIII, "Concerning the final cause of theology," discusses the usefulness *(utilitas)* of theology, its necessity for humanity, whether it is a theoretical or practical discipline, and the significance of its having been written down. Articles IX–XIII examine what might be called the chain of efficient causality characteristic of theology, beginning with the unmoved mover (God), proceeding to the moved and moving (the teachers and preachers of the science), and then to the moved (its students or audiences). Thus, Articles IX and X are on the author or 'effector' of theology and the authority of holy Scripture respectively. Article XI considers the teacher *(doctor)* of theology under seven headings. Is God alone the teacher of theology? Can a woman teach it? Can a young man? A religious? Indeed, a sinner? Did the first teachers of the science have to be simple and uneducated folk *(simplices et idiotae)*? Did its subsequent teachers have to be instructed and learned in secular sciences? The listener or student *(auditor)* of theology is the subject of the following article, the parallelism with Article XI being marked. Can a woman be a student of theology? Can a young man? A sinner? Someone who wishes to adhere to natural reason? Someone who is not instructed or learned in secular sciences? Then the emphasis shifts, as Henry asks if theology is for everyone (questions 6–8).

This section ends, quite logically, with an analysis of the way in which men can acquire or learn theology (Article XIII): can it be learned by man? does such learning require special divine ilumination? does it require the illumination of faith? does the illumination of faith suffice for learning it? or is the illumination of grace *gratum faciens* necessary? does the learner acquire a knowledge which is beyond faith? does that further knowledge co-exist with faith? can a man learn theology by himself, without a teacher? do the writers of this science have perfect understanding of it? Articles XIV–XVIII concern the formal cause of theology in all its ramifications: the various scientific and didactic *formae* or methods (*modus tradendi*) used in the Bible; its various 'senses' or types of meaning (principally the literal, allegorical, tropological and anagogical senses) and the concomitant methods of textual exposition or *modus exponendi;* the people to whom and by whom it should be expounded. The next part of the prologue provides an account of the material cause of theology, followed by an excursus on the kinds of speech or style through which the subject matter of Scripture is communicated. Here Henry discusses the way in which language concerning God and divine matters is used in theology, and how this discourse is to be expounded.

From this impressive array of interrelated topics we may single out those relating to a major relationship, that between divine authority and human fallibility and defect. By this I mean the different types of limitation which, from Henry's point of view, seemed to impinge on theology as transmitted by the scriptural authors, expounded by the teachers of theology and received by humanity at large. How can the unity and singularity of holy Scripture be reconciled with the apparent differences between the prophets, historians, disputants, and evangelists who inscribed the divine Word, and with the Bible's wide range of styles and genres, which in Henry's day were conceived of as methods of scientific procedure (the *modus agendi* of the earlier *accessus* having been identified as *modus procedendi,* under the stimulus of notions concerning scientific methodology which owed much to "the Medieval Aristotle")? Then again, how can one square the superlative truth and value of theology with the fact that certain biblical authors (e.g., David, Solomon, Paul) were or had been sinners, and that on many occasions the sacred text seemed to contain and condone fictions, falsehoods, and lies? Even more problems arise further down the channel of transmission of theology, since some present-day teach-

ers of the science seem to lack the requisite knowledge or maturity—
or, much worse, are obviously steeped in sin. Finally, those on the
receiving end, the *auditores* (hearers, listeners, pupils) of theology, are
often limited as well, whether by age, sin, or indeed by gender, the
issues of whether women should be taught or teach the subject being
singled out by Henry for special treatment. Henry's answers to these
questions will now be considered in turn.

1. PRIMARY AND SECONDARY AUTHORSHIP
OF SCRIPTURE

What is immediately striking about Henry's discussion of the
authorship and authority of holy Scripture is his clear reluctance to
entertain any idea which might threaten the indivisible unity of the
Bible or detract in any way from its divine origins and objectives. It
is this bias which largely determines his version of the ideology and
idioms of efficient causality as applied in an exegetical context.

According to the Aristotelian theory of causality, as Christian-
ized by generations of late-medieval scholars, God was the first mover
or primary efficient cause, who moved inferior causes from potentiality to act. The primary efficient cause divulged power to the instrumental efficient causes, each of which set in motion those parts of creation which were under its jurisdiction. Those immediate causes, then,
were allowed a certain amount of individual power; they were not simply mere cogs in a machine of God's ultimate making. [23]

Such ideas had a considerable impact in scriptural exegesis, in
describing the nature of the relationship between God and men in
producing the Bible. In his *Sentences* commentary, Richard Fishacre
(something of an innovator in developing Aristotelian hermeneutics,
as already noted) declared that the various human authors of Scripture had not themselves written, but "God both wrote and spoke by
them, as the principal efficient cause by the instrument." [24] This strategy of treating composite authorship as levels of efficient causality was
elaborated by, for example, Guerric of St.-Quentin in his commentary on Isaiah. That book is said to have a *duplex causa efficiens,* namely
the Holy Spirit (the moving efficient cause) and Isaiah (the moved,
operating efficient cause). [25] Other texts were believed to have an even
more complex motivation. In his commentary on Luke's Gospel, Bonaventure described a *triplex causa efficiens:* the Holy Spirit, divine grace,

and the Evangelist himself.[26] Exegetes of the Apocalypse found a *quad-ruplex causa efficiens* at work there: God, Christ, the angel, and John.[27]

Yet the Aristotelian principles of causality also made provision for the integrity of instrumental causes. In exegesis this usually meant that the inspired human authors who functioned as instrumental efficient causes between the primary efficient cause (God) and the effect (the text) were granted their personal activities and achievements. Divine inspiration did not necessarily entail disregard or destruction of the talents of the original transmitters of theology.[28] Consequently, in much of the most representative of thirteenth-century exegesis, there was a marked emphasis on the human author's individual purpose in writing and his personal credentials, whether literary or moral — the latter sometimes involving confrontation of the moral shortcomings of certain contributors to the Bible.[29] Concomitantly, the ideology of formal causality provided a new framework for discussion of different styles and structures which the various authors had used, or which one and the same author had used in different biblical books.[30]

Henry of Ghent, however, seems to have suspected that such efforts by his predecessors and contemporaries entailed a dangerous devolution of authority from the divine author to the human authors of Scripture. This is most evident in his question "Whether God is the author of holy Scripture" (Art. IX, qu. 2).[31] He begins by adducing arguments in favor of the (utterly unacceptable, of course) proposition that man, not God, is the author of this science. First, he should be called the *auctor* of a science by whose testimony that science is believed — for, as Augustine says, what we believe is due to authorities.[32] But this science is believed by the testimony of man, for we follow what the prophets, apostles, and their successors have transmitted concerning those invisible things which are remote from our interior sense. Since they were men, it would appear that man is the *auctor* of theology. Secondly, the person who shows the image or plan (*exemplar*) of what is to be made is not called the *auctor* of the art in question, but rather the person who actually carries out the work and produces the artifact. As Paul says in Romans 1, the very authors of Scripture described those things which had been revealed by God, therefore since God simply provided the *exemplar* which others brought into being, they should be called the authors of Scripture, and not God.

Then Henry marshals powerful testimonies against this notion. First, it could be said that the son of God or Christ was the *auctor* of Scripture, on the testimony of *De civitate Dei* 11.3, where Augustine declares that God, having spoken what he held convenient, first by his prophets, then by himself as Christ, and afterwards by his Apostles, made what we call canonical Scripture, of most eminent authority.[33] Christ, therefore, should be called the *auctor*, and the others merely ministers. Secondly, the Holy Spirit could be called the *auctor*, on the testimony of 2 Peter 1:21: "Prophecy came not by the will of man at any time. . . ." Holy men of God wrote and spoke this science by inspiration; the source of inspiration, the Holy Spirit, should therefore be called its author. Thirdly, God himself could be called the *auctor* of theology, on the testimony of Jesus as recorded in John 7:16, where he declares "My doctrine is not mine, but his that sent me." Since the one who sent him was God the Father, Christ's doctrine was therefore principally the Father's, and since whoever is the principal source of doctrine is its author, therefore God is the *auctor* of this science.

Having set up the problem in all its complex ramifications, Henry offers his own resolution. In the situation where there is a craftsman who directs and regulates the work, and another person by whose hand the work is carried out in accordance with the rules laid down by the craftsman, the craftsman is called the *auctor*, not the manual worker. For the craftsman knows the reasons and rules of the art, whereas the manual worker does not, as is explained in the first book of the *Metaphysics*. Here Aristotle had said that the master-workers or craftsmen in each skill are more honorable and know in a truer sense and are wiser than the manual workers, because they know the causes of the things that are done, whereas the manual workers indeed act but in an incomprehending way, not knowing what they do.[34] This is true, Henry says, of the other arts and sciences: someone is called, or not called, the *auctor* on the basis of whether, in practicing the art, he knows or does not know the rules of that art. He who knows the reasons and rules of the art, which he can describe to others and which others can learn from him, should be called its primary and principal author, but not the untrained person who practices without premeditation. Here again, incidentally, we may detect the influence of the *Metaphysics,* since Aristotle had cited the ability to teach as one of the identifying characteristics of the genuinely knowledgeable man,[35] in contrast to the man who has mere experience but no theory. Turning now to theology, Henry says that only God can possibly know the reasons and rules of that science, by himself and about himself; no creature can possibly attain such knowledge by his unaided human powers (*ex puris naturalibus*).[36] The clear inference would seem to be that those inspired prophets and apostles were rather like Aristotle's manual workers who acted in an incomprehending way, under the direction of a superior artificer who knew the reasons and rules of which they were ignorant.

But Henry is not prepared to go that far; to argue in that vein would be to demean excessively the inspired authors of Scripture, and perhaps diminish the process of inspiration itself. God alone must be called the *auctor* of the science of theology, and the Scriptures were inscribed by ministering men who in effect co-wrote them and contemplated his wisdom inasmuch as human hearts can attain it. Thus they perfectly (in terms of human perfection, anyway) understood the rules of the art. That is to say, they were *not* solely the instruments and channels through which the words of this science were transmitted; their activities were unlike those of the workman and the painter who execute a task which has been planned by a superior. Indeed, Henry claims, they can be called *secondary authors*.

Before considering the implications of these statements, however, Henry has more to say about the unique authorship of Scripture. The authority of the science of theology is to be traced to divine, not philosophical, authority, because this science was established solely on the basis of divine inspiration, and did not require the cooperation of any human ingenuity (*ingenium*). Because of this, theological truth is infallible. Philosophical science, by contrast, does indeed require the cooperation of human ingenuity in its first invention, and because the human reason is fallible its truth is fallible. Moreover, the divine authorship of Scripture would seem to include form as well as content: Henry quotes Augustine (*On Genesis*) as saying that the inspired authors comprehend through inspiration not only the *sententiae* but also the quality and form of the words they use.[37] Similarly, the *Glossa ordinaria* on 2 Peter 1:21 ("No prophecy ever came from man's initiative") advises us to attend to the prophetic style, for it is from God.[38] This is evident, Henry continues, because prophecy does not employ the words and the manner of speaking which people use in normal speech; neither is it like secular literature. Truly, prophetic speech was not in accordance with the will of the speaker or the hearer, but rather in accordance with the will of the Holy Spirit. Just as it was not in the power of the prophets always to have the Spirit and always predict the future, so they did not teach of their own volition, but they taught only those things which they disseminated from the Spirit. God, therefore, is truly the principal and sole author of theology, it being possible to attribute this authorship in diverse ways to the Trinity and its three persons. However, this science may at least be described by men, and to this extent man can be called its secondary and ministerial author.

What, then, of the argument that it is by the testimony of men that belief is gained in this science? It must be said, Henry admits, that this is true—but it is true not on its own account but because of divine authority, for it was God who verified what the men were saying with signs and miracles. Thus, Mark 16:20 speaks of how the apostles went out and preached everywhere, the Lord working with them and confirming the Word by the signs that accompanied it. Therefore, the authority was not attributable to them. To the second argument, concerning the exemplar being offered to the man who actually does the job, the reply is that here one is talking of the circumstances in which someone simply provides the exemplar without providing the rules of performing the task, those being in the possession of the operator himself, i.e., the man—a veritable craftsman—who produces the artifact. Thus a painter, having been shown an image, will consider it and then proceed to paint a likeness in accordance with the art of painting which he himself possesses. Henry then proceeds to build on what he has already said concerning the distinction between philosophical truth and theological truth by suggesting that the philosophers may be called the principal authors of their secular sciences. Having been shown the exemplar of a creature which was made in accordance with the art of the divine law, the philosophers set to work by applying the reasons and rules of the philosophical disciplines relating to creatures. Although God granted them revelation to the extent that he showed them the exemplar of his creature, natural industry certainly contributed in that they carried out their own investigative work (although humans cannot take full credit for that, because, according to Henry's epistemology, truth cannot be perceived without the aid of the ray of increated light). Therefore, because they had to work to acquire the reasons and rules of their sciences (for God did not simply reveal all that information to them), they are rightly called the authors of their sciences. By contrast, he revealed the reasons of the science of theology to prophets and apostles. And therefore they cannot be called principal authors of the science of theology, as the philosophers can of their sciences.

2. SCRIPTURAL AUTHORITY AND DIVERSITY

Henry, then, is determined to keep the human *auctor* of Scripture firmly in his place, to determine his subservient, if prestigious, status. Similarly, the indubitable range of subjects and styles in the Bible are regarded in a way which keeps the power and the responsibility for the whole operation firmly at the top. Thus, Henry answers the question "did the same author write both Testaments?" (Art. IX, qu. 1)[39] quite predictably with Augustine's view that the Old Testament is nothing other than the occultation of the New Testament while the New is nothing other than the revelation of the Old, whence the divine authorship of the entire Bible is single and supreme.[40] Even more strikingly, the same motive may be detected behind his disagreement with the method of analyzing the "multiple mode" of biblical style which had been established by the *Summa theologiae* attributed to Alexander of Hales.

According to this earlier treatise, the Bible proceeds by way of precept, example, exhortation, revelation, and prayer, because these modes are appropriate to the inculcation of a pious disposition, which is the objective of the science of theology.[41] Defending this position, the *Summa Alexandri* declares that there are three reasons why the *modus tractandi* of holy Scripture must be manifold.[42] First, the Holy Spirit is "single yet manifold" (Wisdom 7:22), and this fact must be reflected in theology. Secondly, the subject of theology is divine Wisdom, which is manifold, and so "in order that the mode may match the subject it too must take many forms." Thirdly, the end (*finis*) of theology is instruction in those matters which pertain to salvation. And the conditions (*status*) of humans are manifold. Some lived in the time of the Law and some after; some in the time of prophecy, some in the time of grace. "Even within these periods," the argument runs, "the conditions of men are manifold. For some are sluggish in matters relating to faith, some are rebellious in matters relating to good morality, and [fall short] in different ways. Some pass their lives in prosperity, some in adversity, some in good works, some in sin." The conclusion is then drawn that the teaching of holy Scripture, which has been ordained for human salvation must employ a multiple mode, so that the mode matches this objective.

All this is attacked in Art. XIV, qu. 1 of Henry's *Summa*.[43] The diversity in question (giving commands, issuing prohibitions, and so forth) does not consist, he claims, "in the mode of treating or handing down this subject-matter, but rather in the subject-matter which is treated of."[44] *Modus* should not be confused with *materia;* one cannot call the *modus* of this science *multiplex* just because its *materia* comprises many diverse things. Turning to the points made by the *Summa Alexandri* concerning the manifold wisdom of God, Henry declares that, while this is certainly true of God, it does not entail a manifold mode for theology. It is incorrect to say that one piece of the manifold science of God is taught in one passage of Scripture and another in another: rather it is true that in each discourse (*sermo*) a manifold knowledge of God is gained in accordance with the multiplicity of textual meaning (*sensus*) and of exposition. This comes very close to the belief, commonplace in twelfth-century biblical exegesis, that the whole truth of the Bible is immanent in its every part.[45]

What, then, of the idea that diverse *modi tractandi* are appropriate to diverse human conditions? Henry says that the logical conclusion of this argument would be the unacceptable proposition that theology "would have to be passed on to one sort of men in one place, and to another sort in a different place, and not in its totality in all places. Thus, it would not be offered in its totality everywhere to every condition of men."[46] This is quite false, he declares, for theology "is offered for consideration in its totality everywhere to every condition of men," there being no grounds for the belief that the different conditions of men require different modes of treatment. He proceeds to attack the notion that all the individual things relating to theology "should be treated separately, and receive different treatment as is best suited to various people, and in so far as [the teachers] can impart information in different ways about different aspects of Christian belief." The truth of the matter, he declares, is that "the mode used ought to be such that disparate teachings (*sententiae*) concerning different subjects and different tenets of belief should be contained in one and the same discourse." Different men may understand this discourse according to their individual capacities, some being content with the literal surface while others look under it for the spiritual understanding. But, considered in itself, the *modus tradendi* of Scripture is "characterized by the utmost simplicity and oneness of form."[47] Behind these statements seems to lie Henry's conviction that there are no divine ideas of individuals, but only of species.

However, it should not be inferred that Henry is in fundamental disagreement with Augustine's appropriation of the essential principles of rhetoric in exegesis,[48] including the ideas that eloquence is by no means antithetical to wisdom and that the teacher of theology, no less than the secular orator, should suit his style to his audience. Arguments of that kind are found later in the *Summa*. A *quaestio* on whether or not Scripture should "speak of divine matters in a style which used words that retain their proper meaning and is clear, or one that is figurative and [deliberately] obscure,"[49] elicits the response that the Bible caters for both *simplices* and more advanced learners: the faithful are given what is sufficient for their salvation by its simpler passages, while the learned are attracted and stimulated by its obscurities (here Henry actually recycles parts of Augustine's *De Doctrina Christiana*).[50] Obscurity gives rise to polysemy; the more obscure a passage is, the more meanings it will yield as different people interpret it in different ways. Such interpretive diversity is fully discussed in an impressive array of *quaestiones* which consider the capacities of exegetes and their several audiences for understanding the stylistic media of Scripture. Scriptural exposition should, he declares, always be prepared with one's specific audience in mind, and since many learners are coarse (*grossus*) and stupid, in their case a broad (*grossus*) and common exposition is, in the main, to be provided. However, more able learners should be offered a proportionately more profound exposition.[51] A particular exposition should not be propounded to someone whose abilities are inadequate to cope with it.[52] Although an exposition may offer subtle and profound doctrine, it should be reserved for those who are able for it,[53] for to others it may be useless and even dangerous. As far as lesser mortals are concerned, exposition should limit itself to what is sufficient for salvation. The desire to avoid piecemeal exposition (as Henry would see it) cannot lead one to the conclusion that everyone should get everything in terms of exposition. Rather exposition should be suitably tempered so that each listener can grasp it in accordance with his capacity. It is up to the expositor, then, to ensure that everyone will get something out of a given passage of Scripture — but not, of course, necessarily the same thing.[54]

In short, Henry explains the need for diversity of interpretation in respect of the differences between human capacities and capabilities (whether in the expositor or the auditor), rather than something inherent in Scripture itself. And so the unity of Scripture is saved. The consistency with what he said when attacking the notion of the *multiplex modus* of Scripture should be obvious. "All Scripture is offered on a common basis to all men for consideration, and it adapts itself to each man according to his capacity to understand"; the same teaching

is "presented to all, but, because of their different capacities, for some
it serves as the milk of faith only, while to others it is solid food."[55]
The *modus* of holy Scripture is singular, but the needs of human beings are diverse — and hence stylistic diversity and pluralism in the
Bible, and exegetical diversity and pluralism on the part of Bible commentators, is fully justified.

   What we are confronted with in Henry's *quaestio* on the *modus
tradendi* of theology are the consequences of his conviction that theology is not primarily affective (an idea found in the *Summa Alexandri*
and elaborated by Henry's arch-opponent Giles of Rome)[56] but speculative. Those who believed the science was fundamentally affective
quite naturally tended to see the diverse biblical styles as having marked
similarities with the various styles and strategies of Ciceronian rhetoric, which were designed to affect and move the audience, different
types of listener requiring different methods of persuasion and information. The assimilation and development of the secular *accessus* by
theologians had, from the twelfth-century Renaissance onwards, in-
dubitably encouraged this attitude. But Henry, who missed no opportunity to affirm the supernatural and superhuman origins of theology,[57] apparently felt that this trend tended to conceal the essential
differences between secular and sacred letters, secular works having
only men as their authors but the holy Scriptures being uniquely possessed of divine authorship and authority.

   This comes out quite clearly in his criticism of one respect in
which, it must be admitted, the early formulation of the *multiplex modus*
of Scripture was quite vulnerable, namely, its listing of the revelatory
mode (*modus revelativus*) as one of the series of distinctive methods of
treatment employed in the Bible — an idea expressed not only in the
Summa Alexandri[58] but by Alexander's pupil and successor in the Franciscan chair at Paris (1244–47), Odo Rigaldi.[59] "The statement that
used to be made," Henry states, "that in the prophets the mode of
this science is revelatory, is absolutely untrue."[60] What is involved here
is not a particular "manner of writing down what has been revealed"
but rather the manner in which the prophets understood what they
had to commit to writing. Henry reduces to absurdity his opponents'
idea by pointing out that, since biblical writers generally got their knowledge through revelation, it could be said that the revelatory mode is
used *throughout* holy Scripture, not just in some parts of it. In other
words, the *modus revelativus* cannot be considered as if it were part and
parcel of an oratorical repertoire of styles.

Moreover, even Henry's choice of the general term *modus tradendi* ('manner of delivering, handing over, transmitting') rather than *modus tractandi* ('manner of treatment') may be significant.[61] The latter term, which derives from the secular *accessus ad auctores* of the 'type C' paradigm, is found frequently in prologues to Bible commentaries.[62] But the term used in the *Summa quaestionum* serves to emphasize that something already complete and perfect in itself is being delivered, theology being transmitted from high to low, perhaps with the implication that it is not something which is "treated" and controlled by human beings in the same manner in which they deploy the strategies of the human arts and sciences. We are dealing with a mode of understanding rather than with a mode of writing.

Henry, who produced one of the most sophisticated amplifications of the theological *accessus* to date from the thirteenth century, seems to have been suspicious of the assumptions which it had encouraged in some of his predecessors and contemporaries.

3. HOLY STYLE AND HUMAN SIN

Another possible threat to the unity and unique status of the Bible was the fact that some of its esteemed "secondary authors" had been somewhat less than exemplary in their lives on earth, and indeed certain biblical passages seemed to be blatantly untrue. For if falsehood can exist within the inspired — and hence utterly true — Word of God, its authority and integrity must be highly dubious, to say the least. Henry treats all the related issues with admirable economy and precision in the question "Whether truth is inherent in every exposition and sense" of Scripture (Art. XVI, qu. 5).[63]

Having affirmed that holy Scripture everywhere contains the truth, Henry notes that sometimes passages must be understood metaphorically, as when in Judges 9:8 we read the "The trees went to anoint a king." Another type of figurative significance is found in Genesis 27:24, wherein Jacob lies to his father Isaac by saying "I am Esau your first-born." This and similar incidents serve a prophetic purpose, Henry explains (citing Augustine),[64] for Jacob represents the Church in its first stage whereas Esau represents the Jewish synagogue.

Other passages which on the face of it contain falsehoods are freed from this charge when the total context is considered. But elsewhere there are actual lies which cannot be explained away thus, as when at Exodus 1:17–19 the midwives lied to avoid having to kill the Jewish babies. Henry, following Gregory as quoted in the *Glossa ordinaria,* takes a strong line here, claiming that "contrary to the assertion of some" such lies are indeed sins; even white lies incur a severe punishment.[65] Thus, the reward which the midwives received for their kindly deed was an earthly rather than a (vastly superior) heavenly one, as when God dealt well with them and built them houses (vv. 20–21). Henry's way of justifying the inclusion of such material in the superlatively and consistently true holy Scriptures consists of the argument—a commonplace of twelfth-century exegesis, with roots in the secular *accessus*—that Scripture shows us what to avoid as well as what to do.[66] It does not recommend that we should imitate the lies uttered by biblical personages, a point made strongly by this passage of Exodus, where we are shown "what a severe punishment is incurred even by such a pious falsehood." Generally speaking, "whatever lies are found in Scripture, it does not proffer to us as being true by positively asserting (*asserendo*) their truth and commending them, but in reporting (*recitando*) them in the text solely for our doctrine"—that last phrase perhaps echoing Romans 15:4, "All that is written is written for our doctrine." The basic distinction between affirming and reporting, as a strategy for reconciling authorities which seemed to disagree, had received its classic statement in the preface to Peter Abelard's *Sic et Non,* though there Henry's actual terminology does not appear;[67] thirteenth-century commentators and compilers did, however, make extensive use of this jargon in several ways, including the disavowal of responsibility on the part of writers, whether inspired or not, for dubious material which, for one reason or another, they were obliged to include in their writings.[68]

Even more revealing about Henry's priorities and prejudices is his treatment of the case of David and Uriah: David, that great prophet and "secondary author" of Scripture, had connived at the death of his faithful soldier Uriah in order to possess his wife Bathsheba. The *Glossa ordinaria,* declares Henry, interprets the situation mystically as meaning that David represents Christ whereas Uriah represents the devil (this being utterly typical of twelfth-century commentary on this matter).[69] But Henry, although he was prepared to accept the allegorical explanation which the *Glossa* offered of Exodus 1:17–19 (as we have just seen),[70] balks slightly at treating 2 Kings 11 in the same way. Can this be "a true allegory," he asks, in view of the principle that "the cause of understanding one opposite is not given by another?"[71] He manages to resolve (or at least shelve) the problem by distinguishing between the substance of the action and the quality of the action, i.e., the way in which it was done. In terms of the quality of the action, no true exposition in a good sense can be obtained, but in terms of the substance of the action "a true exposition is indeed possible."[72] For one can accept that a prince could order the death of a knight and take his wife for himself, for perfectly good reasons, no blame being attached to him. The action in question, in other words, is not necessarily bad in itself. And this justifies the interpretation of the story of David and Uriah which is offered by the *Glossa.*

This cannot be called one of Henry's most successful arguments. The contrast with the Psalter-commentary which Thomas Aquinas wrote between 1272 and 1273 (at Naples) is instructive. In his exposition of the fiftieth psalm (believed to express David's recognition of guilt and declaration of his remission), Aquinas chooses to treat the incident with Bathsheba as a matter of historical record, eschewing allegorical interpretation and presenting David as a superlative *exemplum* of the truly penitent man who is rewarded with divine mercy.[73] Similar positions are adopted in the Psalter commentaries of the Paris Dominican Nicholas Gorran (written sometime during the period 1263–85)[74] and the great Franciscan exegete Nicholas of Lyre, whose monumental *Postilla litteralis* on the whole Bible was completed in 1331.[75] Henry's position, therefore, seems to be quite conservative inasmuch as he defends the allegorical justification, yet he seems to be quite aware of the difficulties of such a defense. Once again, his concern to affirm the unique status of holy Scripture and its divine inspiration has directed him towards a view of biblical authorship and authority which is more in line with twelfth-century exegesis than with the innovative commentary-tradition of the thirteenth century. His use of and agreement with the *Glossa ordinaria,* here as in so many other parts of his account of the four causes of theology, are clear symptoms of that.

4. SIN IN THE TEACHER

So much, then, for Henry's response to the suggestion that the inspired text of Scripture might contain actual falsehoods and that its "secondary authors" might be less worthy than expected. His argument that, *proprie loquendo,* God is the only true *auctor* of Scripture, is echoed and paralleled by his affirmation of what might be described as the divine doctorate: i.e., if the term *doctor* is used in the strictest sense, God alone can be said to be the teacher of theology. Men can learn natural things without a teacher, because such knowledge depends on (God-given) human reason, but theology is divine in origin, and hence requires the light of faith for its comprehension (cf. Art. XI, qu. 1, resolutio).[76] It might well be inferred, then, that the human *doctores* of theology—those men who lecture on the biblical text and/or preach its message—are actually "secondary and instrumental teachers" of the subject, just as the human authors of holy Scripture are "secondary and ministerial authors." However, in his *Summa* Henry was far more willing to concede that these subsequent transmitters of theology could be sinners (more precisely, could teach in a state of sin) than he was in respect of its "secondary authors." Ample evidence of this is afforded by a matching pair of *quaestiones,* "Whether a sinner can be a teacher of theology" (Art. XI, qu. 5)[77] and "Whether a sinner can be a student of theology" (Art. XII, qu. 3).[78]

On the first of these problems Henry brings to bear the apparatus of Aristotelian causality (particularly the theory of instrumental causality) and Aristotelian psychology (particularly the theory of *habitus* or stable mental condition). He begins by marshaling two arguments in favor of the proposition that the *doctor* of theology need not be a just man. First is the story of the man who did not walk with Christ, whom the apostles wished to prohibit from teaching. But Christ said, "Forbid him not," on the grounds that "he that is not against you is for you" (Luke 9:50). Insofar as he did not remain with Christ he was evil, but if it was not permissible for him to teach theology he should have been prohibited. The second argument in favor is found in Philippians 1:15–19, where Paul says that some of his brothers who are announcing the message are doing it just out of rivalry and competition (whereas the rest preach Christ with the right intention), thereby not caring if they make the Apostle's chains heavier to bear. From this it is certain that they were evil, this being emphasized by the *Glossa ordinaria.*[79] And yet the Apostle declared himself to rejoice in their teaching: "But what then? So that by all means, whether by occasion or by truth, Christ be preached: in this also I rejoice, yea, and will rejoice" (v. 18).

Then two arguments against are offered. At Matthew 10:2ff. the twelve apostles are identified by name, and the *Glossa ordinaria* lists their qualities, qualities which are appropriate to *doctores,* for only those who are illuminated by the light of wisdom, obey the precepts of God, and strongly suggest them to others are suitable for the high office (*magisterium*) of *doctor*. [80] Secondly, as Chrysostom says concerning Matthew 5:19 ("He that shall do and teach, he shall be called great in the kingdom of heaven"), to teach without acting condemns the teacher. [81]

Henry begins his response to the question of whether a sinner can be a *doctor* of theology with a crucial distinction. Someone may be said to be a *doctor* in two different ways: because he is capable of teaching or because he has the office of teaching (*officio docendi*).

In the first sense, one is said to be a *doctor* by dint of his state or condition (*habitus*) of knowledge and consequent ability to teach. Such a *habitus* is not dismissed by the act of sinning, any more than it is acquired by virtuous action, save in terms of disposition, i.e., to the extent that the *habitus* of virtue disposes one to the acquisition of knowledge, as "the Commentator" (Averroës) says in his commentary on Book 7 of the *Physics*. [82] In the passage under discussion Aristotle had explained that knowledge can be acquired only when the soul settles down from the restlessness natural to it. As Averroës put it, "cognitio existit in nobis in principio per quietem anime, et rectitudinem accidentium . . . ,"[83] while in his commentary on the same passage Thomas Aquinas (writing at Paris in 1271), noted that understanding, i.e., speculative thought, and prudence, i.e., practical reason, come to the soul through the rest and abating of corporeal motions and sensible affections. [84] The obvious inference is that moral virtue, whereby the restless passions are controlled, is therefore in a sense conducive to intellectual virtue. The process involved is like polishing metal so that it might become a mirror and receive light, to adopt a metaphor used by Averroës. [85] Aristotle had proceeded to say that the passions may hinder the operation of the soul's intellectual part, as when a man who is sleeping or drunk or diseased is unable to use his intellect. But there is, Aquinas declares, a habitual potency "for the suitability of knowledge" in humans; i.e., to be restored to the appropriate state in which he could use his knowledge. [86] And therefore, exercise of the moral virtues, through which the passions which disturb the reason "are curbed, is especially effective for acquiring knowledge," i.e., it creates the best possible conditions in which knowledge can be acquired. [87]

But Henry concentrates on the idea that the state of knowledge, once it actually *is* acquired, is there to stay, and cannot be lost through immoral behavior. In this sense a man who is evil and a sinner can be called a *doctor* of this science, for he is able to have correct doctrine just like the just man, and indeed he may be better educated than the just man in respect of the relevant *habitus* of knowledge. He is in this way a *doctor* of another person by dint of his possession of the *habitus* of this science, and may be compared to the craftsman (*artifex*) who practices his skill in accordance with the *habitus* of that art. With this craftsman metaphor Henry is returning to an image he used in his discussion of the authorship of Scripture, but here it is applied with a different emphasis and sense. He cites Aristotle in the first book of the *Politics* as saying that it is not necessary for the craftsman to be morally virtuous in order to exercise his craft.[88] In order that he might make good knives, Henry elaborates, he requires not moral virtue but mere proficiency in the art of knifemaking; that is, the "perfection of the art" of knifemaking is simply—good knives. The inference is that the good *doctor* (on Henry's first definition) does not have to be a morally good man.

The second sense relates to the audience's reception of the teacher rather than his mental state and personal abilities. On this definition, a teacher is someone who holds the office of public teaching (*officium publice docendi*). This can be bestowed only by those who are to be taught, and only those on whom this office is bestowed can teach them. Here the analogy is with the doctor of medicine rather than the craftsman. A medical doctor would not be permitted to perform his function in a given city unless he was useful to it. No matter how experienced (*peritus*) he was in his profession, he would not be allowed to practice unless he was disposed to help the sick to recover their health. So, if he were irascible, and thereby provoked all his patients to anger, which inevitably would endanger their health, no matter how expert he was or what good medicines he gave, he would not be permitted to practice in the city. Likewise, with the doctor of theology: no matter how skilled (*peritus*) he may be, if he cannot exercise his *officium doctoris* without imperiling his audience, then he should by no means be permitted to teach or to be a teacher of theology. It is necessary to have both the *habitus* of knowledge, as explained above, and a good reputation (*fama bone vitae*). Therefore, in the *doctor* who *de iure* and *ex officio* can and ought to teach this science, two things are required: knowing (*scientia*) by dint of which he can teach, and a life by dint of which he can teach wholesomely.

Henry proceeds to develop this argument by enlisting the aid of the Aristotelian theory of causality and instrumentality. A *doctor* of sacred Scripture is, as it were, an instrument and organ (*instrumentum et organum*) of the word of God, in teaching the faithful with regard to their individual, and general, spiritual health or profit (*utilitas*). Whence the *Gloss* on Matthew 3:3 ("a voice crying in the wilderness . . ."), identifies John the Baptist as the voice and Christ as the Word which cries in John.[89] For just as with an instrument or organ, the formal disposition and its own constituent material is determined by its objective or end (*finis*) and the material in respect of which it functions. At this point Henry draws on the second book of the *Physics,* where Aristotle had explained that certain things are necessary in order that a given product can come into being, but the product comes to be for an end, not on account of those necessities.[90] He uses the example of a saw, which is designed to carry out something and for the sake of something; this end, however, cannot be achieved unless it is made of the right stuff. If we are to have a saw and perform the operation of sawing, it must be made of iron. As Averroës puts it, the action of sawing cannot be achieved except on account of the form and material of the saw.[91] Thus, to return to Henry, the end determines the material, the end being impossible to attain without the necessary material. Henry gives an elaborate version of this example and makes his own application of the underlying doctrine. In order that a saw can cut straight through tough wood, it must be made of strong and firm metal and it must have teeth: that is to say, the material out of which the saw is made (strong metal) and its formal disposition, pattern, or shape (its teeth) are determined by its end or objective (cutting the wood) and the material on which it works (the hard wood). The material with which the teacher of holy Scripture has to work are the faithful whom he must instruct; the end towards which he works is their own (spiritual) health or profit and that of others through instruction; the material employed in this work is his knowledge; the formal disposition necessary in himself in order that he might realize his objective is a holy life—he himself must first do the things which he teaches others to do.

Any unlearned man, Henry continues, who usurps the office of teaching and does not announce Christ with sincerity deserves utter damnation. Just as the saw, if it is made of soft metal, cannot divide the wood, so if an individual is learned but unjust in his behavior, although he may be able to instruct the faithful he can neither "enform" or shape them in holy life nor maintain them therein. As Chrysostom says on Matthew 5:13 ("you are the salt of the earth"), the *doctor* should be adorned with all the virtues, so that he is able to prompt the lazy and sluggish to perform good works, by his example rather than by mere words.[92] The good manner of life of a priest may, irrespective of words, maintain the holy in sanctity by its example, but without words he cannot lead the ignorant to the knowledge of truth. On the other hand, words, without the example of good behavior, can lead a certain ignorant person to the knowledge of truth, but he cannot remain in faith or holiness without the example of good behavior. A priest whose life does not match his words is a source of scandal. Even though he may perhaps lead the good to the knowledge of truth, he will tend rather to keep bad people away from the truth. Thus, as Chrysostom says concerning Matthew 5:16 ("Let your light shine before men, that they may see your good works . . ."), whoever does not perform what he teaches, does not teach others but rather condemns himself.[93] And it is better to do and not to teach than it is to teach and not to do. For he who does, albeit he is silent, corrects others by his example, whereas he who teaches and does not act not only fails to correct anyone but manages to give offense to many. The person who is not inclined to sin is confused when he sees that the doctors of piety are themselves sinners. Then Henry turns to that great seminal work on the responsibilities of the preacher, Gregory's *Cura pastoralis,* which is quoted as saying that the *magisterium* of pastor is confounded when one thing is done and another is taught; and so, when someone's life is despised it follows that his preaching will be condemned.[94] To which Henry appends that Aristotelian saw. Just as, if a saw is without teeth it cannot directly attain its end in cutting, so no *doctor* who is not "enformed" by familiarity with holiness can wholesomely teach others. It must be said, therefore, that the proper teacher of this science must not only be competent to teach the truth but also be good and just, so that he should enact the same. Acts 1:1 tells how "Jesus began to do and to teach," which the *Gloss* explains as meaning that the good teacher should first do and then teach, in that order, so that his word is not destroyed by his work.[95] And Chrysostom, expounding Matthew 5:13 and 5:14 ("You are the salt of the earth" and "You are the light of the world"), says that you are first called "salt" and then "light," because the first thing to do is to live well and the second, to teach well.[96] The sinner or unjust man cannot, therefore, be a *doctor* of this Scripture.

However, there are degrees of prohibition, it would seem, some errant teachers being more relevantly sinful than others. Henry distinguishes between different types of evil and the corresponding types of sinful teacher. Either such a person believes what is contrary to true doctrine, as the heretic does, or he acts against true doctrine, like the man who sins in his behavior. Someone who is a sinner in the first sense cannot teach at all, nor be a *doctor* of this science, for he is excommunicate and he will corrupt his audience. In the second sense, the sinner is one of the faithful and has sound doctrine, but does not lead a good life. This amounts to a contrast between sins of thought and sins of deed.

A further contrast, between public sin and private sin, is then posited. We must ask if the sinful teacher's sin is hidden and he is of good reputation or whether it is manifest, the man being infamous on account of his evil life. If it is hidden, the sinner may be teaching to flatter and please, or out of vainglory,[97] or he may be a sinner because he is jealous, covetous, lustful, or the like. In the first case, we are dealing with sins perpetrated in the very act of teaching. The man who is steeped in those sins should not teach of his own volition, but rather should hold back. Yet it is undeniable that the Gospel should be proclaimed. Philippians 1:18 declares that "by all means," whether in pretense or in truth, Christ should be preached. This, explains the *Gloss,* describes the kinds of bad and good *doctor* who all preach of Christ but not in the same way.[98] Three types are identified: the good pastor, the mercenary, and the rogue. The good pastor proclaims the truth in truth, the mercenary occasionally proclaims the truth, while the thief and rogue denies the truth and makes away with it. The good pastor is to be valued highly, the mercenary tolerated, and the rogue is to be treated with suspicion. A mercenary is said to be someone who preaches for gain. The thief is indeed the heretic who preaches falsehood. The (good) pastor, however, is the man who preaches what is true and in accordance with God.

Henry then proceeds to make his own view crystal-clear. Some treat the mercenary just as if he were a heretic, for they say that the mercenary preacher who sins in his behavior albeit not in a public manner nevertheless acts contrary to what he teaches, and therefore sins by so doing; therefore he should not teach, because no one should do what they personally condemn. But this, Henry declares, is not reasonable. For if a sinner who is living in sin can, by good actions which fall inside the parameters of goodness (*de genere bonorum*), put himself in the position whereby he could receive *gratia de congruo,* it is not appropriate to say that he sins by so doing. Moreover, he may do other things *de genere bonorum* which are of benefit to others. In sum, by helping others he may help himself spiritually.

How, then, should we regard the teacher whose sin is secret, when this sin is what one might call a matter of personal morality rather than anything to do with the very act of preaching itself, providing that such a person does not teach anything against Christian truth (in contrast with the heretic) and is not therefore excommunicate? Here it must be said that, although he secretly fails to practice what he teaches, this type of teacher is useful to others, and because he may make personal spiritual progress by so doing (as with other works of mercy performed in this life), it is perfectly lawful for him to teach, and for him to be a *doctor* of theology.

And what of the teacher whose wicked life is manifest and infamous? He should not, insofar as it lies within his own power (*quantum est ex parte sui*), teach at all, because he will scandalize his audience. However, on account of the faithful (but not his own account) he may be heard, providing that he has sound doctrine and is permitted to teach by the Church, not having been removed from his office. Concerning this the Lord says in Matthew 23:2–3 that the scribes and the Pharisees now sit "on the chair of Moses"; so "whatsoever they shall say to you, observe and do: but according to their works do ye not. For they say, and do not," failing to practice what they preach. The *Gloss* interprets "the chair of Moses" as meaning that the scribes and Pharisees teach what Moses taught, while "whatsoever they shall say to you" means the things which pertain to that seat.[99] These things should be "observed and done" on account of the seat being Moses', but certainly not on account of the lives of the teachers. If, however, they are rejected by the Church, they should not be listened to by any means.

This discussion has a definite context, which is essential to know for full appreciation of the significance of Henry's statements. As David d'Avray has pointed out, "there is no direct connection between Paris's achievements in scholastic theology and its role as a centre of mass communication," i.e., wherein sermon models and preaching aids were produced, yet there were many ways in which scholastic theology may be said to have helped preachers, one of which concerned the formation of "the preacher's self-image," the "development of an ideology of the preacher's role."[100] For, as Jean Leclercq has demonstrated, between *c.* 1240 and *c.* 1312 there was considerable discussion at the University of Paris on matters relating to the "office" (*officium*) or "mastership" (*magisterium*) of the preacher, the main areas of debate being the preacher's authority and authorization, the knowledge and preparation necessary for proper performance of his task, and his personal character and disposition.[101] It is within the last of these categories, of course, that Henry's *quaestio* on the sinful *doctor* falls. His approach affords interesting comparisons and contrasts with the one taken in another major document of the debate, an anonymous quodlibet (in Paris, Bibliothèque nationale, Lat. 3108) on the subject, whether to preach in a state of mortal sin is itself a mortal sin or not.[102] One of the arguments against this proposition is that, just as a man who is in a state of mortal sin may give alms and pray and do other good works, by the same token he can preach and direct the people to good works: this, as we have just seen, is very much Henry's line. In reaching his own conclusion, the anonymous disputant makes distinctions between preaching *ex officio* and preaching in special circumstances, and between sins which are public knowledge and those which are secret. The sinner who, not required to preach by virtue of office, actually does so out of devotion or owing to the wish of another, does not sin by preaching, providing that his sinful state is concealed. If, however, his sin is manifest, then, irrespective of whether he is preaching *ex officio* or not, he sins mortally on account of the scandal he creates. Similarly, writing much later (*c.* 1340), Thomas Waleys, in an *ars praedicandi* rather than a *quaestio,* attributes to *doctores theologiae* the view that anyone preaching while in a state of mortal sin sins in that very act of preaching.[103] Both these accounts seem to be putting forward a view which, as we have seen, Henry regarded as unreasonable, on the grounds that it puts the mercenary preacher on a par with the heretic. Debate like this represents the struggle to balance the conflicting claims of idealism and pragmatism, and affords a good instance of how scholasticism could generate thought about society and take actual society into account in its thought. Viewed in this light, the strengths of Henry's excursus are as considerable as they are obvious.

Many of the ideas canvassed here are, however, so startling that their origins require investigation, particularly the notion that intellect and knowledge need not co-exist with moral virtue. Like so many of his contemporaries who worried over the same issue, Henry was heavily influenced by (although he does not mention it in the present *quaestio*) Aristotle's distinction between art and virtue as propounded in the second book of the *Ethics*.[104] Averroës, commenting on the relevant passage, explains that, for a craftsman to attain perfection in his art it is enough that the artifacts he produces are good.[105] By contrast, for a man to lead a virtuous life he must be virtuous in himself and perform virtuous actions, these things being equally necessary. For example, he should both perform just and chaste (*castus*) actions and himself be just and chaste. Similarly, Aquinas, expounding the same passage, describes Aristotle's central point as being that "there is no similarity in art and virtue since works of art have in themselves what belongs to the perfection of the art," whereas virtues are principles of actions that do not go out into external matter but rather remain in the agents.[106] Hence actions of this kind are perfections of the agents. And that is why, Aquinas continues, Aristotle asserts that, in order that actions be justly and temperately performed, it is not enough that what is done be good, but the agent must work in a proper manner. His account of the three aspects of this "proper manner" follows and elaborates on what Averroës had said in his commentary.[107] First, the person performing a virtuous action should do it not just by chance or fluke; he should know what he is doing. Secondly, it should not be done out of passion, as when a man performs a good action out of fear. Neither should it be done for any motive other than the wish to do good, "as when a person performs a good action for money or vainglory." Rather, good actions "should be done for the sake of the virtuous work itself which, as something agreeable, is inherently pleasing to him who has the habit of virtue." Thirdly, people should be virtuous consistently, without variation or vacillation.

Here is the wherewithal necessary to distinguish between art and virtue. Only the first of these requirements for virtue, namely knowledge, is required in the arts. A man can be a good artist, Aquinas declares, even if he never chooses to work according to art and does not persevere in his work. But in the moral sphere, action and perseverance really matter; doing is more important than knowing. Action produces the moral *habitus,* rather than the other way round; by performing just and temperate actions a man becomes just and temperate. Hence, "knowledge has little or no importance in a person being virtuous," this being Thomas's phrasing of Aristotle's own statement (as rendered by a version of Robert Grosseteste's translation) that mere knowledge has little or no importance to the virtues: *Ad virtutes autem scire quidem parum aut nihil potest.*[108] That dictum was to resonate through generations of scholastic treatments of the nature of ethics, of the relative merits of intelligence and action, of the qualities essential for the Christian teacher. In this particular context, the point is that knowledge and moral virtue are distinct because the end of moral science—like, we may add, the end of the science of theology—is not knowledge alone, "which those enslaved to passion can perhaps gain" (to quote a gloss from an earlier part of Aquinas's *Ethics* commentary). [109] This is a concomitant of the principle that the conditions and operations which produce a moral *habitus* are quite different from those which produce an intellectual *habitus*. As Aquinas says elsewhere (in his *Summa theologiae*), for a human to act well "it is requisite that not only his reason be well disposed through a habit of intellectual virtue, but also that his appetite be well disposed through a habit of moral virtue." [110] Socrates' belief that as long as a man possesses knowledge he cannot sin is, therefore, "based on a false supposition." (This notion was, of course, criticized in Aristotle's *Ethics*. [111]) Can, then, intellectual virtue exist without moral virtue? After all, "intellectual virtue, which is perfection of reason, does not depend on moral virtue, a perfection of the appetitive part." [112] Aquinas's response is that intellectual virtues can indeed exist without moral virtue (with the exception of prudence). And this — to return to Aquinas's commentary on the *Ethics* — is why Aristotle and his interpreters reject the opinion of those who, thinking "they can become virtuous by philosophizing," talk about virtues rather than exercising them. [113] To which it should be responded that "as those who listen to the advice of doctors and disregard it will never have a well-regulated body, so those who listen to the warnings of moral philosophers and do not heed them will never have a well-regulated soul." Moral virtue is not a matter of theory alone; it requires appropriate behavior of the teacher and of the taught.

Here, then, is the intellectual tradition behind Henry of Ghent's two definitions of the *doctor:* someone who is capable of teaching because he has the requisite *habitus* of knowledge, and someone who has the office of teaching (*officio docendi*), being acceptable to an audience who, because of his own good life, trust him to do them some good. Henry's *quaestio* seems to be somewhat unusual, however, when placed in the persepctive of the other (quite numerous) Parisian *quaestiones* on the same and related issues, because they tend to focus on the *praedicator* rather than work with his more inclusive term *doctor,* and some of them make the relevant Aristotelian distinction between moral and intellectual virtues altogether more cogent by identifying the respective duties of the *praedicator* and the *lector.* An excellent example of this is afforded by part of the anonymous quodlibet in Paris, B.N. Lat. 3108, on which we have already drawn. [114] Here it is argued that although sinners should not preach they may be permitted to "read" (i.e., lecture on) the sacred page. The preacher, because of his office, is bound to the cure of souls, and therefore he owes his flock his devotion (an argument very much in line with Gregory's *Cura pastoralis*).[115] A lecturer or master in a school, by contrast, does not have this obligation to his pupils; his brief is simply to improve their minds, not save their souls. Therefore, in the case in which the *lector* is a sinner, he is not depriving his charges of anything, because he does not owe them his devotion, and so in his very act of lecturing he does not sin mortally. Furthermore, lecturing is not the purely spiritual work that preaching is, whence a layman may lecture on Scripture; the office of lecturer is not primarily conducive to the cure of souls but rather to the instruction of the auditors in some science. Knowledge (*scientia*) is not a moral virtue, the schoolman continues, because, as Aristotle says, it does little or nothing to lead one to the virtues—a reference to the seminal passage from Book 2 of the *Ethics* which we discussed above. *Ad virtutes autem scire quidem parum aut nihil potest.* In sum, here the roles of the *praedicator* and *lector* are conceived of as being distinct, each office having its special procedures and objectives.[116] Similarly, in his *Forma praedicandi* (1322) Robert of Basevorn argues that, in sharp contrast to the *praedicator* whose duty is to make others good, "a lecturer (*lector*) in a school may be in mortal sin and teach in it, and because his act of itself is not immediately directed to making others good as such, I do not believe that he sins mortally [i.e., in his act of teaching]."[117]

The fundamental difference between this type of approach and Henry's is striking. Certainly Henry had no hesitation in employing the basic distinction between preaching and lecturing in several of his subsequent *quaestiones,* for example in the one which investigates whether or not everyone should hear the science of theology (Art. XII, qu. 6).[118] Here Henry divides the human race into two large groups. One consists of those who have the responsibility simply for their own salvation; they should not take upon themselves the care of others and insist on teaching them, for that would cause the greatest possible confusion among the people. All they need to hear is what suffices for salvation, and hence preaching will serve all their needs. It is not appropriate that they should be listeners of this science in the sense of hearing lectures on it (i.e., intellectual instruction in scholastic science). The second group consists of those who do have the responsibility for teaching others. They, the clergy, should be auditors of theology not only by hearing preaching but also by hearing lectures, for preaching alone cannot instruct them to the extent that they become capable of teaching others.

This is, to be sure, some distance away from the contrast between the (acceptable) sinful teacher and the (often offensive) sinful preacher as found in other *quaestiones* of Henry's day. One can only wonder what effect *that* distinction would have had in his *quaestio* on the sinful teacher. It could be suggested that Henry's discussion of the *doctor* as the person with the *habitus* of knowledge, and hence the capability of teaching, could have been sharpened by its deployment, for the juxtaposition of knowledge and immorality takes on its most extreme form in the case in which the *doctor* is a *praedicator*. Turning to Henry's discussion of the *doctor* as possessor of the *officium docentis*, the force of this is perhaps diluted by the claim that the *doctor* should lead a virtuous life, for surely this is crucial for one type of *doctor*, the preacher, but not for the other type, the school lecturer (to adopt the approach of the other clerics we have cited above)?

But Henry's method is quite impressive in its own terms and may be justified on several grounds. For a start, it may be pointed out that the *praedicator-lector* distinction simply did not fit the pattern Henry wished to follow in tracing and describing the chain of efficient causality from author to audience. Since he had taken the *doctor* as the central subject of an entire article (within his sequence *auctor-doctor-auditor*, in Articles IX through XII), this distinction could not have been used in any major structural sense. Then again, it may be suggested that he wished to treat the problem of the sinful teacher in its most comprehensive and widest aspect and hence the term *praedicator*, being too specific, was passed over in favor of '*doctor*' as the central term. There is, however, a further possibility, this being the one which personally I find most persuasive. Henry may have found the distinction, as applied in this context, far too reductive and misleading, perhaps even quite at variance with the truth of the matter as he saw it. For an essential part of the message of his *quaestio* on the sinful teacher is that even an immoral preacher (whether his immorality was concealed or public knowledge) could be conceived of as having some function as a teacher, if not as a living *exemplum* of good conduct. Such a person's knowledge, in other words, is worth something; it does have value in itself and it may lead certain auditors to the ideal combination of good thinking and good deeds. For the failure of the *mercenarius* is not one of knowledge; that is the sin characteristic of the heretic. Therefore, these types of teacher should not be put on a par — hence Henry's disagreement with the author of the B.N. Lat. 3108 *quaestio* and Thomas Waleys. In spirit he was following Philippians 1:18 by affirming the supreme importance of proclaiming Christ. But this is somewhat speculative. Whatever the exact nature of his motivation, the strengths of Henry's approach to the problem are indubitable, consisting largely in his awareness of expediency as well as high principles and a willingness to discuss how things are alongside how things should be.

5. SIN IN THE TAUGHT

Aristotle's *Ethics,* so important in Henry's investigation of sin in the teacher, also plays a vital part in his inquiry into sin in the taught, the *auditores* of theology. In particular, the young man is particularly prone to sin, being led by his passions, and so Henry poses two related questions: can the young man be an *auditor* of theology (Art. XII, qu. 2;[119] cf. much of the discussion in question 3, "Whether a sinner can be a student of theology"),[120] and can he be a *doctor* of theology (Art. XI, qu. 3)?[121]

The young man, Aristotle states in Book 1 of the *Ethics,* "is not a good student of political science, for he is inexperienced in the ways of life that are the starting point and subject matter of this science." Moreover, "because he is strongly influenced by his emotions, he will study political science without result (*inaniter*) and uselessly (*inutiliter*), for the end of this science is not knowledge but human action." Aristotle proceeds to distinguish between the immature in age (the young) and the immature in character (the incontinent), explaining "that the deficiency is not due to time but to a life lived according to the passions and to the pursuit of each object of passion."[122] Aquinas, commenting on this passage, explains that when Aristotle refers to "the ways of life that are the starting point and subject matter" of political science, he means that the principles of this science "proceed from what pertains to and also treats of the actions of human life."[123] Moral science is known mostly by experience, which is precisely what the young lack, since they simply have not lived long enough. Aristotle, then, affirms that the person "who is ruled by the emotions will study this science in vain, that is, without any result and uselessly without attaining its proper end." For "the end of this science is not knowledge alone, which those enslaved to passion can perhaps gain" (that being the crucial concept for the issue of whether a sinner can be a *doctor* of theology, as we have seen above). Rather the end of political sci-

ence, "as of all practical sciences, is human action."[124] A later commentator, Walter Burley (writing between 1334 and 1337), sought to
improve on this monolithic definition by affirming that the end of
moral science is in fact twofold, namely *immediatus et mediatus.*[125] The
finis immediatus is to speculate about those matters which relate to that
science, whereas the *finis mediatus* is to act in accordance with what
this science teaches — thereby the speculative aspect of ethics is given
its due, but its operational aspect accepted as paramount. Because
this is so, "those who follow the emotions do not attain virtuous acts,"
to return to Aquinas's close reading of Aristotle's text.[126] And so, in
this regard "it makes no difference whether the student of this science
is immature in age or immature in character, that is, a slave of the
emotions." This is because, just as the person immature in age fails
to achieve the end of this science that is knowledge, so the immature
in character fails to achieve the end that is action." The deficiency of
the latter type, the incontinent man, is not due to age or time "but
to the fact that he lives according to his emotions, seeking everything
to which the emotions incline." For such men the knowledge of this
science is useless.

This doctrine was of considerable use to many of the late-medieval
schoolmen who considered the nature of the science of theology: they
could apply the ideas directly and precisely since theology was not
simply a speculative science but offered principles and patterns of good
behavior, thus occupying much of the territory covered by Aristotelian theories of ethics and politics. Although the science of theology
is primarily speculative, declares Henry in his *quaestio* on the sinful
auditor (Art. XII, qu. 3), it teaches not only those matters pertaining
to faith so that we should know God but also those things which pertain to life and behavior, so that we should become good. Moreover,
the listener of this science should be more worthy than the *auditor* of
any secular science whatever. But the sinner who is led by his passions
is, as "The Philosopher" says in the first book of the *Ethics,* unsuitable
as a student of political science. Therefore, someone like that certainly
should not be a student of theology. Political science and theology may,
therefore, be compared, but the superiority of theology is indubitable.[127]

Theology, then, like political science, involves not just knowing
but doing. And, in terms of morality, we cannot know unless we do.
The *auditor* does not attain the end (*finis*) of theology just by understanding those things which pertain to faith — rather its end is to be
reached through performance of the appropriate kinds of living and

behavior. In both these respects, the sinner is deficient as an *auditor* of theology because he lacks the requisite knowledge and fails to conduct himself in the right way. And to illustrate this point, Henry turns to an old favorite of his, Chrysostom's commentary on Matthew's Gospel; specifically, to his exegesis of Matthew 22:31, where Christ reproved the Sadduccees for raising quibbling questions about the Resurrection. [128] "Have you not read that which was spoken by God," he asks them, the point being, Chrysostom explains, that because they do not believe the Scriptures it is as if they have not read them. It is as if someone were to explain the art of war to a farmer who lacked the will to fight, or teach agriculture to a warrior who did not wish to cultivate the land: even if these individuals were to hear the teacher's words of explanation all day long, they could not understand or comprehend anything, because they lack the desire for his discipline. [129] As Chrysostom (on Matthew 21:24) says, just as the blind person cannot see in the splendor of light, neither can the malicious or ill-disposed man understand the mysteries of piety. [130] And therefore it is said of sinners in Wisdom 2:21–22, "their own malice blinded them. They knew not the secrets of God."

Henry then returns to Aristotle's statement in the first book of the *Ethics,* concerning the *auditor* of political science, that the person who follows the passions vainly and uselessly (*inaniter et inutiliter*) hears this science "vainly," i.e., without any effective result, in that he fails to achieve the end of this science which is knowledge of its principles, and "uselessly," in that he does not pursue the end of this science which is the activity relevant to those principles. "The Commentator" on this passage of the *Ethics*—Eustratius, as translated by Grosseteste—says that the *auditor,* if he should properly and appropriately hear, should live beyond the enslaving passions. [131] It is not solely on account of his youth that the young man is an unsuitable *auditor* of political science, but also on account of his being debilitated by passions. Since he is weighed down by the fetters of evil thoughts and is looking at the ground, he cannot care for the good, neither in knowing nor in acting. All this applies to theology, Henry adds, inasmuch as theology teaches things to be done and therefore has the same problem with its *auditores.* And this science addresses itself directly to the problem of the enslaving passions. (Clearly, Henry and his colleagues were anxious to overgo Aristotle here; political science could not save the Christian soul.) [132]

In *De doctrina Christiana,* Augustine likens theology to a medicine, whereby the sickness of the human will is aided.[133] Just as medicine benefits the sick body, so the Word of God benefits the sick soul. Henry then turns to the extended use of this same metaphor by Eustratius ("Moralis et civilis medicinalis est animarum. . . ").[134] There are two kinds of medicine: one which preserves health, and one which cures illness. Applying the first sense, the *auditor* of theology can only be a good man, who is conserved in its goodness and directed in his behavior. Applying the second sense, it is very appropriate that the man who is evil and follows passion, whether he be old or young, should be an *auditor* of this science, in accordance with what "the Commentator" says concerning the first book of the *Ethics*. This refers to Eustratius's exegesis of the passage in which Aristotle compares the person immature in age with the person immature in character, and concludes that for both these types the knowledge of political science is useless.[135] But Henry is anxious to affirm that the superior science of theology *is* of use to the young and the incontinent alike. It is not by any means without use to the depraved, he argues, *providing* that they realize the extent to which they are evil and how far they have to go to improve themselves. Unless they are utterly lacking in intelligence they will have a certain desire for direction, and thus by improving little by little they will indeed get better. For it would be inconsistent for the body to be helped by that which has the power to cure it, and for rational souls not to be helped by their appropriate medicine. Here Henry is applying to theology what Eustratius had said concerning ethics.

To clinch the matter he brings in Chrysostom on Matthew again.[136] Matthew 6:22 describes the eye as the lamp of the body; if your eye is sound, your whole body will be sound, but if your eye is diseased your whole body will be all darkness. In order that sight may be restored, the blind person must know the cause of his disease. This is evil concupiscence, which infects the pupil of one's eye, like some malign fluid, and utterly obscures it with thick mist. But it is easy to diminish and disperse that mist, Chrysostom assures us, if the sinner will admit the ray of Christ's doctrine. Similarly, constant hearing of the Word will destroy the fetter of concupiscence which binds fast the hearer.

But will this spiritual medicine be equally effective with all sinners? Henry, again drawing on Eustratius's *Ethics* commentary, admits that it will not, and distinguishes between the hopeless cases, who are really hardened in malice so there is no hope of their conversion, and the hopeful cases, who do have a chance of recovery.[137] He has been speaking concerning the latter. But concerning the former it must be said that it is useless for them to be hearers of such doctrine. Armed with this valuable distinction, Henry returns to the arguments in favor of the proposition that the sinner can be an *auditor* of theology with which he began this *quaestio.* The words of Matthew 9:12, "They that are in health need not a physician, but they that are ill," is said to be true to the extent that the sick man is curable of his illness; i.e., he has to be one of those hopeful cases as described by Henry. But if one considers medicine as maintaining and directing health, then it must be said that it is principally for the just and healthy. The same applies to the second argument, viz., that this science of theology was instituted for the benefit of the sinner (cf. 1 Timothy 1:9). This proposition is true insofar as it was instituted for (redeemable) sinners as opposed to those who are actually just — which is not, of course, to say that it was exclusively established for such sinners.

In the course of this argument Henry has inevitably moved away from the special moral problems of the young man, and taken for granted Aristotle's grouping together of the young and the incontinent, since it is with the sinful auditor in general that this *quaestio* is concerned. The previous *quaestio* had focused on the problem of whether or not the young man can be an *auditor* of theology, and so we must now turn to it.[138] Predictably, the discussion begins with citation of the first book of the *Ethics.* Maturity and a settled disposition are required more in the *auditor* of this science than in the *auditor* of any secular science, because this is the science of the Christian religion. But, as "the Philosopher" says, a young man is not a proper *auditor* of political science, therefore. . . . (This argument is, of course, identical with the Contra argument at the beginning of the *quaestio* on the sinful auditor, as described above.) Besides, as the Apostle says in Hebrews 5:14, "solid food is for the mature," and the *Gloss* identifies that solid food as sacred Scripture.[139] But against this would seem to be the words of Ecclesiasticus 6:18, "My son, from thy youth up, receive instruction: and even to thy grey hairs thou shalt find wisdom." The *Gloss* explains that those who in their youth study sound doctrine gather in their old age the sweet fruits of wisdom; this is healthy doctrine from which the fruits of wisdom are expected.[140]

Here Henry's response turns on the familiar distinction between preaching, which is for all Christians, and school lecturing, which is for the elite only. It is perfectly appropriate for the young man, in

terms of his status, to listen to preaching, whereby he is instructed
in what to believe and what to do; neither age nor sex is a barrier
to the hearing of theology in this way. It is, however, a very different
story when one speaks of the *auditor* of theology as someone who attends the lecture of a master wherein the occult mysteries of Scripture
are investigated. Henry introduces a comparison with the proper servant, who is said to be the one who is suitable and useful to his lord,
inasmuch as he conforms with and is compliant to his lord in all things
and is in total agreement with his lord's will. The bad, unsuitable,
and useless servant, on the other hand, is said to be the one who does
not do any of these things. Similarly, the proper *auditor* of a science
is said to be the man who is apt for the science and brings himself
into conformity with all things relating to it, while the man who is
neither suitable nor conforms to it at all is said to be not its proper
auditor. Returning to the young man, due to his age he is inclined
to slip easily into vices and is insecure in knowledge. Thus the *Gloss*
says concerning Lamentations 3:27 ("It is good for a man [when he
hath borne the yoke from his youth]"), that it is good for a youth to
abstain from vices and, being uncertain and confused, to flee from
error.[141] For youths are weak and insecure in knowledge, and incon-
stant. In accordance with this, therefore, the young man by reason
of his age is an inappropriate and profitless *auditor* of this science of
theology. Inappropriate (*inconveniens*), in that he is instable in mind
and reason; profitless (*inutilis*), in that he is prone to the vices. (This
vocabulary echoes Aristotle's declaration that the young man will study
moral science *inaniter et inutiliter*.) The proper and appropriate *auditor*
of this science, by contrast, is someone who is able to grasp its profound truths and to judge concerning those things which he hears of
the science, accepting things which are well said and refuting the con-
traries. This cannot be done unless one is firm and stable in reason
and intellect and has stable knowledge concerning those things which
fall within the boundaries of the science, because, as "the Philosopher"
says at the beginning of the *Ethics,* only the person who knows can
judge well.[142] But the young man, by dint of the age of his mind and
reason, is not stable, and neither does he have fixed knowledge of those
things pertaining to theology which are especially important to be
known on account of faith. Therefore, the young man is not an appropriate *auditor* of a lecture in this science, in which the more difficult things are treated, for it is first necessary (cf. Hebrews 5:12–14)
that he should be taught "the first principles of God's word," because

he needs milk, not solid food. The *Gloss* explains the first principles of God's word as the simple teaching of the articles of the faith, which is like milk to infants who cannot yet receive solid food, that being the doctrine of the hidden God.[143]

Throughout this discussion much of Henry's language is heavily influenced by Aristotle's treatment in the *Ethics* of the young man as an unsuitable *auditor* of political science, as should be obvious. It is to the *Metaphysics* that he turns for the resounding declaration with which he begins his response to the question, "can a young man be a *doctor* of theology?" (Art. XI, qu. 3),[144] though it is interesting to note that this is the passage with which Thomas Aquinas began his commentary on the *Ethics. Sapientis est ordinare.* "The wise man must not be ordered but must order, and he must not obey another, but the less wise must obey him."[145] Youths are moved by the passions, whereas the old are not and hence the the rational judgments of the old are more sound. According to Aristotle, teaching is a work of the wise man and of wisdom, whereby the doctor uses his wisdom to teach others; since wisdom is greater than the other sciences it should be taught last in sequence and thus not until an advanced state of life. Therefore in the regular course of events a youth should not be a doctor of this science. Whence, at the University of Paris no one can become an inceptor in the faculty of theology until he is at least thirty-five years old. Ezekiel, David, John the Baptist, and Christ himself were in their maturity filled with the divine wisdom in order that they could proceed to teach, because it was appropriate to them as mature men and provided an example of future practice.

In sum, the clear consensus of all the experts, whether Christian or pagan, scriptural or secular, or ancient or modern, was that subtle theology is lost on the young, given their youthful limitations, and hence they should not be permitted to profess it. But young men can grow out of their weaknesses, leave their limitations behind—a process of improvement which, according to the belief of Henry and his contemporaries, was generally denied to women, their imperfection being regarded as constituting a permanent human condition. "Frailty, thy name is woman!" declares Hamlet,[146] and Henry, following the common clerical opinion of his day, could only have agreed. What is impressive, however, is the unusually large (in respect of thirteenth-century *summae* and quodlibetal collections) amount of space he found for discussion of whether women should be taught or indeed teach theology. If Henry was typical of his age in his view of the status of women in the Church, he was unusual in the degree of importance he afforded the matter.

6. FEMALE FRAILTY

Can a woman be a *doctor* of the supreme science of theology?[147] After all, Proverbs 4:3 can be interpreted as meaning that Solomon was taught by his mother. Besides, there is the relationship between prophecy and teaching. The former is certainly not inferior to the latter; moreover, prophets must teach publicly those things which have been revealed to them. As 1 Corinthians 14:3 says, he who prophesies speaks to men for their edification and encouragement and consolation. Since it is accepted that certain women have prophesied — such as Miriam (Exodus 15:20), Deborah (Judges 4:4), Huldah (4 Kings 22:14) and Anne (Luke 2:36) — it must be concluded that female teachers have existed. Then again, in 1 Peter 4:10 we read that everyone who has received a gift should employ or manage it to common benefit, and since women sometimes receive the gift of this knowledge, therefore they should employ it for others, which they cannot do unless they teach. Thus, Mary and Martha received the gift of different tongues along with the Apostles, and were sent to teach and preach publicly just as those men were. But against the proposition stands the firm injunction of Paul (1 Timothy 2:12): "I suffer not a woman to teach."

In his response Henry first makes the general point that here, as in the other *quaestiones* concerning those who are permitted to have the *officium doctoris,* he is speaking of the ability or capability for teaching (*potentia docendi*) rather than teaching *de facto,* in terms of statutory permission rather than of what can actually happen. It is plain that, *de facto,* any knowledgeable person, whether a man or woman, an old man or a youth, whether religious or secular, whether cleric or lay, can teach what he or she knows. And so it must be said to this question on a woman teaching as to the others, that teaching can be either by office (*ex officio*) or by special privilege, promotion, or benefit (*ex beneficio*). In order for someone to teach *ex officio,* Henry continues, four things are required, two of which refer to doctrine and two to the audience. First is constancy of teaching; the teacher should not diverge from what is known to be true. Second is effectiveness of performance; no weakness should retard such work. Third is the authority for teaching: the teacher must have this in order that his listeners defer to him by believing what he says. Fourth is strength and vigor of speech, whereby the teacher directs his audience to the virtues by gnawing to pieces the vices.

Because of her deficiency in each of these four respects, a woman cannot hold the office of teacher. Women, Henry declares, can neither be constant in teaching nor effective in its communication since they are the weaker sex, this being why the commission of preaching was given to men. And hence the Apostle in 1 Timothy, after saying that he does not permit women to preach, adds, as if by way of explanation, that Adam was formed first, then Eve; and Adam was not deceived, but the woman was deceived and became a transgressor (2:13-14). Henry then says that women are unable to make the physical effort required in teaching; because of the fragility of their sex, they simply lack the strength to speak at length and labor in public. And that is why the Apostle, having said womankind is not allowed to teach, adds that she is to be "in silence" (1 Timothy 2:12). Concerning the third quality necessary for teaching *ex officio,* namely authority, a woman cannot have this because of her inferior status, which is attested by Genesis 3:16, where God tells Eve that she will be under the power of the man, and he will rule over her. Hence Paul, after saying that no woman should teach, immediately adds that she should not have authority over men. At this point the *Glossa ordinaria* affirms that woman is denied the authority necessary for teaching.[148] Likewise, in 1 Corinthians 14:34, after saying that women are not permitted to speak in church, Paul immediately adds that they "should be subject," as the law says. Concerning vigor and liveliness of speech, the speech of women does not lead to mortification but rather provokes sins, which is why the *Gloss* on Paul's prohibition of women from teaching (at 1 Timothy 2:12) says that a female teacher would greatly incite men to lust — kindle it like a fire, to adopt the idiom of Ecclesiasticus 9:9 — and sexually excite the males in her audience.[149]

To speak, however, about teaching which is *ex beneficio* and due to the fervor of charity, it is perfectly permissible for a woman (as anyone else) to teach, if she has sound doctrine and providing that this is done privately rather than publicly and in church, for that is allowed only to those who teach *ex officio,* and women are not allowed to hold the *officium doctoris.* Paul's statement in 1 Corinthians 14:3 (as cited at the beginning of this discussion) should not be taken as meaning that women can teach in public just like men. It was in order to make this very point that, later in this same chapter (14:34), Paul said that women are not allowed to speak in church. Women are indeed allowed to teach appropriate doctrine in private. However, their audiences should consist chiefly of other women and girls, but not men, because female speech would inflame men to lust, as has already been said; besides, men would regard it as unseemly and shameful to be taught by a female.

The problem of Solomon having been taught by his mother (Proverbs 4:4) is addressed with two different arguments. First, if she indeed had taught him, this would have been private teaching of the kind whereby the mother teaches the son in his minority. Secondly, there may be a misreading of the text involved: it is better, Henry says, to follow the interlinear part of the *Glossa ordinaria* and interpret the passage as meaning that Solomon's *father* taught him, not his mother.[150] What, then, of those female prophets referred to in the Bible? Henry argues that their gift was given for private rather than public instruction, and if men were taught thereby this was by a special dispensation, wherein divine grace did not respect sexual difference. In accordance with this Colossians 3:10 refers to the new man which is renewed in the image of its Creator, this being neither masculine nor feminine. But public instruction remains a male prerogative. Finally, Henry returns to 1 Peter 4:10. Everyone who has received a gift should indeed employ it for the benefit of others, but the principle of decorum and appropriateness applies, so that men should employ their gift in public while women should employ theirs in private. The text of 1 Peter proceeds by describing the "good stewards of the manifold grace of God" who render it by the strength which God supplies in order that in everything God may be glorified (vv. 10–11). The inference is that if God should supply women with the strength necessary to further his own glorious purposes this should not be gainsaid, but certainly cannot be regarded as normative. Grace sometimes does not respect the difference between the sexes, and in those exceptional cases the public preaching of women is quite acceptable. But Henry emphasizes that there is always a special reason for such occurrences. There were certain Old Testament women who did indeed prophesy. But this was a deliberate affront to men, because they had become effeminate. Therefore, in these very special circumstances, and to make this very special point, women were set above men in a position of pedagogic superiority. Similarly, in the early Christian church as chronicled in the New Testament (Acts 21:9), it was granted that Martha and Mary should preach, and the four daughters of Philip should publicly prophesy. But this, in Henry's view, was due to a shortage of skilled labor in those productive times: since there were many harvests (of converts) and a small number of harvesters, the aid of women was necessary.

But if women cannot teach theology, except in the most special and limited of contexts, can they at least be *auditores* (listeners, pupils) of this science? Henry asks that question in the first *quaestio* of Article XII.[151] A woman should know those things which are necessary for her salvation, and she cannot learn unless by being a pupil, and these things cannot be learned except from this science. Besides, nothing which is imperfect should be impeded from pursuing its perfection. Woman is imperfect in sciences and virtues, just as a man is, and therefore she should be instructed in this science. On the other hand, women cannot hear public lectures in the subject — i.e., attend the lectures held in theological schools, in accordance with yet another of Paul's injunctions concerning women in 1 Corinthians 14, "if they would learn anything, let them ask their husbands at home" (v. 35). Since this science is conveyed by public lecture, whoever cannot learn through this method of instruction cannot learn the science, which would seem to exclude women.

Henry's response is as follows. Being a student of a science means being instructed in those things which pertain to that science. And whoever is instructed in a certain science or in those things which pertain to it, must in a certain way be its student (*auditor*). There are certain aspects of this science, relating to both life and behavior, which are necessary for men and women alike to know. In this sense, then, it is necessary for women to hear this science. Then Henry, drawing on Augustine, proceeds to identify two ways in which we can be instructed in faith and behavior.[152] In one way, in order that one knows what to believe and what is to be done in order to achieve eternal life. In another way, so that one gains knowledge whereby he can help the pious and oppose the impious. Being an *auditor* of the science in this latter sense entails being thoroughly instructed in its depths, and equipped to persuade others publicly about those truths and to defend them against adversaries. In these terms, a woman cannot learn theology, for women cannot teach publicly, as Henry has already argued (here he refers back to the question of the female *doctor* of theology). Indeed, on account of the weakness of woman's natural capacity (*ingenium*) it is not possible for her to attain such a degree of perfection in this science. Assuredly, if she expends herself in searching out its hidden mysteries she is more likely through error to fail rather than make headway. Few people flourish in this science—and women certainly are not among that number.

Turning to the former sense (i.e., learning what must be believed and how to act accordingly), Henry introduces a second distinction. One can be taught things which are necessary for one's station in life, or things which are not suitable to it. In this second sense, a woman cannot be a pupil of this science inasmuch as she should not know things which are inappropriate to her status. Whence a discreet teacher (*doctor*) should propound to the woman only what it is her business to know from this science, and not go beyond that—even if she wishes to do so, for women are curious to know things which they do not need to know. And therefore, Henry protests, they act very foolishly who instruct women in this science beyond what is decent and necessary for them to know—especially those who disclose the secrets of Scripture and translate them into the vernacular (*in vulgari sermone*) so that women may read them. Little wonder that Henry was such a favorite with those later bastions of orthodoxy, the conservative theologians who sought to refute the errors of the Wycliffites. He sums up this phase of his argument by declaring that to "hear" this science in the sense of learning those things which are necessary for salvation and relevant to one's station in life is perfectly allowable to women; indeed, this is highly useful to them in their lives, and a similar argument can be made in respect of every man.

Clearly, this is an application and development of the distinction between basic knowledge (for humanity in general) and specialized knowledge (for an elite of mature males) which, as we have seen, runs through Henry's entire article on the *auditor* of theology. He proceeds to offer another variation on the same theme by appropriating the distinction between teaching and preaching. There are two ways in which theology may be heard: by hearing a lecture wherein the sequence of sacred Scripture is expounded, or by hearing preaching, whereby only what is expedient is made known from Scripture. It is not possible for a woman to be an *auditor* of lectures on theology on two grounds: because in a lecture difficult and secret things are expounded from Scripture which are not appropriate for a woman to hear, and because it is not permitted for a woman to be taught in public, in accordance with 1 Timothy 2:11 ("Let the woman learn in silence"). By contrast, in preaching, whether public or private, a woman may hear this science, because, in preaching, deep matters are not propounded, but rather those things which are appropriate for the general run of humanity. It is of this type of hearing that Deuteronomy 31:11–12 speaks: "thou shalt read the words of this law before all Israel, in their hearing. And the people being all assembled together, both men and women, children and strangers, that are within thy gates: that hearing they may learn, and fear the Lord their God, all the days that they live in the land. . . ." If women wish to learn anything further they should not publicly question the preacher but ask their menfolk in the privacy of their own homes, as the full passage from 1 Corinthians 14 which was partly quoted above makes clear: "Let women keep silence in the churches. . . . if they would learn anything, let them ask their husbands at home" (vv. 34–35). Thus Henry returns to the text which had proved so invaluable in his rejection of the notion that a woman should teach theology, even repeating the *Glossa ordinaria*'s explanation of v. 35 ("For it is a shame for a woman to speak in the church") that this is against the law of the church.

From all this, Henry concludes, the reply which should be made to the first of the initial arguments is obvious, for it is perfectly permissible for a woman to be an *auditor* of this science in order to hear what is necessary for her to know, but not other things, and she should learn not by public lecture but by preaching. In regard to the second initial argument, while it is true that woman is imperfect (just as man is) with regard to this science, it does not follow that she should achieve knowledge of those things pertaining to this science just like a man should. It is not permissible for her to study towards perfecting herself in knowledge of this science in this life, except inasmuch as is sufficient to ensure that she will pass into eternal glory, where all that is imperfect will be perfected. And that seems an appropriate note on which to end our review of Henry's discussion of divine authority and human imperfection.

SUMMATION: CAUSE AND DEFECT

Henry's achievement as an *accessor* is considerable. He produced a survey of the transmission and reception of theology which is as remarkable for its symmetry as for its scope. It is surely one of the most sophisticated, perhaps even *the* most sophisticated, *accessus ad theologiam* to have appeared in his age. Sometimes, it must be admitted, Henry can be repetitive, but even this can be seen in a positive light, as indicating his awareness of the different points of intersection of patristic thought and Aristotelian science. He was highly aware of the challenges posed by the new Aristotelian learning and tried to meet them with the aid of, in particular, Augustine, Chrysostom, and Gregory, not to mention an impressive grasp of the principles of the new learning itself.[153]

On occasion his fashionable categories may seem to create problems rather than solve them, as, for example, when Henry uses the single term *doctor* to designate both the *praedicator* and the *lector*. But, as I have tried to show, good reasons may be found for his decision not to use that distinction on that occasion. Above all else, the skill with which he could enlist the aid of the secular sciences, yet discard them when he deemed it necessary, is remarkable. For instance, Aristotle's rejection of the youthful auditor of moral science can be used to highlight the inappropriateness of the youthful auditor of theology, yet at another juncture Aristotle can be surpassed by a refusal to debar the young from listening to theology, at least at the level of preaching, for by it they may learn to curb their passions and act in ways which are conducive to the formation of good moral habits.

The *accessus* paradigm which Henry expanded so considerably was, of course, another product of secular science. And it is remarkable, and perhaps on the face of it somewhat paradoxical, that Henry could exploit it so effectively yet be fully aware of what he envisaged as the limitations of its conceptualization for theology. Thus, he rejects the theory of multiple *modus tractandi* in Scripture in favor of the theory of a single and unified *modus tradendi*. Most noteworthy of all, perhaps, is the way in which he created from his reading of Aristotle on the four causes an analytical structure which comprised authority and fallibility, weakness and strength, and (particularly in his description of the sinful *doctor*) brought together cerebral analysis and the recognition that one has to make virtue of social necessity, since Christ must be proclaimed by all means, whether in pretense or in truth (Philippians 1:18). In short, Henry's *accessus* introduces us to an unusually systematic and synchronic view of all the major aspects of the relationship between cause and defect.

NOTES

See Plate 12 (Leuven [Louvain], Bibliotheek-Faculteit der Godgeleer-heid, F° 37 G Henr.), Frontispiece, 2d. ed., *Magistri < Henrici> Goethals a Gandavo, ordinis Servorum B.M.V., Doctoris Solemnis, socii Sorbanici, Archidiaconi Tornacensis, Summa in tres partes digesta. . . .* Ed. Hieronymus Scarparius, O. Serv. (Ferrara: Franciscus Succius, 1646).

1. For a summary account, see Minnis, *Medieval Theory of Authorship,* 2d ed. (Aldershot, 1988), 15–39.

2. R. W. Hunt, "The Introduction to the *Artes* in the Twelfth Century," in *Studia mediaevalia in honorem R. M. Martin, O.P.* (Bruges, 1948), 85–112.

3. On this vocabulary, in addition to Hunt's article, see E. A. Quain, "The Medieval *Accessus ad auctores,*" *Traditio* 3 (1945): 228–242, and Minnis, *Medieval Theory of Authorship,* 19–25.

4. Minnis, *Medieval Theory of Authorship,* 41.

5. Hunt, "Introduction to the *Artes,*" 96 (implied rather than explic-itly stated — Dr. Hunt was indeed more speculative in conversation); Beryl Smalley, "Peter Comestor on the Gospels and His Sources," *Recherches de théolo-gie ancienne et médiévale* 46 (1979): 110–111. Compare G. R. Evans, *The Lan-guage and Logic of the Bible: The Earlier Middle Ages* (Cambridge, 1984), 30–31 and 172, note 5.

6. Minnis, *Medieval Theory of Authorship,* 235, note 13.

7. Ibid., 41.

8. Ibid., 70, 72.

9. See Beryl Smalley, "A Commentary on Isaias by Guerric of St. Quentin, O.P.," *Miscellanea Giovanni Mercati II: Letteratura Medioevale,* Studi e testi 122 (Vatican City, 1946), 383–397.

10. See the remarks by Ignatius Brady in his edition of Alexander of Hales, *Glossa in quattuor libros sentiarum Petri Lombardi,* Bibliotheca Franciscana scholastica medii aevi 12–15 (Quaracchi, 1951–1957) 1:102–103.

11. Brady in Alexander, *Glossa,* 1:1–4, with reference to Paris, BN lat. 14438, fol. 1r.

12. This is the dating given by J. A. Weisheipl, *Friar Thomas d'Aquino* (Oxford, 1975), 69.

13. R. J. Long, "The Science of Theology According to Richard Fishacre: An Edition of the Prologue to His Commentary on the Sentences," *Mediaeval Studies* 34 (1972): 79–89, at pp. 80, 88; U. Köpf, *Die Anfänge der theologischen Wissenschaftstheorie im 13. Jahrhundert,* Beiträge zur historischen Theologie 49 (Tubingen, 1974), 67–69, 277.

14. Robert Kilwardby, *De natura theologiae,* ed. F. Stegmüller, Opuscula et textus historiam ecclesiae illustrantia 17 (Munster 1935), 7–12. Compare the breakdown of the prologue's headings by Köpf, *Wissenschaftstheorie,* 278–279.

15. Kilwardby's use of the new paradigm is discussed at length by Osmund Lewry, "Robert Kilwardby's Writings on the *Logica vetus* Studied with Regard to Their Teaching and Method" (Ph.D. diss., Oxford, 1978).

16. Bonaventure, *Opera omnia,* ed. Collegium S. Bonaventurae (Quaracchi, 1882-1902) 1:1. Compare Köpf, *Wissenschaftstheorie,* 278.

17. Albert the Great, *Opera omnia,* ed. A. Borgnet (Paris, 1890-1899) 25:6.

18. See Minnis, *Medieval Theory of Authorship,* 119-145.

19. In large measure, this changing awareness is due to the work of Raymond Macken, the coordinator of the critical edition of Henry of Ghent's *Opera omnia.* See especially his articles, "La temporalité radicale de la creature selon Henri de Gand," *Recherches de théologie ancienne et médiévale* 38 (1971): 211-272; "La théorie de l'illumination divine dans la philosophie d'Henri de Gand," *Recherches de théologie ancienne et médiévale* 39 (1972): 82-112; "La volonté humaine, faculté plus élevée que l'intelligence selon Henri de Gand," *Recherches de théologie ancienne et médiévale* 42 (1975): 5-51; "Les sources d'Henri de Gand," *Revue philosophique de Louvain* 76 (1978): 5-28; and, of course, *Bibliotheca manuscripta Henrici de Gandavo,* in *Opera omnia* 1-2 (Leiden, 1979). On the volumes of Henry's *quodlibeta* that have already been published in the *Opera omnia,* see the notice in *Scriptorium* 39 (1985): 142*-144*. On this projected edition of the *Summa,* see the introductions in *Henrici de Gandavo Summa (Quaestiones ordinariae) art. 31-34,* ed. R. Macken, with a general introduction by L. Hödl, vol. 27 of *Henrici de Gandavo Opera omnia* (Leuven, 1991). See also Stephen P. Marrone, *Truth and Scientific Knowledge in the Thought of Henry of Ghent, Speculum* Anniversary Monographs 11 (Cambridge, Mass., 1985), and Katherine H. Tachau, *Vision and Certitude in the Age of Ockham: Optics, Epistemology, and the Foundations of Semantics, 1250-1345* (Leiden, 1988), 28-39.

20. I am grateful to Dr. Macken for valuable discussion of this dating. On Henry's process of revision, see Macken, "Les corrections d'Henri de Gand à sa Somme," *Recherches de théologie ancienne et médiévale* 44 (1977): 55-100, to which compare Macken, "Les corrections d'Henri de Gand à ses Quodlibets," *Recherches de théologie ancienne et médiévale* 40 (1973): 5-51.

21. On the development of such prologues in the thirteenth century, see Köpf, *Wissenschaftstheorie, passim;* P. G. Théry, "An Unedited Text of Robert Grosseteste on the Subject-Nature of Theology," *Revue néoscholastique de philosophie* 36 (1934): 172-190; P. W. Nash, "Giles of Rome and the Subject of Theology," *Mediaeval Studies* 18 (1956): 61-92; M.-D. Chenu, *La théologie comme science au XIIIe siècle,* 3d ed., Bibliothèque Thomiste 33 (Paris, 1969); P. Prassel, *Das Theologieverständnis des Aegidius Romanus, O.E.S.A.* (Frankfurt, 1983). Compare A. J. Minnis and A. B. Scott, *Medieval Literary Theory and Criticism, c. 1100-c. 1375: The Commentary Tradition* (Oxford, 1988), 198ff.

22. For the following discussion of Henry's prologue, I rely on two early printings: *Summa quaestionum ordinarium* (Paris, 1520; rptd. Louvain and

Paderborn, 1953), and *Summa in tres partes praecipuas digesta* (Ferrara, 1646).

23. See Minnis, *Medieval Theory of Authorship,* 28–29, 74–84; Minnis and Scott, *Medieval Literary Theory,* 198–199.

24. Long, "Science of Theology," 88.

25. Transcribed from Oxford, New College Library 40, by Smalley in "Guerric of St. Quentin," 388–389.

26. Bonaventure, *Opera omnia* 7:5.

27. See Minnis, *Medieval Theory of Authorship,* 81.

28. Ibid., 82–84.

29. Ibid., 94–112.

30. Ibid., 118–154.

31. Paris ed., fols. 71r–72r; Ferrara ed., 176–178.

32. Augustine, *De civitate Dei* 11.3, CSEL 40/1:513–514.

33. Augustine, *De civitate Dei* 11.3, CSEL 40/1:513–514.

34. Aristotle, *Metaphysics* 1.1 (981a–b).

35. Aristotle, *Metaphysics* 1.1 (981b).

36. On the importance of this concept in later theology, see H. A. Oberman, *The Harvest of Medieval Theology,* rev. ed. (Grand Rapids, Mich., 1967), 47–50; and William J. Courtenay, *Schools and Scholars in Fourteenth-Century England* (Princeton, 1987), 213, 286, 296–297.

37. Augustine, *De Genesi ad litteram* 2.9, CSEL 27/1 (Vienna), 45–47. See also 1.9 (pp. 11–12) and 5.3 (p. 152), as well as Augustine's account of different kinds of vision in 12.6–37 (pp. 386–435).

38. *Glossa ordinaria* on 2 Peter 1:21, as in *Textus Biblie cum Glossa ordinaria, Nicolai de Lyra Postilla.* . . (Basel, 1506–1508), 6:24.

39. Paris ed., fols. 70r–71r; Ferrara ed., 174–176.

40. Augustine, *De catechizandis rudibus* 3.5–6 (CCSL 46.124–126).

41. "Alexander of Hales," *Summa theologica* tractatus introductorius 1.4.1 ad 2 (Quaracchi, 1924–1928) 1:8.

42. "Alexander," *Summa* tract. introd. 1.8.3 resp (Quaracchi ed., 1:10).

43. Paris ed., fols. 99r–100v; Ferrara ed., 247–249.

44. Translated in Minnis and Scott, *Medieval Literary Theory,* 252.

45. Compare Minnis, *Medieval Theory of Authorship,* 46–48.

46. Minnis and Scott, *Medieval Literary Theory,* 252–253.

47. Ibid., 255.

48. As most clearly expressed in *De doctrina Christiana* 4.

49. 20.3, Paris ed., fols. 121r–121v; Ferrara ed., 304–305.

50. The crucial passage is *De doctrina* 2.6.7 (CCSL 32.35–36). Henry does not, however, cite here Augustine's famous interpretation of the Song of Songs 4:2; that appears in his discussion of whether holy Scripture should be expounded in an obscure style (16.9, Paris ed., fols. 90v–91r; Ferrara ed., 276–277).

51. 16.1, "Concerning the mode of expounding this science in respect

of its exposition" (Paris ed., fol. 104r–v; Ferrara ed., 259–261). The notion of "gross" and uneducated listeners who required general, untechnical exposition owes something to Aristotle's account of the scope and status of the science of ethics as understood by thirteenth-century thinkers (see *Nicomachean Ethics* 1.3, 1094b19–21). For example, Giles of Rome had this passage in mind when he declared that "in the whole field of moral teaching the mode of procedure, according to the Philosopher, is figurative and broad (*grossus*)." See his *De regimine principum* (Rome, 1556), fol. 1v, translated in Minnis and Scott, *Medieval Literary Theory*, 248. Similarly in *Rhetoric* 2.8 (1419a), Aristotle had warned against asking something which uneducated listeners would not understand. Commenting on this passage, Giles explains that the audience for rhetorical orations is supposed to be *grossus,* and so the enthymemes must be suited to the capacity of the minds of such "gross" people. See *Rhetorica Aristotelis cum Egidii de Roma commentariis* (Venice, 1515), fol. 117r.

52. See 17.2, which considers whether each and every spiritual exposition should be offered to everyone indiscriminately (Paris ed., fols. 92r–93r; Ferrara ed., 280–282).

53. Such people are not, however, to be given a profound exposition individually. Individuality relates rather to the different capacities of the capable, some being more capable than others.

54. This idea was also elaborated in 17.1, "Concerning the method of expounding this science, in respect to the person to whom it is expounded" (Paris ed., fols. 91r–92r; Ferrara ed., 278–280). God does not indiscriminately dispense all his benefits to the good and bad alike, but only carnal things, the spiritual benefits being reserved for the good. Therefore it must be said that sacred Scripture is not to be expounded to all indiscriminately, but only to those who are receptive to it and who will find it useful, as are the faithful and obedient. Of course, the teaching of the faith is indeed recommended and thus expounded to all — *before* obstinacy sets in. After that happens, only the faithful need be addressed. In 12.8, on the subject of whether every faithful man, without discrimination, should be admitted to hearing the science of theology (Paris ed., fols. 89v–90v; Ferrara ed., 223–224), Henry distinguishes between a *statement* of what must be believed and the *understanding* of what must be believed. There is nothing in Scripture that should not be propounded to every faithful man indiscriminately, but of course not everyone has the capacity for understanding such matters. In this second sense, there are indeed certain things that by profound exposition can be spoken to spiritual men and hidden from carnal men. This, Henry declares, is what Augustine meant in *De doctrina Christiana* 4.9.23 (CSEL 33:132). Similar thinking is found in Henry's *Quodlibet 10* q. 16, "Utrum doctor siver magister determinans quaestiones vel exponens scripturas publice peccet mortaliter non explicando veritatem quam novit." It is a matter of the capacity of one's audience. If a *doctor* fails to convey doctrine that would be "useful, fruitful, and

necessary" to a given audience, then he indeed sins mortally. On the other hand, he is perfectly justified in censoring material. See Henry of Ghent, *Quodlibet 10,* ed. R. Macken (Leuven and Paris, 1981), 304–307.

55. 14.1, translated in Minnis and Scott, *Medieval Literary Theory,* 255. Henry takes the metaphors of milk and solid food from Augustine, *Tract. in Ioh.* 98.3 (CCSL 36.577–588), but see also the remarks on this issue below.

56. See "Alexander," *Summa* 1.8. Giles's views are made very clear in his commentaries on the *Sentences* and the Song of Songs. For the former see *In lib. Sent.* prologus 3.4 resolutio (Cordoba, 1699), 31. The latter is found among the works of Aquinas in several early editions; see, for example, Thomas, *Opera omnia* (Parma, 1852–1872), 14:387–389, and the translation in Minnis and Scott, *Medieval Literary Theory,* 243–247.

57. Hence he argues that its *modus* is narrative rather than argumentative or ratiocinative, i.e., that it is beyond the processes of normal human inquiry. See 14.2 (Paris ed., fol. 104r–v; Ferrara ed., 259–261).

58. "Alexander," *Summa* tract. introd. 1.4.1 ad 2 (Quaracchi ed., 1:8).

59. For Odo's view, see B. Pergamo, "De quaestionibus ineditis Fr. Odonis Rigaldi, Fr. Gulielmi de Melitona et codicis Vat. Lat. 782 circa naturam theologiae deque earum relatione ad Summam theologicam Fr. Alexandri Halensis," *Archivum Franciscanum Historicum* 29 (1937): 42.

60. 14.1 ad 1, translated in Minnis and Scott, *Medieval Literary Theory,* 255–256.

61. It should be noted, however, that in introducing article 13, "de modo tradendi theologiam," Henry does use the term "forma tractandi." Because in the sciences form is twofold, namely *forma tractandi* and *forma tractatus,* he explains, his question on the method of teaching appropriate to theology must likewise be twofold (Paris ed., fol. 99v).

62. For examples, see Minnis, *Medieval Theory of Authorship,* 21–22, 45, 49, 54, 66, 144. Cf. the variant *forma tractandi,* often used within discussions of a biblical text's *causa formalis;* examples on 29, 144, 147, 148.

63. Paris ed., fols. 107v–108r, Ferrara ed., 268–269, translated in Minnis and Scott, *Medieval Literary Theory,* 263–266. This discussion may be compared with *Quodlibet 3* q. 18, where Henry asks whether every passage of Scripture is literally true, i.e., true in its literal sense. See his *Quodlibeta* (Paris, 1518), fol. 79v. As in the *Summa,* ps-Augustine *De praedestinatione et gratia* 1 (PL 45:1666–1667) is quoted as saying that every reader who approaches Holy Scripture with the intention of expounding it, when troubled by some discordant opinion expressed in the sacred writings, must with sure and unshaken faith steadfastly believe that truth is nowhere absent in Scripture, even though understanding does not readily come to those who seek answers, due to the immensity of the subject. In the quodlibet, Henry also cites Augustine's *De doctrina Christiana* as authorizing the belief that when "the letter" does not have a true historical sense, then a mystical sense must be sought.

The only example here of a difficult scriptural expression is Judges 9:8, for which Henry cites with approval Isidore's spiritual explanation in the *Glossa*. Henry adds that this is a case of a passage that is true not *secundum sensum vocum,* but *secundum sensum rerum.*

64. *Contra mendacium* 10.23–24 (CSEL 41.497–502). He also draws on two other works by Augustine, *De civitate Dei* 16.37 (CSEL 50/2: 190–192) and *De mendacio* 5.5, 7 (CSEL 41:419–420, 421).

65. *Glossa ordinaria* on Exodus 1:20 (Basel ed., 1:124v).

66. For discussion, see Minnis, *Medieval Theory of Authorship,* 52–56.

67. PL 178:1341D–1342A.

68. See Minnis, *Medieval Theory of Authorship,* 101–102.

69. See *Glossa ordinaria* on 2 Kings 11 (Basel ed., 2:107v–108v).

70. Moreover, he accepts what the *Glossa* says about Judges 9:8. There Jerome is cited as reading the trees as men, according to the allegorical sense of the text.

71. Paris ed., fol. 107v; Ferrara ed., 268.

72. Paris ed., fol. 108r; Ferrara ed., 269.

73. In Thomas Aquinas, *Opera omnia* (Parma ed., 14:344).

74. Oxford, Bodleian Library, Bodley 246, fol. 89v.

75. Basel ed., 3:157r–158v. Compare Minnis, *Medieval Theory of Authorship,* 108.

76. Paris ed., fol. 77v; Ferrara ed., 192.

77. Paris ed. fols. 79v–81r; Ferrara ed., 199–201.

78. Paris ed., fols. 85r–86r; Ferrara ed., 212–213.

79. *Glossa ordinaria* on Philippians 1:15–19 (Basel ed., 6:35v).

80. *Glossa ordinaria* on Matthew 10:2ff (Basel ed., 5:35v).

81. Chrysostom, *In Matt.* 16 (PG 57:243).

82. *Physics* 7.3 (247a–248a), as in *Aristotelis opera cum Averrois commentariis* (Venice, 1562–1574) 4:322r–323r.

83. *Aristotelis opera* (ed. Venice, 4:323r).

84. Thomas Aquinas, *Super Physicam* 7.6, as translated by R. J. Blackwell, R. J. Spaeth, and W. E. Thirlkel in *Commentary on Aristotle's Physics* (London, 1963), 446.

85. *Aristotelis opera* (Venice ed., 4:322v).

86. Thomas Aquinas, *Commentary on Aristotle's Physics,* 447.

87. By contrast, as Aristotle points out, in matters of learning and making judgments children are inferior to adults owing to the great amount of restlessness and motion in their souls (248a). This is why the young make poor listeners of moral science—and, indeed, of the speculative side of the science of theology, as Henry will argue elsewhere. See Section 5 of the present article.

88. *Politics* 1.13 (1260a–b).

89. *Glossa ordinaria* on Matthew 3.3 (Basel ed., 5:13v).

90. *Physics* 2.9 (200b).

91. *Aristotelis opera* (Venice ed., 4:85r).

92. Ps-Chrysostom, *In Matt.* 10 (PG 46:684–685).

93. Ps-Chrysostom, *In Matt.* 19 (PG 46:685).

94. *Regula pastoralis* 1.1–2 (PL 77:14–16).

95. *Glossa interlinearis* on Acts 1.1 (Basel ed., 6:163r).

96. Ps-Chrysostom, *In Matt.* 10 (PG 46:685).

97. The problem of the vainglorious *doctor* is singled out by Henry in *Quodlibet 1* q. 34. There he declares that the divine *doctor* should in his teaching seek principally the honor of God. If he puts his own honor first, he sins mortally. See *Quodlibet 1*, ed. R. Macken (Leuven and Paris, 1979), 193–194.

98. *Glossa ordinaria* on Philippians 1:18 (Basel ed., 6:98v).

99. *Glossa ordinaria* on Matthew 23.2–3 (Basel ed., 5:70v).

100. D. L. d'Avray, *The Preaching of the Friars* (Oxford, 1985), 179, 184, 203.

101. Jean Leclercq, "Le magistère du prédicateur au XIIIᵉ siècle," *Archives d'histoire doctrinale et littéraire du moyen âge* 21 (1946): 105–147. Compare A. J. Minnis, "Chaucer's Pardoner and the 'Office of Preacher,'" in *Intellectuals and Writers in Fourteenth-Century Europe*, ed. P. Boitani and A. Torti (Tubingen and Cambridge, 1986), 88–119.

102. Transcribed by Leclercq, "Le magistère," 129–130.

103. *De modo componendi sermones* 1, ed. Th.-M. Charland, *Artes praedicandi*, Publications de l'institut d'études médiévales d'Ottawa 7 (Paris and Ottawa, 1936), 330.

104. *Nicomachean Ethics* 2.4 (1105a).

105. *Aristotelis opera* (Venice ed., 3:22v).

106. Thomas Aquinas, *Super Ethicam* 2.4, ed. R. M. Spiazzi (Turin and Rome, 1949), 80; translated by C. I. Litzinger as *Commentary on the Nicomachean Ethics* (Chicago, 1964), 130.

107. *Aristotelis opera* (Venice ed., 3.22v).

108. Text in Thomas Aquinas, *Super Ethicam* (Spiazzi, 79).

109. Thomas Aquinas, *Super Ethicam*, 1.3 (Spiazzi, 11).

110. Thomas Aquinas, *Summa theologiae* 1–2.58.2 resp., as in the Blackfriars edition (London and New York, 1963–1980) 23:69.

111. *Nicomachean Ethics* 6.13 (1144b), and Thomas's comment on the passage (ed. Spiazzi, 346).

112. Thomas Aquinas, *Summa theologiae* 1–2.58.5 (Blackfriars, 23:77). Compare the discussion by H. V. Jaffa, *Thomism and Aristotelianism* (Chicago, 1952), 31–34.

113. Thomas Aquinas, *Super Ethicam* 2.4 (Spiazzi, 81; Litzinger, 131).

114. Text in Leclercq, "Le magistère," 129–130.

115. See the *Regula pastoralis* 1.2 (PL 77:15C–D). See further the in-

teresting elaboration of Gregory's views in the fascinating *quaestio* by Gerard of Boulogne, transcribed from Paris, BN lat. 17485 by Leclercq, "Le magistère," 124–127, discussed by Minnis, "Chaucer's Pardoner," 93–94.

116. This distinction is of course related to the one between academic theology and pastoral theology, as expressed by Thomas Aquinas's contrast between "scholastic doctrine," with which prelates do not greatly concern themselves, and the "doctrine of preaching, which pertains to prelates." See his *Contra impugnantes Dei cultum et religionem* 11, ed. P. Mandonnet (Paris, 1927), 16. Roger Bacon made the same point in a highly combative way by declaring that it is the job, not of academic theologians, but of *prelati* to explain the articles of faith and morals to the people and to preach to them. "Indeed," he grumbles, "we know for certain and see everywhere that one simple brother, who never heard a hundred theology lectures, [or] if he heard them still did not care, preaches incomparably better than the greatest masters of theology." The remark is cited by d'Avray, *Preaching of the Friars,* 181–182.

117. *Forma praedicandi* 4; Charland, *Artes praedicandi,* 241; translated by L. Krul in *Three Medieval Rhetorical Arts,* ed. J. J. Murphy (Berkeley and Los Angeles, 1971), 123–124.

118. Paris ed., fols. 87v–89r; Ferrara ed., 218–221.

119. Paris ed., fols. 84v–85r; Ferrara ed., 210–211.

120. Paris ed., fols. 85r–86r; Ferrara ed., 212–213.

121. Paris ed., fols. 78v–79r; Ferrara ed., 195–196.

122. *Nicomachean Ethics* 1.3 (1095a), and the text in Aquinas, *Super Ethicam* (Spiazzi, 9; Litzinger, 17).

123. *Super Ethicam* 1.3 (Spiazzi, 10; Litzinger, 19).

124. *Super Ethicam* 1.3 (Spiazzi, 11; Litzinger, 19).

125. Walter Burley, *In Eth. Nicomach.* 1.3 (Venice, 1481), unfoliated.

126. Thomas Aquinas, *Super Ethicam,* 1.3 (Spiazzi, 11; Litzinger, 19). Here Burley, following Albert the Great, declares that neither the young man, nor anyone else in whom the passions hold sway, can hope to be an expert in moral science. A "special logic" (*logica specialis*) functions in ethics; its end is not to know but to act well. See Albert, *Super Ethica* 1.2, ed. W. Kübel in *Opera omnia* 14/1 (Munster 1968), 12.

127. Similarly, Robert Grosseteste cites Aristotle's *Ethics* on the unsuitability of the young man as an *auditor* of political science, then proceeds to declare that it is even more fruitless for a young man to study theology: "Quanto magis igitur inaniter a talibus auditur sacra pagina!" See Robert Grosseteste, *Hexaëmeron,* ed. R. C. Dales and S. Gieben (London, 1983), 55.

128. Ps-Chrysostom, *In Matt.* 43 (PG 46:870–871).

129. This illustration is also taken from ps-Chrysostom (PL 46:871).

130. Ps-Chrysostom, *In Matt.* 39 (PG 46:848).

131. *The Greek Commentaries on the Nicomachean Ethics of Aristotle in the*

Latin Translation of Robert Grosseteste, Bishop of Lincoln (d. 1253), ed. H. Paul Mercken (Leiden, 1973–) 1:43–44.

132. See Jaffa, *Thomism and Aristotelianism,* 31–34.

133. *De doctrina Christiana* 2.5.6 (CCSL 32:35).

134. *Greek Commentaries* (Mercken, 46).

135. See the entire discussion in *Greek Commentaries* (Mercken, 41–46). The distinction between the two kinds of medicine occurs on p. 46.

136. Chrysostom, *In Matt.* 12 (22) (PG 57:292–293).

137. *Greek Commentaries* (Mercken, 46). Similarly, Walter Burley speaks of passionate and even incontinent men who are curable. But not every soul is curable. Like Henry, Walter was influenced by Eustratius's teaching, including the metaphor of moral science being medicinal to the soul. Just as bodily infirmity is twofold — curable and incurable — so also is the infirmity of the soul. Some people have become so accustomed to their evil actions that they are obstinate and incurable, vice having become so rooted in the soul that they would need more time than the span human life allows to eradicate it. See Burley, *In Eth. Nicomach.* 1.3 (Venice ed.). The same metaphor, and the same basic argument (in a much shorter form), is also found in the work of Jean Buridan. See his *In Eth. Nicomach.* 1.3 (Paris, 1513), fol. 7r.

138. 12.2 (Paris ed., fols. 84v–85r; Ferrara ed., 210–211).

139. *Glossa ordinaria* on Hebrews 5.14 (Basel ed., 6:142v).

140. *Glossa interlinearis* on Ecclesiasticus 6:18 (Basel ed., 3:393v).

141. *Glossa ordinaria* on Lamentations 3:27 (Basel ed., 4:192r).

142. *Nicomachean Ethics* 1.3 (1095a), in Litzinger's translation (p. 17): "Now everyman is a good judge of the things he knows."

143. *Glossa ordinaria* on Hebrews 5:12–13 (Basel ed., 6:142v).

144. Paris ed., fols. 78v–79r; Ferrara ed., 195–196.

145. *Metaphysics* 1.2 (982a).

146. *Hamlet* 1.2, line 146.

147. 11.2 (Paris fols. 77v–78r; Ferrara ed., 191–192).

148. *Glossa ordinaria* on 1 Timothy 2:12 (Basel ed., 6:119r).

149. *Glossa ordinaria* on 1 Timothy 2:12 (Basel ed., 6:119r).

150. *Glossa interlinearis* on Proverbs 4:4 (Basel ed., 3:313r).

151. Paris ed., fols. 84r–84v; Ferrara ed., 208–210.

152. Here the printed editions refer to book 9 of *De civitate Dei,* which is apparently incorrect. The specific source is unclear, but the general distinction occurs in 20.1 (CSEL 40/2:424–426). Compare 21.5 (CSEL 40/2: 521–523).

153. And, of course, different *quaestiones* would have different circulations and be put to different uses, and so each had to have a large measure of intellectual autonomy.

Denys the Carthusian and the Doxography of Scholastic Theology

Kent Emery, Jr.

"Quidquid RECIPITUR, ad modum recipientis recipitur." What is received by Denys of Ryckel (Dionysius Cartusiensis, 1402–1471) is nearly the whole tradition of Christian thought and practice up to his time. Denys's literary production embraces scriptural, monastic, speculative, mystical, apologetic, canonical, and pastoral works. In this study I shall focus upon Denys's reading of scholastic theology. But one must read Denys's scholastic writings in the broad context of his hierarchically ordered corpus. The rule of faith that he discovered in his scriptural commentaries governs his scholastic thinking, which is likewise guided by, and perfected in, the visions of mystical theology. The order in which Denys executed his literary works follows in outline the order of his intellectual intention. His first work after entering the Charterhouse of Roermond in Limburg in 1424 concerns the Carthusian life.[1] Significantly, his first speculative work is a treatise on the gifts of the Holy Spirit.[2] Thereafter, between the years 1434–1457, he produced commentaries on each book of Scripture. These commentaries expound Scripture according to the traditional four senses, and make an encyclopedia of comments of the fathers and doctors. They provided Denys a storehouse of material to be distributed among other works, and supplied him with a complete set of scriptural references with attached interpretations.[3]

Denys's enormous scholastic erudition is all the more remarkable inasmuch as he did not receive a full university education. He studied only in the arts faculty at the University of Cologne, where in 1421 he matriculated in the *Bursa* founded by Henricus de Gorrichem (ob. 1431), later named the *Bursa Montana* after its second Regent, the Thomist Gerardus de Monte (Gerardus ter Steghen).[4] Denys received a Master of Arts degree in 1424, whereupon he immediately entered the monastery. While at Cologne he wrote a treatise, *De ente et essentia,* now lost. He may also have written a treatise on universals attributed to him by his sixteenth-century editor, undiscovered until recently.[5] We know the character of the first treatise from a remark Denys makes many years later in his *Sentences* commentary:

> When I was studying in my youth and I was instructed in the *via Thomae,* I rather thought that *esse* and *essentia* should be really distinguished. At the time I compiled (*compilavi*) a certain treatise on the matter. I wish that I had it now, for I would correct it. In the meantime, having more carefully considered the matter, often in the past as now, I am convinced that, more truly and probably, the two do not really differ.[6]

Happily, I have discovered three manuscript copies of the treatise on universals of which Denys's editor spoke. Although his authorship must be proved, there are signs of authenticity. The text is a compendium of realist teaching on universals, and in each case was copied by fifteenth-century students of the *via antiqua.*[7]

Denys conceives his intellectual effort within a threefold hierarchical ordering of wisdom that he proposes from his earliest works until his last treatises and commentaries.[8] The order is neatly summarized in one of his last works, *Elementatio theologica, seu Compendium theologiae,* written about 1465.[9]

Properly speaking, the eternal Son of the Father is uncreated wisdom, which every created wisdom reflects. The uncreated wisdom is distributed to created minds eminently through the gifts of the Holy Spirit. The human mind ascends toward the uncreated wisdom in a threefold manner. First, one may ascend through a natural, philosophic wisdom, the highest act of which is the contemplative felicity about which Aristotle speaks in the tenth Book of the *Ethics.* Aristotle calls this "theology" in the *Metaphysics.* Second, there is a supernatural, theological wisdom which good and bad, elect and reprobate alike may acquire. Although founded in Revelation, it is expanded by human inquiry. This acquired wisdom, called "scholastic," is among the charismatic graces bestowed for the good of others (*dona gratiae gratis datae*). Those possess this wisdom who have knowledge of Scripture and are erudite in the theological books of the saints and doctors. Third, strictly speaking, supernatural wisdom is a sanctifying grace and is formed by a savorous awareness (*notitia*) of the divine that is identical with the gift of wisdom. In its highest degree and condition, this wisdom is called "mystical theology" by the "divine Dionysius" the Areopagite.[10]

The order of wisdom engenders an order of theological literacy. The eternal Word or uncreated wisdom diffuses itself in a covering (*tegumen*) and in shadows whereby its infinite luminosity is proportioned to the weakness of human capacity. Hence the evangelical doctrine of Scripture is wrapped in various similitudes, parables, and figures suited to our way of knowing, which ascends from sensible images to a knowledge of immaterial realities and a love of the divine. From the source of Christ's teachings in the four Gospels derive the countless volumes of the saints and Catholic teachers. These pour into a mighty river of lucid water in the *Liber Sententiarum,* compiled (*compilatus*) from the books of the fathers by Peter Lombard. From this river branch so many streams of science in the commentaries and writings of scholastic doctors. In his own *Sentences* commentary, Denys adds, he has attempted to reunite the tributary waters in a single flow: in four huge volumes he has collected in one place the sapiential statements of the outstanding scholastic commentators on the *Sentences.*[11]

Denys's account of the order and course of wisdom, one should note, follows a temporal as well as a logical or natural order. This order of wisdom also suggests a hierarchy of authorities that Denys follows closely throughout his writings. Sacred Scripture is the highest authority, but because of its condescending obscurity it is the most difficult to penetrate and more often than not is the object of dispute. Scripture is a symbolic theology whose meaning becomes evident through intellectual and mystical probings. After Scripture the statements and lives of the saints are authoritative. Who these saints are is indicated by a list Denys writes in the *Protestatio ad superiorem suum* (*c.* 1440–41): Augustine, Ambrose, Gregory, Origen, Gregory Nazianzen, Cyril, Basil, Chrysostom, John Damascene, Boethius, Anselm, Bernard, Bede, Hugh of St. Victor, Jean Gerson, and William of Paris.[12] The greatest authority among the saints is Denys's "most-elect teacher," Dionysius the Areopagite, whose *Mystical Theology* defines and names the highest form of wisdom. For Denys, the teaching of the Areopagite provides a rule of thought analogous to Scripture's rule of faith. With Denys, it is seldom a matter of disputing the Areopagite, but simply of determining what he says.

After the authority of the fathers belongs the authority of scholastic doctors. Their authority is only as strong as their arguments, evaluated in the light of Scripture and mystical theology. Among scholastics, Thomas Aquinas has a certain preeminence, not because his arguments are always the best — sometimes he erred outstandingly — but because he was the only saint among them.[13] Finally, the authority of philosophers rotates from school to school, depending on how much on any given question they adumbrate the truths of Scripture and mystical theology. Proclus' uncanny resonance with Dionysius, for example, assures him Denys's high esteem.[14]

In a remarkably clear way, Denys's ordering of wisdom determined the chronological sequence and generic pattern of his philosophical and scholastic writings. His first mature effort of this kind was *De lumine christianae theoriae,* composed around 1451–1452.[15] Book 1 of this work treats natural, philosophic wisdom, Book 2 supernatural, theological wisdom. Whereas the arguments of the advocates for a Proclean order of Thomas's *Summa theologiae* seem forced,[16] such an order for Denys's *De lumine* is explicit. In the Prooemium, Denys explains that his two-part work is arranged according to the way things go out from the first cause and then return to it. He concludes the introduction with a theorem from Proclus: "Omne causatum et manet in sua causa, et procedit ab ipsa, et convertitur ad ipsam."[17] Book 1 assembles an impressive collection of texts from the philosophers; although these are drawn largely from primary sources, Denys is guided by the digests of Albert the Great, whom he calls the "most skilled" in the doctrines of the Peripatetics.[18] Book 2 on the other hand, draws almost exclusively from one source: for the most part it is a résumé of Thomas's *Summa contra gentiles.*[19] Closely related to *De lumine* Book 1 are two works composed in 1452 and 1455. *De natura aeterni et veri Dei* synthetizes the questions concerning God in *De lumine,* and *De puritate et felicitate animae* does the same for the questions concerning the soul.[20]

Two works bespeak Denys's early attachment to the teaching of Thomas. The *Dialogion de fide* (*c.* 1432), written in a simple dialogue form for novices, adheres closely to Thomas; the treatise *Creaturarum in ordine ad Deum consideratio theologica* abridges Thomas's commentary on the second Book of the *Sentences.*[21] More problematic is Denys's massive paraphrase of Thomas's *Summa theologiae,* composed at the end of his life in 1466, long after he had rejected key tenets of Thomas's thought.[22] Its title is: *Summa fidei orthodoxae, alias Enterione, id est Medulla operum sancti Thomae.* The Greek neologisms in this and Denys's first Thomistic work point to a certain *lumen orientale,* transmitted through Proclus and Dionysius, that suffuses his interpretation of

Thomas. The chronology of these works and their generic form, as well as Denys's accustomed disposition of Thomas's opinions in the *Sentences* commentary, suggest that he thought Thomas to be the best starting point for scholastic exercise and an apt teacher for beginners.

Denys's most ambitious scholastic work is the enormous commentary on the *Sentences* of Peter Lombard. Since he never entered the theology faculty, Denys's commentary is not a youthful, public, university exercise, but a private undertaking that he composed progressively over a lifetime in the solitude of the monastery. He finished around 1464. The accumulating materials extracted from commentary after commentary supplied Denys with a treasure-chest of texts which he thence redistributed appropriately throughout his other works. The private character of Denys's effort is indicated by the fact that, in eight years of searching his manuscripts, I have not found one medieval copy of even a part of the commentary, nor is the title registered in a single ancient library list of the many I have consulted. The autograph volumes, now lost, may be the only copy that ever existed. In the Prooemium to the work, however, Denys speaks about how difficult it was, and the great labor it took, to acquire the books of the many doctors he recites.[23] It seems likely, therefore, that before writing a final fair copy, he wrote down extracts in many other pages. Perhaps some of these will turn up as an anonymous abbreviation of one scholastic doctor or another.

In his *Sentences* commentary, Denys speaks *recitative* and *elective*. In two epitomes of the commentary, written in 1464–65, he speaks *assertive*.[24] In the *Elementatio philosophica* and *Elementatio theologica* he separates what he judges to be the distinctive philosophic and theological issues in the *Sentences*. As the titles of these works suggest, Denys imitates the form of Proclus' *Elements of Theology*: under declarative propositions, imitating Proclus' theorems, he organizes a concatenation of arguments. These works serve as an index to the *Sentences* commentary and are the most direct sources for Denys's independent judgments.

These syncopated works of philosophy and theology prepared Denys for his final, arduous acts of wisdom. Around 1465 he wrote a large commentary on *De consolatione philosophiae* of "noster fidelis Boetius."[25] Denys considers *De consolatione* to be a philosophic work in its literal sense. But Boethius is a Christian who tacitly holds the rule of faith in his mind. Denys unfolds the latent conformity of the work to the mysteries of redemption in "mystical" readings that he appends to his literal comments. Finally, in the years 1466–68, Denys produced his crowning achievement: commentaries on all the works of Dionysius the Areopagite.[26]

In the Prooemium to his commentary on the *Sentences,* Denys expands on the historical progress of wisdom. Although the wisdom accessible to the mind *in via* is meager in comparison to the light *in patria,* nevertheless over time it has become very great. Gregory says that as the progress of wisdom increased in the times before the Savior, so it has continued to increase in the times afterwards. Thus, the wisdom revealed in the time of evangelical law, first through Christ, then through the sending of the Holy Spirit and the Apostles and Evangelists, has steadily grown through the holy fathers and again through the Catholic teachers and scholastics. Especially during the time when Master Peter Lombard assembled his *Sentences* was there a great outpouring in the elucidation of wisdom. The Prophet Isaias foresaw this when he said: "the earth is filled with the knowledge of the Lord" (Is 11:9). What was concealed has been brought to light; the difficulties of Scripture have been untangled; objections to the Faith have been resolved. And indeed, not only the difficulties of Scripture but the obscurities in the writings of the holy fathers have been subtly discussed, magisterially declared, and led to their full Catholic meaning by the Master and those illustrious Catholic men who have written so gloriously over the *Sentences.*[27]

Such praise for an old textbook and its commentators, such confidence in the progress of wisdom, written by a former schoolboy among the Brethren of the Common Life who lived as a monk during the waning of the Middle Ages and the harvest of nominalist religiosity, disturbs somewhat our conventional and emergent historiographies. In balance, we shall see, Denys admits a recent diminution. Through his *Sentences* commentary, by returning to more authentic sources, he aspires to the regeneration of Christian wisdom in his time.

Denys's commentary comprises sizeable recitations and extracts of the arguments and determinations of an array of scholastic doctors. What Denys extracts—usually the conclusion or solution of the argument—he quotes nearly *verbatim* or paraphrases closely. His artful abridgments show a good understanding of his authors. In each recitation he searches the *motivae,* or guiding principles, of the resolution. He explains his procedure in the Prooemium. First he will present the responses of the more famous doctors, Thomas, Albert, Alexander of Hales, Bonaventure, and Henry of Ghent. Afterwards he will present the more outstanding followers, such as Peter of Taran-

taise or Richard of Middleton, who seem to follow Thomas but sometimes disagree with him. Finally, he will report the responses of the
greater doctors and their followers on the other side of the question.
Included here, almost invariably, is Duns Scotus. Denys does not limit
himself to writings on the *Sentences;* where apposite, he will extract from
Summae and other treatises. Accordingly, Denys always recites from
Thomas's *Summa theologiae* after he records the resolution in the *Scriptum;* sometimes he adds something from *Contra gentiles* or the disputed
questions. Likewise he regularly includes material from Henry of
Ghent's quodlibetal questions and Ulrich of Strassburg's *Summa de
bono.* [28]

The form of Denys's compilation does not hang loosely on the
order of questions in the *Sentences.* He calls his work a *collectaneum* or
collectio that gathers into one volume the writings of the scholastic commentators, just as the Lombard collected into one text the words and
teachings of the fathers. Thus, Denys says, his commentary is a "reduction of the scholastic doctors into one"; this rubric is nearly identical
to that of the *Monopanton,* composed for Nicholas of Cusa, which reduces
all of the verses of Paul's Epistles to one continuous text. [29] Denys's
commentary follows the model of the Lombard's book, since it is at
once large and compendious. It is large because it contains a great
quantity of material; it is compendious because of its form. "The *sententia,*" Avicenna declares, "is the most decisive and definite utterance." [30]

Denys's reduction to unity is more than literary. As it descends
from above, the simple, uncreated wisdom becomes more and more
diverse. Whereas the cognitive act of mystical theology is extraordi-
narily unified, [31] the lower degree of scholastic learning is necessarily
various. This variety, however, has its own becomingness:

> There are diverse and various opinions in scholastic materials,
> and it is delightful to know something about all of them. Fre-
> quently, indeed, in order to clarify the conscience, it is whole-
> some to know the teachings of diverse doctors. Nor should one
> cling pertinaciously or incautiously to the opinion of any one
> doctor, as those sometimes do who read only one doctor, or only
> a few of them. Moreover, many useful and beautiful things are
> found in the writings of one doctor that are not found in the
> writings of another. [32]

In light of the scattering of the divine wisdom, eclecticism is a sapiential method and prudential judgment founded on the nature and order
of human cognition.

Denys's irenic attitude does not embrace everyone. He remarks that countless books have been written on the *Sentences* and are still being written. Alas, too many books have been written; by the endless multiplication of their writings, certain recent, less eminent authors have caused the writings of ancient, superior authors to be read less.[33] The inflated currency of the fourteenth century, in other words, has driven out the good coin of the thirteenth-century ancients. Durandus of St. Pourçain is the only fourteenth-century writer whom Denys adduces regularly.

Doubtless, Denys's attitude was affected in general by his schooling at Cologne, but I think that it is possible to point to more specific sources. Recently, Zenon Kaluza has brilliantly documented the origins of the negative attitude towards fourteenth-century thinkers in the early fifteenth century, tracing it to the writings of Jean Gerson and the Parisian master in the arts faculty, Iohannes de Nova Domo (Jan van Nieuwenhuyze). For reasons of piety and a desire to cleanse from theology the terminology of artistic study, Gerson censured the theological endeavors of the *secta nominalium.* Gerson continually urged the theology faculty to return to the writings of earlier masters, specifically, the writings of Thomas, Albert, Bonaventure, Henry of Ghent, and Durandus of St. Pourçain. This is a short-list of Denys's scholastic authorities. Gerson reserved even more aversion for the advocates of the formal distinction, whom he called *formalizantes.* As Kaluza amply demonstrates, Gerson's aversion stems from his understanding of Dionysius the Areopagite's teaching in the *Mystical Theology.*[34] Denys was well acquainted with Gerson, whose works he classifies as written in the manner of the saints.[35] Denys disputes Gerson's affective, anti-intellectual interpretation of mystical theology and dismisses his clumsy reading of Jan van Ruusbroec, whom he considers "another Dionysius."[36] Nevertheless, he confers upon Gerson considerable authority in the lower registers of knowledge and, like him, attacks the formal distinction.

Closer yet to Denys's attitude are Iohannes de Nova Domo's strictures against the *nominales.* Iohannes's grammatical and logical writings, via Heimericus de Campo, migrated to Cologne just at the time Denys studied there (1422).[37] Later, albeit silently, Denys employs Iohannes's texts in his comments on the distinction between *esse* and *essentia.*[38] Iohannes's principle with respect to the *nominales* is simple and decisive: "contra negantes principia non est disputandum." In logic, the nominalists deny the reality of the universal outside the soul; but the universal "is the principle of art and science, indeed, the first, formal object of adequation that every science investigates, and when we do not look upon it, we cannot conceive or understand anything at all."[39] Likewise, in grammar the nominalists deny the *modos significandi,* which are the first principles of correct speech.[40]

Denys does not expressly state Iohannes de Nova Domo's principle, but he certainly applies it. In his philosophic works, the nominalists are mentioned a few times in connection with the doctrine of the immortality of the soul. For Denys, this doctrine is central in establishing the strict analogy between natural and supernatural wisdom.[41] Surveying the various arguments of the Peripatetics on the question, he analyzes the position of Alexander of Aphrodisias, Averroës and Abubather who, because they deny the personal immortality of the soul, place in this life whatever felicity is possible to human beings. At the end of his analysis Denys adds:

> There are certain philosophers of the present time, who are philosophers in name only, who think that Alexander philosophized best about the nature of the soul. Not unreasonably did Albert couple Alexander with those rude and unlearned (*rudibus et indoctis*) philosophers because he alone among outstanding philosophers said that the intellectual power is destructible.[42]

Elsewhere Denys observes that certain *solemn* philosophers argue that Aristotle taught the soul to be inseparable from the body. There are other, not so solemn philosophers, Denys adds, called *nominales,* who agree with Alexander of Aphrodisias that neither Aristotle nor natural reason itself can demonstrate the immortality of the soul. No wonder they assert this, "because when they should look upon the natures and properties of things, they repeatedly turn to terms and sophismata."[43] For this reason they are sometimes called *terminalistae.*[44]

The opinions of the nominalists, then, are unworthy of serious consideration because they never attain the level of philosophy. Denys thus distinguishes them from "solemn" philosophers who otherwise reach the conclusion that Aristotle did not demonstrate the immortality of the soul. Indeed, he eventually came to declare, as a proposition in the *Elementatio philosophica,* that "it is truly difficult to express what Aristotle thought about the immortality of the soul." He draws his arguments in support of this proposition from the "solemn doctor" himself, Henry of Ghent, who had persuaded him of the fluctuations and ambiguities in Aristotle's words.[45]

As the subphilosophic nominalists fail in the first principles of logic, so they fail in the first principles of grammar. In his treatment of the *Sentences* question, "Whether whatever God knew once, he knows and will always know," Denys affirms the arguments of Bonaventure and Thomas. Both trace the arguments to grammatical principles. Those who maintain that God will always know as true what he once knew are called *nominales* because they suppose the unity of the name for the thing signified in such declensions as "albus, alba, album," and in such utterances as "Socrates runs," "Socrates ran." Rather, Bonaventure says, they should distinguish between speaking grammatically, as they do, and speaking logically, whereby different modes of signification designate corresponding differences in the manner of being. Similarly, Thomas distinguishes between speaking materially, with reference to the intentional object of reason, and speaking significantly, with reference to the being of a thing and its various conditions. In significant speech, changes in consignification point to changes in the condition of a thing's being. Thomas notes that the old position of the *nominales* has been rejected by most of the "moderns."[46]

Bonaventure's and Thomas's remarks lead Denys to make his contribution to the vexed taxonomy of the terms "ancient" and "modern." At the end of the question he exclaims how truly Aristotle said that the same opinions are repeated infinitely. Those who William of Auxerre, Bonaventure, and Thomas called *nominales* are now called *terministae,* because they speak only about terms and concepts instead of the natures of things. Whereas Thomas called the *nominales* "ancients," they are now called "moderns," because their teaching has reappeared in recent times. The "moderns" in William of Auxerre's day were called *reales,* and their followers today are called *realistae.* The realists are now called "ancients," because constant in the truth, they follow "the path of the ancient and true Peripatetics."[47]

Today we would more likely label Denys a "Platonist" than a "Peripatetic," but then he considered the author of *Liber de causis* and Avicenna authentic Peripatetics. (Denys doubts Thomas Aquinas's identification of Dionysius the Areopagite as a Peripatetic, however.)[48] Surely our terms "Platonist" and "Aristotelian" are as shifting as the medieval usage of the terms "ancients" and "moderns." In any event, Denys's allegiance to "the ancient and true Peripatetics" and their thirteenth-century followers raises further questions about his judgment of later developments in the theology faculty. In the *Elementatio philosophica,* he reports Henry of Ghent's statement that Aristotle stumbled on questions concerning the eternity of the world, divine providence, the unity of intellect in the human species, and the immortality of the soul.[49] Henry's remark points to the famous Parisian Condemnations of 1277. Before turning to Denys's encounter with these, I shall make some preliminary observations.

Because he lived and worked in the happy seclusion of the Charterhouse, in speculative matters Denys never needed to engage in *viva voce* dispute; nor, because he was not a licensed master of theology, did he need to work under the direct surveillance of ecclesiastical authority. Denys's scholasticism was a literary affair, rather like most of ours: he did his thinking in a network of old texts, which he analyzed privately, set in relation to one another in a personal disposition, and explained in writings that may or may not be read. His several personal confrontations with authorities took place within a monastic ambit, over issues of the religious life. But in speculative matters he was free. He rejected every simply positive notion of ecclesiastical authority. We do not believe the Scriptures because the Church tells us they are inspired by God. Rather, the Scriptures derive their authority "causaliter et exsistentialiter" directly from uncreated wisdom.[50] Thus, a reason of the Scriptures is always there to be discovered, difficult though it may be to discern. Ecclesiastical pronouncements, in turn, are the more binding the more they bear the marks of intrinsic authority, that is, the more evidently they relate to the analogies of faith and right thinking.

Denys confronts the Condemnations of 1277 in the writings of Richard of Middleton and Henry of Ghent, over a limited set of problems concerning angelic situation, locomotion, and individuation, the causality and nature of heavenly bodies, and the "double truth." When he first addresses the question of angelic situation in his *Sentences* commentary, Denys prefers Thomas's argument that, because of their purely spiritual composition, angels can be said to be in a place only by virtue of their action upon a body. Angels are limited by a determined range of power and influence, not by spatial dimensions. Only in passing, in his recitation of Richard of Middleton, does Denys mention that Thomas's position seems to agree with an article condemned at Paris.[51] In a later question, however, he recites the arguments of Henry of Ghent. Henry's first argument reaches the same conclusion as Thomas's, albeit in a typically more complicated way. Denys comments that Henry must add to his response because his first conclusion falls directly under an article condemned by Lord Stephen (Étienne Tempier) at Paris: "Substantiam intellectualem (videlicet angelum aut intelligentiam) non esse in loco nisi per suam operationem: error."[52] Henry's involved, subsequent arguments indirectly confirm the older conclusion that Denys prefers. Henry explores several arguments that would enable one to say that a spiritual substance is determined to a place in some other way than by its action upon a body. None of these arguments survives Henry's criticism of them, and in the end he is forced to confess simply that "unless one believes, he will not understand" (Is 7:9).[53] In response to Henry's statements, Denys notes that many who lived after Bishop Stephen simply acquiesced in the decision of Paris, conceding that an angel is somehow in a place by reason of its substance, even when it does not act upon a body. But Thomas, Albert, and most of the ancient Parisian doctors who preceded Stephen thought otherwise. Since Stephen's decision is difficult to comprehend, many who have come after him — especially those outside Paris — do not pay any attention to the excommunication. They say that a bishop's jurisdiction does not extend beyond his diocese.[54] In short, because it does not square with intrinsic criteria of thought (namely, what follows from the purely spiritual nature of angels), and because it collides with more ancient authorities, this particular article of condemnation looks like modern nonsense.

On the other hand, Denys firmly maintains that angels move, and move through a medium. Against opponents who argue the contrary, such as Durandus of St. Pourçain, he multiplies scriptural and patristic authorities.[55] Thus he upholds Lord Stephen's article: "Quod substantiae separatae non possunt moveri ab extremo in extremum nec per medium seu in medium, nisi quia possunt velle operari in eis: error."[56] Those who argue that angels do not actually move often sound dangerously like the ancient Peripatetics, Denys says, who taught that Intelligences are immobile in their place and operation.[57]

Denys encounters this opinion in the writings of Albert the Great, in a way that involves a far more serious error. From Albert's *Sentences* commentary and *De quatuor coaequaevis* he extracts arguments affirming that angels move from place to place through a medium, and when they are in one place they are not in another. Albert catalogues four errors on this question, including the opinion of Averroës and Maimonides that angels never move because they are unmoving movers of the spheres, through which they influence human hearts and senses.[58] Denys remarks that Albert's words here sound more Catholic than what he says in his commentary on the *Liber de causis*.

There Albert proves by manifold arguments exactly what he otherwise condemns: the Intelligences do not move; each is the first mover in its own order, and remaining immobile, moves the orb or its conjoined soul as the desired moves the desiring. Some may claim, Denys continues, that in the commentary on the *Sentences* Albert speaks as a theologian, but that in his commentary on the *Liber de causis* he speaks as an expositor, defender, and imitator of the Peripatetics and as a natural philosopher. Indeed, Albert himself says in the latter work that he defends the opinion of the Peripatetics denying that an Intelligence is limited to any place and affirming that each Intelligence is always everywhere. Albert speaks often in this way, as does his student Ulrich of Strassburg. To say that "this is true according to natural reason or the teaching of the philosophers or the tradition of the Peripatetics, but not according to Scripture or the documents of faith, as if there could be two truths contrary to one another" is exactly the manner of speaking condemned by Lord Stephen at Paris. Whatever is contrary to Christian faith must simply and absolutely be denied as false, Denys concludes.[59] On this crucial issue, then, he is willing enough to evoke the Condemnations; but one should also note that the "double truth" strikes near the heart of Denys's vision of wisdom, wherein the philosophic truths of the natural order yield a perfectly isomorphic analogy to the theological truths of the supernatural order.[60] Denys's eclectic attitude enabled him always to find some proportionate teaching among the philosophers, and thus preserve the analogy.

Concerning angelic individuation, right reason and ecclesiastical authority are in perfect accord. Denys considers this problem in two questions of his *Sentences* commentary. In the first, he addresses the underlying philosophical issues. Thomas's teaching, in *De esse et essentia* and elsewhere, moves the question. The cause of individuation in any species is the specified or designated matter (*materia signata*), determined in quantitative dimensions, that enters into composition with form to make the essence of a thing.[61] Denys responds with a chain of arguments that are recapitulated in the *Elementatio philosophica*. In general, his determination is governed by the hierarchical principle that the higher reality effects more than the lower one. More specifically, his argument follows Henry of Ghent. He relies upon Henry's distinction between the *esse essentiae* of a being, defined by its relation to the exemplar cause, and its *esse actualis exsistentiae*, produced by the efficient cause. These are intentionally distinct in the mind of

God, understood as distinct by human reason, but really the same in the existing creature.[62]

The reason for the individuation of a thing, Denys says, is its *esse hoc aliquid*. Because each thing has only one specific and substantial being, it follows that its *esse* and *hoc esse* are really identical, distinguishable only by reason. The extrinsic, effective principle of any individual reality is the cause that produces or creates it. The individual is the end reality of the creative act, for to suffer, to act, and to become pertain only to supposites or singular things. It is the intellect that confers universality upon beings. Nothing abstracted by the intellect — neither form nor matter — can be the cause of actual, existential, real being (*esse actuale, exsistentiale, reale*). Hence, a reality is determined or singularized by reason of its very existential being, for being belongs first to supposites. Thus, no logical principle abstracted from actual being, neither matter, nor this matter, nor quantity, can be the cause of the individuation of a form.[63]

To assert that matter or specified matter (*materia designata*) is the principle of individuation, Denys continues, seems to be an uncultivated way of speaking. The specified matter is what is individuated, not the principle of individuation. In itself, matter is the least determined, the most potential and confused; how then can it be the cause of determination and individuation? Form is what is said to distinguish, determine, and beautify the confusion of matter. Moreover, first composition precedes second composition, that is, the composition of substantial form with its matter precedes the composition of the matter with its accidents. Hence, matter is specified by its composition with substantial form before it is determined further by accidents of quantity and quality. Moreover, since form may be understood as *esse* no less communicable to many than matter, there is no greater reason for considering matter to be the principle of individuation than form. Finally, as in abstraction form is considered to confer *esse* on matter, so in reality it must be *this form* that confers *esse* on *this matter*. In any real being, form individuates and determines far more than matter.[64]

Having established the general, philosophical principles, Denys turns to the theological problem of angelic individuation in the next question of the *Sentences*.[65] Here he disputes two opinions. The first, represented by Thomas, argues that because only matter can individuate a species, and because matter does not enter the composition of angelic natures, there are as many angelic species as there are individuals. Elsewhere Denys remarks that those who hold this opinion follow the words of Aristotle "too immoderately."[66] A second opinion, represented by Albert the Great, argues that all angels are of the same species.[67] Against these opinions Denys sets the arguments of Henry of Ghent. Since a creature is individuated by its *esse actualis exsistentiae,* even though lacking composition with matter an angelic species can yet be individuated by means of a purely spiritual composition. Every created essence participates *esse,* and the essence of an angel or Intelligence becomes a person or supposite by no other reason than by the fact that it has spiritual *esse* as an actually subsisting effect of God's creative act. *Esse* adds nothing to essence save a relation to the efficient cause.[68]

Henry confirms his argument by reference to three articles condemned at Paris; Denys makes these his own in the *Elementatio theologica:* (1)"God cannot multiply individuals in a species without matter: error"; (2)"Forms do not undergo division except by matter, error, unless this be understood of forms educed from the potentiality of matter"; (3)"Because Intelligences do not possess matter, God cannot make many of them in the same species: error."[69] Somewhat disingenuously, in light of his previous restrictions, Denys reinforces and extends the authority of these condemnations, pronounced by "Lord Stephen, Bishop of Paris and outstanding doctor in theology, with the approval of all of the doctors of the theology faculty."[70] Denys saves Thomas from the condemnation in the only way he can: chronologically. If Thomas had lived at the time these articles were condemned, or afterwards, he would not knowingly have defended anything contrary to them. How unbecoming it is, then, for any Thomist (*Thomistam*) now to defend a position that so many solemn doctors contradict with good reasons.[71]

In his own response, Denys enacts Henry of Ghent's principle within the hierarchical order of spiritual realities. Although angels are simple forms subsisting as supposites, no one thinks that they are pure acts of being. Rather, they are more or less mixed with some potency as they are more or less distant from the pure act. "Divine Dionysius" affirms that *esse, posse,* and *agere* are diverse in angelic natures, and Boethius says that *quo est* and *quod est* differ in them. These need not be really distinct in the angelic nature, however. One and the same essence is called *quo est, esse,* or "act" insofar as it participates the first pure act; it is called *quod est* or "potency" insofar as it falls away from the purity of the first act. Hence, one may easily understand how angels receive genus and specific difference. Angels are not equal in act or formality; each degree of essential perfection, measured by nearness to the pure act, constitutes a special species, and likewise each degree of essential perfection constitutes a specific difference.[72]

Henry's and Denys's arguments establish the possibility of individuation within an angelic species; they do not establish the fact. Denys is sensitive to the arguments of Ulrich of Strassburg, who otherwise reaches the same conclusion as Thomas, because they rely on the authority of Dionysius the Areopagite.[73] Dionysius says in the *Celestial Hierarchy* that illuminations descend from superior to inferior angels, not only from hierarchy to hierarchy, but from the highest to the mean to the lowest angel in the same order.[74] Does this mean, Denys asks, that each angel is distinct in essential perfection, or only in accidental perfection? He allows that he does not fully understand what "the leader among theologians" (*princeps ille theologorum*), "the most sacred Dionysius," intends in the text. Thus, he will not dare assert that all angels must convene in the same *species specialissima*.[75] Finally, he judges it more probable that angels in the same choir or order share the same species. He adds, however, that in questions about the holy angels, those most "worthy substances, our lords, rulers, helpers, protectors and guardians," one must be careful lest he offend, by incautious assertion and contentious disputation, before their benign and beautiful faces.[76] Only dimly can one discern those beings higher in the order of Intelligences.

Denys's final remark on angelic individuation, in the *Elementatio theologica,* looks to the lowest being in the order of Intelligences. Because the human soul is an individual form that is the term of God's real, creative act, "the opinion affirming that rational souls are individuated by their bodies is nothing."[77]

Questions concerning individuation touch directly the spiritual realities of angelic beings and the human soul; the formal distinction among the divine attributes, proposed by Duns Scotus, touches directly the spiritual reality of God. No less strenuously than Gerson, Denys rejects the formal distinction. He engages the distinction already in his earlier philosophic works. In *De lumine christianae theoriae* he identifies the distinction as arising among doctors of the Franciscan order, now called *formalistae*. Without naming the author, he presents an abbreviated argument for the distinction from Francis of Meyronnes.[78] In this work, Denys appears to follow the opinion of Alexander of Hales that no distinction among divine attributes can be understood except in terms of God's relations to creatures.[79] Denys takes up the question again in *De natura aeterni et veri Dei,* written for a beloved Carthusian confrère. Here, appropriately, after adducing a few arguments from Aristotle and Proclus, he multiplies authorities of the saints against the distinction.[80]

In these works, Denys bases his arguments upon the absolute simplicity of divine *esse,* and the simplicity of the divine act of knowing; he founds the perceived diversity among attributes in the diverse manner of the human knower: "cognitio enim fit secundum naturam cognoscentis." Denys's arguments are only indicative; evidently he was making more extensive preparation to treat the question. The results of his preparation are manifest in the *Sentences* question: "Whether the distinction among divine attributes is real, or formal, or only by reason." This question is the longest in his entire commentary; in it, he displays even more than his usual erudition.[81]

To expound the massive argumentation of this question would require a monograph. But in any case, it is Denys's disposition of recited authorities — in other words, his doxography — that most fully reveals his thought. At the beginning of the question, he announces the intensification of his usual procedure. This question, he says, is one of the outstanding difficulties of the theology faculty, provoking dissension, minute inquiry, and out-and-out combat. For this reason he must linger over the material, and with extreme care adduce the words of the doctors.[82]

Denys first presents the writings of Thomas Aquinas, whose position remains largely his own: distinctions among the divine attributes are perceived by reason alone, although they have a real foundation in the plenitude of perfection in the simple divine *esse.*[83] Denys, however, here omits a statement by Thomas in a later article that will play an important role in the further unfolding of the question. The distinction among divine attributes derives from reason and intellect, Thomas states, but not in the reason of the human intellect alone, but also in the reason of the angelic and divine intellects.[84]

Denys follows Thomas with the arguments of doctors whose conclusion is essentially the same, Peter of Tarantaise and Richard of Middleton.[85] He further reports certain objections of Giles of Rome against Thomas's expression, answering each of them and striving to show that Giles has misread what Thomas says. Giles anyway reaches the same conclusion as Thomas.[86] Denys next recites the similar opinions of Alexander of Hales, Bonaventure, and William of Auxerre.

These hold that the plurality of divine attributes is only a distinction of reason, understood in terms of God's many relations to created perfections. If, unlike Thomas, these doctors do not speak of the foundation of attributes in the divine perfection, they perhaps even more affirm the divine simplicity.[87]

Denys concludes the first movement of his question with the teaching of Albert the Great. He has postponed Albert because a slight variance from Thomas's position seems to echo Alexander of Hales's understanding. The difference between Thomas and Albert, Denys notes, has been magnified by Albert's contemporary followers. They say that Thomas posits a *distinctio rationis rationabilis* among the divine attributes, whereas Albert posits only a *distinctio rationis ratiocinantis.* Denys tests this against Albert's texts, does not find the difference, and reconciles the teaching of the two doctors.[88] Throughout his recitation of the ancient doctors, Denys makes every effort to find the underlying unity of their teaching in order to set them in a common front against Duns Scotus. Before turning to Scotus, however, Denys will put forward the arguments of one who seems to occupy a middle ground, and who introduces the decisive new element in the discussion: Henry of Ghent.[89]

With utmost care, Denys rehearses Henry's version of the traditional argument. Considered in terms of God's relations *ad extra* to creatures, the plurality of ideas correspond to *imitabilitates* of the divine nature. These exist indistinct in act in God, and are known by him in all of their diversity in a single act of comprehension corresponding at once to the simplicity of his nature and the multiplicity of his relations to creatures. God knows this multiplicity *a priori,* according to the plenitude of his divine perfection; the created intellect, by a natural light, knows this multiplicity of conceptions *a posteriori,* according to the multitude of created perfections.[90]

At this point, Henry enlarges his argument by a distinction among corresponding terms. Until now, he has spoken of a plurality of "ideas" corresponding to perfections participated by creatures; now he will speak of "attributes" corresponding to perfections considered absolutely, that is, perfections considered abstractly as what it is better to have than not to have. These may be said to exist independently in God, without reference to creatures. Among them there is a certain plurality, known to the divine intellect *ad intra.* This plurality derives from the plurality of personal, trinitarian emanations, for all the divine attributes may be reduced to intellect and its operations (e.g., wisdom) or will and its operations (e.g., goodness). Now, from eternity God knows himself as true and thereby generates the Word, and loves himself as good, and thereby breathes forth the Spirit. Hence from eternity the divine reason knows a distinction of absolute perfections; through the divine light, the minds of the Blessed also perceive this distinction. This distinction, however, is no more real than the personal distinction to which it relates. One may now fill in the corresponding sets of terms. As by a natural, philosophic light the created intellect may discern a plurality of ideas corresponding to the many ways creatures partake the simple *esse* of God *ad extra* by virtue of being created, so by a supernatural, theological light the created intellect may discern a plurality of attributes corresponding to perfections, reducible to the divine persons, existing absolutely in God *ad intra* and bestowed upon creatures in gracious *bene esse*.[91]

Denys makes no immediate response to Henry's resolution, which, it seems to me, owes its structure to the movement from Book 5 to Book 6 in Bonaventure's *Itinerarium*.[92] Later in the question Denys aligns Henry with the ancient doctors, remarking that Henry goes beyond them all, showing how there is a distinction of reason among the divine attributes not only in the human mind, but in the uncreated intellect and the conceptions of the Blessed as well. Denys adds that Henry's position seems more reasonable than Alexander's, which posits a distinction only in relation to creatures.[93] Later in his *Sentences* commentary Denys adopts Henry's doctrine of a special, supernatural illumination of theological verities.[94] After reading Henry, he no longer treats this question concerning the divine attributes as a philosophical one; after the *Sentences* commentary, he assigns it to the *Elementatio theologica*.[95]

According to Denys's disposition of the question, Henry's determination gives rise to the formal distinction in Duns Scotus. Denys affords Scotus ample space to speak his case, although not so much as Henry of Ghent.[96] For Scotus, the crux of the question is this: Henry argues that there is a distinction *ad intra* of divine attributes related to the distinction of personal emanations, saying that this is a distinction understood by the divine reason. But the distinction among personal emanations is real. No real distinction presupposes a merely rational one, as no real being presupposes a mere *ens rationis*. A real being is distinguished from an *ens rationis* precisely because it exists independently of any action of intellect upon it. An *ens rationis*, then, is posterior to real being; thus, the distinction of divine attributes that derives from really distinct personal emanations must in some way be *ex natura rei*.[97] Elsewhere, Denys rejects Scotus's notion of a real, absolute distinction among the properties of the divine persons upon which Scotus founds his objection to Henry.[98] For now, he follows Scotus's explorations, which lead Scotus to conclude that although the divine attributes are not really distinct, there is a certain non-identity and formal difference among them *ex natura rei* before any consideration of the intellect, divine or human. This distinction is signified by a formal distinction, which lies between real and rational distinctions.[99]

Here Denys takes an unexpected turn, leading the reader into an obscure, textual forest. To clarify the many difficulties of Scotus's teaching, he resorts to a compiler no less able than himself: Peter of Candia. Here, finally, in the heat of battle, Denys enlists troops from the fourteenth century. From Peter of Candia's encyclopedia of opinions, he seizes now welcome arguments of William of Ockham and Gregory of Rimini against the formal distinction among divine attributes. He selects only those arguments, of course, that deny the formal distinction and affirm the divine simplicity. He could not accept, for example, William of Ockham's conclusion that the divine attributes are only mental signs or concepts and have no real foundation in the divine essence.[100] After all has been said, Denys—like the ancients before him and many after—cannot find a formal distinction between a real or a rational distinction.[101]

Reciting Francis of Meyronnes's ("the leader of the Scotists") manifold distinctions about the distinction, Denys gives the *formalistae* one more chance.[102] He counters Francis, finally, with Durandus of St. Pourçain. Durandus brings the question back down the ladder it has climbed. First he denies the formal distinction; then Henry of Ghent's distinction in the divine mind; then Thomas's foundation for the plurality of attributes in the plenitude of divine perfection. With Alexander, Durandus concludes that there is only a distinction of reason among the attributes corresponding to God's relations with things really distinct in creatures.[103]

Denys has allowed the ancient scholastics to show the truth, the moderns to expose falsehood. Scotus is the inventor of a novelty never thought of by "the holy doctors and most-excellent masters of theology who went before him."[104] The authorities Scotus invokes in fact all militate against him. To prove this, and to affirm the absolute divine simplicity and identity of attributes in the divine *esse*, Denys calls forth his own authorities, among the philosophers, Aristotle, Proclus, the *Liber de causis,* and among the saints, Augustine, Bernard, Anselm, and most of all, "divinissimus, sacratissimus et theologicissimus Dionysius."[105]

Three concluding remarks point to the deep reasons for Denys's hostility to the formal distinction. In his commentary on the *Sentences,* Denys says that those who put forward a formal distinction in God have not "subtly enough contemplated the divine simplicity, in which undoubtedly every perfection is contained, not formally as they imagine to themselves, but supereminently as divine Dionysius teaches."[106] Similarly, he judges in the *Elementatio theologica* that the formalists have not attained to "sincere contemplation."[107] In *De natura aeterni et veri Dei,* after citing his reasons and authorities against a formal distinction among attributes in God, he counsels his beloved confrère. The divine simplicity is something that can be talked about and believed, but can be seen only by the pure in heart. Let us therefore not be empty assertors about it, as many are, but rather sincere contemplators of it, as — alas — too few are. Let us then simplify our hearts, and fasten them on the unchanging good, for all perfection consists in a deiform simplification and loving conversion to the simplicity of the divine mind.[108] This text draws a full circle from Denys's first monastic work, which treats purity of heart,[109] to the great Dionysian commentaries.

The *nominales* never pass beyond the concepts that their terms signify; nor, in fact, do the *formalistae,* who, worse, reify their concepts and project them into the divine mind. At the root of their errors is their mistaken notion of the univocity of the concept of being.[110] Only an analogical understanding of being at once preserves the transcendence of divine *esse* and shows the human soul a way to ascend towards God. It also establishes what Denys calls "the beautiful rule" of knowing: "modus agendi sequitur modum essendi, et proprietas actionis, naturam agentis."[111] According to this principle, the human soul's spiritual individuation, assuring its separate substantiality, allows for the spiritual cognitions of mystical theology testified to by the saints and verified in Denys's own experience. In his commentary on the Areopagite's *Mystical Theology,* Denys teaches that in the highest form of union possible in this life, the soul, although not attaining a vision of God *quid est* through an uncreated species, may yet attain an intuition of God *quia est* above every created species.[112]

In this context Denys reproves Thomas's oft-repeated statement that the soul must return to a phantasm in every act of cognition. Even more than a disagreement over speculative principles, Denys's difference with Thomas is a matter of interpretation: interpretation of the words of "the most blessed Dionysius." To support his position, Thomas frequently alleges a text from the *Celestial Hierarchy:* "the divine ray cannot enlighten us unless it is wrapped up in the various veils of sensible forms."[113] This text refers only to the first information of the soul, Denys says.[114] Among other reasons, this is why Thomas is suited for beginners. What does Thomas think the saint means at the beginning of the *Mystical Theology* when he says: "In mystical visions, rise up in an absolute ascent beyond all things, detached from them all, to the ray of the supersubstantial obscurity, withdrawing absolutely from all things by means of a forceful beating down and abandoning of the senses and intellectual acts, all sensible and intelligible realities, and all existing things, even yourself." Certainly one cannot rise above intelligible realities if he cannot rise above sensible ones.[115] In the same chapter Dionysius says: "the sole cause of all things truly appears without veils to those who transcend all unclean and material realities, and all of the supercelestial souls." Do you hear what he says, Denys asks, he says *incircumvelate.* And if in this intuition one must rise above even the most-pure angelic minds, how much more must he rise above the lowly material phantasm? If what Thomas says is true, then what David (Ps 1:8, 2 Kings 23:2–4) and the saints have said about anagogic, purely mental contemplation and the illustrations of the Holy Spirit cannot be true.[116]

Perhaps ironically, Denys of Ryckel, who so loved the ancients, anticipated in one sense the most modern: for the human mind, save mystical vision, truth is foremost a matter of interpretation. Of course, Denys thought himself to be measured by authoritative texts, rather than to measure them according to slight disclosures of mundane experience. Even so, he apparently has had his modern readers. Several features of his scholastic doxography may have a familiar ring. Students at Toronto were sometimes told how a line of French scholars, from Victor Cousin to Étienne Gilson, as a first step of inquiry surveyed the topography of a question in Denys's commentary on the *Sentences*. They dipped less often, it would seem, into the pages of mystical theology. Remotely and unknowingly, in any event, we may all have partaken Denys the Carthusian's textuality and his disposition of medieval scholastic discourse.

NOTES

1. Denys's first monastic writing (before 1430) is *Contra detestabilem cordis inordinationem in Dei laudibus horisque canonicis vel Laus Cartusiana* (*Opera omnia* 40:191–259). See Kent Emery, Jr., "Denys of Ryckel and Traditions of Meditation: Contra detestabilem cordis inordinationem" in *Spiritualität Heute und Gestern*, Analecta Cartusiana 35/3 (Salzburg, 1983), 69–89.

2. *De donis Spiritus Sancti* (*Opera omnia* 35:155–262). The first three tracts were written around 1430; the fourth tract was compiled about 1446.

3. The scriptural commentaries are published in *Opera omnia* 1–14. For their chronology, see A. Stoelen, "De Chronologie van de Werken van Dionysius de Karthuizer: De eerste Werken en de Schriftuurkommentaren," *Sacris erudiri* 5 (1953): 361–401.

4. P. Teeuwen, *Dionysius de Karthuizer en de philosophisch-theogolische stroomingen aan de Keulsche Universiteit* (Brussels and Nijmegen, 1938), 15–18. A more detailed account of Denys's career at Cologne is given in my *Dionysii Cartusiensis Opera selecta 1* (*Prolegomena*). *Bibliotheca manuscripta 1A: Studia bibliographica* (CCCM 121 [1991]: 15–18).

5. See Emery, *Dionysii Cartusiensis . . . Bibliotheca manuscripta 1A* (CCCM 121:122–128).

6. *Sent.* 1.8.7 (*Opera omnia* 19:408D): "Postremo, quamvis in adolescentia dum eram in studio, et in via Thomae instruerer, potius sensi quod esse et essentia distinguerentur realiter (unde et tunc de illa materia quemdam tractatulum compilavi: quem utinam nunc haberem, quia corrigerem); interim tamen diligentius considerando, non solum hac vice, sed et ante frequenter, verius ac probabilius ratus sum quod non realiter ab invicem differant."

7. The three manuscripts are now in Prague. The manuscripts, and the evidence for and against Denys's authorship, are discussed in Emery, *Dionysii Cartusiensis . . . Bibliotheca manuscripta 1A* (CCCM 121:122–126).

8. See Kent Emery, Jr., "Twofold Wisdom and Contemplation in Denys of Ryckel (Dionysius Cartusiensis, 1402–1471)," *Journal of Medieval and Renaissance Studies* 18 (1988): 99–134.

9. *Opera omnia* 33:105–231. For the date, see A. Stoelen, "Denys le Chartreux," *Dictionnaire de spiritualité* 3 (Paris, 1957), 433.

10. *Elem. theol.* prooemium (*Opera omnia* 33:111–112).

11. Ibid. (112).

12. *Protestatio ad superiorem suum* (*Opera omnia* 1:LXXI).

13. In *De sacramento altaris* 28 (*Opera omnia* 35:425A'), Denys says that Thomas is "Doctor ille inter doctores scholasticos praecipue sanctitatis, illuminationis et auctoritatis." In his early *Contra detestabilem* 8 (*Opera omnia* 40:202D'), he calls Thomas "meum patronem." In *De donis* 1.8 (*Opera omnia*

35:165C), he calls Thomas "doctor inter modernos eximius," and in *De con-templatione* 2.7 (*Opera omnia* 41:244B') he calls him "insignem philosophum atque profundum egregiumque theologum."

14. See Emery, "Twofold Wisdom," 105, 111–117; Werner Beierwaltes, "Philosophische Marginalien zu Proklos-Texten," *Philosophische Rundschau* 10 (1962): 60–64.

15. *Opera omnia* 33:233–513. For the date, see Stoelen, "De Chronologie," 371.

16. I refer to the argument for the neo-Platonic, *exitus-reditus* structure of the *Summa* in M.-D. Chenu, O. P., "Le plan de la Somme théologique de S. Thomas," *Revue Thomiste* 45 (1939): 93–107, and in *Introduction a l'étude de Saint Thomas d'Aquin* (Montreal and Paris, 1954), 255–276. For a review of subsequent arguments and criticisms, see Otto Hermann Pesch, "Um den Plan der Summa theologiae des hl. Thomas von Aquin," in *Thomas von Aquin,* ed. Klaus Bernath (Darmstadt, 1978), 1:411–37. The pattern fits Denys's two-book *De lumine* easily.

17. *De lumine* 1 prooemium (*Opera omnia* 33:235). I cite the edition in C. Vansteenkiste, "Procli Elementatio theologica translata a Guilelmo de Moerbeke (Textus Ineditus)," *Tijdschrift voor Philosophie* 13 (1951): 263–302, 491–531 and 14 (1952): 503–546. The edition of Moerbeke's translation by H. Boese (Leuven, 1987), was unavailable to me at the time of writing. Denys here combines *Elementatio* theoremata 30–31: "Omne quod ab aliquo pro-ducitur immediate, manet in producente et procedit ab ipso; Omne pro-cedens ab aliquo secundum essentiam convertitur ad illud a quo procedit" (Vansteenkiste 13:278).

18. *Sent.* 2.3.3 (*Opera omnia* 21:221C–D). It is a common formula of fifteenth-century Albertists that Albert "longius et profundius laboravit" than others in the doctrine of the Peripatetics; see Zenon Kaluza, *Les querelles doc-trinales à Paris: Nominalistes et réalistes aux confins du XIVe et du XVe siècles* (Bergamo, 1988), 122.

19. See Teeuwen, *Dionysius de Karthuizer,* 131–135.

20. *De natura aeterni et veri Dei* (hereafter *De nat.*) is printed in *Opera om-nia* 34:7–97; *De puritate et felicitate animae* (hereafter *De pur.*) is printed in *Opera omnia* 40:393–443. For the dates, see Stoelen, "Denys le Chartreux," 433–434.

21. The *Dialogion de fide catholica contra gentiles* is printed in *Opera omnia* 18:269–530; *Creaturarum in ordine ad Deum consideratio theologica* is printed in *Opera omnia* 34:99–221. See Teeuwen, *Dionysius de Karthuizer,* 110–124.

22. Stoelen, "De Chronologie," 372.

23. *Sent.* 1 prooemium (*Opera omnia* 19:37).

24. Denys applies this terminology to Peter of Candia in *Sent.* 1.2.2 (*Opera omnia* 19:167C').

25. Denys's commentary on *De consolatione* is printed in *Opera omnia*

26. For the epithet, see *Elementatio philosophica* 81 and *De lumine* 2.52 (*Opera*

omnia 33:89C, 439C). In *De lumine* 1.68 (*Opera omnia* 33:314C) Denys says of Boethius: "Noster autem Boetius . . . subtilissimam atque veracem induxit de rerum regimine philosophiam." For Denys, Boethius is the model for the Christian philosopher, strictly speaking, as distinct from the theologian. For Denys's rather modern conception of Christian philosophy, evident in this typology of Boethius, see Emery, "Twofold Wisdom."

26. Denys's commentaries on the works of pseudo-Dionysius are printed in *Opera omnia* 15–16. These include the various Latin translations of ps-Dionysius's writings, and I shall cite from them.

27. *Sent.* 1 prooemium (*Opera omnia* 19:36).

28. Ibid. (37).

29. *Sent.* 1 prooemium (*Opera omnia* 19:36). In the list of his works contained in Trier, Stadtbibliothek Hs. 631/1562 4°, the title for the work is "Super quatuor libros sentenciarum scripta doctorum scholasticorum reducendo in unum" (f. 227r). Denys's *Monopanton* (*Opera omnia* 14:465–537) is a work "Epistolas beatissimi Pauli quasi in unam redigendo epistolam" (467).

30. *Sent.* 1 prooemium and expositio prologi (*Opera omnia* 19:36, 57A′–B′).

31. See Emery, "Twofold Wisdom."

32. *Sent.* 1 prooemium (*Opera omnia* 19:37): "scholasticorum materiarum in quibus sunt opiniones variae ac diversae; estque delectabile de omnibus aliquid scire. Imo frequenter pro serenatione conscientiae, est salubre diversorum doctorum doctrinas agnoscere, nec opinioni unius incaute aut pertinaciter inhaerere, sicut interdum his accidit qui pauca aut unum dumtaxat doctorem legerunt. Multa quoque pulchra atque utilia inveniuntur in uno doctore, quae in scriptis non habentur alterius."

33. *Sent.* 1 prooemium (*Opera omnia* 19:36).

34. I refer to Kaluza's *Les querelles doctrinales*. Kaluza delineates Gerson's attitudes on 13–86, and gathers in Appendix 1, 127–144, texts of Gerson's remarks on the Scotists.

35. *Protestatio ad superiorem suum* (*Opera omnia* 1:LXXI), where Denys lists Gerson among the "saints" and not the doctors. The classification is formal.

36. See Emery, "Twofold Wisdom," 130–133 and notes.

37. The original study of Iohannes de Nova Domo, Heimericus de Campo, and the Cologne Albertists is: G. Meersseman, *Geschichte des Albertismus, 1: Die Pariser Anfänge des Kölner Albertismus* (Paris, 1933), and *2: Die ersten Kölner Kontroversen* (Rome, 1935). My "Twofold Wisdom," 111–112, n. 48, gives subsequent bibliography. See also Kaluza's notes, 107–120.

38. Teeuwen, *Dionysius de Karthuizer,* 70–72, 75, 92, 98.

39. Kaluza, *Les querelles doctrinales,* 94–95. The text comes from the preface of Iohannes's *De universali reali,* which may have been added by a la-

ter writer. It conforms, however, to statements throughout Iohannes's works.

40. Kaluza, *Les querelles doctrinales,* 92–94. The fifteenth-century revival of the *modi significandi* by Gerson, Iohannes de Nova Domo, Heimericus de Campo, Denys, and others merits further study.

41. Emery, "Twofold Wisdom," 110–111, 118–120, 123–124, and throughout. For a fuller study of Denys's concern for the philosophic demonstrability of the immortality of the soul, see Emery *"Sapientissimus Aristoteles* and *Theologicissimus Dionysius:* The Reading of Aristotle and the Understanding of Nature in Denys the Carthusian," in *Mensch und Natur im Mittelalter,* ed. A. Zimmermann and A. Speer, Miscellanea Mediaevalia 21/2 (Berlin, and New York, 1922), 572–606.

42. *De lumine* 1.50 (*Opera omnia* 33:292C′): "Sunt autem et praesentis temporis quidam, vel re vel potius nomine tantum philosophi, qui Alexandrum de natura animae optime philosophatum reputant: quem tamen Albertus rudibus et indoctis philosophis non irrationabiliter comparavit, eo quod solus inter omnes egregios philosophos, intellectualem virtutem destructibilem dixit." Gerson likewise adopted Albert's doxography linking the ancient Epicureans and modern *nominales,* projected it to the terminists, and termed them "rudes" (Kaluza, *Les querelles doctrinales,* 14–15, 39–40, and throughout). In *Dialogus disputationis Christianum et Sarracenum* 10 (*Opera omnia* 36:468C′), Denys joins the terms invidiously: "Mahon autem secutus est quosdam Epicureos rudissimosque philosophos, qui felicitatem hominis in delectationibus sensualibus gustus et tactus constituerunt."

43. *De lumine* 1.101 (*Opera omnia* 33:363C′–D′).

44. *De pur.* 64 (*Opera omnia* 34:436D).

45. *Elem. phil.* 98 (*Opera omnia* 33:61A–62A). Denys quotes Henry of Ghent, *Quodl. 9* q. 14 (Macken, 247–248). For Henry's influence upon Denys in this matter, see Emery, *"Sapientissimus Aristoteles."*

46. *Sent.* 1.41.4 (*Opera omnia* 20:551B–555A′). Denys recites Bonaventure, *Sent.* 1.41.2.2 (*Opera omnia* 1:739–41); Thomas Aquinas, *Sent.* 1.41.5 (Mandonnet and Moos 1:375–76) and *Summa theologiae* 1.14. ad 3. Iohannes de Nova Domo traced most of the terminists' errors to their expansion of material supposition to the exclusion of "simple" supposition; see Kaluza, *Les querelles doctrinales,* 103–105.

47. *Sent.* 1.41.4 (*Opera omnia* 20:554D′–555A′). William of Auxerre's classification is reported by Denys in *Sent.* 1.39.1 (*Opera omnia* 20:469B–D); see William of Auxerre, *Summa* 1.9.2 (Ribaillier, 1:180–81).

48. Denys says that of all the Peripatetics, Aristotle and his followers, Avicenna spoke most profoundly about human felicity; see *De lumine* 1.48 (*Opera omnia* 33:290B′–291C′). In *Sent.* 1.8.6 (*Opera omnia* 19:390A), Denys states: "quamvis liber de Causis ex libro Procli sit sumptus, tamen ut ait Thomas in suo commento super librum de Causis, auctor libri de Causis Peripateticus fuit, non Platonicus." Following Thomas Aquinas, both Ger-

son and Iohannes de Nova Domo identify pseudo-Dionysius as a Peripatetic; see Kaluza, *Les querelles doctrinales,* 47, 123. Denys demurs on this point in the late *Elem. theol.* 60 (*Opera omnia* 33:160C′): "Interim his objici potest quod Thomas in Scripto secundi affirmat, beatissimum Dionysium Aristotelem esse secutum pene in omnibus . . . Ad quod videtur dicendum . . . quod gloriosus praesul, doctor et martyr Dionysius, in valde multis ab Aristotelis recessit."

49. *Elem. phil.* 98 (*Opera omnia* 33:61B–C). See Emery, *"Sapientissimus Aristoteles."*

50. See *Sent.* 3.24.unica (*Opera omnia* 23:420C′–421C), where Denys responds to the opinion of Durandus of St. Pourçain that in relation to us, the authority of Scripture is based solely on the Church's word that it is inspired. See Kent Emery, Jr., "Theology as a Science: The Teaching of Denys of Ryckel," in *Knowledge and Sciences in Medieval Philosophy: The Proceedings of the Eighth International Congress of Medieval Philosophy* (S.I.E.P.M.), vol. 3, ed. R. Työrinoja, A. I. Lehtinen, and D. Føllesdal (Helsinki, 1990), 196–206.

51. *Sent.* 1.37.3 (*Opera omnia* 20:450C′–455A′). Denys recites the solutions of Thomas Aquinas, *Sent.* 1.37.3.1–2 (Mandonnet and Moos 1:869–875), and Richard of Middleton, *Sent.* 1.37.2.1 (1:325–326).

52. See Tempier, Parisian Condemnations 204 (CUP 1:554).

53. *Sent.* 2.2.5 (*Opera omnia* 21:168B–170C′). Denys nicely abbreviates the solution of Henry of Ghent, *Quodl. 2* q. 9 (Wielockx, 58–72).

54. *Sent.* 2.2.5 (*Opera omnia* 21:170C′–B); see also *Elem. theol.* 86 (*Opera omnia* 33:180A′–D′). By reporting what others say, Denys's rejection of the Parisian article is indirect and refers to geographical, not temporal, extent.

55. *Sent.* 1.37.3 (*Opera omnia* 20:458C′–459D′).

56. Tempier, Parisian Condemnations 204 (CUP 1:554): "Quod substantiae separatae sunt alicubi per operationem; et quod non possunt moveri ab extremo in extremum, nec in medium, nisi quia possunt velle operari aut in medio, aut in extremis. —Error, si intelligatur, sine operatione substantiam non esse in loco, nec transire de loco ad locum."

57. *Sent.* 2.2.6 (*Opera omnia* 21:177D′–178A).

58. *Sent.* 1.37.4 (*Opera omnia* 20:466B′–468A′). Denys recites from Albert the Great, *Sent.* 1.37.24 (*Opera* 26:264–266) and *Summa de creaturis* 1: *De quatuor coaequaevis* 4.59.1–3 (*Opera* 34:621–631).

59. *Sent.* 1.37.4 (*Opera omnia* 20:468A′–469A). Denys recites Albert the Great, *Liber de causis et processu universitatis* 2.2.3 (*Opera* 10:482–84). Denys (468C′–D′) also quotes exactly from Albert's *Liber* 2.2.1 (*Opera* 10:477–78): "Peripaticorum enim his rationem defendimus, qui negant intelligentiam loco diffiniri: dicentes omnem intelligentiam esse ubique et semper." In condemning the double manner of speaking, Denys would seem to refer to Tempier, Parisian Condemnations 90, 146 (CUP 1:548, 552).

60. Emery, "Twofold Wisdom," 123–125 and throughout.

61. *Sent.* 2.3.2 (*Opera omnia* 21:216B–C).

62. Denys resumes at length Henry of Ghent's teaching concerning the distinction between *esse* and *essentia* in spiritual beings in *Sent.* 1.8.7 (*Opera omnia* 19:405D–408A'). There he extracts from Henry's *Quodl. 1* q. 9 (Macken, 48–56) and alludes to *Quodl. 10* q. 7, where, he says, Henry "de hac ipsa materia multo diffusius scribit." Later, in *Sent.* 2.3.1 (*Opera omnia* 21:191B'–196D), Denys again extracts generously from Henry's teaching on the matter, this time from *Quodl. 3* q. 9 (Badius Ascensius, fols. 60v–61v) and from *Quodl. 10* q. 7 (Macken, 145–197). Denys's own arguments in *Sent.* 2.3.2 (*Opera omnia* 21:216C–217A') are based on these earlier treatments. In conclusion, Denys says (217D–A'): "Istud scholastice dictum sit, ut studiosis praebeatur inquisitionis acutioris occasio. Nec enim in opinabilibus istis materiis, in quibus etiam magni tam diversimode opinantur, aliquid cum temeraria assertione est proferendum aut quasi certitudinaliter determinandum: quanquam nonnulli in talibus nimis assertive loquantur, quasi ipsi soli sano ac praecellenti pollerent ingenio."

63. *Elem. phil.* 38 (*Opera omnia* 33:44B–A').

64. Ibid. (44A'–C').

65. *Sent.* 2.3.3 (*Opera omnia* 21:217D'–237D): "An omnes angeli sint eiusdem speciei."

66. *Sent.* 2.3.3 (*Opera omnia* 21:220C–221C'). Denys extracts from Thomas Aquinas, *Sent.* 2.3.1.4 (Mandonnet and Moos 2:97–98) and *Summa theologiae* 1.50.4. Denys makes his remark in *Elem. theol.* 64 (*Opera omnia* 33:164B).

67. *Sent.* 2.3.3 (*Opera omnia* 21:221C–222B'); Albert the Great, *Summa theologiae* 2.2.8 (*Opera* 32:137–38).

68. *Sent.* 2.3.3 (*Opera omnia* 21:225D–226A'). Denys extracts from Henry of Ghent, *Quodl. 2* q. 8 (Wielockx, 43–52) and alludes to *Quodl. 11* q. 1 (Badius Ascensius, fols. 438r–439v).

69. *Sent.* 2.3.3 (*Opera omnia* 21:225B'–C'); *Elem. theol.* 64 (*Opera omnia* 33:164D–A'). Denys quotes the Parisian articles directly from Henry of Ghent, *Quodl. 2* q. 8 (Wielockx, 45); see Tempier, Parisian Condemnations 96, 191, 81 (CUP 1:549, 554, 548).

70. *Elem. theol.* 64 (*Opera omnia* 33:164D).

71. *Sent.* 2.3.3 (*Opera omnia* 21:226D–A').

72. Ibid. (228D'–229A).

73. Ibid. (222B–D').

74. Ps-Dionysius, *De coelesti hierarchia* 10, trans. Eriugena (in *Opera omnia* 15:190–91).

75. *Sent.* 2.3.3 (*Opera omnia* 21:229A–C).

76. Ibid.

77. *Elem. theol.* 64 (*Opera omnia* 33:164D'–165D').

78. *De lumine* 1.13 (*Opera omnia* 33:247A'–248D), Denys remarks that

advocates of the formal distinction try to demonstrate it in a fourfold way: "per viam divisionis . . . per viam definitionis . . . per viam oppositionis . . . Quarta via . . . est demonstrationis via." This distinction comes from the third part of Francis of Meyronnes's treatment in *Sent.* 1.8.1 (fol. 44r^a–44v^a, c–i). Like Gerson, Denys in his writings views the distinction through the perspective of ps-Dionysius's teaching about the divine transcendence in the *Mystical Theology* and engages Duns Scotus and Francis of Meyronnes chiefly in their arguments over *Sent.* 1.8, which concerns the divine attributes (see Kaluza, *Les querelles doctrinales,* 53). Denys certainly read Gerson's *Contra vanam curiositatem* and his *Notulae* over mystical theology at an early date; it is in these texts that Gerson most often makes his strictures against the Scotists (see Kaluza, Appendix 1, 127–144). Thus, Gerson's writings may have first alerted Denys to the "danger" of the formal distinction. Denys, however, is nowhere as "superficial" (Kaluza's word) as Gerson in his understanding of his opponents' arguments; he attends their words carefully. He certainly does not, as Gerson does, classify Henry of Ghent among the formalists with Duns Scotus (Kaluza, 60). The rest of my study will make this evident.

79. *De lumine* 1.57 (*Opera omnia* 33:299B'–301B'; see esp. 301B–C).

80. *De nat.* 35 (*Opera omnia* 34:58D–61C).

81. *Sent.* 1.2.2 (*Opera omnia* 19:149–77).

82. Ibid. (149C').

83. *Sent.* 1.2.2 (*Opera omnia* 19:149C'–152C'); Thomas Aquinas, *Sent.* 1.2.1 (Mandonnet and Moos 1:66–71) and *Summa theologiae* 1.13.

84. Thomas Aquinas, *Sent.* 1.36.2.2 ad 2 (Mandonnet and Moos 1:842): "quamvis relationes quae sunt Dei ad creaturam, realiter in creatura fundentur, tamen secundum rationem et intellectum in Deo etiam sunt; intellectum autem dico non tantum humanum, sed etiam angelicum et divinum."

85. *Sent.* 1.2.2 (*Opera omnia* 19:153A–154A').

86. Ibid. (154A'–155A).

87. *Sent.* 1.2.2 (*Opera omnia* 19:155A'–D'). Denys extracts from the conclusion of Bonaventure, *Sent.* 1.35.3 (*Opera* 1:608), and the solution of Alexander of Hales, *Summa theologica* 1.1.3.1.4 (1:130–131, n.80).

88. *Sent.* 1.2.2 (*Opera omnia* 19:155D'–156D'); Albert the Great, *Sent.* 1.8.3 (*Opera* 25:224–25).

89. Denys quotes at length from Henry of Ghent, *Quodl. 5* q. 1 (Badius Ascensius, fols. 150v–154r). He extracts from all the parts of the argument, not just the solution.

90. *Sent.* 1.2.2 (*Opera omnia* 19:157A–158B).

91. Ibid. (157D'–159B; answers to objections, 159C–162A).

92. Bonaventure, *Itinerarium mentis in Deum* 5–6 (*Opera* 5:308–12). In chapter 5, Bonaventure considers God as *Esse,* the divine simplicity, and divine attributes; this is the way of Moses, the Old Testament, and of philosophy. Rising higher, in chapter 6 he considers the Trinity of Persons under

the name of *Bonum;* this is the way of Paul, his disciple Dionysius, and in general, of Revelation.

93. *Sent.* 1.2.2 (*Opera omnia* 19:171C'-172B).

94. See Raymond Macken, "L'illumination divine concernant les vérités révelées chez Henri de Gand," *Journal philosophique* 5 (1985): 261–271; Emery, "Theology as a Science."

95. *Elem. theol.* 25 (*Opera omnia* 33:131C-133D'): "Inter attributa divinae naturae non est realis neque formalis distinctio, sed rationis dumtaxat; nec praeter ac ultra personalem distinctionem est ponenda in divinis ulla distinctio ex rei natura, ut aliqui opinantur."

96. *Sent.* 1.2.2 (*Opera omnia* 19:162C-164B). Denys quotes Scotus from the *Opus Oxoniense.* He follows Scotus's text very carefully and traces all of the parts and turns of the argument. Compare Scotus, *Ordinatio* 1.8.1.4 (*Opera* 4:230-68 nos. 157-209).

97. *Sent.* 1.2.2 (*Opera omnia* 19:162A'-B').

98. *Sent.* 1.36.2 (*Opera omnia* 20:213B-215A'); *Elem. theol.* 36 (*Opera omnia* 33:133D'-134D').

99. *Sent.* 1.2.2 (*Opera omnia* 19:163D-164D').

100. *Sent.* 1.2.2 (*Opera omnia* 19:164A'-167C'). Denys takes the opinions of Gregory of Rimini and William of Ockham from the text of Peter of Candia. There is yet no complete printed edition of Peter's commentary on the *Sentences,* but introductory materials have been edited by S. F. Brown in "Peter of Candia's Sermons in Praise of Peter Lombard," in *Studies Honoring Ignatius Charles Brady* (St. Bonaventure, N. Y., 1976), 141–176, and in "Peter of Candia's Hundred-Year History of Theology," *Medieval Philosophy and Theology* 1 (1991): 175–190. See also the study by F. Ehrle, *Die Sentenzenkommentar Peters von Candia,* Franziskanische Studien 9 (Munster, 1925). Peter paraphrases (166D-D') William of Ockham's responses in *Sent.* 1.2.1-2 (*Opera* 2:17-20, 61-69) and quotes directly (167B'-D') from his argument against Scotus and William Alnwick in *Sent.* 1.2.1 (*Opera* 2:14.8-16). From Gregory of Rimini Peter reports "septem rationes contra Scoti opinionem" (166D'-167B'); see Gregory, *Sent.* 1.8.1.2 (fols. 66v^a-67r^a, L-Q, A-C). Denys remarks that Peter favors the position of Scotus (167C'). Although Denys can admit William's logical arguments and authorities against Scotus, he could not affirm the underlying principle of his resolution: "dico quod non sunt nisi quidam conceptus vel signa quae possunt vere praedicari de Deo, et magis proprie deberent dici conceptus attributales vel nomina attributalia quam perfectiones attributales. . . . Et ideo dico quod attributa divina quae sunt plura non sunt realiter essentia divina, sed attributa, quae sunt conceptus" (*Sent.* 1.2.2, in *Opera* 2:61, 66). Denys only alludes to this argument (166C'), which does not serve his own. In *Elem. theol.* 25 (*Opera omnia* 33: 133C'-D'), Denys notes that William concedes formal distinction among the personal trinitarian relations and the divine essence, but not among the at-

tributes; see William of Ockham, *Sent.* 1.2.11 (*Opera* 2:358–79). William does not admit formal distinctions in creatures.

101. *Elem. theol.* 25 (*Opera omnia* 33:131B′–C′): "... inter distinctionem realem et rationis non videtur media esse: quoniam idem et multa, idem et differens, passiones et proprietates sunt entis; sed nil est nec esse potest nisi ens reale, quod habet esse praeter operationem animae, et ens rationis, quod habet esse per solam animae actionem: ergo praeter distinctionem realem et rationis alia non est. — Praeterea, quidquid convenit rei ex sua natura, convenit ei remota omni operatione intellectus. Si igitur inter attributa Dei sit formalis distinctio ex rei natura, omni operatione intellectus seclusa, illa esset realis: quod nullus admittit. — Insuper, non est sine necessitate ponenda in eodem pluralitas." Denys will adopt the principle of economy when useful.

102. *Sent.* 1.2.2 (*Opera omnia* 19:164A′, 167D′–169C′). Here Denys reports all four parts of Francis of Meyronnes's question, *Sent.* 1.8.1–2 (fols. 43r^a–44v^a): "primo, quid sit distinctio; secundo, quot modis sumatur; tertio, qualiter possit investigari; quarto an in divinis sit distinctio" (167D′).

103. *Sent.* 1.2.2 (*Opera omnia* 19:169C′–171B′). Denys extracts generously from Durandus of St. Pourçain, *Sent.* 1.2.2 (fol. 18r^a–v^b nos. 7–15).

104. Sent. 1.2.2 (*Opera omnia* 19:173C′–D′).

105. Ibid. (172C′–D′).

106. Ibid. (177D–A′).

107. *Elem. theol.* 25 (*Opera omnia* 33:133C′–D′).

108. *De nat.* 35 (*Opera omnia* 34:61B′–C′). Despite the tenor of this advice, Denys is not counseling a resort to simple piety. The work in fact is intended to urge upon the modern devout the importance of intellectual inquiry and speculative thought. See Emery, "Fondements théoriques de la réception de la beauté sensible dans les écrits de Denys le Chartreux (1402–1471)," in *Les Chartreux et l'art XIVe–XVIIIe-siècles: Actes du Colloque de Villeneuve-lès-Avignon*, ed. D. Le Blévec and A. Girard (Paris, 1989), 310–314.

109. See Emery, "Denys of Ryckel and Traditions of Meditation," 80–82.

110. Against Duns Scotus's doctrine of the univocity of the concept of being between God and creatures, Denys affirms the teaching of Henry of Ghent and adds his own arguments in *Sent.* 1.3.1 (*Opera omnia* 19:217D′–220C). He treats the topic again in *Sent.* 1.8.6 (*Opera omnia* 19:390D′–401B): "An Deo conveniat ratio universalis, seu generis aut speciei." There he concludes: "quam inconviens et absurda sit quorumdam opinio, dicentium quod ens non solum univoce de Deo et creaturis dicatur, sed item quod Deus sit in praedicamento ac genere, in tantum ut quidam dixisse legatur, quod Deus seu divina essentia in quantum quidditas, non est dignior quam quidditas asini: quod auribus vere religiosis detestabiliter sonat, et honorificentiae superdignissimi Dei contrariatur, de quo cum omni reverentia et timore loqui debemus . . . ut beatissimus Dionysius et Damascenus affirment. . . . Itaque

dico quod divina essentia in quantum quidditas, secundum quod quidditas convenit ei, non solum quidditate asini, sed etiam quidditate excellentissimi angeli, in infinitum praestantior est. Nec in hoc simile est de Deo et creaturis . . . de Deo tamen majestatis et excellentiae penitus infinitae loqui sic nefas est" (400A–D). Again, Denys's concern is the unknowable transcendence of God, as taught by ps-Dionysius. In *Elem. theol.* 84 *(Opera omnia* 33:91C–D), Denys asks: if the more profound philosophers declared God to be above and outside of every genus, "quanto magis Christianos hoc fari faterique decet, cum et divinus ac magnus Dionysius, praesertim in libro de Mystica theologia, tam evidenter edoceat hoc?" See also *De lumine* 1.82–83 *(Opera omnia* 33:255A'–257C); *De nat.* 61 *(Opera omnia* 34:95D–96B'); and, as the problem relates directly to mystical theology, *Difficultatum praecipuarum absolutiones* (in ps-Dionysius's *De myst. theol.*) 2 *(Opera omnia* 16:486D–487A').

111. *Diff. praecip. absol.* 2 *(Opera omnia* 16:489D), and throughout Denys's writings.

112. *Diff. praecip. absol.* 2 *(Opera omnia* 16:487A'–488C). For Denys's doctrine concerning the highest mystical cognition, see Emery, "Twofold Wisdom," 124–133.

113. Ps-Dionysius, *De coel. hier.* 1, trans. Eriugena (in *Opera omnia* 15:6).

114. *Diff. praecip. absol.* 2 *(Opera omnia* 16:489B'–C'). On this issue, see Emery, "Twofold Wisdom" and *"Sapientissimus Aristoteles,"* throughout, and "Did Denys the Carthusian Also Read Henricus Bate? *Bulletin de philosophie médiévale* 32 (1990): 196–206.

115. *Diff. praecip. absol.* 2 *(Opera omnia* 16:489C'–D').

116. Ibid. (490A–B).

SCHOLASTIC EDITIONS CITED

Albert the Great. *Sancti Alberti Magni . . . Opera omnia.* Edited by A. Borgnet. 38 vols. Paris, 1890–99.

Alexander of Hales. *Doctoris irrefragabilis Alexandri de Hales Summa theologica.* Edited by Fathers of the College of St. Bonaventure. 4 vols. (vol. 4 in 2 pts.), with 2 vols. of indices. Quaracchi, 1924–29.

Bonaventure. *Doctoris seraphici s. Bonaventurae Opera omnia.* Edited by Fathers of the College of St. Bonaventure. 10 vols. Quaracchi, 1882–1901.

Denys the Carthusian. *Doctoris ecstatici D. Dionysii Cartusiani Opera omnia.* Edited by Monks of the Carthusian Order. 42 vols. in 44. Montreuil-Tournai-Parkminster, 1896–1913, 1935. (Cited as *Opera omnia*)

Duns Scotus, John. *Doctoris subtilis et mariani Ioannis Duns Scoti . . . Opera omnia.* Edited by C. Balić and others, 18 vols. to date. Vatican City, 1950–.

Durandus of St. Pourçain. *D. Durandi a Sancto Porciano . . . in Petri Lombardi*

Sententias theologicas Commentariorum libri IIII. 2 vols. in continuous foliation. Venice, 1571; reprinted Gregg Press, N. J., 1964.

Francis of Meyronnes. *In libros Sententiarum, Quodlibeta, Tractatus Formalita-
tum . . . De univocatione.* Venice, 1520; reprinted Frankfurt/Main, 1966.

Gregory of Rimini. *Gregorii Ariminensis O. E. S. A. Super primum et secundum
Sententiarum.* Venice, 1522; reprinted St. Bonaventure, N. Y., Louvain,
and Paderborn, 1955.

Henry of Ghent. *Henrici de Gandavo Opera omnia.* Leuven, 1979-.

————. V: *Quodlibet I.* Edited by R. Macken, 1979.

————. VI: *Quodlibet II.* Edited by R. Wielockx, 1983.

————. XIII: *Quodlibet IX.* Edited by R. Macken, 1983.

————. XIV: *Quodlibet X.* Edited by R. Macken, 1981.

————. *Quodlibeta Magistri Henrici Goethals a Gandavo.* Edited I. Badius Ascensius. 2 vols. in continuous foliation. Paris, 1518; reprinted Louvain,
1961.

Richard of Middleton. *Super quatuor libros Sententiarum.* 4 vols. Brescia, 1591;
reprinted Frankfurt/Main, 1963.

Tempier, Étienne. Parisian Condemnations of 1277: Edited by H. Denifle
and E. Chatelain in vol. 1, n. 473, pp. 543-558 of *Chartularium Universitatis Parisiensis.* 4 vols. Paris, 1889-97. (Cited as CUP.)

Thomas Aquinas. *Scriptum super libros Sententiarum.* Edited by P. Mandonnet
and M. F. Moos. 4 vols. Paris, 1929-1947.

William of Auxerre. *Magistri Guillelmi Altissiodorensis Summa aurea.* Edited by
J. Ribaillier. 4 vols. (vols. 2-3 in 2 pts.). Spicilegium Bonaventurianum
16-20. Paris and Grottaferrata, 1980-87.

William of Ockham. *Guillelmi de Ockham Opera philosophica et theologica.* Edited
by members of the Franciscan Institute, St. Bonaventure University.
10 vols. St. Bonaventure, N.Y., 1967-86. I cite from vol. 2: *Scriptum
in librum primum Sententiarum Ordinatio.* Edited by G. Gál and S. Brown,
1970.

Errata

P. 293, line 31: "humans" should read "man."

P. 319, line 20: "this" should read "the."

P. 320, n. 50: "fols. 90v–91r" should read "fols. 110v–111r."

P. 321, n. 52: "fols. 92r–93r" should read "fols. 112r–113v."

P. 321, n. 54, lines 1–2: the quote should read "Whether theology is to be expounded indiscriminately to everyone."

P. 321, n. 54, line 3: "fols. 91r–92v" should read "fols. 111r–112v."

P. 321, n. 54, line 20: "sivet" should read "sive."

P. 326, n. 142: "everyman" should read "every man."

The following plates are printed with the permission of the respective libraries.

Plate 1: Frankfurt am Main. Stadt- und Universitätsbibliothek. Ms. Barth. 32, f. 5r. Psalm 4

Plate 2: Göttweig. Stiftsbibliothek. Cod. 30, ff. 20v–21r. Psalm 1

Plate 3: Dillingen. Studienbibliothek. Fragm. 25. Psalm 130

Plate 4: Wolfenbüttel. Herzog August Bibliothek. Cod. Guelf. 33 Weiss., f. 5r. Isaiah

Plate 5: Bamberg. Staatsbibliothek. Bibl. 22, f. 5r. Song of Songs

Plate 6: Bamberg. Staatsbibliothek. Bibl. 22, f. 5r. Song of Songs

Plate 7: Oxford. Bodleian Library. Ms. Rawlinson G. 163, f. 92r. Psalm 67

Plate 8: Oxford. Bodleian Library. Ms. Bodley 862, f. 85r. Psalm 67

Plate 9: Oxford. Bodleian Library. [Impr.] Auct. Z. III. 2. Psalm 67

Plate 10: London. British Library. Ms. Harley 3095, f. 40v. Boethius, *De consolatione philosophiae*

Plate 11: Paris. Bibliothèque Nationale. Ms. lat. 15355, f. 162r. Henry of Ghent, *Summa*, art. 34, q. 5. Authorial corrections on the apograph. The manuscript was later owned by Godfrey of Fontaines. See R. Macken, "Les corrections d'Henri de Gand à sa Somme," RTAM 44, (1977): 55–100.

Plate 12: Leuven (Louvain), Bibliotheek-Faculteit der Godgeleerheid, F⁰ 37 G Henr. Frontispiece, 2nd ed. *Magistri < Henrici > Goethals a Gandavo, ordinis Servorum B.M.V., Doctoris Solemnis, socii Sorbonici, Archidiaconi Tornacensis, Summa in tres partes digesta. . . .* Ed. Hieronymus Scarparius, O. Serv. (Ferrara: Franciscus Succius, 1646).

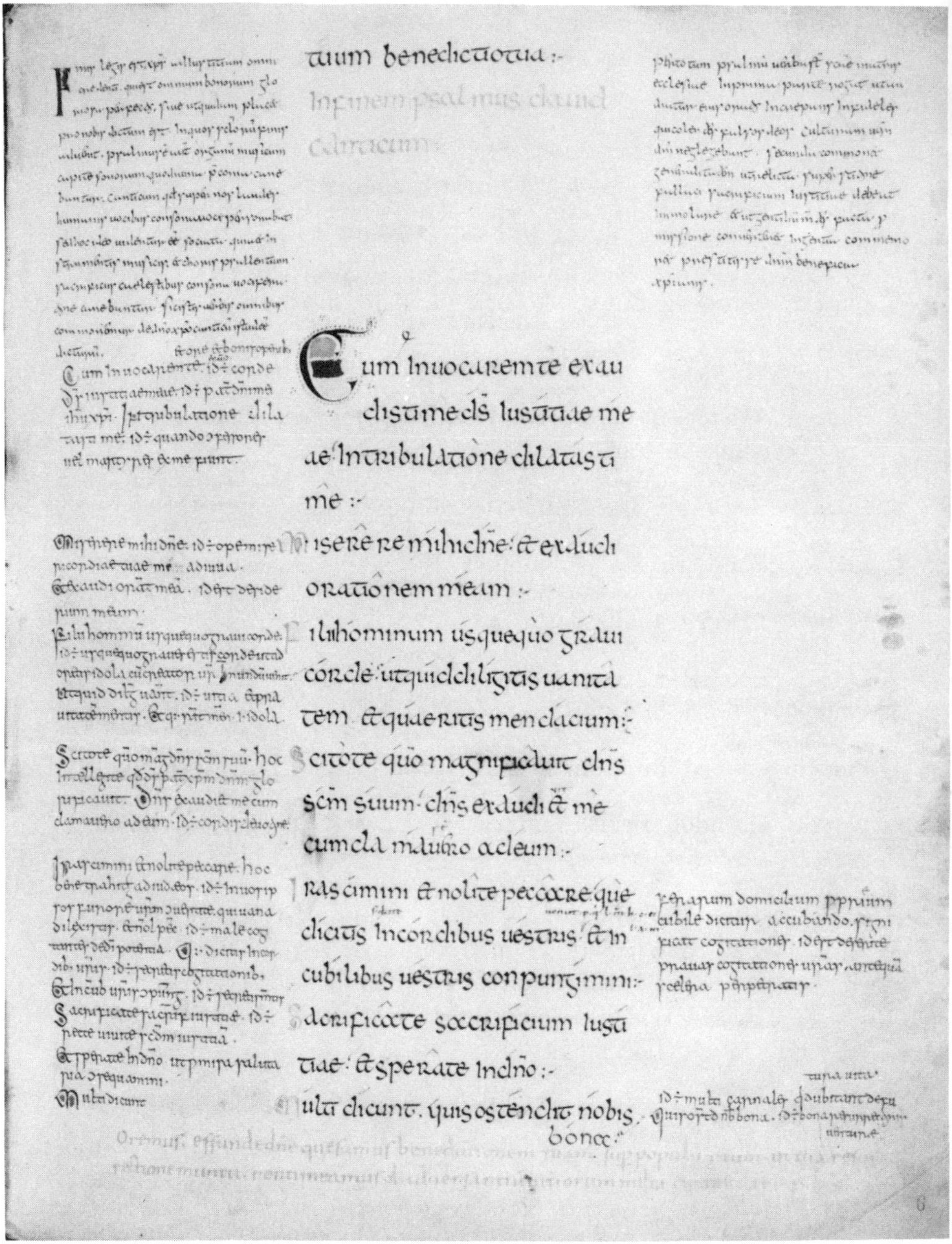

tuum benedictio tua :·

Infinem psalmus dauid

Cum inuocarem te exau
disti me ds iustitiae me
ae Intribulatione dilatas ti
me :·

isere re mihi dne et exaudi
orationem meam :·

ilii hominum usquequo graui
corde ut quid diligitis uanita
tem et quaeritis mendacium :·

citote quo magnificauit dns
scm suum dns exaudi et me
cum clamauero ad eum :·

ras cimini et nolite peccare que
dicitis incordibus uestris et in
cubilibus uestris conpungimini :·

demni ficate sacrificium iusti
tiae et sperate indno :·

ulti dicunt quis ostendit nobis
bona :·

Plate 1

Plate 2

Plate 3

INCIPIT LIB
ISAIAE PRPH

V ISIO ISAIAE · FILII AMOS
quam uidit super iudam
& hierusalon In diebus
ozie ioathan achaz ezechie
regum iuda · Audite caeli &
auribus percipe terra quo dns
locutus est · Filios enutriui
& exaltaui · ipsi autem spreue
runt me · Cognouit bos pos
sessorem suum · & asinus psepe
dni sui · Israhel non cognouit &
populus meus non intellexit ·
Uae genti peccatrici · populo graui
iniquitate · semini nequam · filiis
sceleratis · Dereliquerunt dnm ·
blasphemauerunt scm irt abalie
natisunt retrorsum · Super quo
pcutiam uos ultra addentes pre
uaricationem · Omne caput
languidum & omne cor merens ·
a planta pedis usq; aduerticem
nonest ineosanitas · Uulnus & liuor

Plate 4

Plate 5